Landscapes of Privilege

Landscapes of Privilege

*The Politics of the Aesthetic
in an American Suburb*

James S. Duncan and Nancy G. Duncan
University of Cambridge

ROUTLEDGE
NEW YORK AND LONDON

This book was developed for Routledge by the Center for American Places, Santa Fe, New Mexico, and Harrisonburg, Virginia (*www.americanplaces.org*).

Published in 2004 by
Routledge
29 West 35th Street
New York, NY 10001
www.routledge-ny.com

Published in Great Britain by
Routledge
11 New Fetter Lane
London EC4P 4EE
www.routledge.co.uk

10 9 8 7 6 5 4 3 2 1

Library of Congress Cataloging-in-Publication Data

Duncan, James S.
    Landscapes of privilege : The Politics of the Aesthetic in an American Suburb / James S. Duncan and Nancy G. Duncan.
        p.   cm.
    Includes bibliographical references and index.
        ISBN 0-415-94687-5 (alk. paper)—ISBN 0-415-94688-3 (pbk. : alk. paper)
        1. Landscape architecture—New York (State)—Bedford (Westchester County)
        2. Landscape assessment—New York (State)—Bedford (Westchester County)
        3. Landscape protection—New York (State)—Bedford (Westchester County)
        4. City Planning—New York (State)—Bedford (Westchester County)   I. Duncan, Nancy, 1948–   II. Title
    SB470.54.N6D86   2003
    712′.6′09747277—dc21

                                                                2003009898

For John
Friend, Teacher, Colleague

Contents

List of Figures

List of Tables

Acknowledgments

We began studying Bedford in 1971, Jim's first year in graduate school. Inevitably, when one has been working for so many years on a topic, even in fits and starts, many people influence the direction one takes. Among the most important are the late David Sopher, who first taught us cultural analysis in his rather Zen-like fashion, and John Agnew, who in the mid-1970s convinced us that cultural analysis should have a political bite. Elihu Gerson, in his own inimitable way, bullied and encouraged us in the beginning of this project, teaching us an interactionist and relational perspective that even through our poststructural adventures we have never abandoned. We would also like to thank David Lowenthal for taking an interest in the first paper we wrote on Bedford and suggesting that we send it to the *Geographical Review*.

A number of people aided us in our research. Our research assistant in 1996, Luis Luhan, enriched our understanding of the Latino perspectives on Mount Kisco. Rosemary Woods of the Bedford Historical Library was generous with her extensive knowledge of Bedford. Mike Kerchoff was an accommodating cartographer. Jo Sharp walked with us through Bedford's woods and down its dirt roads helping us take the photographs.

Our debt to our informants in Bedford is enormous. Unfortunately, our policy of not revealing informant's names doesn't allow us to thank by name those who helped us the most. They offered us their time and their extensive insight and knowledge. We hope that they will find this book, if not the flattering portrait that they have come to expect from those who write about the town, at least a thought-provoking examination of how its beauty is sustained. We wish also to thank our informants from Mount Kisco for generously offering us their time and opinions on the sensitive subject of the day laborers.

For reading and critically commenting on earlier drafts of this book in part or in whole, we are grateful to John Agnew, Stuart Corbridge, Dydia Delyser, Maruja Jackman, Michael Landzelius, Phil MacIntosh, David Robinson, Jo Sharp, and Judy Walton. We have received valuable feedback on our ideas when presenting bits of this book over the years at conferences and in seminars at the following universities: Bergen, British Columbia, Cambridge, Durham, Harvard, Kentucky, Oxford, Queen's Belfast, Royal Holloway, and Syracuse.

Inevitably many colleagues past and present have an important impact on one's work. In this regard, we would like to acknowledge especially Trevor Barnes and David Ley at the University of British Columbia; John Agnew, Mike Heiman, Don Meinig, John Mercer, David Robinson, and John Western at Syracuse University; Matt Potteiger and Elen Deming at the State University of New York; and Peter Burke, Stuart Corbridge, Phil Howell, Gerry Kearns, Larry Klein, Satish Kumar, Michael Landzelius, Linda McDowell, and Sarah Radcliffe at the University of Cambridge.

We would also like to acknowledge our present and former graduate students, now friends and colleagues in cultural geography with whom discussions over the years have helped us think more clearly about this project. They include Kay Anderson, Patty Butler, Dydia Delyser, Lorraine Dowler, Steve Frenkel, Liz Gagen, Nalani Hennayake, Shantha Hennayake, Nic Higgins, Dave Lambert, Steve Legg, Luis Lujan, Judith Kenny, Nuala Johnson, Gerry Pratt, Mitch Rose, Pilar Saborio, Rich Schein, Heidi Scott, Jo Sharp, Jonathan Smith, and Judy Walton.

George Thompson and Randy Jones of the Center for American Places have been patient with us over the very long haul. We thank them for their help and understanding.

And finally, we are grateful to all our family for their support, good humor, insight, and tolerance. Special thanks to Jimmy for moving over, to Miriam for joining him, and to Em for being Em. And last but not least, to Sally, whose landscape taste we will never, ever share.

Earlier versions of portions of Chapter Four appeared in "Sense of Place as a Positional Good: Locating Bedford in Time and Space." In P. Adams, S. Hoelscher, K. Till (eds), *Textures of Place, Geographies of Imagination, Experience, and Paradox*. Minneapolis: University of Minnesota Press. (with N.G. Duncan), 2001; of Chapters Two and Six appeared in "The Aestheticization of the Politics of Landscape Preservation" *Annals, Association of American Geographers*. 91:387–409 (with N.G. Duncan), 2001, and of Chapter Eight appeared in "Can't live with them. Can't landscape without them": Racism and the pastoral aesthetic in suburban New York," in *Landscape Journal: Design, Planning and Management of the Land*, volume 22 (with N. Duncan), 2004.

CHAPTER 1

Introduction

One morning in 1993 we were sitting in the archives in the Bedford Town Hall leafing through the correspondence on a zoning controversy. An elderly gentleman walked into the room and said with a faint smile on his face, "So you're back, are you? What are you finding we've done wrong this time?" We recognized him as J. Halstead Park, a descendant of the first white settlers in Bedford—an affluent suburb not far from New York City—and former chairman of the local historical society. We had interviewed him in the early 1970s for an article in which we argued that there were social divides in Bedford between an old WASP elite, a new upper middle class, and an old working class, and that landscape tastes played an important role in the performance of these groups' identities. Halstead Park explained to us, "Don Marshall [the town historian] came to dinner one night to discuss what we should do with your article. We decided to bury it. It would have ruffled too many feathers." With that, he wished us a good day, and was gone.

In 1999, the writer Alex Shoumatoff wrote an article for *Vanity Fair* on the "new" Bedford. He knows the town well, having grown up there, and his perceptive piece, part sociological study and part exposé, focuses on the decline over the past two decades of an old Anglo Bedford upper class, of which his family (as Russian aristocracy) are well entrenched honorary members, and the rise of a new, more ethnically heterogeneous, ultra-wealthy elite. His article attracted a lot of letters to the editor in various local newspapers. One paper, the *Record Review*, published some interviews with long-term residents about Shoumatoff's portrayal of the town (Lynch 1999b). Among those who felt aggrieved was Jim Renwick, a member of the Town Board whose family is descended from the first settlers. He dismissed the article as "trite, because it was about money, a very shallow subject."

Before the middle of the nineteenth century, Bedford was a farming community dominated by a few families, some of whom trace their roots back to the first white settlers in 1680. In the 1870s, it began its long, slow transition into the affluent outer suburb that it is today. Since that time, there has been a tension between various social groups in town with differing claims to status, based upon wealth, education, taste, length of residence, and genealogy. We had touched on this tension in our article in the early 1970s when the old Bedford patrician elite was still a force to be reckoned with. Halstead Park "buried" our piece, not because he thought we were wrong, but because he believed that such status

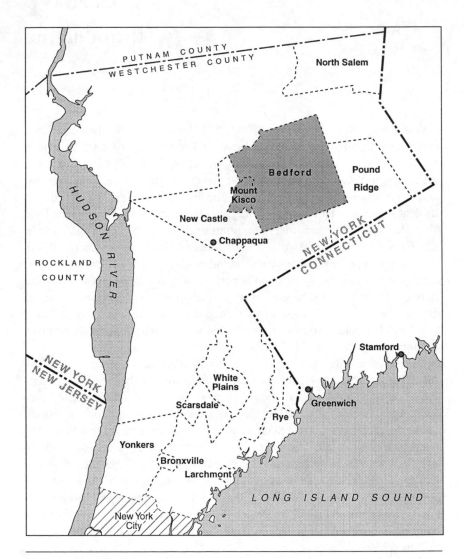

Fig. 1.1 Map of Westchester County.

battles are best not aired in public. Class is considered a private topic that many Americans are reluctant to discuss. We were intruders and consequently our intervention was "airbrushed" out of town history. Shoumatoff's more recent intervention, at a time when various traditional elites were feeling overshadowed by wealthy newcomers, was seen as a threatening, even traitorous act. We might add that it was also treated with bemusement by some who didn't recognize "their Bedford." But while an obscure article in the *Geographical Review*

(Duncan 1973) can be buried, one in *Vanity Fair* cannot, and so it was dismissed by many as wrongheaded, trite, and vulgar, although it was much talked about and admired by some for its insightfulness.

Local histories in the United States are rarely critical or overtly sociological; they are usually celebratory and serve to inculcate residents with traditional values. They are designed to fill them with pride and a sense of belonging. Such a commemorative history of Bedford written in 1955 by the town historian, funded and sold by the town, describes Bedford as "men and women and children who live together in a community, who have a common purpose and a common heritage from history, out of which they have fashioned a philosophy to be followed in striving for the fulfillment of that purpose." And yet we can see even in such a celebratory statement an acknowledgment that homogeneity is achieved in part through imagination. An imagined community[1] is created out of historical narratives selected to shape the values of the town. The author admits as much when he says:

> [S]ince the 250th anniversary in 1930 [when Bedford's history had last been celebrated publicly] many new families have moved into the Township. Since then, moreover, hundreds of young people have been born in Bedford and some of them have grown to maturity. For these two classes of Bedford folk, there has been but little opportunity of readily obtaining authoritative information with regard to the Town's history and traditions. (Barrett 1955, 6)

In this history and in a series of newspaper articles titled "Bits of Bedford History," the town's historian hoped to create a sense of community and a love of Bedford so that its new citizens would help to preserve it as a sanctuary from what he terms, "the buffetings of a too competitive world" (Barrett 1955, 112). He concludes, "To those who know its rich store of natural resources and its priceless heritage from history, the Town of Bedford is such a sanctuary" (Barrett 1955, 112).

We realize that our present book will be scrutinized by some residents anxious to see whose ox is being gored. In truth, we have no stake in the various status battles in town. Rather, our commitment is to describing in our own words, and in those of our informants, the role that aesthetics plays in the production of place and of identities, while commenting on the wider social consequences of such an aestheticized view of the world. Some, no doubt, will find it focuses on a Bedford that appears largely irrelevant to them. We readily acknowledge that it is selective in its focus principally on pastoral Bedford and on historic Bedford Village, only one of the three hamlets in the town. We explore the ways people produce their identities in and through places, especially homeplaces, such as houses, gardens, and home communities. We are interested in investigating some of the more conservative, defensive attempts at using one's surroundings to establish individual, familial, and community identities. These identities are defined in large part *against* and in contrast to an outside world, what some have termed "a constitutive outside." Homeplaces are the subjects of conscious design effort, even struggle, on the part of those who can afford to shape them aesthetically. But they are equally the materialization of inherent antagonisms, exclusions, unarticulated racism, and reactions to global complexity as a threat to "the local." We explore the idea that place-based identities can be insecure, even among those with the resources (time, money, and skills) to create ideal settings in which to substantiate desired social identities. We argue that such a high degree of attention on the part of suburban residents to the visual, material, and sensual aspects of place and place-based identity leads to an aestheticization of exclusion. A seemingly innocent appreciation of landscapes and desire to protect local history and nature can act as subtle but highly effective mechanisms of exclusion and reaffirmation of class identity.

We have attempted to supplement existing studies of the constitution of places through exclusionary zoning and environmental legislation with a more social psychological understanding of the politics of place-making and attachment to homeplaces. We hope to achieve a fuller understanding of the cultural practices of producing places and place-based identity. The structural and institutional bases of reinvigorated localism in a globalizing world have too often been studied without more than a cursory reference to the sentiments and emotions behind place-making practices. Similarly, studies of sense of place, place attachment, and belonging are too often studied in isolation from the political-economic flows and processes that are central to place production.[2] Although the former more than the latter is the focus of our attention, we believe both need to be considered in their mutual constitution. We have attempted to discover something of the hopes and fears, longing to belong, sense of community, and insecurities of the residents of a town that is both inwardly focused and defensive of its imagined uniqueness and—at the same time—highly enmeshed in a regional, national, transnational, as well as global production of socio-spatial relations.

Bedford is a very old settlement, having been an agricultural village of the Canitoe and earlier Indian tribes before the arrival of English settlers in 1680. But it is the waves of urbanites who have moved there during the late nineteenth and early twentieth centuries who have had the most impact on the town, turning it into the affluent, Anglophile "lifestyle island" (Dorst 1990) that it is today. While keen to portray itself as a 300-year-old rural community, as a place apart from New York City—forty-four miles away—Bedford is, in a very real sense, a 120-year-old suburb, very much dependent on its socio-spatial and economic relations with New York City and several other sprawling centers of economic activity in Westchester sometimes referred to as "edge cities,"[3] including White Plains, Purchase-Rye, and the Tarrytown area.

Bedford evolved from a community of modest farmers dominated by a small local elite in the mid-nineteenth century into a suburb whose landscape was dotted with large gentlemen's estates by the late 1920s. In the decades following the Depression and World War II, many of these large estates declined and some were subdivided. By the 1960s, Bedford had achieved a seedy look of elegant decay, a kind of classic upper-class American version of a picturesque English landscape, so aptly described by Lowenthal and Prince (1965). A second wave of settlement began after World War II, producing a mixture of large and relatively more modest houses.

In the 1980s and 1990s, in the years when Wall Street boomed, some new mansions were added to the landscape. Although these houses produced a degree of infill, residential zoning requiring four-acre minimum lot sizes in much of the town ensured that the landscape never changed dramatically from the time of the great estates. Wealthy New Yorkers and West Coast actors disillusioned with the glitzy, fast-paced life in Hollywood have found in Bedford a quiet retreat from the city and the social whirl. It would appear that in Bedford, as in many other places, with escalating globalization there is an increasing fear of place-lessness[4] and a longing to belong that produces a kind of reterritorialization and search for traditional values, including localism and reinvigorated nationalism. In the United States, among other things, globalization has produced a nostalgia for small town communities. It is a longing for simpler, quieter, more whole-some places that have an air of historical authenticity and an aura of uniqueness about them, without forcing oneself to be divorced from the many benefits of globalization enjoyed by the more privileged members of society.[5] The sense of community that is longed for is more a symbol or aesthetic of community than the reality of close-knit social relations. In fact, as we will argue, community in places like Bedford has to a large extent been reduced to NIMBYism[6] and the collective consumption of romanticized landscapes of community. Whereas the residents of Bedford and similar communities are remarkably successful in their quest for autonomy, this is at least partially illusionary. As we will show, the town's borders are in danger of being disrupted and transgressed by various transnational flows, most visibly migration from Central America.

We focus particular attention on Bedford Village and a surrounding estate area characterized by a beautiful landscape of rolling hills with horses grazing on open meadowland. Such a landscape requires a large amount of care and maintenance. It needs not only a lot of labor, but also a highly sophisticated political organization. Residents are extraordinarily vigilant and at times aggressive in protecting the quality of the landscape. Conservationists protect its brooks, ponds, bogs, and forests of spruce and hemlock with zeal. A majority of the town's residents insists that Bedford retain its many miles of dirt roads, and the Historical Preservation Committee feels so strongly about preserving the villagescape that it has bought, restored, and continued to maintain many of the white wooden shops in the Bedford Village.

A 1997 article in the *New York Times* (West 1997), titled "Who needs a house in Beverly Hills? Stars now flock to wealthy but unassuming Bedford, N.Y.," tells of "quiet Bedford" being transformed by stars into an "in" place. As evidence, a map is produced showing all the famous people living in Bedford,

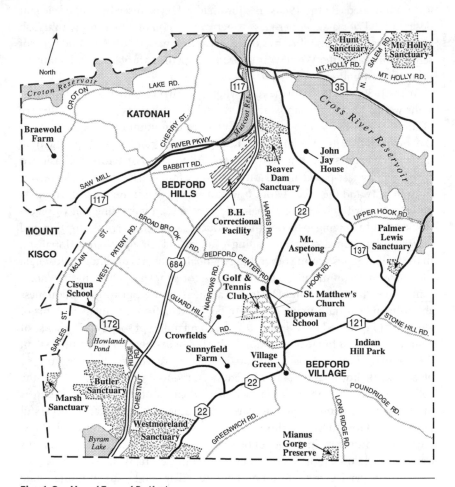

Fig. 1.2 Map of Town of Bedford.

including, among others, Mariah Carey, Chevy Chase, Glenn Close, Michael Crichton, Ralph Lauren, I. M. Pei, and George Soros. For many residents who had only known Bedford as the well-to-do, but sleepy town it was for a half century, its newly found popularity with the rich and famous beginning in the early 1980s has not been an entirely pleasant surprise. Longer-term residents are both proud to be associated with a landscape that attracts the attention of celebrities and worried that newcomers may bring unwanted changes to the landscape. Like Western tourists who seek "unspoilt" countries where they can return in fantasy to simpler ways of life, so Bedford and other attractive country towns located near large cities are sought out as places where one can lead a more wholesome, authentic life. The irony, as with tourism, is that the more people arrive seeking unspoiled landscapes, the more likely it is that the qualities that attracted them will disappear. The residents of Bedford are well aware of this dilemma and their attempts to deal with it have produced a virulent politics of anti-development. One of our tasks in this book is to explore the intended and unintended consequences of these politics. Another task is to examine the role of the landscapes of Bedford as a symbolic resource employed in the quest for social distinction—how residents are invested in this place, socially, psychologically, as well as economically.

Landscapes are produced and lived in an everyday, practical, very material, and repetitively reaffirming sense. Identities are performed in and through landscapes. Here we use the terms "perform" and "performative" as J. L. Austin (1975) defined them—productive, in contrast to denotative—and also as Judith Butler (1990) uses them[7]—to mean everyday embodied practices, embedded in a spatial context that is as much constituted by social practices as it is constitutive of them. As performances of varying types of identity come together to produce a common landscape, it tends to become contested and potentially destabilized. Bedford is a site of aesthetic consumption practices in which the residents achieve social status by preserving and enhancing the beauty of their town. They accomplish this through highly restrictive zoning and environmental protection legislation and by preserving as much undeveloped land as possible through the creation of nature preserves. Thus we argue that romantic ideology, localism, anti-urbanism, anti-modernism, and an ethnic- and class-based aesthetic all lend a political dimension to the desire to live in a beautiful place such as Bedford. Further, we believe that the celebration of the natural environment, historic preservation, and the claimed uniqueness of a local landscape has often diverted attention away from the interrelatedness of issues of aesthetics and identity on the one hand and social justice on the other. The desire to protect nature and history and the seemingly innocent pleasure derived from natural landscapes has a complex cultural and political history that we explore in Chapter Three. Our thesis is that landscape as an aesthetic production acts as a subtle but highly effective mechanism of exclusion. The numbers and types of people who can live and work in Bedford are restricted through various social, economic, political, and legal practices, backed up by appeals to an unquestioned desire to preserve a valuable and unique sense of place. This might not have any significant social consequences if Bedford were, in fact, unique. However, as we demonstrate in our discussion of affordable housing in Chapter Five, many of New York City's northern suburbs are characterized by similar exclusionary and aesthetic practices. As we explain, these practices are in effect subsidies to the rich that have the effect of reducing available land for the potential development of affordable housing.

Andrew Sayer (2000, 169) has argued that "contemporary cultural studies' preoccupation with aesthetic values is evident in its focus on style and taste, indeed in the definition of its object of study as 'the stylization of life' (Featherstone 1994). There is less interest in moral-political values." We agree; however, we also believe that these two types of value are in actuality inextricably bound and can be best theorized via the concepts of aestheticization and complex complicity. This we see, in part at least, as a process of displacement whereby moral-political issues can become obscured by attention to aesthetic concerns. We argue that the *merely* aesthetic often isn't *mere* at all. The moral questions here are complicated by the issue of complicity. Christopher Kutz (2000) argues that individuals' actions and lifestyles are implicated in harm done to others through their association with many other people and institutions. He says (2000, 1),

> We find ourselves connected to harms and wrongs, albeit by relations that fall outside the paradigm of individual, intentional wrongdoing... [Although] we stand outside the shadow of evil, we still do not find the full light of the good.

Kutz offers a theory of complicity to replace the deeply ingrained modern individualistic conception of moral agency that exempts individuals from being held accountable for the consequences of joint action where their own contribution is small. He continues (2000, 5), "The individualistic conception drives a wedge between me and us, between private and public." Because there is "no legitimate moral subject," he argues (2000, 5), "corresponding to the we, responses to collective harms find no proper target." We hope in this book to bring to peoples' attention the interdependence between issues that are too often seen as separate. We hope to show that certain unquestioned goods, such as environmental conservation and historic preservation, may have unintended negative consequences for which individuals may not be accountable qua individuals, but with which they can be seen as complicit.

People in Bedford see landscapes as communicative of identities and community values. They speak of landscapes symbolizing—and even inculcating—political and moral values, as well as creating and conveying social distinction. They also know that their landscapes depend upon a politics of anti-development. But while at a certain level being aware of this, for the most part they tend to naturalize their privilege, having no reason to trace the far-reaching, unintended consequences and unacknowledged conditions of that privilege. This naturalizing tendency is greatly aided by the spatial structuring and fragmentation of local governments, which results in a high degree of local autonomy and inward focus that to a large extent obscures the regional impact of the collective consequences of their individual actions from them. Clearly our informants are far more knowledgeable than we are about many of the issues that we discuss. We reject any implication that people are in any sense mere agents of the structural processes that we attempt to illuminate. We do think, however, that human agency is a relational achievement with far-reaching institutional and natural histories that are difficult to trace. Consequently, we try to interpret our informants' own interpretations from a critical, structural, and relational standpoint few of them would share, given the prevalence of the individualistic conception of moral agency.

A place like Bedford is highly interconnected into transnational flows and networks of power, privilege, and as we shall see in Chapter Eight, economically and politically driven migration. In fact some very well-known actors in these global networks live in Bedford. People like the financier George Soros; presidents of major New York banks, multinational companies, law and stock brokerage firms, and major world airlines; and large manufacturers such as Ralph Lauren live there. Regional and national level political organizations, such as the Civil Liberties Union, the Westchester Hispanic Coalition, the Center for Immigrant Rights based in New York City, as well as the Nature Conservancy and Westchester Land Trust, are examples of large-scale institutions that have been enrolled into networks that connect the towns of northern Westchester to the wider region, the nation, and beyond. It is clear that as institutions, such as foreign language newspapers and transnational labor migrant and other political organizations, move into the suburbs, towns like Bedford and Mount Kisco are becoming more highly connected and, from the point of view of nativist residents, increasingly exposed to unwelcome penetration by outside forces.

Since the late nineteenth century, Bedford's elite has been cosmopolitan and urbane in its public and business life, but deeply anti-urban in many aspects of its private life. Bedford has been produced as a highly controlled space, a semi-privatized domain in which supposedly authentic rural republican American identity can be nurtured. Its landscapes are treated as aesthetic productions, highly controlled so that as far as the eye can see, even if one drives or rides on horseback for many miles, one views nothing industrial or distasteful. Residents of Bedford maintain the illusion of disconnection through the spatial separation of home and work and an aestheticized attitude that conflates images of the English country gentleman, owner of all he surveys, with the sentimental pastoralism of the Jeffersonian American small farmer and individualistic agrarianism. This ambiguity can be seen in the language of residents as found in interviews, newspaper articles, town and club histories, and real estate advertisements in which the terms "aristocrat," "great estate," and "commanding distant views" sit comfortably alongside terms such as "the simple country life," "rustic," "rural charm," "farmer's club" (actually an exclusive, elite institution), "studied seediness," and "old colonial simplicity." Self-assured in their attempts to maintain open green space, the residents' aesthetic pleasures are sustained through spatial separation. Residents spatially and visually insulate themselves from uncomfortable questions of race and poverty and keep out of sight as many reminders of the social consequences of what has been referred to as "painless privilege" (Pile 1994) as possible. It might be noted, however, that intra-class questions of race, religion, ethnicity, and gender relations, and styles of consumption, especially conspicuous consumption, are not as easily erased from sight and can lead to insecurity and—despite material wealth—can sometimes lead to psychically painful privilege.

In order to maintain such pleasures, Bedford residents participate in what Steve Pile (1994) has spoken of as a "renewed struggle for coherence, boundedness, and homogeneity that can only be secured by exclusion." Bedford's residents have tried and largely succeeded in producing the town as an island of nostalgic retreat from the perceived negative impacts of increasing globalization and encroaching ethnic hybridity. These responses to contemporary complexity require us as geographers to reconceptualize such popularly celebrated concepts as place, locality, localism, and landscape in order to understand how in places such as Bedford they are refortified as conservative forces in the face of increasingly complex, globalizing geometries of power that threaten and to a degree penetrate Bedford's defenses (Harvey 1989; Massey 1993; Smith 2001).

Organization of the Book

In the next chapter we situate Bedford within its geographical and historical context, and then outline the theoretical framework we employ to analyze our data. In Chapter Three, we discuss the major discourses embedded in the landscape of Bedford: the pastoral, the wilderness, and the New England village. We then show how local real estate agents reproduce and reinforce these ideas and images in the marketing of property in town. Chapter Four examines the role of Anglophile landscape tastes in the practices of place-based identity. We argue that people's sense of the beauty of Bedford is very much in relation to a set of aesthetic and social judgments about the appearance of surrounding towns. While people take pleasure in the beauty of Bedford, they are anxious about the decline of that beauty due to overdevelopment. Such anxieties lay the foundation for an exclusionary politics that attempts to keep Bedford from looking like other affluent suburbs in Westchester judged to be less visually appealing. Chapter Five explores the manner in which a particular aesthetic based upon the discourses outlined in Chapter Three are encoded in local zoning law and how these serve as a barrier to landscape change in town. We first examine the various town zoning codes, which form the legal framework, and then reveal how citizens make use of this framework as they organize in an attempt to block development. In Chapter Six, we discuss the production of nature in Bedford and examine how tax law provides yet another tool to halt development. We show how gifts of land to the local nature preserves and the granting of conservation easements to land trusts are seen as effective ways of saving the landscape. We go on to argue that nature in Bedford is produced and delimited as much by nineteenth-century romanticism as by twentieth-century ecological thought. The power of the latter is marshalled largely to add scientific legitimacy to what has been a hundred-year-long mission to protect the rural beauty of the town. Chapter Seven explores the aestheticised view of local history in town, with specific reference to historic Bedford Village. We argue that members of a town gentry with ties to the "founding fathers" have used historic preservation as a way of putting forward their status claims in the face of a flood of wealthy newcomers to town. Chapter Eight explores the situation of the Latino day laborers who in increasing numbers are employed to maintain the landscape of Bedford. While relatively few of these workers have found housing in Bedford, many have settled in the adjoining village of Mount Kisco where they are considered an unaesthetic element of the streetscape and are made to feel unwelcome. The exorbitant price paid for low-quality rental housing by Latino laborers in Mount Kisco is complexly but unquestionably related to the preserved beauty of Bedford and similarly exclusionary towns. Because this relation between Bedford and Mount Kisco is diffuse, and certainly not isolated from a much larger spatial, political and environmental context, the solutions to the problems are not immediately obvious. The goal in this chapter is not to offer solutions but to explore the lived reality of the production of space in Mount Kisco. In doing so, we examine the systematic attempts by the village to drive the day laborers away and the Latinos' relatively successful resistance to these attempts. We show that the success of this resistance is attributable in part to translocal and national networks of individuals and institutions, which the Latinos have been able to mobilize. Finally we examine the often contradictory attitudes of residents of Bedford who want low-wage Latino labor, but don't want them to live in the area. We show that both their desire to have labor and to banish them as local residents is based primarily on aesthetic grounds.

CHAPTER 2

Bedford in Context

Westchester County

Since ancient times urban elites have been building residential areas away from the crowding, crime, and pollution of cities. Kenneth Jackson (1985, 12) opens his book *Crabgrass Frontier: The Suburbanization of the United States* with a telling quotation: "Our property seems to me the most beautiful in the world. It is so close to Babylon that we enjoy all the advantages of the city, and yet when we come home we are away from all the noise and dust (written in cuneiform on a clay tablet in 539 B.C.)." Although suburbanization in the United States began well before the Revolutionary War, mass suburbanization is largely a twentieth-century phenomenon. As late as the 1920s cities were still draining rural areas of people (Fishman 1995, 395), but powerful forces were pressing inexorably toward suburbanization as a macroeconomic solution to problems of undercon-sumption by providing an alternative locus of capital investment (Harvey 1989, 2000; Smith 1996; Walker 1981, 1995; Zukin 1991, 140). Suburbs created a phenomenal growth in demand for private and collective consumption. As David Harvey (1989) points out, although suburbs were privately developed, they profited from large government subsidies in the form of government-backed housing finance and public investment in highway construction and other in-frastructures. This massive building program has changed the residential, man-ufacturing, and service sector landscapes of the United States as manufacturing and service industries have also suburbanized at an increasing rate. Since the end of World War I, 85% of all new housing has been built in the suburbs (Zukin 1991, 140), and by 1950 one quarter of all Americans lived in suburbs. Fifty years later, over half of the population live in suburbs and only a third live in cities (Kasinitz 1995, 387). 1992 marked the first federal election in which suburbanites constituted the majority of the voters. The United States has be-come, in the words of William Schneider (1992, 33), "a suburban nation with an urban fringe and a rural fringe."

Westchester is a suburban county within the New York metropolitan area. The region is one of the largest and most complex urban areas of the world; it includes both sprawling edge cities and relatively rural outer suburbs, sometimes known as "exurbia." It is also the most globalized metropolitan economy in the world (Warf 2000). According to the U.S. Census of 2000, Westchester has a population of 923,459. Bounded by Long Island Sound and the state of Connecticut on the east and the Hudson River on the west, it has 457 square miles of varied terrain ranging from sea level to over 900 feet. It has a mix of urban and suburban communities.

Westchester is within the oak-hickory zone of the eastern woodlands of northeastern United States (Shoumatoff 1979; Pregill and Volkman 1993). Pre-colonial Westchester was a complex cultural landscape. Shaped by thousands of years of Native American occupation, the forests the Dutch and English colonists found there were not virgin forests as local lore would have it (Cronon 1983). The Indians had, however, allowed much of the area now known as Westchester to remain forested for hunting. They cleared meadow-like openings in the forest to encourage tender growth for game (Pregill and Volkman 1993, 325). In the late seventeenth century, a typical, uncleared acre, according to Shoumatoff (1979, 25) would have contained eighty enormous trees. But he goes on to say that Westchester had been 80% cleared by the end of the nineteenth century.

Many different Algonquin-speaking tribes belonging to a political organization known as the Wappinger Confederation were living in Westchester when the first white settlers, the Dutch, the English, and the Huguenots arrived. In the eighteenth century, large landholders and tenant farmers populated the county. Later in the nineteenth century, "summer people" and "weekend people" had begun to build houses and estates. Laborers, mainly from southern Italy, came with them to work on the estates and also to build reservoirs for New York City. John Stilgoe (1988, 68), in his study on the origins of the American suburb, quotes the nineteenth-century writer Nathaniel Willis as saying that by the 1850s southern Westchester had become inundated by newcomers seeking an idyllic life in the country. He said, "You find yourself in a region of 'country seats'—no poor people's abodes or humble belongings anywhere visible . . . Miles upon miles of unmitigated prosperity weary the eye . . . Lawns and park gates, groves and verandas, ornamental woods and neat walls, trimmed hedges and well placed shrubberies, fine houses and large stables, neat gravel walks and nobody on them—are notes upon one cord." Stilgoe comments, "Willis discovered a new spatial creation overwhelming—not simply overlaying—an older spatial order, a creation that had driven away the poor folks, the farmers." But the poor had not been driven entirely out of Westchester; rather, they had been forced out of view of those who traveled through the elegant countryside. Towns like Bedford in northern Westchester experienced a similar transformation thirty years later. This wave of newcomers was much like the later waves of the 1920s and again in the last decades of the twentieth century, the newcomers being criticized locally for their ornamental plantings, overly neat trimmed hedges, and pristine rebuilt walls. And like Willis, some people today still worry about the homogeneous prosperity of northern Westchester's landscape reflecting an artificial situation in which young teachers, firemen, and policemen can no longer afford to buy a home and some of the older residents can no longer afford to keep theirs. As we can see, what often underlies this concern to "take care of one's own" is a worry about being taken care of oneself should the need arise.

With the coming of the railroads in the mid-nineteenth century, southern Westchester became a manufacturing and residential base. Real estate developments cropped up along the railroad line in places like Rye near the shore of Long Island Sound and Tarrytown on the Hudson. The population grew by more than 50% in the first decade after the rail lines were laid. Between 1850 and 1860, the population of Westchester grew by 75%. In southern Westchester, the population more than doubled. An English traveler of 1855 spoke of suburban villas "springing up like mushrooms on spots which five years ago were part of the dense and tangled forest" (Jackson 1985, 36). Southern Westchester was also a destination for daytrips and vacations in the countryside, along the shores of Long Island Sound and on the banks overlooking the Hudson River. Yonkers, the largest city with a population of 40,000 in 1900, became a major industrial center with a large working-class population including many Irish, Poles, Ukrainians, and Italian immigrants as well as African Americans. Yonkers's industrial growth continued well into the twentieth century (Friedman 1984, 75). But from the mid-twentieth century on, Yonkers declined as the northeastern United States deindustrialized. Disinvestment, unemployment, substandard housing, and racial tensions among whites, blacks, and an increasingly large Hispanic population characterize Yonkers and the rest of the southern industrial region of the county today (with some small, exclusionary residential neighborhoods and towns like Bronxville, Rye, and Scarsdale being notable exceptions).[1]

Central Westchester developed only slightly later; White Plains, the capital of the county, experienced its greatest growth during the twentieth century as it began to attract the development of corporate headquarters and professional and managerial employment to the county. The city also has several large malls with branches of some of New York City's big department stores. The CEOs and board members of corporations wished to bring their offices closer to where they lived; they also wanted to take advantage of a large pool of highly educated women with children who preferred to work flexible hours and not commute to New York City. Only the highest paid employees find Westchester housing affordable, however, and many long-term residents who own houses they couldn't afford to buy today find the property taxes a heavy burden. Large numbers of people commute long distances from Putnam and Rockland Counties to work in White Plains or along the Cross Westchester Expressway called the "platinum mile" (because of its world corporate headquarters) and in the other edge cities of Westchester. Sharon Zukin (1991, 164) says, "With 'local actors' like IBM, General Foods, and Union Carbide, business planning in Westchester is permeated by companies with global concerns." But she says they are hardly indifferent to their surroundings. There is as much sentiment, it would appear, as economic sense in their locational decision-making. As she states (1991, 164–65),

> Westchester's corporate legitimacy feeds the market for more upper class real estate development. Although that conflicts with employers' needs to ensure housing for their work forces, as well as the requirement of light manufactures and warehouse owners, it is the main focus of place-based elites. . . . Few localities in this day and age are able to keep the social or spatial qualities that attracted the early residents. Yet Westchester County has remained a striking contrast to both suburban sprawl and urban blight. The continued visual homogeneity of this landscape reflects a carefully crafted commitment to a kind of planning that keeps property values high. These in turn safeguard the county's social homogeneity— at least outside the former industrial towns. Unlike many other places, Westchester County explicitly contradicts the idea that suburbs don't plan their growth.

It is the cultural history and the hegemony of the landscape tastes of such place-based elites with their deep-seated abhorrence of suburban sprawl—matched only by their aversion to urban ugliness—that we have tried to understand in this book.

As we show in Chapter Eight, the demand for gardeners and cleaners, restaurant employees, and various unskilled and semi-skilled laborers, as well as low-waged clerks and casual flexible labor is bringing new immigrants, especially Latinos, into northern Westchester. The subsequent pressure on the lowest end of the housing market has resulted in their exploitation by the owners of the relatively small number of rental housing units as well as some cases of homelessness. What are seen as urban problems in the suburbs are very distressing to those longtime residents used to enjoying their painless white privilege[2] without visual reminders of poverty.

The landscape of northern Westchester where many of the CEOs live remains relatively undeveloped. In the 1920s, local elites brought in strict zoning codes to ensure that mass suburbia never came to the rolling, wooded hills and pastoral landscapes of that part of the county. Even though Pepsico and IBM have built corporate offices in northern Westchester, most of the landscape has maintained its rural look. Zoning laws have ensured that the few large companies that are located there have large campus-like facilities set far back from the road among hills, lakes, and forests. Furthermore, as Zukin (1991, 171) says, zoning prevented working- and middle-class people as well as small businesses from gaining a foothold in Westchester.

Using Westchester as a key example of the suburbanization of corporate headquarters, Zukin (1991, 136) points out that the Cross Westchester Expressway between Tarrytown on the Hudson and Greenwich, Connecticut—the "platinum mile"—resulted from the relatively high cost of labor and real estate in cities along with suburban tax inducements and changes brought on by mergers and acquisitions. Of course, Westchester County was not unique in this regard. Still, she explained, it was Westchester's local elites who shaped development through the manipulation of zoning laws and urban planning. It is this hidden history of such place-based elites that we wish to understand—how their private lives and their love of history and nature collectively and cumulatively with others like them from other towns have impacted the social and economic geography of the county. We have attempted to delve deeply into what Zukin (1991, 138) refers to as the "long term efforts of local actors with enormous power over place" who early in the twentieth century realized that property development built around social homogeneity would effectively drive out industrial uses. For places like Westchester, the nineteenth-century suburb served as the ideal model, "where owners of villas consumed 'nature' in country clubs, on parkways, and the grounds of their own estates." But as she says (1991, 138), Westchester also looked forward to corporate and commercial landscapes carefully located so as to retain the favored pastoral aesthetic in much of the county.[3] This fragmentation that Zukin refers to is central to our argument that the politico-spatial structure of Westchester is as important a factor as the aesthetic orientation toward landscape in explaining Bedford today. Individuals, whether acting alone or in groups such as homeowner's associations, may appear to possess a great deal of freedom in shaping the landscape. But local societies and town boards are in fact constrained—and, just as important, enabled and enhanced—by the structures of authority and a "mobilization of bias" in favor of current residents over potential residents, businesses, or developers.

New York State is fragmented into several thousand units of government. Although the cities and towns that make up the state are legally the creation of the state, they have considerable home rule and taxing powers. Property taxes support town services. Towns raise a large percentage of the money spent on schools, especially in wealthy towns. Consequently, the quality of education and other services is very uneven across communities. Towns also have considerable zoning powers, as we will show in Chapter Five. Planning is carried out at both the town and county levels, but the county planning role is largely advisory. In Bedford, for example, town planning is very inward looking and not particularly concerned about the regional scale (personal communication with the town planner). As we shall see, the landscapes of power referred to by Zukin are to a large extent generated by this considerable autonomy of individual towns. Power in small Westchester towns resides not with politicians, developers, or other business interests, nor with the poor and the institutions that represent them, but overwhelmingly with middle- and upper-income residents.[4]

Bedford's History 1680–1980

Before the arrival of the Europeans, a small group of Native Americans called the Cantitoes lived in the area that is now Bedford.[5] They belonged to the Wappinger Confederation. During the early seventeenth century, the Wappingers strenuously resisted Dutch encroachment on their lands and in the early 1640s drove the Dutch out. In 1645, an army of Dutch and English soldiers attacked and set fire to a sleeping Wappinger village on land that was later to become part of Bedford. The Dutch estimated that 700 Indians died and only seven escaped. This was the last major act of resistance to European expansion in Westchester.

From the beginning, the English settlement of New England was a highly structured process. In seventeenth-century Massachusetts, for example, the general court asserted control over the initial location, size, and affairs of towns (Zuckerman 1970, 12–14). The chartered town became the highly standardized instrument of land division and expansion (Wood 1991, 34). By 1635, this system had begun to spread from Massachusetts into Connecticut (Meinig 1986, 92). It was within this institutional framework that Bedford was settled. By the middle of the seventeenth century, Stamford, Connecticut, was a thriving coastal town and in 1680, twenty-two of its residents purchased a 7,673-acre tract just beyond the edge of town from Chief Katonah. The founders of Bedford paid twelve Indian coats, six blankets, 300 guilders wampum, two yards of red broadcloth, six yards of red cotton, and approximately nine pounds in unitemized expenses (Town of Bedford 1966, 1). The total cost of the land was the equivalent of forty-six pounds. Each of the twenty-two settlers who purchased land was assigned a house lot of no less than three acres of Indian agricultural land as well as lower quality wet meadows and some uplands. A three-acre common (today's village green) was also laid out for grazing animals. Each of the original settlers contributed two pounds to the purchase price, and anyone who met with their approval could join them by paying a like amount into the town treasury. In return, they would receive not only land, but also all the rights of citizenship (Wood 1925, 620).

Property and ecological relations among the Native Americans were neither fully understood nor respected by the settlers. Sale of land to colonists was a complicated affair because of differing conceptions of property, and competing sovereignties and jurisdictions under which the differing rights of ownership were recognized. Each native village held its territory for the use of all its members. Rights to territory were vested in a village leader called a "sachem" who looked out for the immediate and changing land needs of his people. Individuals had the right to farm the fields they had cleared, but once they began to revert to forest, the former users lost their rights to the site. Transfers of land were seen as temporary and for particular uses. Native Americans did not recognize the authority of the colony of Connecticut or the English crown's legal system of fully alienated land. They assumed that any transfers of land would allow them to continue using it along with the English (Cronon 1983, 66–67). Although there was some degree of sharing with hunters, with increasing English migration into the area, Indian agricultural use became more and more restricted.

In 1683, the settlers sought permission from the general court in Hartford to consider their settlement a legal town named Bedford. However, in that same year, Bedford was transferred from the colony of Connecticut to the province of New York. The town protested the transfer until 1700 when King William III ended the dispute by proclaiming Bedford to be a part of New York State. Today the residents of Bedford still cherish its epithet "the only New England Village in New York State." Within five years of Bedford's founding, nine of the original twenty-two families had moved back to Connecticut. By 1710, only seven of the twenty-two founding families were still living in Bedford (Marshall 1980, 6). The original purchases from the Indians were by then divided into lots of fifty or more acres, and the system of land for common use was not extended. The town's citizens rapidly adjusted to the New York land system based upon large manorial holdings. Jacobus Van Cortlandt, a wealthy and influential New Yorker of Dutch ancestry, was allowed to purchase an estate of eight square miles in Bedford. Similarly, Colonel Peter Matthews, a lobbyist who procured the Bedford town patent from New York in 1704 was given an estate of two square miles as his fee (Marshall 1980, 18–19). While Bedford still had more small holders than many other places in the province of New York, as early as two decades after its founding, it no longer resembled the stereotypical New England village so celebrated in its history today. Two men between them owned nearly one-third of the town's land.

During the American Revolution, Bedford lay in the neutral ground between the British and American colonial lines, and the residents of the town were divided in their loyalties. The majority of poor farmers, who had been relatively isolated both economically and socially from the national centers of power, had little interest in the conflict until July 11, 1779, when a detachment of British and loyalist troops burned the village. After the American Revolution, Bedford was chosen as one of two county seats in Westchester. The county built a new courthouse and jail in 1786 to replace the public buildings burned by the British. At this time, Bedford had a population of 2,466 people and was the largest town in the county.

In 1801, the American Revolutionary hero John Jay retired from public life and moved to a 750-acre country retreat in Bedford that was part of the Van Cortlandt estate he had inherited from his wife's family. It remained in his family until the 1950s when it became a New York State historic site. Bedford continued to be a large and politically important town within the county until after the middle of the nineteenth century. In 1840, its population of 2,822 placed it second to Yonkers whose population had grown to 2,969. White Plains, the other county seat, had a population at the time of 1,087. With migration out of New York City facilitated by the coming of the railroad in the 1840s, the balance of population began to shift away from Bedford toward the southern part of the county. The railroad also brought industry into the county, beginning a trend toward the suburbanization of manufacturing and services that continues to this day. The increased ease of travel removed the need for two county seats, and consequently in 1870, White Plains became the sole county courthouse, after which the Bedford courthouse served as a town hall and more recently a museum.

The railroad passed through two of Bedford's three hamlets,[6] Katonah and Bedford Station (later renamed Bedford Hills). This bypassing of Bedford Village, which shifted the balance of the population away from that part of town and reduced it to an economic backwater, turned out to be its salvation as far as contemporary preservation-oriented residents are concerned.[7] While the twice-daily rail service allowed local dairy farmers to access markets in New York City, their prosperity was short-lived as decreasing transportation costs soon also allowed milk and beef to be shipped to New York from more fertile lands to the west. While a small amount of subsistence farming continued into the twentieth century, it became progressively more marginal to the life of the town.

From the 1870s on, many farms were bought by wealthy New Yorkers and converted into country estates. Small farmhouses were transformed into care-taker's cottages or pulled down and replaced by mansions. The age of mansion building reached a peak around 1885. Bedford Village was transformed during these years as well, by cleaning up the muddy village and moving a number of charming, "colonial-style" buildings from elsewhere in town to the village center, bringing it closer to the nineteenth-century romantic ideal of the pic-turesque New England village.[8] Toward the end of the century, the ethnic mix began to change as the gardeners, stonemasons, and unskilled laborers—many of southern Italian and Irish origin—who came to build the estates settled in the town, although even more of the immigrants moved to Mount Kisco where there was more affordable housing. The railway not only brought about the physical and social transformation of Bedford, but it also created a new geogra-phy within the town itself (Howard 1902). The railroad depot of Bedford Hills progressively became the most densely settled hamlet. Typically, the New York-ers, or "Hilltoppers" as they were called, disembarked from the train at Bedford Hills and took carriages to their estates in the pastoral areas of town. A second building boom took place during the 1920s as old estates were refurbished and new ones created. During these years, two institutions were formed that were to have a profound impact on the future development of the town: the zoning code, which established a minimum four-acre lot residential zone throughout 80% of the town, and the Bedford Historical Society, which has taken a very active role in preserving Bedford Village. Each in different ways sought to preserve a particular romantic landscape taste in the face of social and economic change.

From the Depression until the end of World War II, there was relatively little new development in Bedford. As the landscape became increasingly wooded, the large estates and their gardens took on a seedy look of elegant decay that came to be valued by many residents who wanted an understated, casual lifestyle. How-ever, the prosperity following the war ushered in a wave of new development, including the subdivision of large estates. In response to this subdivision, in the mid-1950s, a number of wealthy families who had lived in the town for several generations deeded land to nature preserves. Notwithstanding these moves, throughout the 1960s and 1970s, four-acre lots were beginning to be carved out of larger estates. The Town Development Plan of 1972 expressed concern about the rate of development and passed the Wetlands Law to help restrict it. Nevertheless, as there was a lot of land that could still be legally subdivided into four-acre lots, the slow breakup of many of the large estates continued. In 1989, the town government, with the backing of the large majority of the population, sought to stave off suburbanization through "steep slope" legislation, which further restricts development. During the 1980s and 1990s, a new group of very wealthy urbanites came to Bedford. Along with financiers, lawyers, and advertising executives came celebrities seeking an alternative to the fast-paced life in New York City and Los Angeles. The arrival of these wealthy outsiders has meant that while there are still subdivision pressures, many estates are being preserved intact and other large estates have been created by assembling blocks of land of several hundred acres. Houses that had been referred to in the 1960s as "white elephants" haven't been torn down as many had expected, but have been renovated, often by young families.

Contemporary Bedford

The town of Bedford, which occupies thirty-nine square miles, is one of the largest towns in northern Westchester County in terms of area. The majority of the town is very low density, as 80% of the land is zoned for single family houses on a minimum of four acres and 95% for houses on one or more acres. The three hamlets have higher densities. Bedford Village, the oldest and smallest, has become what the Bedford Historical Society has termed "a living museum," replete with a village historical tour, two museums, and restored buildings with little plaques. Over the past several decades, a drugstore, hardware store, and large grocery have relocated to a small shopping center outside of the village proper. A clothing store closed as local people were drawn to better prices and greater selection in central Westchester. The wider range of businesses previously located in the historic village proper have been replaced by real estate agencies, antique stores, and gift shops.

The second hamlet is Katonah. As early as 1878, civic-minded village residents established a village improvement society that organized opposition against the city of New York's plan to expand its reservoir system by flooding the village center. These efforts failed, and in 1897, the people of the hamlet moved the best large Victorian houses on great timbers dragged by horses along a wooden track. (The houses were lined up and moved slowly while people continued to live in them.) A new village center was laid out by the famous architectural firm of Frederick Law Olmstead. The village, an early planned community, was designed in the shape of a Celtic cross, with a broad esplanade lined with 250 trees down the center. The individual lots were deed restricted, forbidding the sale of alcohol, banning the keeping of pigs and vicious dogs, and outlawing noxious businesses such as tanning. Houses were to have a minimum value of $2,500 and property could not be sold to Italian Americans (Duncombe 1978).

All restrictions but the last (overturned in the 1950s) remain in force today. Contemporary Katonah has a comfortable late-nineteenth-century feel to it with a main street of single- and two-story shops and side streets lined with Victorian houses with flower beds and lawns stretching down to the sidewalks. It is the kind of village, with its little local markets and shops, which corresponds to an American archetype of a self-sufficient small town.

The third hamlet in town is Bedford Hills, created in the nineteenth century as services cropped up around the railway station. It is here as well as in Mount Kisco that immigrant laborers found modest places to rent and where Bedford's small black and Hispanic populations largely live today. To many residents of the town, Bedford Hills seems more like the adjoining town of Mount Kisco. In fact, Bedford Hills flows into Mount Kisco along a strip of small shopping malls, supermarkets, and car dealerships interspersed with stores and small houses.

Despite its reputation, Bedford is not homogeneously affluent. In fact, the median single family house price in Bedford in 2000 was $519,000. This puts the town only $112,000 over the Westchester County average and more than $300,000 less than the most expensive towns in Westchester (Bronxville, Harrison, and Scarsdale). This is not to suggest that there is not vast wealth in Bedford, but rather that in parts of town, especially in Bedford Hills and Katonah, there are concentrated pockets of much less expensive housing. There is relatively little multi-family housing in Bedford (99% of the town is zoned for single family housing on one or more acres). The presence of even a small amount of multi-family housing in town has forestalled an exclusionary zoning suit of the sort faced by Newcastle, often known as Chappaqua (the name of one of its hamlets), in the 1970s.[9] Indeed, the town of Bedford has maintained that it is not exclusionary because of its small pockets of affordable multi-family housing.

Bedford is of course prosperous relative to the United States as a whole and even Westchester County. Median household income in 1990 was $73,357, over double the national average, and the number of executives and professionals (46.58%) was just under double the national average.

Similarly, the residents of Bedford are highly educated relative to the national and county averages. The percentage of residents with graduate and professional degrees is particularly marked. In 1990, 20.75% of Bedford residents had graduate or professional degrees, while the national average was 7.22%.

Having described the landscape tastes of Bedford as Anglophile, it is interesting to examine the ethnic and national origin of residents of the town. Table 2.1 shows that the town of Bedford is overwhelmingly white, and Bedford Village stands out as the whitest and least Hispanic part of town.

Table 2.2 reveals that while the population of Bedford increased between 1990 and 2000 at a slightly faster rate than Westchester County as a whole, the population of Bedford Village declined during this time by 5.7%. Bedford's growth rate is substantially less than that of neighboring Mount Kisco, and

Table 2.1 Number and Percent of Population 2000[10]

	BEDFORD TOWN	BEDFORD VILLAGE	MOUNT KISCO	WESTCHESTER COUNTY
Total Population	18,133	1,724	9,983	923,459
White	15,867 (87.5%)	1,668 (96.75%)	7,766 (77.8%)	655,614 (71.0%)
Black	1,291 (7.1%)	5 (0.3%)	598 (6.0%)	129,276 (14.0%)
Hispanic	1,372 (7.5%)	40 (2.3%)	2,450 (24.5%)	144,124 (15.6%)

although many Hispanics work in Bedford, the number residing in the town as a whole between 1990 and 2000 is small relative to Mount Kisco and Westchester County. In fact, the number of Hispanics living in Bedford Village declined by 16.7% during the time, while their number more than doubled in Mount Kisco.[11]

The national origin[12] of residents of Bedford is of interest in terms of the town's dominant landscape narratives. The four dominant groups numerically in Bedford in 1990 are Italian Americans (14.2%), Irish Americans (12.3%), English Americans (11.7%), and German Americans (11.6%). Bedford is less Italian American and more Anglo than the neighboring town of Mount Kisco (24.5% Italian) and Westchester County (21.4% Italian). The difference is particularly marked if one looks at Bedford Village. Here people of English ancestry are the numerically dominant group, comprising 19.2% of the population.

Our study focuses primarily on Bedford Village and the "estate area" of town, which is generally considered an idyllically beautiful landscape of gently rolling hills. Tall maples and oaks overhang dirt roads lined with stone walls and wild flowers. Although they are hidden from view, the hilltops are dotted with late-nineteenth- and early-twentieth-century mansions, obscured by tall trees and approached by long winding gravel driveways. The aesthetic value of having a rural landscape is seen by most all of the residents of the town as unquestionable. According to an aestheticized view of nature, Bedford's many acres of pasture, forests, and large wooded house lots indicate that it has more nature than if the

Table 2.2 Percentage Population Increase 1990–2000

	BEDFORD TOWN	BEDFORD VILLAGE	MOUNT KISCO	WESTCHESTER COUNTY
Total Population	+7.3%	−5.7%	+9.6%	+5.6%
White	+6.6%	−6.7%	−1.1%	−5.8%
Black	+2.0%	−61.5%	−20.1%	+7.4%
Hispanic	+12.2%	−16.7%	+121.1%	+67.2%

Fig. 2.1 Pastoral Bedford.

town were composed principally of houses surrounded by manicured lawns. This romantic discourse, which we examine in Chapter Six, lends support to the exclusionary structures and practices that maintain Bedford's scenic landscapes.

Bedford Village is no longer a rural village, but a rural-looking suburb, or exurb. Many people in Bedford claim to hate suburbs. In fact, to contemporary residents, suburbia conjures up a terrifying vision of spreading so-called "placeless" and "ticky-tacky" Levittowns of the early postwar period. They fear being swallowed up by this suburban sprawl. In fact, suburban towns vary considerably.[13] American suburbia includes many types of community that are far more planned and controlled by resident's associations than Bedford, which despite its highly restrictive zoning code and long history of institutionalized planning, has evolved incrementally over centuries according to the wishes of countless individual decision-makers with a long tradition of individualism and antipathy toward homogeneous placelessness. Examples of more highly planned suburban communities include the early garden cities,[14] contemporary CIDS (common interest housing),[15] and MPCs (master planned communities).[16]

Bedford should also be distinguished from contemporary neotraditional villages that have resulted from a movement against the so-called "placelessness" of MPCs. Neotraditionalism looks toward traditional, prewar suburbs and even pre-industrial agrarian-style villages (Dowling 1998; Duncan and Lambert 2002; Ellen 1996, 74; Falconer Al-Hindi and Staddon 1997; McCann 1995; Till 1993).

It values both the elegant countryside and historic villagescapes of towns such as Bedford, but these have become so expensive that they are out of reach of many middle- and even upper-middle-class buyers (Ellen 1996, 74–75). Consequently, neotraditional communities are now being built to satisfy some of this demand.

Bedford in Theory

As the visible, material surface of places, landscapes can evoke powerful images and sentiments, helping to constitute community values and playing a central role in the performance of place-based social identities and distinction (Cosgrove 1993; Daniels 1993; Graham 1994; Lowenthal 1991; Matless 1998; Rose 1995). Members of certain types of small, affluent, and relatively homogeneous communities are able to mobilize enough economic and cultural capital to create landscapes that have the power to incorporate and assimilate some identities while excluding or erasing others. These landscapes serve as scarce positional goods charged with an aura of the particularity of place. In capitalist societies such as the United States where identity is linked to possessions, the aesthetic often plays an important role in depoliticizing class relations (Harvey 1989).[17] Class relations as constituted by power, authority, and production practices become aestheticized.[18] By this we mean that they are obscured, becoming incorporated into categories of lifestyle, taste, patterns of consumption, and appreciation of the visual, the sensual, and the unique. As we (Duncan 1973) have argued,

> ... since it is usually easier to make or lose money than it is to gain or lose status, those in privileged status positions seek to dissociate status from class, that is to urge that status reflects factors such as family origin, manners, education or the like—attributes that are more difficult to obtain or lose than economic wealth. Landscapes become possessions for those with the wealth and power to control them.

Although certain geographers and sociologists have long understood that landscape taste is an important positional good (Duncan 1973a, 1999; Firey 1945; Higley 1995; Hugill 1986, 1989; Ley 1993, 1995; Lowenthal 1991; Lowenthal and Prince 1965; Pratt 1981; Wyckoff 1990), we would argue it is more important as a form of cultural capital (Bourdieu 1984) than many academics have recognized. Because landscape taste is an issue that preoccupies the affluent more than any others in society, it usually has been seen as relatively inconsequential and thus rarely investigated by academics. However, we would argue that its consequences are more far-reaching than may at first appear.

Don Mitchell (1994, 9) points out that much of the recent geographical work on landscape has been consumption oriented, arguing that landscapes "retain their ontological status in geography as evidence and as reflection of social and cultural processes rather than as determinants in these structures." For example, one can point to individuals who construct and maintain landscapes and others who spend their leisure time enjoying them. Clearly, a class analysis can be applied to understanding the labor relations involved in producing them. Nevertheless, production and consumption are often inseparable, as we hope to demonstrate in this study. In fact, Mitchell (1994, 10) himself states this as clearly as anyone: "Landscape is best understood . . . as a certain kind of produced, lived, and represented space constructed out of struggles, compromises and temporarily settled relations of competing and cooperating social actors. It is both a thing and a social 'process,' at once solidly material and ever changing."

Wealthy suburban communities surrounding global cities such as New York are particularly good examples of a phenomenon found in many places in the contemporary world: a retreat from the perceived impersonality of modern mass society and from the psychologically unsettling processes of globalization. Therein, social relations are increasingly disembedded and reconnected into complex and heterogeneous networks of abstract social and economic relations (Beck, Giddens, and Lash 1994; Giddens 1991). As David Harvey (1989, 292) says, "The revival of basic institutions (such as the family and the community), and the search for historical roots are all signs of a search for more secure moorings and longer lasting values in a shifting world." This reaction is evident in a militant localism (Probyn 1990), regionalism, ethno-nationalism, or what Harvey (1989, 305) calls "the reactionary politics of an aestheticized spatiality." Although not *all* localism is militant or reactionary, as Harvey (1989) or Neil Smith (1996) sometimes appear to imply, it tends to be exclusionary. The retreat into localism is often manifested in the celebration of place and tends to be more widespread and insidious than is often acknowledged. It can be argued as well that there is an aesthetic of community that celebrates "sign-values" of close neighborly relations that obscure a lack of more fully developed communal relations.[19] This is often based in an aesthetic of anti-modernity, which both provides a sense of disconnection from global networks and reembeds one in place.

We aim to repoliticize the naturalized categories of the subjects of our study rather than take them for granted ourselves. We attempt to avoid a compartmentalization of issues that can allow casual, everyday mobilizations of power to go unrecognized by those who suffer the consequences as well as those who benefit. We wish to avoid separating aesthetics from issues of social justice and the danger of alienated complicity that comes with sharing in an unproblematized aesthetic attitude toward beautiful landscapes such as the rolling green hills of Bedford. The beauty of such landscapes obscures the exclusion as well as the exploitation that produces them. Mitchell (1996a) provides a similar example in which the beauty of California's San Joachim Valley belies the struggle and exploitation that constitutes its landscape. Whether it is or is not in the interest of members of a particular class or group to take a critical view of hegemonic ideologies, few people question the broad ideological frameworks within which they make their day-to-day decisions. Alternatives to many of the existing local political structures, such as those that effect housing opportunities, are rarely considered because of the spatial dispersion of populations of people who as a group might otherwise raise challenges, if only there were a form of organization to bring them together.[20] Those without property in an American town are unable to obtain standing in a court of law to challenge exclusionary practices. In fact, most court cases against exclusionary zoning in the United States have been brought to court by developers hoping to build multi-family and other more affordable types of housing. Developers must first buy property in a town and only then can they challenge its zoning laws if they can afford to do so. Most federal programs offering incentives to these developers to build affordable housing were dismantled during the 1980s and thus there have been relatively few court cases challenging exclusionary zoning since then. This "structuring out" of any potential resistance to exclusion occurs because of the relative autonomy of towns and the power of residents, especially in a residential town such as Bedford. We agree with Ed Soja (1989, 6), who states that "we must be insistently aware of how space can be made to hide the consequences from us, how relations of power and discipline are inscribed into the apparently innocent spatiality of social life, how human geographies become filled with politics and ideology."

Kevin Hetherington (1997) points out that the "new cultural geography" has tended to focus on marginality and acts of resistance to the social order. We have chosen instead to look primarily at privileged groups with resources and power to build landscapes, to protect themselves with invisible walls of zoning, and to shape their own identities through these landscapes. The ways that these orderings are mobilized are unseen by those who happen to drive past admiring the beauty of the landscape. Deeply embedded in the landscape are human costs invisible to the eye. Landscapes are thus not as innocent as they appear.

We believe that the swing in the field of geography toward an emphasis on individual human agency, autonomy, and intentionality, often at the expense of structures, structuring, and stabilizing practices, was at one time a necessary corrective to structural determinism. However, this liberal, individualistic orientation can sometimes deflect attention away from a critical, grounded analysis of the workings of successful hegemony, structured inequalities, unintended externalities, unknown conditions, and complex complicity across far-reaching networks. While we share with other cultural geographers an interest in uncovering resistance movements, revealing fragile hegemonies, and exploring contested geographies, we also assume that the degree of hegemony and success of resistance must remain open empirical questions. In places like Bedford, resistance to exclusionary practices and structures is fractured and minimal. Practices of domination and conservation of the status quo are sometimes seen by the residents as struggles against inevitable economic forces and processes of modernization rather than as relations of domination. By employing a nonindividualistic theory of agency, we believe an understanding of diffuse complicity through enabling structures and networks of individuals, institutions, and other resources may be possible. We would like to show how people share in responsibility through heterogeneous networks of organized, structured relations, institutions, and other resources.[21]

Residents of Bedford and similar towns manage to combine reappropriated "weapons of the weak" (Scott 1985) with the heaviest weaponry in the arsenal of the rich and powerful. Their actions demonstrate that weapons of the weak should not be uncritically celebrated by liberal planners and others seeking ways to augment the power of local groups to fend off developers and agents of corporate capitalism. We take the perhaps unpopular view that as critical geographers we should be in a position to analyze invisible interconnections and structural conditions (including historical discourses) that residents often fail to recognize. In doing this, we understand the many reasons why the residents *could,* but would choose not to, reflect on the consequences of their privilege.

We aim to achieve a balanced view of how hegemonic ideas are reproduced. While recognizing a high degree of self-consciousness, intentionality, and strategizing, we oppose any simplistic manipulation thesis, seeking instead to place primary emphasis on only partially articulated class reproduction practices. As Terry Eagleton (1990, 4) says, "I do not intend to suggest that the eighteenth century bourgeoisie assembled around a table over their claret to dream up the concept of the aesthetic as a solution to their political dilemmas." Similarly we offer no such simplistic explanation of historically complex practices. Our perspective harks back to the early work of Paul Willis (1977, 2) who stated, "Class identity is not truly reproduced until it has properly passed through the individual and the group, until it has been recreated in the context of what appears to be personal and collective volition." We are concerned both with what people sincerely believe and what they strategically profess. We are also aware that the line between these is sometimes difficult to discern and that often people have varying degrees of knowingness about the often small part their individual actions play in reproducing local structures. Likewise, we pay attention both to taken-for-granted ideas that support successful relations and conditions of domination and coercion through legislation. All are important to a full understanding of exclusionary practices. We explore the way attachment to place, heritage, nature, and place-based identities have been developed and practiced in places such as Bedford. While we investigate a type of alienation or cultural repression that results in a failure to recognize the unintended consequences of place attachments and celebration of localities, we are equally interested in the knowingness entailed in deciding that certain issues of social justice ought to be sacrificed in the interest of preserving an aesthetic.

We are interested in how landscapes are integral to social and political processes and how they embody past and present social relations (Duncan 1990; Mitchell 1996a; Schein 1997). We adopt a hermeneutic approach[22] to understanding how landscapes are central to the performance of social identities, investigating how they are read both consciously and practically (nondiscursively) by the people who produce, value, and engage within them. Of particular interest are the social and political consequences that flow from these various readings (Duncan and Duncan 1988, 1997; Duncan 1990). Because landscapes are integral to identities and because of deep emotional attachments to places, threats to the landscape are often interpreted as threats to identity. Thus the reaction to what some may consider trivial questions of differing aesthetic judgments may be surprisingly intense.

One of the most interesting geographical aspects of this particular case study is the success of the hegemony that is achieved in part through the fragmentation and the spatial exclusion of potential resistance. The overall structure of landscapes is relatively fixed and largely beyond the control of most people and institutions, except the wealthiest. However, in certain types of communities, residents have gained control over their landscapes. Having a territorial, material basis, these landscapes are privatized through various mechanisms of appropriation and exclusion, private (including institutional) ownership, and local legislation. Power relations and exclusion are aestheticized through the design of landscapes and thereby tend not to enter the terrain of explicit contestation. Exclusion, rather than being recognized as anti-democratic, acquires an aura of scarcity and becomes a form of cultural capital. In place of the negatively charged words "exclusion" and "exclusionary," one finds the positively charged term "exclusive." An exclusive neighborhood thus is a positional good—consequently one that is highly sought after.

Landscapes, especially those that are highly controlled, are integral to the performance of social identities. Collective memories, narratives of community, invented traditions, and shared environmental concerns are repeated, performed, occasionally contested, but more often stabilized or fixed in artifactual form. As Harvey (1996, 8) says, "We are in daily practice surrounded by things, institutions, discourses, and even states of mind of such relative permanence and power that it would be foolish not to acknowledge those evident qualities." One of the more common means of ensuring that landscapes are transformed into cultural capital (positional goods) and communicate social identities is through exclusion. Various social, economic, political, and legal practices have been devised to create or stabilize the association between landscapes and particular desired social identities. These exclusionary practices are not always recognized as such; often they are defined as preservation. And in fact, as we will illustrate below, exclusion in itself is often not the goal, but the means for preserving the "look of the landscape." The aim is not to intentionally exclude *types* of people, but to prevent an overall increase in the *number* of people and houses in the town. In this respect, Bedford may not be typical of suburban landscapes more generally, as we will explain. Indeed, in the case of nearby Mount Kisco, it is the Latino day laborers, their physical appearance, their deportment, and their ways of using space that are the cause of strong feelings of aversion.[23]

The higher one goes up the scale of wealth in a community, the more control the owners of property expect to have over their residential spaces. In the poorest neighborhoods, people may have little choice about the interiors of their rooms or apartments. Moving up the scale of wealth, people begin to have control over their interiors and, if they own property, their front and back yards. With more money to spend, the rich can display more personal choice in producing a well-designed house and garden. The richest people, having both the greatest resources and feelings of entitlement, attempt to control long-distance views. They often go to great lengths to ensure that nothing they see from their own property and nothing they pass by when they drive around their towns is unattractive. The pleasure they take in their property as well as its economic value thus depends greatly upon control over the aesthetic and spatial practices of a whole community. As residents of Bedford and similar towns believe, ownership of land gives them the right and responsibility to produce a town's landscape as a coherent whole, a visual production, or a unique "work" to use Henri LeFebvre's (1991) term. "Sense of place"—meaning a locale possessing an aura of uniqueness as well as historical and environmental value—is the veneer that obscures practices of social homogenization and "spatial purification" (Sibley 1995).

Our view of identities is similar to our view of place; although we see them both as fluid, performed, fragmented, multiple, and contested (Butler 1990), we find that people continually attempt to stabilize and establish secure identities and, more often than not, anchor them in place. As Gerry Pratt (1998, 27) argues, "Denial of [place-based] boundaries would seem a luxury affordable only to those not trapped by them." Or, we would add, not threatened by their absence or excluded by them. She goes on to say, "The same is probably true for the romanticization of them." In other words, stabilized identities and bounded places whether positive or negative, protecting or entrapping, enabling or constraining, are not always but often the empirical reality. This reality challenges contemporary theoretical predilections toward celebrating instability and permeability of borders and boundaries. Thus, we are in agreement with Harvey (1996, 8) when he says,

> While I accept the general argument that process, flux, and flow should be given a certain ontological priority in understanding the world, I also want to insist that this is precisely the reason why we should pay so much more careful attention to 'permanences' that surround us and which we also construct to help solidify and give meaning to our lives.

If places are seen as borderless, blurred, and chaotic, one will be unable to understand the "multiple processes of boundary construction" (Pratt 1998, 44) well enough to disrupt them. We see Bedford as lying somewhere toward the more stable and relatively less contested end of a continuum of boundary construction projects and reterritorializations of identity found within the United States today. Thus our primary focus is on subtle naturalizing and aestheticizing attitudes that reinforce social and spatial boundaries.

We have not attempted to produce yet another study of the suburban politics and legislation behind exclusionary zoning; instead we wish to present an in-depth study of relatively hegemonic aesthetic values and the historical and cultural reasons why these values should be so secure in a county within the New York metropolitan area where the pressure to develop land is great. We attempt to show how the logic of aesthetics parallels the logic of hegemony so that class inequalities are refigured and depoliticized as questions of landscape taste or environmental ethics. We investigate the reasons for the success of the dominant ideologies of nature, history, and individualism, as well as the failure of an effective resistance to these ideologies to materialize.

What does it mean to view something aesthetically? Although a variety of different, loosely related aesthetic discourses have developed since the Enlightenment, in practice they have become conflated (Eagleton 1990). The most common contemporary view assumes an engaged or immersed quality of the aesthetic as a realm of immediate, unarticulated response to the materiality of art or nature or whatever objects one adopts an aesthetic attitude toward. Often unarticulated except in naturalized, unself-conscious terms, the aesthetic is largely separated from the realm of the cognitive. The aesthetic disposition in this sense is related to ideology in that it refers to the unarticulated, unmediated, and naturalized pleasure one takes in the concrete materiality of things in themselves. Although visual pleasure is often based on learned taste or so-called "refined" appreciation, part of the learning process is to internalize the taste so that it appears a self-evident inclination, a "habit of the heart" (Bourdieu 1984). As such, the aesthetic refers to a sensuous, bodily pleasure and immediacy of response that is thought to be shared with others (Kant 1987, 20)—self-evident, yet subjective rather than objective, eliciting a spontaneous agreement. As Terry Eagleton (1990, 28) puts it,

> The aesthetic is from the very beginning a contradictory, double edged concept. On the one hand, it figures as a genuinely emancipatory force—as a community of subjects now linked by sensuous impulse and fellow-feeling rather than by heteronomous law, each safeguarded in its unique particularity while bound at the same time into social harmony . . . On the other hand, the aesthetic signifies what Max Horkheimer has called a kind of "internalized repression," inserting social power more deeply into the very bodies of those it subjugates, and so operating as a supremely effective mode of political hegemony.

The aesthetic attitude is closely linked to European romanticism in that both valorize lived particularity over abstracted generalization (Lash and Urry 1994, 49; Pepper 1984), the locality over centralized governance, and embeddedness in place over the global interconnectedness of social relations. To take an aesthetic, as opposed to a critical, attitude toward a landscape is to be in one sense alienated from it by rendering it naturalized, autonomous, and self-evident, as well as sensually pleasurable. Harvey (1996), following Raymond Williams (1960, 1990), believes that it may not be possible to have a nonaestheticized reconciling of place-based particularisms with spatially extensive processes not directly accessible to direct local experience. In this, his view is more measured and pessimistic than Doreen Massey's (1991a, 1991b, 1993) "progressive" or inclusionary sense of place. While Harvey (1996, 32–33) speaks hopefully about "potentially progressive" and "tangible" "solidarities organized in affective and knowable communities" that consist in "a reaching out across space," he nevertheless fears reactionary as well as "militant particularisms." While not wishing to generalize about the inherently conservative or progressive qualities of place, we see such attachment in Bedford as highly conservative.[24] Hence, we focus here on the dark side of aestheticism and romanticism as leading toward the inward-looking "pursuit of personal, national and racial idiosyncracies" (Pepper 1984, 71).

To say that the aesthetic is seen as spontaneous and naturalized does not contradict the fact that there is also a belief in the "refinement" of taste and that this very refinement is itself a form of cultural capital. As Pierre Bourdieu (1984, 36) discovered in his comprehensive study of bourgeois aesthetics in France, taste is learned mainly within the context of the family, most effectively over generations through practical experience in a class or cultural habitus and yet it *appears* paradoxically to be an arena of great freedom and individual expression. Bourdieu (1984, 56) states, "Each taste feels itself to be natural—and so it almost is, being a habitus which amounts to rejecting others as unnatural and therefore vicious." Fine social distinctions are based on a demonstrated appreciation of the aesthetic. While this appreciation can be learned deliberately over a relatively short period of time, it is often believed that the least self-conscious and elegantly demonstrated aesthetic sensibilities are inculcated over a lifetime. Thus, as we found out in Bedford, for example, many people often have little knowledge of the history and textual basis of their landscape taste; they do not need to know this because they have learned it in a nondeliberate, experiential sort of way. Their taste is performed and practiced as a general appreciative approach to living life that closes the gap between art and life—making of one's life and landscape a work of art with the aura of the unique (see Campbell 1987, 183, 199).

Taste has come to be seen as the property of individuals. Each person is assumed to be entitled to his or her own taste. This produces a sense of community based on the idea of autonomous individuals sharing taste. From this point of view, the aesthetic has the same qualities as hegemony. The question about what is attractive, it is believed, cannot be logically argued or subjected to rigorous analysis, but inspires unself-conscious consent from individuals. These judgments are seen as coming from a realm of the aesthetic separated from ethics, ideology, or politics, further securing the hegemonic effect (Eagleton 1990). Through the sensuous, passionate, apparently autonomous subjective experience of individuals who appear to obey no laws except those internally imposed, hegemony is achieved because agreement appears spontaneous. Furthermore, unlike the realms of politics or ethics and unlike the realms of cognition and of reason, the aesthetic commands the most secure hegemony because it appears to relate to nothing but itself. Thus the aesthetic parallels Antonio Gramsci's (1991) concept of hegemony that sees consensus across classes achieved without coercion. Hegemony is based on a type of alienated thought by which the interests of the dominant classes in society are naturalized and universalized to the point of being seen as coincident with the interests of all classes.

While we do not wish to overplay the extent of consensus, we have found it to be considerable. In our various research projects on the landscapes of Bedford and Mount Kisco over the years, we have interviewed people from a wide range of income and educational backgrounds.[25] While there are some differences of opinion and awareness of exclusion, in general we were struck by an overwhelming sense of consensus that tends to support the status quo. The fragility, fragmentation, and superficiality of hegemony, however, must always be acknowledged and the extent to which dominant ideas go unquestioned can never be assumed but should be seen as open empirical questions.

Eagleton (1990, 20) writes,

> The ultimate binding force of the bourgeois social order . . . will be habits, pieties, sentiments and affections. And this is equivalent to saying that power in such an order has become *aestheticized*. It is at one with the body's spontaneous impulses, entwined with sensibility and the affections, lived out in unreflective custom.

Normally to take an aesthetic attitude toward something is to react to it sensually, not analytically—not looking beneath its surface to study or criticize the underlying social relations and other conditions of its production or reproduction. Bourdieu (1984) says something similar when he claims that certain practices become "enchanted," that is, naturalized, taken for granted, and invisible. While they certainly can be questioned, in practice they tend not to be. Of course it is also possible to take an aesthetic attitude *as well as* a practical stance toward something. Often the aesthetic response is secondary but sequestered in one way or another, temporally or spatially. In other words, it is thought about by the same person wearing different hats in different contexts. Whatever is aesthetic—a picturesque landscape, for instance—is seen as having value in its own right. Its existence is necessarily interdependent with other (often unjust) processes—economic, political, or social—that remain unappreciated. To the extent that the aesthetic is a sensibility that is seen as separated from the cognitive or the moral, to the extent that it is unable to be clearly articulated, then one wonders what politics follow from such an attitude? Can one talk about the political implications of taking pleasure in landscapes (Rose 1993)?

Aesthetic values are sometimes seen by local decision-makers as positive values to be weighed against other issues they have responsibility over. But even with people in such positions, interdependence is often underappreciated. Even when it is recognized that trade-offs have to be made between aesthetic and other goals such as social justice, safety, economic gain, or convenience, it is rarely recognized that aesthetics itself can be ideological nor is it always recognized that there may be a class and ethnic basis to a particular aesthetic that helps to secure the hegemony of certain groups. In other words, what we are arguing here is that there is often an aestheticization of decision-making about aesthetics, because while the aesthetic is seen as vulnerable to politics, it is usually not thought to be ideological or political in and of itself.

Methodology

We used a variety of research methods in this study, including seventy-six semi-structured interviews (fifty-one from Bedford and twenty-five from Mount Kisco) and the analysis of various written texts, including town histories, planning texts, two townwide surveys of the residents of Bedford, and one townwide survey of the residents and business owners of Mount Kisco.[26] Real estate advertisements, newspaper articles in several local and regional newspapers, and the *New York Times* not only served as an important source for tracking local controversies, but offered a wealth of information on the opinions of town officials and residents alike. We also analyzed the landscape itself, a text (among other things of course) whose meaning tends to be "read" inattentively and uncritically by residents because it is thought to be politically neutral rather than normative.

Our Bedford interview sample of fifty-one people included both long-term and more recently arrived residents.[27] We interviewed people from a range of occupational, educational, and income levels, although as we were primarily interested in the views of affluent residents, we drew most heavily on that group. Relatively few cultural and historical geographers have studied elites due in part to perceived difficulties of access and political commitment to studying the less privileged.[28] Notable exceptions are Cosgrove (1984), Daniels (1993), Higley (1995), Hugill (1986, 1989, 1995), Ley (1987, 1993, 1995), Lowenthal and Prince (1965), Pratt (1981), Woods (1998), and Wyckoff (1990). In fact, elites remain generally understudied in academia (Woods 1998).[29] However, most of the social issues that researchers are concerned with are thoroughly relational. There is a whole spectrum of highly mediated, structurally enabled and constrained relations between classes. As such, it makes little sense *not* to study locally and globally powerful elites and the issue of their complicity in oppressive relationships for which they may not *individually* be held accountable (Kutz 2000; Young 1990). Their social practices—including apparently independent decisions about where and how to live their personal lives—are complexly interrelated with the lives of others. Hughes and Cormode (1998b) state, "In researching the myriad processes which forge contemporary landscapes of power, it is important to know more about and critically engage with, the people who are most influential in shaping these processes, along with those affected by them."[30]

We also questioned people whose occupation made them of particular interest to us, such as town officials, local real estate agents, developers, and environmental activists. Our questions to residents focused on issues such as what people value about Bedford, what changes in the town they have noticed, why they moved to the town, what they thought about land development issues and nature preservation, and the impact of Bedford's zoning on the surrounding area. The interviews varied greatly in length, the shortest being thirty minutes and the longest over six hours. We used the same set of questions for each respondent, but the longer interviews took off in various unplanned directions. Some people were interviewed more than once. A few were people we had known for a very long time or had interviewed for earlier projects (Duncan 1973, N. Duncan 1986; Duncan and Duncan 1984, 1997). We found this to be an advantage, as a number of the issues we were touching on were sensitive and having a long-term association with the town and a close relationship to some respondents allowed us to get more candid interviews.

We assured all those we interviewed that we would not identify them by name or in any other way reveal their identities. In a few instances we, therefore, changed an informant's occupation to a similar one in order to guarantee anonymity. The only residents we identify by name are those in official positions or whose opinions and activities have been reported in previously published material (mainly newspapers). The respondents were very willing to talk to us.[31] Some were even disappointed that they would not be named in the book. No one we approached refused to be interviewed. In many cases, this willingness came from an intense interest in the town and its landscape. There was also an assumption (which we specifically tried *not* to foster) that because we wished to discuss aesthetic issues (in particular such things as historic preservation and environmental conservation) that we would agree with the opinions being expressed. The preservation of history and nature were seen as self-evidently valuable practices.[32]

In our Mount Kisco sample, we focused principally on Latino laborers because we already had a good sampling of non-Latino attitudes from newspapers and the Mount Kisco town survey and because we were interested in the attitudes of day laborers working in Bedford. We also interviewed a number of village officials, local Latino advocates, and non-Latino residents. We conducted our interviews in Spanish with day laborers and in English with other residents and officials. Luis Lujan, a research assistant and graduate student at the time, conducted some of the interviews. Approximately two-thirds of these respondents were men, reflecting the overrepresentation of men among day laborers. A few of the interviews conducted on the street were short, others lasted as long as two hours. The Mount Kisco interviews centered on housing and the "day laborer issue" and a semi-structured questionnaire was focused around a series of controversies in the village.

A survey conducted in 1997 by the Bedford Conservation Board in connection with the Bedford Master Plan was mailed to each of the 6,200 households of Bedford. Five-hundred-and-fifty questionnaires were returned, a response rate of 8.87%. The 1999 Bedford Master Plan Questionnaire was prepared for the town by the Center for Governmental Research Inc. in Rochester, New York. Surveys were mailed to one thousand residents, 649 of whom responded at a 64.9 % return rate. The sample was chosen from the list of property owners using a random stratified technique. Residents of the different hamlets were targeted in order to sample opinions in each part of town. Both surveys sought to elicit resident opinion about the future of the town by asking them about development and their attachment to various parts of town. The 1999 Mount Kisco villagewide survey (Frederick Clark Associates) was sent to 5,500 residents and returned by 710 of them, at a rate of 13%. The sample, which drew upon homeowners, renters, and store owners, sought opinions about the social and developmental issues facing the town as it developed its new Master Plan (Clark 2000). These three surveys addressed many of the same issues that we raised in our qualitative interviews. While such surveys lack the ability to probe resident opinion deeply, they add breadth to our interview data. Thus, we used these survey data as a check on our interpretations and at times as a guide to what issues we might probe in our more in-depth interviews.

CHAPTER 3

The Narrative Structures:
The Cultural Codes of a
Landscape Aesthetic

Here we maintain a country feel. We are very English.
—man who moved to Bedford from Scandinavia
several decades ago

I think I learned my landscape taste from the landscape itself. I
identify with the land in Bedford.
—woman who grew up in Bedford

Introduction

In the last chapter we saw how Bedford began to be transformed both visually
and socially after the middle of the nineteenth century, as affluent urbanites
converted declining or derelict farms into country estates. Bedford was being
reshaped by new aesthetic ideals based on the landscape tastes and cultural consumption practices adopted and developed during the nineteenth century by
urban elites. As signifying systems, the landscapes of Bedford not only communicated a gracious, country house way of life, but they also played a substantial
role in constituting this aestheticized way of life. Landscapes are, of course,
much more than signifying systems. As the visible surface of places, landscapes
are ensembles of physical elements and economic infrastructure—hills, fields,
streams, dirt roads, barns, mansions and cottages, railroads, offices, stores and
villagescapes, as well as images, views, and individual and collective memories.
They are media molded into grand compositions that are enacted within the
framework of culturally and historically particular discourses. As we have argued, landscapes, especially landscapes of home, become incorporated into the
formation and performance of individual, familial, and community identities.
The meanings of places upon which people base their identities are contested
and assembled from very loosely articulated cultural discourses.

In the case of nineteenth-century Bedford, newcomers from the city brought
with them an ambivalent anti-urbanism and romanticized images of the countryside as a principal site of stable and healthy social relations. A dominant set
of discourses, juxtaposed and amalgamated in various ways, became embedded

and naturalized in the landscapes of Bedford at that time. These various discourses of country life are loosely related and of diverse origin and varying degrees of compatibility. They have been open to varied interpretations and negotiations. While individual strands have gained and lost prominence over time, this complex of narratives and ideologies and their interrelations can be traced back historically, although we will not attempt this here. The discourses include Arcadian ecology; the romantic idea of wilderness; Thoreauean transcendentalism; a Jeffersonian agrarian vision of the virtuous yeoman farmer; aristocratic stewardship of land; rural republicanism; the English pastoral ideal including the country cottage, wild garden, and country house; Puritan New England democratic values; and historic preservationism.[1] In the twentieth century, new narratives were added to this interacting, intertextual melange including the anti-suburban back-to-the-land movement, an enhanced ecological consciousness, and scientific and aesthetic environmentalism. These discourses (fragmented and sometimes contradictory among themselves) have evolved and combined to create a "moral geography" (Matless 1998) for Bedford—an imagined geography with performative (rhetorical) power to commit individuals to collective action. This imagined geography has shaped Bedford in its mutually constitutive relations within the physical, political, economic, and regional geographies of the New York metropolitan area.

The terms "ideology" and "discourse" signal something more than consciously held ideas. They allude to broad taken-for-granted frames of reference, including practical knowledge that results in embodied material practices of engaging with the world. Discourses contain commonsense ways of knowing, valuing, and doing—for example, knowing what one likes without knowing how to explain why, or seeing any reason to do so. Discourses contain morally charged tales and loosely linked pieties that connect landscapes to places and places to lifestyles and political and religious ideologies, shaping them all into a dominant aesthetic. Rather than try to trace the multiple origins and intricate workings out of each of the discourses mentioned above, we will focus on what we consider to be three key discourses (defined broadly enough to encompass many aspects of the others), which appeared frequently as underlying themes in our interviews: the wilderness, the New England village, and the pastoral. All three were first inscribed on Bedford's landscape in the late eighteenth and nineteenth centuries, a landscape that had been lived in and loved by poor farmers in ways much less influenced by these romantic and aesthetic ideals.

W. J. T. Mitchell (1994, 2–3) states that a full account of landscape should trace the process by which the landscape effaces its own readability and appears to naturalize itself. He adds that we must understand that process in relation to what might be called "the natural histories" of its beholders. He goes on to state that like money, "landscape is a social hieroglyph that conceals the actual basis of its value. It does so by naturalizing its conventions and conventionalizing its nature."[2] In other words, the histories of landscape as a medium of identity

formation and power relations can be interpreted as the history of the naturalizing of ideologies as they become materialized in the landscape. We intend in this
chapter to briefly trace this history for Bedford. Mitchell (1994, 3–4) adds that
while landscape in the form of the picturesque "may be an 'exhausted medium,'
at least for the purposes of serious art or self-critical representation; that very
exhaustion, however, may signal an enhanced power at other levels . . . and a
potential for renewal in other forms, in other places." The physical landscape of
rural New England (including Bedford) is one such place.

The three principal discourses of the wilderness, the New England village, and
the pastoral are highly intertextual in that they are expressed in literature, painting, film, advertisements, and the landscape itself. These media have become
intertwined, reinforcing, and mutually constitutive. Each symbolically encodes
narratives that not only define Bedford as a landscape, but as a whole aestheticized way of life. In later chapters, we will demonstrate how these discourses
underpin contemporary zoning legislation, as well as historic preservation and
nature conservation. We find, not surprisingly, that people have only a very diffuse knowledge of the history of the landscape tastes they have adopted. Rather,
their knowledge is " practical" (Giddens 1979). That is to say that although most
residents have only a vague discursive knowledge of the basis of their taste, they
effectively put it into practice and make a whole series of decisions and social
judgments based upon that knowledge.[3]

Wilderness

Wilderness is a complex concept whose meaning has changed considerably over
the centuries. It is a concept composed of diverse narratives of evil, savagery,
heroism, redemption, godliness, freedom, utility, refuge, fragility, and protection. As Peter Schmitt (1990, xvii) points out, "[W]ild nature has changed
almost as much as an image in American rhetoric as it has in its physical features." Certainly, the idea of wilderness as something valuable to be preserved is
relatively recent. The English colonists who arrived on the eastern seaboard of
the United States in the early seventeenth century described the land they saw
before them as a "hideous and desolate wilderness . . . full of wild beasts and
wild men . . . and the whole country full of woods and thickets" (Thomas 1983,
194). In his account of the historical geography of American forests, Michael
Williams (1989, 11) points out that the forest was seen as a "dark and sinister
symbol of man's evil, where one was beyond the reach of redemption and where
even a civilized man could revert to savagery if left too long." Within this narrative framework, the clearing of the forests was a form of redemption, for "in the
clearings God could look down benevolently on their efforts to reestablish order
and morality" (Williams 1989, 12). The colonists expressed no sentiments about
the beauty of the forest; they held a utilitarian view that "the forest was good
only inasmuch as it became improved land or lumber, or the site of settlements"
(Williams 1989, 11). This would have been the attitude of the first white settlers

in Bedford who chose the site because it had already been partially cleared of forest and then set about further clearing to create additional farmland.

By the eighteenth century in Britain, among the elite at least, attitudes toward forests had changed; deforestation had proceeded at such a pace that there were sound economic reasons for reforestation. The cutting of trees such as elm, oak, and ash beyond a specified age and size was outlawed (Daniels 1988), while these same varieties were planted for timber to help defray the cost of the enclosure (Bermingham 1986, 9). Tree planting during this time was seen as an aristocratic venture signifying a "complex mixture of social assertiveness, aesthetic sense, patriotism and long term profit" (Thomas 1983, 209). As such, trees became an indispensable part of the scenery of upper-class English life. As the wild forests, disappeared to be replaced by replanted forests, they ceased to terrify and appall, becoming romantic sources of inspiration and pleasure. The commercial and aesthetic value of forests was further reinforced by a growing religious conception of nature that saw all God's work as serving a purpose. In fact, by the latter part of the century, an aesthetic appreciation of wild nature was considered a fundamental aspect of religious faith. Wild nature had come to be seen as beautiful, morally healing, and spiritual. Thomas (1983, 216, 259–61) says, no other people went so far in this "divination of nature" as the English.

Such aesthetic attitudes toward forests are based on a romantic appreciation of the picturesque and the sublime as symbolic freedom. At its height in the late eighteenth century, the picturesque movement became equated with English scenery—irregular mountains, shaggy trees, woodlands, winding country roads, and old, overgrown gardens. Wilder scenery, such as that found in the Alps, was considered sublime (Bermingham 1986, 57, 63). Uvedale Price in his 1810 essay on the picturesque and the sublime speaks of "the love of seclusion" as "not less natural to man, than that of liberty." This love of seclusion in old, even derelict gardens resonates with contemporary descriptions of Bedford by some of our informants and can be found reflected in local real estate advertisements. Such eighteenth- and nineteenth-century English ideas of wilderness were influential among Americans, especially the east coast elite. After the American Revolution in 1776, as they set out to invent a new national identity, Americans ironically drew upon English romanticism to refashion themselves as products of the American wilderness (Schmitt 1990, xvii). The romanticism of William Wordsworth, Samuel Taylor Coleridge, and Percy Bysshe Shelley blended deism, primitivism, the picturesque, and the sublime. Popularized in America by Ralph Waldo Emerson, William Cullen Bryant, and other American intellectuals, it had a profound impact upon the urbanized upper classes. The wilderness was celebrated in the paintings of Thomas Cole, Frederick Church, and the Hudson River School; the novels of James Fenimore Cooper and Washington Irving; and the transcendental philosophy of Henry David Thoreau, which taught such values as simple living and stewardship of nature.

Like other Americans of his class, Thoreau saw the forest as a revered place to be returned to for spiritual strength and regeneration. Such romanticism was popular with the educated elite who saw forests as God's first temples (Thomas 1983, 216). In fact, some have argued that by the end of the century nature had become a new religion in America and lamented that Christianity had been "almost wholly an indoor religion" (Schmitt 1990, 141). In 1896, Charles Eliot wrote of forests as the "cathedrals of the modern world," and in 1912 John Burroughs wrote, "If we do not go to church as much as did our fathers, we go to the woods much more" (Thomas 1983, 216, 269). In his classic study *Wilderness and the American Mind,* Roderick Nash (1982) states that "appreciation of the wilderness began in the cities." He goes on to say that "the concepts of the sublime and the picturesque led the way by enlisting aesthetics in wild country's behalf while deism associated nature and religion." English romanticism's appreciation of the wilderness made its way into American culture first through an intellectual elite and later with members of a business elite who had the means to build summer camps and weekend houses in the woods. Preservation of the rapidly disappearing forests became an influential movement, as stories of heroic struggle against a hostile nature were slowly replaced by one of shame at capitalism's plundering of America's most fragile and precious heritage. As we shall see below, this heritage was valued not only for aesthetic and moral reasons, but for health-related (for example, protection of watersheds) and economic reasons as well (Nash 1982, 120–21). By the mid-nineteenth century, the government began to set aside preserved land. Yellowstone National Park was established in 1872 and in 1885 the Adirondack region of New York State became a forest preserve.

Late-nineteenth-century English romanticism was politically conservative in the older aristocratic sense that it was opposed to the spatial expansion of industrial capitalism (Weiner 1981). It incorporated an anti-urban aesthetic and sensibility, held to ambivalently by those who lived in cities or whose family money came from industrial capital. Such elitist romanticism included a nostalgic affinity for an old English aristocratic order that favored noble simplicity over an industrial complexity, feeling over rationality, and aesthetics over utilitarianism (Pepper 1984, 76–78). It was a reaction to what romantics saw as a mass urban-industrial society that alienated individuals and, more important, their bodies from their true natures. By returning to nature in the wilderness, it was thought individuals could regain the health, morality, and freedom that had been corroded away by modern society. There was a heroic, individualistic quality to this intensely aesthetic and sensual response to nature (Oelschlaeger 1991, 110–11).

From the 1870s on, gentlemen farmers began to convert dying farms into picturesque estates by planting trees and allowing pastures to revert to woodland. A local writer (Shoumatoff 1979) states that according to a land study conducted in the 1880s, Westchester County was 80% clear. To judge from early photographs, it was a bleak wasteland of boulder-strewn pastures and long stone fences. He says that only on the ridge and hilltops and down in the ravines where it was too steep and rocky to farm were the woods intact. He goes on to say that contemporary Westchester is more than 80% wooded.[4]

Romantic views of wilderness interacted in complex ways with material conditions. By the late nineteenth century, the demand for timber in New York was such that by 1870, the state was importing over a million tons per year (Williams 1989, 17). At this time, there were renewed calls for the preservation of wilderness. For some, wilderness preservation took on the character of a moral crusade against lumbering interests, which were demonized as sinful and self-interested (Schmitt 1990, 144). In 1895, in response to pressure from preservationists, the state constitution created state forests in New York within which lumbering was highly restricted (Schmitt 1990, 14). For conservationists, who see nature as a valuable resource to be husbanded, properly maintained forests were seen as potentially sustainable.

North American flora and fauna were objects of intense scientific interest during the eighteenth century. The study and classification of nature offered another rationale for preservation. Religious and scientific views of nature were sometimes conflated. In the metaphor of nature as a "great chain of being," every element has an essential place in a hierarchy such that if one link in the chain is removed the whole is threatened. Yet another metaphor sees nature as a book that one must learn to read in order to know God's purpose (Pepper 1984, 42, 43, 69). By the late nineteenth century, such taxonomic and scientific interest was institutionalized in the formation of societies such as the Agasiz and the Audubon Societies, branches of which were formed in Bedford at this time, the Sierra Club, the Society of American Foresters, the National Geographic Society, and a number of academies of science. The late nineteenth century also saw the rise of professional nature guides and naturalists as educators, who would diffuse the idea of the importance of wilderness to the middle classes (Wilson 1992, 56). It was considered especially important that children be exposed to the physical and moral benefits of nature. By 1915, summer camps where children could become morally and physically healthy had become common. Ninety percent of them were in New England, the closest source of wilderness for the urban elites of the eastern seaboard (Schmitt 1990, 96).

During the late nineteenth century, changes in transportation technology made nature increasingly accessible to affluent city dwellers. The twentieth-century parkway was not only a road to nature, it was itself a "nature road" designed to allow drivers to view nature as they traveled to recreate their minds and bodies in the countryside.[5] These parkways re-created key symbolic landscapes: the forest edge, the lake, and the stream (Wilson 1992, 34, 37). Some of the best known of these parkways are in Westchester County; they include the Hutchison River, Merritt, and Taconic Parkways, as well as the Sawmill River Parkway that runs through Bedford.

The New England Village

As we saw in the last chapter, Bedford was once part of the state of Connecticut and thus founded as a New England village. But this is not to say that it originally corresponded to nineteenth- and twentieth-century romantic images of what a New England village should look like. As we show, this was a conscious achievement. For many white middle- and upper-class Americans, particularly in the east, this landscape image embodies the essence of American history and the ideals of close-knit community and participatory democracy. As such, it is one of the key symbolic landscapes in America today (Meinig 1979). Because of this symbolic power, key elements of the New England village landscape—village greens, clusters of white wooden houses, and white churches with steeples—have been reproduced up to the present in towns and suburbs around the country. The most recent manifestation has been the vogue for neotraditional planned developments.

Over the past several decades, a body of scholarship has challenged received notions about the appearance of the original colonial New England villages. J. R. Wood (1982, 1984, 1986, 1991, 1997), for example, has argued that the classic model of the nucleated New England village composed of farmhouses around a meetinghouse on the green was in fact rare. John Stilgoe (1982, 44–45) points out that as early as 1654 there were few towns in Massachusetts that were nucleated around the meetinghouse. Rather, this form was an ideal that often appeared in town plans and was encouraged by the clergy so as better to keep an eye on their flock. The reality, however, was that farmers preferred the convenience and freedom of living on dispersed farmsteads, coming into the village center only to attend to their religious and secular duties. Such was the case with Bedford Village. The classic Christmas card New England village is largely a nineteenth-century invention of colonial tradition. It owes its presence not so much to seventeenth-century Puritan settlements as to eighteenth- and nineteenth-century shire and market towns like Bedford, aestheticized by nineteenth-century romanticism. As Wood (1991, 41–46) points out, there were many towns in the nineteenth century whose economic and population growth was stunted because they had been bypassed by the railroad. Some of these were "romantically reconfigured as symbols of the past" by summer people who "restored" them as romantic embodiments of the imagined colonial New England village (Butler 1985). Before the 1830s, village life was thought by the urbanized elite to be dull and backward (Stilgoe 1988, 78–79). As late as 1850, Andrew Jackson Downing decried the ugliness of villages caused in large part, he said, by Irish immigrants. The Irish, who were too poor to farm, lived in shacks in villages and kept pigs that roamed freely and devoured vegetation. Downing said, "Wherever they settle, they cling to their ancient fraternity of porkers, and think 'it no free country where pigs can't have their liberty' " (quoted in Stilgoe, 1988, 86). As we shall see in Chapter Eight, contemporary ethnic antagonism is again expressed in terms of aesthetics and differences in spatial practices, leading to segregation and attempts at exclusion. Downing also spoke of the necessity of planting shade trees to beautify villages: "A village whose streets are bare of trees, ought to be looked upon as in a condition not less pitiable than a community without a schoolmaster, or teacher of religion" (quoted in Stilgoe 1988, 86–87).

Until the 1840s, a typical New England village green remained the functional, if ugly, mess of mud and weeds that it had long been. But by the late 1840s, some of the members of the old rural elite with connections to the urban and national elites influenced by romanticism and transcendentalism sought to re-create an image of republican simplicity in the country and began to clean up villages and their greens. These re-created colonial villages were in fact composed primarily of newly popular building styles that had not been present during colonial times. These included Greek revival, neo-Gothic, and Queen Anne (Jackson 1985, 71; Stilgoe 1988, 31). The newfound love of "invented villages" was reinforced before World War I when more Americans traveled to England and discovered the English village. They began at that time to evaluate their own villages by English standards (Stilgoe 1988, 217–19). This hybrid blend of the New England village, the Jeffersonian farm, and the English village thus became naturalized as the traditional rural ideal.

Early in the twentieth century, affluent Americans became keenly interested in the colonial past and began to discover American pine, cherry, and walnut antiques, seeing them as especially appropriate to rural and village settings, while dark mahogany and oak English antiques were seen as more appropriate to formal city settings. By the 1920s, this now widely shared love of antiques spread to a revaluation and restoration of old houses. Those who could not afford an old house bought an old-looking new one (Stilgoe 1988, 290–93). The *Ladies Home Journal* promoted colonial houses and sold mail order plans (Lynes 1980, 210). A developer-led building boom in the prosperous years after World War II has reinforced this trend so that colonial, loosely defined, is the most common house style in east coast suburbs at present. Although the elite who inhabit Bedford wish to distinguish their large colonial mansions built in the 1920s from post–World War II middle- and working-class suburban colonial-style houses on smaller lots, this house style and the desire for this style have a common history.

The Pastoral Idea in England and America

The third and most important landscape narrative in Bedford is the pastoral. Before the middle of the seventeenth century, the English government opposed the enclosure of common lands and sought to curb the power of large landowners (Bermingham 1986, 9). A century later, however, the enclosure movement had gained momentum as the percentage of England and Wales controlled by large landlords rose from 70% in 1700 to 85% in 1800 (Butlin 1982). During the eighteenth century, wealth was still derived from the great English estates, but increasingly such estates became high-status retreats for the leisured classes (Bunce 1994, 78). Landscape designers such as Capability Brown were hired by wealthy landowners to design vast parks created out of newly enclosed lands. The enclosure movement made possible a controlled landscape of large open fields interspersed with woodlands. The fields were kept cropped and fertilized by grazing animals. Brown and others were responsible for the spread of the lawn as a miniaturization of the pastoral, as well as the mix of meadow, water, trees, and grazing animals that we associate with the natural, romantic garden (Jenkins 1994, 10–15). Although Brown's landscapes were criticized after his death as a form of conspicuous consumption (Daniels 1993, 83), the criticism was of their large scale rather than their "natural", romantic design. Henceforth, gardens, whether on the grand scale of Brown's or at a more modest scale, were designed to create the illusion of wild nature, rather than the formality that characterized French and earlier English gardens of the elite (Crandell 1993, 117).

Although the lawn is now thought to be a quintessentially American landscape feature, the first European colonists found no perennial lawn or pasture grasses in America (Jenkins 1994, 10–15). The common east coast grasses were annuals such as broomstraw, wild rye, and marsh grass; these were rapidly killed off by European cattle, sheep, and goats. More nutritious European grasses and clover were imported and gradually replaced them. European immigrants to America in the seventeenth and eighteenth century brought their traditional garden designs of mixed herbs, vegetables, and flowers with them. In the eighteenth century, wealthy Americans often had a flower garden rather than a lawn in front of their house, while ordinary people had bare, packed dirt or uncut native grasses. An elite eighteenth-century English landscape tradition of lawns studded with trees was introduced into America in the latter part of that century. Wealthy Americans learned of the English aristocratic tradition through books, paintings, and travel, and produced them with the help of English indentured gardeners who scythed them and dug weeds by hand (Jenkins 1994, 15).

In the postrevolutionary period, some of the most distinguished patriots quite consciously emulated English styles. Among the best known of the English-style pastoral estates were Chancellor Livingston's late-eighteenth-century estate on the Hudson, the Gore estate in Massachusetts, and the Penn estate outside Philadelphia. William Hamilton, who spent time in England touring estates after the revolution and was an avid reader of romantic British writers, built Woodlands, a 500-acre English-style country seat outside Philadelphia, at the end of the eighteenth century. Thomas Jefferson noted in 1803 that Woodlands was "the only rival which I have known in America to what may be seen in England" (Jenkins 1994, 16–17 [ref. 51]); Stilgoe 1988, 135–36). George Washington followed English models at Mount Vernon and employed English landscape gardeners. His estate had a deer park and a bowling green protected by a "ha-ha," a ditch designed to keep animals out. A Polish guest at Mount

Vernon observed, "The General has never left America; but when one sees his house and his home and his garden, it seems as if he had copied the best samples of the grand old homesteads of England." Due to Washington's popularity, views of Mount Vernon were reproduced and sold widely during the late eighteenth and early nineteenth century, greatly helping to popularize the English pastoral landscape style in America (Jenkins 1994, 16 [ref. 48–49]).

While minister to France from 1785 to 1789, Thomas Jefferson spent time in England where he was influenced by the great aristocratic estates. He created his own estate, Monticello, as a model English pastoral estate. As the best-known garden designer in the United States, he diffused English landscape tastes to an elite postrevolutionary population (Jenkins 1994, 16 [ref. 42–45]). Leo Marx (1964, 73–75, 88) has argued that a fully articulated pastoral ideal in America emerged by the end of the eighteenth century. Jefferson blended Virgilian pastoralism with Enlightenment beliefs about radical primitivism, perfectibility, progress, and the condition of man in the state of nature. The Jeffersonian model of rural life was a moral and political as well as a practical guide for life. Jefferson and others such as Benjamin Franklin saw the independent farmer as the building block of American democracy. The sturdy yeoman farmer shielded from the artifice of city life was seen as the foundation of a truly virtuous and prosperous society (Schmitt 1990, xvii).

Ordinary American farmers, such as those who lived in Bedford struggling to earn a living, would have been much less familiar with these romantic ideas (Williams 1989, 14). However, wealthy families in Bedford, as elsewhere, with ties to a national elite and to England, such as the Jays and the Woods, took their lead from English aristocrats, transforming their working farms into picturesque estates. The best known of the late-eighteenth-century estates in Bedford was that of John Jay, who built an English-style manor house and adopted the pastoral aesthetic. In the 1860s, John Jay II built Bedford's first ha-ha, creating the pleasing picturesque illusion of a natural landscape unmarked by traces of human labor. And by the end of the nineteenth century, new gentlemen farmers, summer residents, and commuters came to Bedford thoroughly versed in the romantic aesthetic.

In England during the early nineteenth century, a tension had developed between the old rural elite and nouveaux riche industrialists who set themselves up on country estates. Members of the old elite attempted to reinforce their claims to distinction through a newfound interest in genealogy and the picturesque landscape style with its emphasis on the old and the rustic (Bermingham 1986, 74). But the old elite ultimately fought a losing battle to distinguish themselves from the new capitalists who quickly appropriated their style (Weiner 1981); between 1835 to 1889, 500 country houses were built or remodeled in Britain (Jackson 1985, 88). As early as the late eighteenth century, the middle classes were also beginning to discover the countryside as a site for leisure activities and ultimately as a source of their own cultural capital (Bermingham 1986, 10). Just as Humphrey Repton reduced the scale of Capability Brown's designs, bringing them within the reach of the upper middle classes, so landscape architects like John Loudon in the first half of the nineteenth century brought the picturesque and the pastoral within the reach of the middle classes. Loudon was best known for the gardenesque style, a small-scale version of older, grander landscape gardens. He said of his designs, "The suburban residence, with a very small portion of land attached, will contain all that is essential to happiness, in the garden, park and demesne of the most extensive country estate" (Bermingham 1986, 170). This miniaturization of the great estate provided an affordable pastoralism as the middle classes fled cities by railroads to the newly created suburbs.

Referring to the United States, Michael Bunce (1994, 101) argues that "although the idealization of agrarian society is associated most directly with Jefferson, much of the persistence of the agrarian myth in the American mind can be attributed to fictional literature and, more recently, to the portrayal of farm and country life in film and television." Although Thoreau is often thought of as a philosopher of wilderness, he also contributed to the spread of the pastoral impulse in American thought at mid-century.[6] His insight was to see the pastoral as a "middle landscape combining elements of both wilderness and civilization . . . both cultivated fields and forest within the reach of the city" (Nash 1982, 94–95). As such, he was an early theorist of suburbia or what Stilgoe (1988) calls "the borderland."

American landscape gardeners were also influential during this period. *The American Gardener's Calendar,* written in 1806 by Bernard McMahon, advocated an English pastoral landscape of great lawns, copses of trees, massed shrubs, serpentine walks, and water features (Jenkins 1994, 23). Arguably the most influential American landscape designer of the nineteenth century was Andrew Jackson Downing. Born in England in the 1820s and brought to America as a child, Downing's importance was not only as a codifier and popularizer of the English pastoral, but as miniaturizer and hence democratizer of the style. Downing's *A Treatise on the Theory and Practice of Landscape Gardening,* written in 1841, was based on a book with a similar title by the great English landscape architect Humphrey Repton. In this and *The Architecture of Country Houses* (1851), Downing outlined an ideal model of the American country house, based upon the miniaturization of the eighteenth-century English country estate. Echoing Jeffersonian ideas and those of other nineteenth-century romantics, a house in the country surrounded by gardens was seen as a moral bastion against the corruption of cities (Jenkins 1994, 20). Downing built himself a small estate of five acres in Westchester overlooking the Hudson. The Gothic revival house and great lawn were designed as a showplace to demonstrate that the beauty of the English estate writ small was within the reach of the upper middle classes (Lynes 1980, 23–24).

Downing, who was influenced by Loudon's gardenesque style, also wrote a highly influential book titled *Cottage Residences* (1842). The idea of the country cottage as a lower priced alternative to the villa drew upon Anglophilia and disappointment with the American farm, which, although romanticized in the Jeffersonian tradition, was considered too utilitarian and unattractive by many bourgeois suburbanites. Around mid-century, writers and landscape designers such as Nathanial Willis, Frederick Law Olmsted, Nathanial Hawthorne, and Andrew Jackson Downing toured England and encountered what Stilgoe (1988, 28–30) called "the magical world of artists and literature" centered around the landscape of the English cottage. By mid-century, the cottage had replaced the farm as a symbolic site of rural virtue. The cottage was not necessarily small but it was simple, blending English picturesqueness with republican sympathies (Stilgoe 1988, 30–32). In 1847, Downing urged readers of his journal *The Horticulturalist* to choose building sites with old trees to "dignify" a newly built house making it appear old. By the 1890s, second growth on abandoned farmland had matured sufficiently for developers in Westchester to find such picturesque lots (Stilgoe 1988, 118, 186). While estate landscapes of lawns, copses, waterways, and vistas were possible on the larger properties, developers of small lots signified the English estate through the use of lawns and small clumps of trees (Jenkins 1994, 27).

The lure of the countryside during the nineteenth century for both British and American educated classes was fostered by the romantic idealization of the countryside in the writings of Wordsworth, John Keats, Shelley, Alfred Tennyson, and William Morris. These writers presented readers "with a vision of an English countryside in which woods, wildflowers, grassy banks and birdsong were at the center of the idyllic scene." Painters such as Holman Hunt reproduced these same images on their canvases. Similarly, a romanticized version of bourgeois country life was presented to Victorian readers by Jane Austen, George Eliot, the Brontes, and Anthony Trollope (Bunce 1994, 41). The mid- to late nineteenth century saw the emergence of childhood literature that sentimentalized the countryside (Bunce 1994, 50, 63) and in the twentieth century, authors such as Beatrix Potter, Kenneth Grahame, and A. A. Milne continued the genre (Bunce 1994, 50, 51, 66). From early in the twentieth century, images of the pastoral were fed by country life magazines and later by glossy coffee table books. Victorian images were supplemented by twentieth-century romanticizers of the countryside such as Evelyn Waugh, P. G. Wodehouse, and James Herriot, all popular in the United States as well as in England. The power of these images has been further increased by the representation of Waugh's and Herriot's stories on television and in film, bringing together for today's audience the literary and the painterly ways of seeing.

From the latter part of the nineteenth century on, country life magazines aimed specifically at suburbanites proliferated. Such magazines had little to do with the technical aspects of farming, and everything to do with the healthy pleasures of the simple life in the country (Jackson 1985, 72; Schmitt 1990, 16). At the end of the nineteenth century, one increasingly found gardening advice published in newspapers for the new suburban residents. Around the same time, the American garden club movement was founded by well-to-do suburban women. A founding chapter of the Garden Club of America was started in Bedford in 1913. These clubs sought not only to beautify cities and suburbs but to provide models of taste for the middle and lower classes as well as immigrant groups (Jenkins 1994, 27, 38).

By the beginning of the twentieth century, the pastoral ideal had become so subconsciously ingrained in the minds of east coast American suburbanites that the knowledge of specific historical connections of the landscape to a pastoral literary and philosophical tradition—so clear among the middle and upper classes in the nineteenth century[7]—was largely lost to all but a highly educated few. In many ways, Bedford's landscape at present can be seen as the result of a move begun by authors such as Jefferson and Thoreau: the conversion of pastoralism from a literary tradition into a whole aestheticized way of life. A dominant landscape taste now flourishes largely independent of the literature that once popularized it. It has become a form of practical, largely unarticulated, knowledge informing everyday practices of producing and consuming landscapes.[8] It is naturalized as the indisputably beautiful—as simple, natural, good taste and an example of intertextual practice that knows itself in only the vaguest of terms. It is this process of cultural forgetting to which Pierre Bourdieu's (1984) concept of enchantment refers. Although the textual bases have become largely disconnected from the landscape practices they underlie, the narratives of pastoralism, wilderness, and the New England village have entered social memory through evocative phrases, images, pictures, historical vignettes of beautiful landscapes, novels, films, and advertisements. It is such landscapes that give residents a sense of Bedford as the place they know and love and a sense of themselves as belonging in its landscapes. In fact, the principal text in which these ideas are inscribed is now the landscape itself, as the quotation at the head of this chapter exemplifies. Pastoral, woodland, and village views (past and present) conjure up strong emotions and drive people to great expenditure of time, physical effort, and money in order to maintain and defend the landscape of rural Bedford as they know and remember it.

Narratives and Social Memory as Reproduced in Contemporary Real Estate Advertisements

Real estate advertisements in the *New York Times*, local newspapers, and brochures for properties in Bedford typically employ fragments of a narrative such as "gentleman's farm" or a series of fragments such as "pastoral views, estate area, historic New England village." These fragments act as synecdoches for narratives preserved in social memory. Real estate agents create advertisements by classifying properties according to a taxonomy of locally resonant narratives (New England village, English estate, romantic cottage garden, forest glade, and so on). These fragments of description accompany photographs of an aspect of the property composed to make the property visually fit the description. Real estate advertisements articulate a model of rurality for those for whom it is already firmly embedded in social memory. In so doing, local real estate agents not only market land and houses, but reproduce an alluring picture of Bedford and its "historic" estates as a desirable setting in which to establish social distinction. They are, in other words, selling a place, a way of life, and placed-based identity. This is clear from the fact that in the shorter advertisements the houses and the land they sell are often not described in much detail. Information such as the number of rooms are often left out in favor of small evocative elements such as "babbling brook" or "rock outcroppings" that signify a whole country way of life.

It should be noted here that, as one real estate agent told us, the advertisements are written as much to please an owner's sense of pride and thereby secure listings as it is to attract buyers. Among the best known examples of lifestyle advertising in national publications today are Ralph Lauren's Polo advertisements, whose soft focus and Anglo-American country house images promise 1920s-style upper-class "WASPdom" to all who buy his line of clothing and accessories. We use the term "WASP" (white Anglo-Saxon Protestant) here advisedly, knowing that Jews, Roman Catholics, blacks, and other non-WASPs have not simply adopted an English landscape taste, but have appropriated it for themselves and changed it from an ethnically specific style into a more generalized symbol of social class. Whether there is a possibility of unwitting complicity or evocation of a disquieting history of ethnic and racist exclusion tainting the history of this aesthetic is a difficult matter of interpretation that we will not enter into here. We will say, however, that an English landscape aesthetic has at times been consciously employed to distinguish the dominant white, Anglo elite from all others and that there is today among some of our interviewees a nervousness about ethnic Others appropriating what they see as their own codes of distinction.[9] Our informants expressed to us in various ways that while successful mimicry drives them to ever more subtle codes, what they loath most are poor copies that spoil what they see as a vulnerable landscape. An example of successful mimicry is Ralph Lauren, because he has spent several tens of millions of dollars to create the ideal English country house in Bedford. According to almost everyone we interviewed, he has managed to re-create a dignified version of a mature English country estate.

While Americans hold on to a belief in an inviolate inner self, their actions show that they also subscribe to the idea that "possessions maketh the man." Such views are perhaps less contradictory than they at first appear. Because identities are performed and articulated in part through consumption practices, taste comes to be seen as a window into the inner person as well as a badge of belonging because the "inner person" is always already thoroughly social. Advertising spins narratives that relate an object for sale to a whole constellation of places, practices, and other objects. In order to be efficacious, these narratives draw upon culturally ingrained symbolic systems that resonate with the consumer. Running throughout the real estate advertisements in Bedford are words that create fantasies of a gracious, propertied way of life that comes with owning land in Bedford. These narratives are framed within nineteenth century, anti-urban, romantic attitudes toward nature and history. Bedford is portrayed as a site that blends the picturesque wilderness with the pastoral countryside. The real estate advertisements script Bedford as not only a refuge from the city, but a retreat back in time to the eighteenth- or nineteenth-century countryside of a grand manor house, a quaint and cozy farmstead, English cottage, or a picture postcard New England village.

Nowhere in these advertisements is the word suburbia mentioned, as it has become a signifier for placelessness, an undistinguished middle-class lifestyle, small lots, and uninteresting tract housing. However, while the advertisements allude to an escape from urban modernity, they often point out that Bedford is not isolated from urban amenities. Bedford is close enough to New York City for daily commuting and access to its airports. Typically, advertisements will say, "One hour from Manhattan," "50 minutes to La Guardia airport," or "5 minutes to Route 684." But none of this seems to undermine the imagery of an escape. We sense a knowingness about the imagery that they realize is an illusion and yet is deeply pleasurable in its associations nevertheless. One could say that there is a kind of cultivated fantasy, a belief that one wishes to retain in the face of contradictory evidence, not unlike an older child's belief in Santa Claus.

The Pastoral

The following are the first words or phrases used as titles in advertisements: "35 picturesque acres in foremost estate area. Gently rolling fields, stone walls and high woodlands," "Giant trees, old stone walls, pastoral views," "Open pasture—Rolling fields with spectacular southern views and woodlands—picturesque fields," "Bucolic views," "Rambling stone walls and a pond," "7 high acres of rolling lawns with huge shade trees, stone walls, and a park-like English country setting," "Long, winding drive leads to over 20 private acres of rolling lawns, orchards and fenced paddocks." Many advertisements employ painterly descriptions and words—"Majestic maples line the entrance drive," "Reflections of fruit trees and stone walls in the peaceful lake," "Verdant lawns," "An 18th century painting—Time has not changed the views from this spectacular 12 acre pastoral hilltop"—designed to summon up images of landscape in the minds of readers. The "estate," as it is used in advertising in Bedford, sometimes draws very explicitly upon fantasies of upward mobility. Such fantasies are overwhelmingly Anglophile; "English Manor House," "English Country Home," "English Stone Tudor," "Stone Cotswold," "English Fieldstone Victorian," "Walled English Garden," "Parklike English Country Setting," and "English Country Garden" are typical. Another evocative, if none too subtle, advertisement is titled "Born

Aristocrat" and goes on to mention an "English country setting." The principal house on many of these properties is referred to as a manor. For example, a number of advertisements have as their title "Stone Manor House" and "Early Victorian Manor House."

Another prominent theme in the selling of Bedford is equestrianism; this can be seen in the horse and hound logos of several real estate offices in Bedford. This signifier is part and parcel of the pastoral imagery, as riding or hunting with hounds is central to the rural upper-class lifestyle. Consequently, the following types of advertisements are common: "Bedford Riding Country," "Horses and Hills," "The Narrows, quiet dirt road in the heart of the horse country. Stone walls, stream, hardwoods, 4 acres." Other advertisements—"Hunt Country Estate," "Listen to the hunting horn—in an area of fine horse farms," "Horses, hounds! 10 rolling, private acres"—imply that Bedford is hunt country. Here again such advertisements convey a mood rather than give detailed information about the house or property. Numbers of bedrooms, for example, are often left out.[10] They are intended to appeal to those seeking a country house image, rather than conveying useful information. For example, while Bedford has several hundred miles of bridle paths, hunting with horses and hounds actually takes place in the nearby town of North Salem.

The past, both real and imagined, is a source of prestige for those who can claim connection with it. While few can trace their ancestors back to the twenty-two families who settled in 1680, those willing and able to spend a large amount of money can purchase a bit of Bedford's history. There are relatively few eighteenth-century buildings left in Bedford, but when they appear on the market, their age is their most prominent selling feature. Most of these eighteenth-century houses are of modest size, as Bedford did not become prosperous until it became a commuter suburb of New York in the late nineteenth century. However, a few of these properties have recently come on the market for as much as $3.7 million in part because of their charm and acreage. Titles of these advertisements read, "18th Century Gem" or "18th Century Gentlemen's Farmstead." Another advertisement reads, "1700's Gentlemen's Farm—Stately and Serene, a Step Back into Bedford's Past!" However, buyers are reassured, "completely updated with original detailing remaining." This, of course, is what an aestheticized view of history requires.

Such lifestyle advertising also appeals to the graciousness of an earlier age—"Colonial stone manor house with gabled slate roof. Built in the late 19th century," "A throwback to the lifestyles of gentleness and refinement," or "Elegance and opulence reminiscent of the golden age." This golden age, built upon fortunes quickly amassed with highly exploited labor, could hardly be characterized as gentle. But this fantasy is untroubled by the fact that much legislation has been required to prevent such a "golden age" from returning. (It might be noted, however, that there is evidence in Bedford today that such a "golden age" is to an extent returning and not simply as a fantasy. Such gains as the labor movement was able to secure have been rapidly eroded away. Large estates, thought of in the 1960s as unsaleable "white elephants," are now are being restaffed from a new pool of relatively unprotected immigrant laborers from Central America.[11]) The early twentieth century is a source of historical fantasy as well. An advertisement for a 1920s house suggests, "Roll back time to an unspoilt era." Another reads, "Turn of the century country grandeur—Unsurpassed, unspoiled. Long drive opening out on nearly 17 acres of 1900's romance . . . An historic hidden wonderland." Here the past is "romance," a "wonderland" from a time before the landscape became "spoilt." This is the well-known pastoral lament of longing for a recent, more idyllic past that has been expressed over the centuries (Williams 1973).

One of the most common themes in these advertisements is privacy, which is in part at least an aesthetic category closely related to individualism. Long driveways figure prominently in advertisements because they create privacy. As one advertisement says, "Long, Long Drive to Total Privacy." Other advertisements emphasizing privacy read as follows: "11 acre retreat in total privacy," "Neighboring expansive estates and nature preserve provide further seclusion and protection," and "Private hilltop with views for miles." Privacy is also a mark of wealth, for in the relatively densely populated New York metropolitan region, privacy is a scarce and costly commodity. Increasingly, however, trees and hills are not seen as providing sufficient privacy. Recent advertisements read, "Gated and fenced for the ultimate in privacy" and "Complete privacy with complete security."

The Small Farm

An image of the New England farmstead with allusions to democracy, individualism, and self-sufficiency is used to sell some of the smaller properties in Bedford. Some are sanitized farms from the eighteenth and nineteenth centuries, while others are quaint reproductions. While it is no longer possible to earn a living by farming the land in Bedford because of the high cost of land and property taxes, these farmsteads stand as synecdoches for a "wholesome," physically engaged way of life that exists in Bedford primarily in social memory. A working farm with its efficient metal silos and modern farm equipment would be considered an eyesore. We find a seeming paradox of the aesthetic ideology in that only a farm made affordable by urban-based capital is seen as an adequate signifier for the self-sufficient farm with all of its anti-urban resonances. But the paradox is more apparent than real because self-sufficiency is an aesthetic more than a material reality. The rurality of Bedford does not replace the city in the lives of its residents—it decenters and revalues it. The city is a necessary lifeline to cultural and technological sophistication. It is also a connection to a globalizing world and, for many, a place of work. Bedford creates a retreat for families with multiple positionings in society and a taste for a variety of lifestyles. It provides a private space away from the urban public sphere.

While advertisements for the estates in Bedford often look back to England as the cultural model, advertisements for the small farms draw more often on American themes—for example, "Meadows, oaks, old stone walls. All the charm of old Vermont on quiet country road. Historic colonial." Another reads, "A walk thru history. 19th century New England farmstead. Sparkling renovation based on historical research. Picturesque property with weathered barn." This latter advertisement touches upon several key elements in the aesthetic, including picturesque decay, with the assurance that the property is renovated to contemporary standards of luxury. Potential buyers are further assured that this renovation has been "based on historical research," given the stamp of scholarship.

Other advertisements—"Step into Bedford's Past! Circa 1740 antique colonial . . . Completely charming," "Colonial farmhouse ca 1790 . . . impeccably restored," "Near the Mighty Oak. Charming 1800's farm house. Quiet dirt road, old stone walls, rolling lawn, babbling stream," "Romantic 1800s colonial farmhouse"—recast property not simply as heritage for sale, but as an opportunity to experience a distillation of the best the past has to offer. A number of themes recur, especially an experiencing of the past through the possession of property and picturesque imagery similar to that used to market larger estates, without the more obvious language of distinction. Adjectives selected are instead drawn from the discourse of the picturesque and include "charming" and "romantic." The word "charming" appears over and over again as a code for what (in the Bedford context) is a relatively small property. As in the advertisement titled "Eighteenth Century Painting" mentioned above, some properties are directly compared to pictures—for example, "Picture Book Farmstead" and "Currier and Ives. 19th century Bedford captured forever."[12] The sensibility exhibited here comes virtually intact from the eighteenth- and nineteenth-century picturesque way of seeing, where travelers were urged to find landscapes scenes that corresponded to particular paintings and poetic descriptions. The phrase "19th century Bedford captured forever," suggests that just as an artist can capture the values of a time and place forever so can a purchaser of property.

The Cottage and Historic Village Houses

The cottage in Bedford draws its imagery principally from nineteenth-century English romantic anti-urban images of the cottage and its garden, in which city dwellers find opportunities to commune with God or their own inner selves through the therapeutic experience of gardening (Thomas 1983, 236). Present-day advertisements still appeal to such sensibilities. Examples include "Gardener's Eden," "Queen Anne's Lace," or "Romantic Cottage. A quiet oasis in the heart of Bedford—a pond, a brook, a gardener's delight." Another ad reads, "Country cottage retreat. An antique showcase for the romantic at heart." The term "showcase" in this advertisement is telling for it suggests that while one might wish to retreat from the competition of the urban marketplace, one's attitude to the home is still informed by the market mentality displaying one's taste and social status as an urban merchant would display his goods. Yet another advertisement—"The completely renovated country kitchen features many modern amenities . . . yet retains the charm of an old cottage with its exposed beams"—demonstrates the fantasy of retreat with an aesthetic emphasis.

One can see the self-conscious employment of intertextual allusions in the titles of advertisements, such as "Storybook Cottage," evoking the romantic rural childhood literature that originally shaped the tastes of the buyers. Some of the advertisements for the smaller properties—"English Country Home. Circa 1920 English home in the heart of Bedford's historic district. Charm and history combine!"—refer specifically to English themes. The English imagery in this advertisement was probably chosen because the house is stuccoed rather than clad with the more common American clapboard. Occasionally the style of the house need not have anything to do with England for this imagery to be adopted. For example, a small stained-shingle ranch-style house built in 1935 was advertised as "English Cottage. Country charm." Apparently the association was based on the fact that it had a "wide cobblestone walkway" leading to the front door. Some advertisements—"Antique Cottage. The ambience of colonial craftsmanship"—blend their imagery. Others are written as if they describe English picturesque landscape paintings—for example, "Country Romance—Ca 1834. Fabulous restored cider mill perched over rushing river and set amid 3 waterfalls—Over 2 acres nestled in a hollow fringed with elm, spruce and balsam—bucolic flavor to this sylvan retreat—For sophisticated country weekends."

As we have seen, Bedford Village is portrayed in the local histories and town promotional literature as an authentic New England colonial village, and not surprisingly, this is how real estate agents market properties near the village green. Headings for advertisements commonly read, "Historic Bedford," "A Walk Through History," and "Bedford Historic Charm." The few eighteenth-century houses that remain in Bedford command particularly high prices and their pedigree is prominently displayed—for example, "A Bit of History—Across from 18th century school house on Bedford's famous Green—A colonial gem circa 1790 restored to perfection," or "On the Village Green—The oldest house in Bedford's historic district. Registered in the Library of Congress—servants' quarters." The themes in these advertisements are variations on the themes discussed above—for example, historic fantasies, romanticism, the aesthetic, and distinction through the possession of property. An advertisement for a late-nineteenth-century house is titled, "Practically a Landmark!" while another is advertised as "A Country Village Victorian." Early-twentieth-century houses are marketed as "historic." Yet another reads, "Currier and Ives . . . historic village home, charmingly redone." Recently built village houses are advertised as having connections to the historic district—for example, "Executive Colonial Near

Historic District" and a "Quaint Village Street." The title of an advertisement for an early-nineteenth-century village house sums it up best: "History for Sale."

The House in the Wilderness

The advertisements usually convey the idea that a property is simultaneously remote and near, rustic and yet complete with modern conveniences—for example, "The Perfect Weekend Home. Romantic stone lodge set in wooded seclusion in Northern Westchester . . . yet only an hour from Midtown" or "Rugged country road leads to hilltop vistas. Transformed by well-known family into cosy retreat. Heated pool." Another advertisement—"Artist's Sanctuary. Down a meandering dirt road—draped with fresh pines—this woodland site enjoys quiet and seclusion"—constructs the buyer as landscape painter. Another reads, "Find seclusion among mature plantings and hidden rockeries." It is common to find such titles of advertisements as "Woodland Glade," "White Birch Grove," or "Nestled in Woodland Setting."

Some advertisements highlight rock formations that were an important part of the nineteenth-century picturesque—for example, "3 private acres. Dramatic rock outcroppings and meandering stream" or "Quiet woodland setting. Dramatic rock outcroppings." Many of the advertisements feature water—for example, "Woodland waterfall, pond, river. Total privacy yet so convenient—the perfect hideaway" or "Woodland waterfall. Cool rushing river known for its trout fishing! Protected privacy. Nestled among magnificent hemlocks. Once a fishing camp. This home was totally renovated in 1974 and 1989 . . . Gourmet kitchen overlooking herb garden. $1,225,000." Other details so commonly expected in real estate advertisements elsewhere (numbers of bedrooms and bathrooms, as well as the presence of a garage or playroom) are frequently replaced by more evocative details such as "herb garden." The above property provides perhaps the perfect aestheticized experience of the wilderness for an upwardly mobile urbanite: a fishing camp an hour from New York converted into a million dollar weekend retreat.

Conclusion

As we have argued, taste is a form of cultural capital that people acquire often without knowing its origins. People from similar social and regional backgrounds develop common sensibilities and aesthetic appreciations; shared taste is mobilized as the basis of group belonging and equally as the basis of social distinction or exclusion. Some images are widely shared; however, fine distinctions within this discourse are used to establish the status of some and to exclude others. An example from Bedford might be the appreciation of the old and decaying as a central value in the picturesque. A certain studied seediness, such as unrepaired stone walls, a heavy old iron gate, and a gravel or dirt driveway, make reference to history that is valued by some and rejected by others. Landscape taste plays an important role in the cultural reproduction of a local and national elite. As we hope to demonstrate, this aestheticization and stylization of life are not superficial values because they are in a profound sense constitutive of people's identities. They can lead to deep emotional attachments and sincere feelings that help explain how trivial (to an outsider) landscape changes or threatened changes can provoke anxiety, fear, aversion, anger, and hatred toward others. As we will show, they become the basis for a sometimes virulent politics of exclusion.

CHAPTER 4

Anxious Pleasures: Place-Based Identity and the Look of the Land

Ever since I first saw English country houses in the movies, I dreamed of one day having a country estate with a large wrought iron entrance gate. When my husband and I decided to move out of the city, we came to look at houses in Bedford. I took one look at this place and said to him, "This is where I have always wanted to live."

—woman who bought a recently built house in Bedford on
four acres

I guess you can tell from my answers that I want Bedford to stay the same as it was when I was young. In fact, if I had my way I would want to go backward in time and freeze Bedford. I'd like to go back to a time when Bedford was more pastoral, when people were less concerned about saving every last tree. I so wish that the new houses had never been built. Basically, for me Bedford is a retreat from some of the evils of the modern world. And new houses in Bedford seem like modern evils to me.

—woman who has lived in Bedford all her life

Introduction

Residents of Bedford tend to have very strong place-based identities. The town is known throughout the New York metropolitan area as one of the most beautiful, and consequently one of the most expensive, outer suburbs. Residents not only have an emotional stake in preserving the look of the land, but also a very large financial stake as well. While there exists among residents a general consensus on the broad narrative structure of Bedford, the details are very much open to interpretation. Hence, as the two opening quotations suggest, one woman's dream house is another woman's nightmare. Although both expressed to us a wish to shut the door on new development, for the long-term resident, new houses not only spoil previously cherished views, but by the very fact of being new, they inauthentically represent Bedford in her mind.

When we asked our informants why they were attracted to Bedford, many stressed that they were looking for a rural setting within commuting distance of New York. A Wall Street broker said, "It's the first town within an hour of New York that offers a real rural setting. That's why I moved here." Another person said, "Because it is a beautiful country setting and you can't find it any closer. It's a quality of life issue." Yet another said, "We had heard that Bedford was a pretty town. We needed somewhere close to New York and to an international airport. We're not city dwellers. We're rural people." We might add that this interviewee needs to be near an airport because her husband's work requires him to fly to Europe and Asia on a monthly basis. The woman and her husband fit the description of jetsetters as well as anyone. And yet she refers to themselves as "rural people," a term that one does not normally associate with jetsetters.

Some of the people we interviewed had lived in New York before buying a weekend place in Bedford or moving there permanently. An example of this is a banker:

> I work in the city, but got sick of living there. So where am I going to live? Long Island? No thanks. Closer towns like Scarsdale or Bronxville? I'm not really into Tudor suburbs. In Bedford, I can live in the country and still get into work in a little over an hour. It's a question of lifestyle. I have to work in New York but I don't have to live with all those people.

The choice to leave the city is one of lifestyle. The question for these people of how one chooses to live is very much a question of where one chooses to live. The decision to leave the city is not simply one of country versus city, nature versus culture; it is about distinction as well, for a country house in a place like Bedford is a positional good, a mark of distinction, a sign to oneself and one's colleagues in the city that one has arrived financially. Another man, whose business is based in New York City, sees the choice as simple: "If you work in New York City but want a quiet place to live that's not too isolated socially, it's either Bedford or the Hamptons [on Long Island]." It is interesting to note that the canons of distinction narrow the effective choice of those who by some measures are faced with unlimited choices.[1] The wife of a man in the film business who moved to Bedford thirteen years ago explained why she and her husband moved there: "People don't mind driving fifty minutes to get to a home in the country. It's privacy versus people hounding you. You have relief here. The quality of life is better here. You have normalcy here." Her comments echo a late-nineteenth-century notion that the city is a place of nervous agitation and cutthroat impersonal relations, and that the countryside is an antidote to this. The city is a kind of infirmity of the spirit and the countryside is a cure or "relief," as she puts it.

A local clerk who used to live in the Bronx and moved to Bedford Hills nearly twenty years ago expressed some of the same views as this woman, but in stronger language: "People live out here to get away from New York City. It's a mindset thing. Studies have shown that the closer you are to New York City, the more stressed you feel. This is called the country. You come home from work and relax. Somehow people turn into animals by the time they get to Grand Central Station." The view of the city as productive of social and physical illness is echoed by another woman who has lived all her life in Bedford and whose husband works on Wall Street: "I'm a country person. I think I would get physically sick if I was forced to live in the city." This woman's visceral reaction shows how embodied her place-based identity has become.

Bunce (1994) suggests that the idea of the rural is vague and open to multiple interpretations. Guided by differing interpretations of how Bedford should look, people subdivide land, build houses, and lay out gardens. But because the look of Bedford is so very important to its residents, the putting into practice of one person's vision of the rural can destabilize and undermine another's vision. A lack of agreement over landscape aesthetics creates conflict among residents and has led to an increasing institutionalization and bureaucratization of taste through a proliferation of boards and advisory committees and subcommittees whose job it is to administer zoning and environmental laws. Because Bedford is a town and not a private gated community, the legislation of taste is limited. Except in the small village historic district, there is no control over the design and color of buildings. As a consequence, much of the legislation seeks to block virtually all new building of any sort. Attempts to subdivide land and build new houses are invariably greeted with cries of outrage that the rural nature of Bedford is being destroyed. It is worth remembering, however, that most people who buy brand new million dollar houses would be staggered to think that they are destroying anything. As we saw in the lead quotations to this chapter, despite a shared desire to retain an exclusive residential landscape, differences in taste and judgment concerning authenticity produce tension and miscommunication.

While the landscape of Bedford is clearly structured by the narratives of pastoralism, wilderness, and the New England village, our informants seem to know relatively little of the history of these landscape ideas. Although they are highly articulate people adept at putting the ideas into practice, many couldn't say much about the look of the town aside from using words like "beautiful," "rural," "wooded," "pastoral," and "New England village." Their knowledge was often practical and naturalized rather than discursive. When probed about the origins of their landscape taste, they spoke of learning from their parents or in some cases of seeing it on television, in films, or in magazines, but most often they would say things like, "I don't know. I have always loved the country," or "I'm a country person."

The textual, historical basis of taste, therefore, is often simultaneously present and absent; it informs practice but largely escapes consciousness. In fact, we encountered in a few respondents what might be called, following Steven Levine (1972), "sacred inarticulateness," an inability to speak about something despite, or perhaps because of, its being held in such high regard. For example, we asked a man who has lived in Bedford for many years and deeply loves the look of the town to describe it. He responded, "How would I describe Bedford?" He paused for a moment, then added, "Beautiful, how else? What more can one possibly say?"

The residents we interviewed often found it easier to describe contemporary Bedford in relation to other places and in relation to how they remembered it in the past. Depending upon how long they had lived in Bedford, interviewees compared Bedford in the present to Bedford at different periods in the past. Interestingly, despite the variation, certain commonalities emerge because, we suspect, the broad cultural narratives traced in the last chapter impose a degree of homogeneity on disparate experiences. Bedford can be seen as a positional good (Hirsch 1976) as the residents judge the town to be aesthetically and socially superior to other towns in the region. And yet for many long-term residents, Bedford's position is insecure. The town is not, they claim, as bucolic or as distinctive as it was in the past, and as such, it runs the risk of losing its positional advantage. To those who worry about the changing look of Bedford, the blame appears to lie with developers who have built on open land and newcomers with different tastes who have settled in the town. This fear has led to a politics of exclusion that attempts to halt most new development in Bedford, through the adoption of highly restrictive environmental legislation. This politics of exclusion centers on aesthetics much more than on social issues. Most residents we spoke to said that they don't care who their neighbors are as long as the rural ambience of the town doesn't change. This is not so much a tolerance of social difference as it is a belief that a properly controlled landscape gives the illusion of a socially homogeneous place and, as ever, it is the look that matters.[2]

Although with few exceptions, people's views of Bedford are generally positive. However, as we probed more deeply, we found that many residents are ambivalent about the landscape of the town. Feelings of sadness, loss, disapproval, and even anger emerged as they described changes in the look of Bedford over the years. Drawing on resident surveys from 1997 and 1999 in preparation for the town's Master Plan, and asking residents directly about their attitude to changes in town, we explored the question of what they thought Bedford should ideally look like. We focused on certain key elements in the landscape about which we knew there had been controversy, including house and garden styles, the shifting balance between forest and open fields, the rise in gated properties, the dirt roads, and stone walls. What emerged was a complex and ambiguous set of attitudes toward Bedford and its connection to their identities.

Sense of Place as a Positional Good

The residents of Bedford, it would appear, situate their town conceptually somewhere between the rural and the suburban. A real estate saleswoman said, "Bedford is less suburban than other towns. It's more rural." A homemaker claimed that "Bedford is on the borderline of the suburb." Another homemaker said, "It's not suburban. That's more like Scarsdale. North Salem is rural. Bedford is in-between." Some qualified what they meant by the term "rural." A banker who has lived in Bedford for thirty years described the town as follows: "Parts of it are rural, but gentlemen farms, because rural in America, aesthetically speaking

Table 4.1 Percent Disagreeing with the Statement "Our Rural Character Is Not Important to Me"

A. *By Length of Residence*

Total	10 Years or Less	11–20 Years	More Than 20 Years
91%	96%	92%	86%

B. *By Area*

Total	Bedford Village	Bedford Hills	Katonah
91%	90%	90%	91%

(529 = Total Number)

Source: Town of Bedford 1998.

means it is hideous. When I think of rural—and you don't have to drive too far north of Bedford to find this—I think of trailers, abandoned equipment, and peeling paint." A homemaker compared the rural of Bedford to that of less affluent counties to the north: "Bedford is beautiful in comparison to Patterson and Putnam Counties. They are disgusting looking, full of junk and clutter spoiling a beautiful landscape. I hate rural poverty. I don't mind city poverty so much. A city's just cement and buildings, so it's not going to look nice anyway." Here we see the aestheticized view of life, where even poverty is evaluated in aesthetic terms. Urban poverty is more acceptable because in her view the urban landscape is blighted anyway. Bedford to these people is the beautiful rural, the ideal of rurality rather than the reality. It is, in the words of a real estate salesman, "deluxe rural."

The 1997 survey conducted by the Bedford Conservation Board reveals that residents think of their town as rural. In response to the statement, "Our Rural Character Is Not Important to Me," 91% disagree. As Table 4.1 demonstrates, newer residents feel even more strongly about this than do longer-term residents, and there is little variation by area within Bedford.

There are twenty-nine active farms in Bedford at present. Of these, three raise rare breeds of cattle and other livestock, four are nurseries or tree farms, and twenty-two are horse farms. In 1999, an attempt was made to get tax relief for these farms from the new Agricultural and Farmland Protection Board (Chitwood 1999d). Two years later, the state approved the creation of a special agricultural district within the Croton Watershed to help preserve farmland.[3] In the last few years, increasing numbers of sheep can be seen in Bedford. These are not kept for commercial purposes, but rather because, in the words of a reporter who wrote an article in the local paper extolling the value of keeping sheep, they "bestow a strong pastoral character to nearly any estate on which they graze" (Mandelker 2000). But while residents love to see sheep, horses, and rare breeds of cattle grazing in the distance, some, especially those raised in the city, don't want to hear or smell farm animals or see farm equipment. For example, a resident had her application to keep pet goats denied by the Board of Variance because neighbors complained that the goats were noisy (Heppner 1998). Another resident, who has lived in town for eleven years, said angrily of a new neighbor,

> Why have these people moved here if they want to change everything? They should stay in the city if that's the lifestyle they want. There is real tension between the older and new people on our road. One new neighbor complained that another had a tractor and a pig and some chickens. It's not like he had a real farm and anyway he was there first. Why did the woman move in if she didn't want to be in the country?

At issue here is not, as our informant suggests, a choice between an urban and a rural lifestyle, but rather differing conceptions of the country.

One interviewee distinguished Bedford from other suburbs thus: "Thanks to four-acre zoning, we don't have houses on top of one another like in Rye and Larchmont." However, the three suburbs that are most often compared to Bedford are Greenwich, Scarsdale, and Chappaqua. Greenwich is seen as formal, Scarsdale nouveau riche, manicured, and formal, while Chappaqua, although wealthy, is seen as a glorified middle-class suburbia of developments, albeit unusually well landscaped with mature trees and impressive houses. A landscape architect said, "Greenwich is manicured. Here in Bedford we let nature do its own thing." A real estate saleswoman stressed bodily and lifestyle differences: "Bedford isn't flash like Greenwich. Here you don't have to wear makeup all the time and wear a fur coat. Everyone there has their Mercedes. Here we have our station wagons and jeeps." Another respondent concurs, "The biggest contrast is with Greenwich people. It's the social scene there. Few people move from there to here. It's a millionaire's ghetto." She sees the homogeneity of Greenwich as confining. In fact, this woman reveals her limited mental map of Greenwich, for as a small city, it has a more heterogeneous population than Bedford. In sum, Greenwich is cast as an admired, formal elegance that lacks the "honest simplicity" and "down-to-earth" wholesomeness of Bedford's country charm.

A local businessman contrasted the casual style of Bedford to the formality of Scarsdale: "Bedford isn't like Scarsdale with the lawn mowed right up to the street and every tree a specimen." A resident generalizes about the look of the landscape: "In Scarsdale, every inch of property is cultivated. Here we maintain a country feeling. We are very English." A banker described neighboring Chappaqua as "suburban houses on very large, wooded lots." A homemaker said that Bedford was "definitely not as suburban feeling as Chappaqua. Even though there is a lot of money there, it doesn't have the estate look of Bedford." She and others worry that the increasing number of trees in Bedford is undermining the pastoral, estate nature of Bedford making it look more like Chappaqua.

Underlying all of these comparisons with other suburbs is the belief that simplicity, naturalness, and getting back to basics are central to definitions of Bedford. A woman captures this at the level of the aesthetics of landscape when she says of one of the most fashionable roads in Bedford, "Guard Hill is elegant, casual country. There are well-to-do people, but it has all the country feeling of horses and even some run-down places along the way." Her approval of "run-down" places is a classic statement of the picturesque with its emphasis upon charming decay.

Anxieties about Bedford

While residents deem Bedford superior to other suburbs, many fear that new development is eroding that difference. Everyone we talked to who has lived in Bedford for at least a decade agrees that Bedford is changing. One person explained, "It's still rural but modernization is coming." Here the link between the countryside and premodernity is made explicit. Others place the town further along the trajectory from countryside to suburb: "Bedford is suburbia. It's a bedroom community. It has always been suburbia, but it didn't use to feel that way." All figure such change as a loss of both individuality and distinction.

Driven by anxieties of impending loss, the town began preparing its new Master Plan in the mid-1990s. Such anxiety is in fact heightened by anti-development efforts in town, as town boards and local newspapers insistently argue that the rural nature of Bedford will cease to exist unless development is curtailed. As an editorial in one of the local papers said, "As history has proved, Bedford's most beautiful views, its most pristine tree-lined drives are also its most vulnerable areas for development" (*Record Review* 1996). The 1997 survey asked residents whether such things as Bedford's "rural character" and "open space" are improving, staying the same, or getting worse. In both cases, the vast majority think Bedford is losing its rural quality and becoming more developed.[4] Those who have lived in Bedford Village longer feel this somewhat more strongly.

In 1999, several town meetings were called to sound out resident opinion on the shaping of the Master Plan. It would appear, however, that another purpose was to raise awareness and reinforce anti-development sentiment. Members of various town organizations exhorted the residents to be vigilant and actively work to protect the town's "rural character and ambiance, scenic views, stone walls and roads" (Marx 1999b). Typical of newspaper articles about the Master Plan and of letters to the editor at the time is the following by a man who has since been appointed town historian:

> Quality of life in Bedford is made evident in those things natural, that is, of nature. Rolling hills, streams, horse farms, dirt roads, wild flowers, open spaces, and nature preserves enhance our "quality of life." Anything that takes away vistas, quietness and habitat or that imposes urban character, such as curbing, unnatural overhead lighting, private entrance gates, totally uniform stone walls, construction vehicles, limousines and developments of any kind, detract from our quality of life. It's almost that simple. (Stockbridge 2000)

One respondent to the town's 1999 Master Plan questionnaire wrote to the paper, "Sadly, as riding trails are blocked off by some new homeowners, fences and security gates are erected, more traffic lights blink with lines of snaking vehicles and new houses erupt on environmentally sensitive parcels, the essence of the community's rural character inevitably suffers" (*Record Review* 2000). An interview with one long-term resident was dominated by a tirade about the evils of the DOT (New York State Department of Transportation), which he feels imposes a great excess of modernization in the form of road signs that spoil Bedford's historical character. He said, "I've counted them along our road and the road into Bedford Village. It's disgusting how many unnecessary signs there are. One for every slight curve in the road." Anxiety about the aesthetic vulnerability of Bedford was brought sharply into relief in a number of controversies over the aesthetics of landscape. We will turn to these now.

House and Garden

There is no question that the most feared potential change in Bedford is new houses. This was evident from the results of the 1999 Master Plan survey. The survey posed the question, "How important to you is each of the following problems facing Bedford as it revises its land use Master Plan?" It listed a series of "problems," such as "traffic and safety on local roads," "loss of community character as new homes replace undeveloped land," "rising property taxes," "loss of diverse population as property values rise," "inadequate retail shops and private service providers," and "threat to environmental quality from uncontrolled growth as new housing replaces undeveloped land."

Residents were then asked which among the aforementioned "problems" posed the "single most important challenge facing Bedford." More people chose "loss of community character as new homes replace undeveloped land" than any other "problem." Interestingly, the more recently a person moved to Bedford, the more likely they were to list this as the most important challenge. As might be expected, concern is greatest in the less densely developed parts of Bedford.

Our interviews explored these attitudes in more depth. A man who has lived in Bedford for thirty-one years has this to say about the changes in town:

> There are areas of Bedford that have been suburban, and by that I mean developer houses on small lots, since before I came here. But now what I see is the spirit of suburbia coming into Bedford in the form of giant million dollar plus developer houses that unfortunately are cropping up in some of the most beautiful parts of town. These people probably don't think that what they are creating is suburbia because they are spending so much money, but they are. Suburbia is a style.

Suburbia for this person is an aesthetic category. It has to do not with how much money one has, but with how one chooses to spend it and what this says about oneself. A businessman who has been a long-term resident is even more explicit that the changes he objects to in Bedford are changes in taste:

> Some of the new developments are in bad taste. They look like puffed-up middle-class suburban housing that has been quadrupled in size and put on a large lot. The problem is Bedford has become fashionable, and people with suburban tastes and lots of money have moved here. I wish nobody had ever heard of Bedford.

Table 4.2 Response to the Question, "What is the Single Most Important Challenge Facing Bedford?"

A. *By Length of Residence*

	<5 Years	5–9 Years	10–19 Years	20 Years+
Loss of Community Character as New Homes Replace Undeveloped Land	32.2%	29.7%	23.0%	21.2%
Threat to Environmental Quality from Uncontrolled Growth	20.1%	30.4%	22.0%	19.3%
Rising Property Taxes	24.0%	20.0%	26.5%	33.4%
Traffic and Safety on Local Roads	18.6%	15.0%	20.0%	17.3%
Loss of Diverse Population as Property Values Rise	3.0%	3.3%	5.5%	5.9%
Inadequate Retail and	2.1%	1.6%	0.0%	0.2%
Service	0.0%	0.0%	3.0%	2.7%
Providers Other				

B. *By Area*

	4 Acre+	1–4 Acre	Bedford Village	Bedford Hills	Katonah
Loss of Community Character as New Homes Replace Undeveloped Land	41.9%	23.0%	17.6%	9.3%	20.0%
Threat to Environmental Quality from Uncontrolled Growth	21.0%	22.7%	23.0%	17.2%	24.2%
Rising Property Taxes	19.4%	27.3%	12.1%	39.1%	35.8%
Traffic and Safety on local roads	15.0%	20.9%	37.4%	23.4%	7.4%
Loss of Diverse Population as Property Values Rise	1.3%	4.0%	4.4%	4.7%	10.5%
Inadequate Retail and Service Providers	1.0%	1.7%	0.0%	1.6%	0.0%
Other	0.4%	0.4%	5.5%	4.7%	2.1%

(649 = Total number)

Source: Town of Bedford 2000.

We asked people what they considered to be appropriate styles of housing for Bedford. One thing that emerged was the belief that Bedford should not only have a variety of house styles but also of scales:

> I'm in favor of a variety of sizes of properties. A healthy community has a mix. Whereas I find some of the big old estates very attractive, and I'd hate to see that land broken up, there were always small, often quaint little houses on small lots that preexisted the zoning. This is an essential part of the Bedford look.

Fig. 4.1 An Eighteenth-Century House.

One woman who grew up in Bedford described the archetypal Bedford house as follows:

> The houses that seem most Bedford-like to me are the big old rambling white colonial houses with barns and detached garages, dirt driveways, rhododendron bushes, fields, and overgrown gardens. I know there are some very handsome brick sort of Georgian-style houses but these tend to be invisible from the road so I don't associate Bedford with them as much.

Another person listed those styles that are appropriate and those that aren't:

> Only certain styles of houses are appropriate for Bedford. Colonials are, but raised ranches are not Bedford. Bedford is historic. Capes are appropriate but modern architecture isn't. It doesn't blend into the landscape. Certainly no condos. Bedford is traditional. Why change it?

For another man, the issue was much less clear cut, for appropriateness was not only defined by style but by age as well:

> I guess there are lots of styles that are appropriate. Although it's funny that almost no style seems appropriate if it has just been built. I've seen a few nice colonial reproductions in Bedford, but part of the key is mature planting to soften the house. You see large new houses with tiny little shrubs around them. They look so new and unfinished.

Fig. 4.2 A Rambling Classic Bedford House and Garden.

It may seem odd to the reader that people react so strongly against the new houses. It is not immediately obvious why landscapes should look finished in a culture that normally puts a lot of value on newness. The idea that old houses have more charm is a familiar, if not always shared, view in the United States and Europe. However, there is nothing natural—only naturalized—about the idea. We are reminded of an English friend who said of the United States after his first trip to Florida, "it's so unfinished looking." One woman told us:

> It's very hard to say when something is appropriate because you can have a style that is appropriate and yet it is built in a way that makes you want to throw up. There are some styles, however, that are simply inappropriate. I can think of a place made out of cedar that looks like it should be on the west coast. There are international-style boxes that seem inappropriate, Spanish haciendas look ridiculous, and postmodern houses with Palladian windows that remind me of what every developer has thought is fashionable for the past ten years.

We asked one informant what he thought of postmodern-style houses. He answered, "I like postmodern architecture in a city, but I don't want Bedford to look postmodern. I don't even want it to look modern. What Bedford represents is history. Bedford for me is an escape from my world in New York." Here once again, we have Bedford figured as aestheticized history and the antithesis of urban capitalist modernity. It stands for the lost normalcy that a romantic mythology hopes to recover for late capitalism.

Others try to describe how Bedford is changing by claiming that its houses are increasingly coming to resemble those in other suburbs. For some, Bedford is becoming like Greenwich. One person who replied to the 1999 survey wrote, "Please help us protect this unique town. We do not need another Greenwich, Connecticut. We need to discourage the builder of McMansions from coming. I'll do anything to help." Another informant said, "The old Bedford lifestyle is slowly vanishing. People who are fixing up homes that the old Bedford people lived in are different. Bedford has become another Greenwich, which I have nothing against. They certainly have beautiful places in Greenwich." Another resident had the following to say about the small area of conservation zoning in Bedford: "I hate it. You get all the houses along the road and it looks just like Scarsdale." One woman we spoke to compared the different aesthetic of the two places: "There are some people who move here and try and make it look like Scarsdale. They cut down trees and plant little plants. I know a woman who realized her mistake and set about correcting her property by making it look more wild . . . not so manicured." Jane Schewior, chairman of the Bedford Tree Advisory Board, had this to say about plans for planting at a traffic improvement project in town: "We don't want it to look like Scarsdale—all landscaped and manicured. We just want it to look natural, as if nothing ever happened" (Nardozzi 2001e).

Being from Scarsdale has become to some a term of abuse to describe people who move to Bedford with the "wrong" aesthetic. One person said, "Some of these new people who have come from Scarsdale or somewhere want to change the place." Another said, "Bedford used to look much more low-key and casual. It used to look like old money. I'm afraid that it has changed for the worse over the past ten years. Everywhere you look, a fancy developer-special has popped up on a four-acre lot. It doesn't look like Bedford anymore; it looks like Scarsdale . . . it looks nouveau riche." Scarsdale generates such hostility in some quarters that a new word has been invented by locals to describe a disapproved aesthetic. A real estate broker described changes in town as "the Scarsdalification of Bedford with those big houses on little lots with their formal little gardens and the big tacky gates."

The local newspaper joined in the attack on large new developer houses, dismissing them as "McMansions" and "starter castles." In an editorial, it stated, "Homes in our area just keep getting bigger and bigger. We all have our dreams, nevertheless our neighbors have dreams too, including open space or wooded vistas" (*Record Review* 1998). Some wished that Bedford could have been frozen at some time in the past, such as one woman who said, "For aesthetic and nostalgic reasons, I wish there was just the variety [of housing] there used to be in the 1950s. And even though I know it is unrealistic, I wish that building had stopped then." Another man, in response to the question, "what do you consider appropriate housing styles," replied angrily, "I don't want to see another building of *any* kind in Bedford."

On the other hand, a proposal that all new house plans within the town of Bedford be submitted before a local Architectural Review Board has been presented to the town board several times over the years, but has never passed. Those in favor of such a review board argue that it would ensure that builders only construct houses that are "tasteful" and "blend" with their surroundings, while those opposed argue that taste is subjective and should not be legislated (*Patent Trader* 1986). However, by the late 1990s, the idea of an Architectural Review Board was gaining in popularity. In the 1997 survey, which was part of the Master Plan, in response to the question, "Is the town of Bedford doing enough to control the architectural review of new developments?" the majority thought not.[5]

Several people we spoke with wanted an Architectural Review Board to block the "McMansions" on four-acre lots and also to stop people building houses in certain styles. As one said, "Mediterranean-style houses aren't appropriate here. This is a colonial town." While we will discuss the Master Plan meetings in detail in Chapter Five, it is worth noting here that they became a forum for the discussion of, among other things, what constitutes a suitable style of house in Bedford. At one such meeting in April 2001, the Master Plan Committee criticized "extra-large houses built on 'small' (four-acre and less) lots." Singled out for abuse was a new 6,000-square-foot white colonial-style house on a four-acre lot on one of the more prestigious roads in town. Neighbors complained about the look of the house to the Planning Board and the Master Plan Committee and consequently the town planner spoke to the owners of the house, who decided to construct a berm and plant it with trees and shrubs in order to partially hide the house from the road. The local newspaper reported the committee's negative comments about the house and published a photograph of the house on the front page of the paper under the heading, "Master planners look askance at 'McManse'" (Nardozzi 2001o). The following week, the paper printed two letters to the editor that were critical of the coverage of the meeting. While the newspaper had a policy of "naming and shaming" residents who violated the town's environmental ordinances, at least two residents felt that the paper had gone too far in trying to shame the builders and owners of a new large house that the newspaper found unattractive. One resident who said he moved to Bedford seven years before called the article a "mean spirited and sanctimonious attack on a particular home" (Fillipone 2001). The other writer who noted that she had lived in Bedford for over fifty years wrote that while she disapproved of "overbuilding," "was it really necessary to describe the house as 'horrible' . . . ? To make matters worse, your paper had to publish a picture of the house on the front page" (Burke 2001). We spoke to a long-term resident who said, "It's actually quite a handsome, big white colonial, like so many others in Bedford. It's impossible to know why it would be singled out, except it's close to the road." Having said this, many residents are becoming concerned that the town is soon to be overrun by "McMansions" and phoned the town offices and members of the Master Plan committee to voice their concerns. In response to citizen pressure, in July of 2001, the town supervisor proposed an amendment to the town code in line with proposals coming from the Master Plan Committee. It would temporarily halt the construction of houses over a certain height or over a certain floor area to building lot ratio (Nardozzi 2001p). A month later, the newspaper increased the pressure by publishing an editorial titled "Prepare for McGeorgians" (*Record Review* 2001). Its latest foray into the taste wars played the class card, equating large developer houses with lower-class taste: "Someday we may look forward to potential new home builders steering clear of ostentatious fortresses in humble neighborhoods, the same way so many of us steer clear of dangling fuzzy dice above our dashboards and decorating our smiles with gold teeth." It is worth noting that the house prices in some of these "humble neighborhoods" average over one million dollars. At a well-attended town board meeting in late August, the town planner deflated some of the panic about "McMansions" by stating that of forty-five permits for new house construction issued over the past two years, only five would be in conflict with the moratorium (Nardozzi 2001q). After two more board meetings, it was decided that the floor ratio rule might encourage the construction of ranch-style houses and the proposal was dropped. However, this abortive attempt to ban "McMansions" has moved the town closer to forming an Architectural Review Board (Nardozzi 2001r, 2001s, 2001t).

But not all residents we interviewed felt that there was a narrow range of acceptable house styles or that recently constructed houses are inappropriate. One newly arrived person we spoke to said, "There are lots of house styles that are appropriate in Bedford. I guess you could say that since this is a colonial town, the houses should be in a colonial style, but that would be really boring. I live in a contemporary and wouldn't consider living in an old house. It just isn't me. It's the variety of different types of housing here that give this place its character." A woman who moved to Bedford four years ago said, "Bedford to me is a real town, unlike many planned communities. It has evolved over centuries, and you can see the accumulation of different architectural styles including contemporaries. I would always prefer a contemporary to a reproduction. Grand manors had their day and age. To reproduce one today seems artificial." Another person said, "We bought a new colonial last year and we just love it. We have always wanted to live in the country. We looked at quite a few houses in the area and in the end chose a new house because the good ones don't look any different from the old ones and you won't have problems with it." Yet another person who bought an old house on eight acres said,

> You should have seen this place when we bought it [four years ago]. The house was really run down. It looked like it hadn't been touched in decades. We have had to redo the whole place. The garden had also been very neglected. It was wild. We have cleaned it up and extended the lawns and flower beds and we are in the process of rebuilding the stone walls that have fallen down. There are still

Fig. 4.3 A Recently Built House.

a lot of places in Bedford that are like ours was. But slowly it's changing and they are getting fixed up. There is no question that Bedford is looking better and better. That's why so many people want to move here.

Trees and Fields

The history of Bedford is in part a struggle over how wooded the town should be. Opinion has shifted back and forth over the centuries on this issue, reflecting shifts in the economy and aesthetic values. Two centuries after the Europeans displaced the Mohicans, an agricultural landscape of open fields dotted with sections of forest had been created. Over the past century, the adoption of a new aesthetic centered on the picturesque demanded a more heavily treed landscape than two centuries of farming had produced. As a consequence, fields were allowed to revert to woodland cut only to create views with eye-pleasing arrangements of pasture surrounded by woodland. Since the mid-twentieth century, open fields have been progressively decreasing, so much so that one of the things older people who grew up in Bedford tell us is how much less open the land now looks. This century-long swing toward valuing forest is based on a picturesque balance between trees and open land. Many would claim that the landscape is out of balance again. The increase in forest since the 1970s has been driven by a number of factors, including anti–tree-cutting legislation. As we shall see in Chapter Five, those who want to open up more fields or views often find themselves on the defensive, having to apply for permits to cut or cutting surreptitiously so that neighbors don't notice.

The tree, at present, has been elevated to a position of supreme importance in Bedford, by a combination of an aesthetic that romanticizes history and nature and a desire for privacy. The trees are protected institutionally by a set of laws and public beliefs that combine nineteenth-century spiritual romanticism with late-twentieth-century scientific ecology. A longtime resident of Bedford said, "The people who want to stop all development want everyone to think that there have never been fewer trees in Bedford than there are today. This simply isn't so, but it doesn't stop them from saying so." That this relatively new attitude toward trees has been effectively diffused to many recent arrivals in town is evidenced by the following exchange we had with a resident. A woman who moved to Bedford in the late 1980s told us, "I wanted to clear some of my property of the dead underbrush and small trees. But I kept the big old trees." She then added rather defensively that she liked the "more open look." When we told her that Bedford had been much more open thirty years ago, she was amazed: "You know, I felt very guilty about cutting down those trees. What you've said makes me feel better."

This woman is not alone. There are many people in Bedford who value trees, but feel that the veneration of the tree has gone too far. There are some that feel that the town is losing the pastoral quality, while others feel that the picturesque quality of Bedford is being threatened as the mix of trees and open spaces is altered. A woman in the real estate business, who knows Bedford and the surrounding area well, believes that landscape taste can be largely explained in terms of national background. She told us, "Pound Ridge is more forested and it appeals more to Germanic, Jewish, artistic, avant-garde taste. Bedford is more pastoral, but it is losing that quality because there are fewer people in town with conservative Anglo taste and newcomers don't seem to distinguish between valuable old trees and second growth." One man worries that in winning the battle against development, the town might lose the pastoral landscape and, through legislation like the tree-cutting code, produce a forested landscape that he finds less visually appealing: "It's a dilemma. Basically I'm in favor of the [tree-cutting] code because if we let people cut down the trees, we'll see all the new houses. The problem is, if you don't cut down some trees, they'll take over the fields." Evidence that this man's perspective is widely shared is found in the 1997 survey. Sixty-one percent of residents feel that scenic vistas were getting worse while only 3% feel they are improving.

Additional support for the importance of the pastoral can be found in the same survey where residents were asked to name their "favorite Bedford view". Of the 447 people who responded to the question, 126 chose farms, a further thirty-five chose the pastoral views at the top of Guard Hill Road, and eighteen chose the Bedford Oak, a classic pastoral scene. This represents 179 out of 447,

Table 4.3 Response to the Questions, "What Is Your Favorite Bedford View?" and "What Place in Bedford Should Be Kept Intact at All Costs"

"Favorite View" Number of Mentions		*"Kept Intact at All Costs"* Number of Mentions	
Total	447	Total	393
Farms	126	Bedford Village	76
Reservoirs	71	Existing Farms	57
Bedford Village	44	Hamlets	50
Top of Guard Hill	35	Open Land	36
Bedford Oak (See Chapter Nine)	18	Katonah	27
Katonah	15	All of Bedford	22
Nature Preserves	13	Bedford Oak	21
		Town Parks	19
		Nature Preserves	18
49 Other Sites	125	BRLA Trails (Bridle paths)	10
		Other	57

Source: Town of Bedford 1998.

or 40%. By contrast, only thirteen (2.9%) chose the nature preserves, the most forested landscapes in town.[6] Another measure of support for the pastoral can be found in the same table where 33.8% of those places that residents thought should be preserved at all costs were pastoral. Again, forested landscapes scored much lower (4.5%).

A real estate broker who says his aesthetic commitment is to the picturesque, which he defines as a mixture of open spaces and trees, argues that pastoral land is the most economically valuable in Bedford. He says that to him, and to many of his customers, "economic value has everything to do with aesthetics." "Open land broken up by beautiful groupings of trees is land you own. Look at the edge of my property over there," he said, pointing to a mass of trees and dense underbrush forming a visual barrier. "What is the point of owning fifty acres of forest beyond that point when twenty feet will screen my land every bit as well? It's simply a waste of money, because it's as if I didn't own anything but the first twenty feet." He argues that his opinion is supported by the market value of land: "There is little premium for having a property that backs up on one of the nature preserves in town because the same could be accomplished by a hedgerow. On the other hand, there is a real premium for land that is up against Sunnyfield [a large horse farm] because of the views of pastoral lands." He further argues that "the least expensive thing that you can do to improve the value of your land is to cut trees down to create a view." He went on to explain that such cutting had to be done "tastefully" and that large, fine trees should, of course, be preserved. He estimated that if one could expose a fine view through cutting, the value per acre of a property would be increased fourfold. "There are risks, however, in opening up land in this way," he said. "People fear change. You have a beautiful view of fields and woods one day and the next day you are looking at some awful new house. It's definitely a risk." He argued that trees can still be cut, but because of the tree-cutting ordinance it has become a long, slow process.

Another real estate broker told us that there are potential problems from an economic standpoint if one owns many acres of open fields. He gave as an example Sunnyfield Farm. "There is no way that if that property was sold that it could be divided up into four-acre lots even though it is in four-acre zoning. Because people can see those rolling horse fields and ponds from the roads, the town says that it is in the 'public domain.' They would argue that it shouldn't be divided on those grounds, and on environmental ones." When we asked what environmental grounds, he replied, "The town can simply argue that the subdivision has to take place in a way that has less environmental impact. Eventually you would be able to subdivide the land but certainly not into four-acre parcels. The downside [for owners] of open land like this is that it's hard to subdivide."

Both those who wish to stop development and those who wish to subdivide land are becoming increasingly sophisticated about such public claims to an interest in views over private property. In 1993, a seminar was conducted at St. Matthews, Bedford's establishment Episcopalian church, on what has come to be called the "taking issue." Environmental lawyers and other specialists in such public claims over property were brought in to advise people on what they could do to combat subdivision of "view properties." At least one property owner we know took steps to forestall such a move to "take" her property. A neighbor who knows her told us that, "She planted a 'wall' of conifers all along one edge of her property to shield the vista from the road in order to protect her property for future development. She told me that if she didn't do this she was sure that the town would 'take' her land." We drove by that property recently and all one sees from the road is a wall of trees. The view is now private and hence is unlikely to be "taken."

The Aesthetics of Gates

Another controversial issue in Bedford is the growth in the number of gates at the entrance to properties. Thirty years ago, large properties were likely to have wooden or stone gateposts and perhaps wrought iron gates. Typically the entrances to these properties would have a rural route mailbox and perhaps a sign with the name of the property. The houses on some of the larger properties were large brick or stone buildings often in the Georgian style, which, though imposing, nevertheless had acquired an air of relaxed, slightly unkempt informality about them over time. The horse farms were fenced for obvious reasons while the other properties typically had wooded boundaries marked more often than not by old, dry stone walls in various states of disrepair. These dilapidated stone walls were thought to convey the romantic, irregular, picturesque look of the countryside. Properties of four acres or less very rarely had gates or posts on either side of their driveway. Owners of such properties would typically have had a rural route mailbox with their last name printed on it. This studied simplicity stemmed from the fact that people then saw gates as suitable for large estates, but unsuitable, and even ridiculous, on small four-acre properties.

Although this landscape model still predominates in Bedford, one increasingly sees many exceptions. Since 1980, many large, formal houses have been constructed on four-acre lots. The entrances to these new houses are designed to look imposing. It is now increasingly common on lots of four acres or less to see large posts framing the driveway. These posts are sometimes of wood but more often of brick or stone. It is not uncommon to see cast cement lions or other heraldic objects on top of these posts. Some long-term residents see such objects as symbolic of social change. As an editorial in a local newspaper pointed out, "Here in Bedford the lion's popularity may be more evidence that the town's aesthetic of understatement no longer reigns unchallenged" (McCarthy 2001). In keeping with this new formality, newer houses are often framed by manicured lawns dotted with flower beds and copses of small ornamental trees. Whereas gates were used on the large farms in the past to keep animals in, the gates at the entrances to smaller properties, which are often unattached to fencing, are more symbolic than functional.[7]

Increasingly one sees electronically controlled gates and prominent signs advertising that the property is electronically protected. When we asked people about their gates, most said that they were concerned about burglary or had them for their family's personal safety. Statements included, "I feel we need security," "I think it will discourage burglars," "Unfortunately you have to be security conscious nowadays, even here," "We are high-profile people. We just can't take a chance on someone coming in," and "It protects our privacy." One man said, "When we bought this place it didn't have a gate. We saw other people's gates and they just seemed to finish off the place nicely." A woman, who moved to Bedford in 1998, said, "Everyone has gates here. It's part of the Bedford look."

In the early 1980s, as the renewed[8] fashion for gates was beginning, Foxy Gwynne (1983, 4) who in her regular editorial column in a local paper often acts as a spokesperson for what many old-timers in Bedford privately think, tried to discourage their construction by dismissing the grand entranceways on the new houses as "the phony wrought iron gates at the entrance to make one think the owners are opulent dukes or princes." Most of the people we interviewed who didn't have gates were also critical of them. Many of the older residents said that the gates are eyesores that directly contradict what Bedford represents to them, which is a relaxed country setting away from both crime and urban formality. The claim that protection is needed in Bedford is often dismissed out of hand. As one longtime resident said, "These people who put up huge gates, high fences, and elaborate alarm systems must think that they are still living on Long Island or Queens or wherever it is they come from. Who do they think that they are protecting themselves against?" A woman who has lived in Bedford for eight years said, "Gates are silly, affected, not necessary. People say they are for security, but Bedford is very safe. The police told me that there hadn't been a break-in in the area for two-and-a-half years. We only lock the doors at night. Our house has a alarm system, but we never use it." A Bedford policeman we interviewed confirmed this saying, "This is a safe place to live. The gate thing started in 1978 with the murders.[9] Also, the celebrities came here and they need gates." Others stressed that gates were a "sign" of the types of people who had moved to Bedford since the 1980s. One man said,

> Ten years ago you didn't see these gates. They are typical of new rich people coming to Bedford from their New York City apartments and putting on airs. There's no danger here in Bedford. Do you know that in the forty-four years that I have lived here I have never once locked my doors? I don't even own a house key; this is Bedford. Of course I have dogs, which would be pretty good protection.

A young man who has lived in Bedford all his life said,

> These new people in town can't relax about their land; they need to mark it out. I know a person who spent $40,000 on their gate. Why do you think they spend this amount? For protection? I'll tell you why; it's all about status. You can't see the really expensive houses from the road because they are so far back. So people show off their money with fancy gates. They are markers of wealth. People know how much different kinds of gates cost. It's like designer clothes. They can't put their checkbook out there so that people can see how much they have in their accounts, so they build gates.

We interviewed the owner of a company that installs gates and he had this to say about why his customers purchase gates: "Some are for security, but mostly it's a fad; keep up with your neighbor. A lot of houses aren't visible from the street, so they want something at the street to indicate that there is an important property back in there. A lot of it is just show money. They want gates commensurate with their house. We've put in gates that cost in excess of $100,000. We do the automation and everything." The editor of one of the local newspapers put it less sympathetically, "Folks need walls and gates not to enforce their security but to combat their insecurity. If I live in a big house behind a big gate, I must be a big shot, mustn't I?" (Tucker 1995). We asked some of the people who were critical of the new gates what they thought of the old gates, some of which have been in Bedford since the turn of the century. One long-term resident said, "The old heavy wrought iron gates are ok and at least they were in proportion to the property. The new ones are flimsy or look ostentatious because they are out of proportion to the house and

Fig. 4.4 A Dirt Road with Dry Stone Walls.

property. Maybe some of the old ones looked ostentatious in the 1920s but they have acquired a certain respectability with age." He continued, "The ones that Ralph Lauren did look great, very solid and elegant. But it is very difficult to do a good entrance gate. When I first came here the only entrance gates you saw were old ones mostly in disrepair. But even if they were falling down, they looked substantial." A real estate salesman said, "Some of the old gates are fine but, to tell you the truth, no gates are best. The new gates make Bedford look like Scarsdale."

Stone Walls

Many residents and members of various town boards who are instrumental in framing the new Master Plan consider the dry stone walls that line Bedford's roads to be central to the rural ambience of the town. However, since the early 1980s when wealthy new residents began moving to Bedford in increasing numbers, there has been a controversy over how these walls should look. Twenty years ago, Foxy Gwynne (1983) in her influential local column chastised newcomers for "not knowing how to behave in the country." She cited as an example, "the friendly old stone walls sagging or tumbledown are rectified into a harsh, straight line."

Over the past two decades, a large number of new walls have been built and old ones repaired. The *Patent Trader* published an editorial titled "Walls" urging newcomers to the town not to build anymore. The editor wrote, "the builders of these walls insist that security, not ostentation, is their intention. In all but a few instances, such claims are preposterous. Burglary, vandalism and kidnapping are negligible concerns in our community" (Tucker 1995). In 2000, the Bedford Coalition, an umbrella group of local and regional organizations, joined the fray. They made clear in a public meeting that stone walls are on the "A-list" of what the coalition wants to save in Bedford. But again, they worried about the "wrong" kind of walls being built. A member of the coalition said, "Many people make mistakes, take down their stone walls, or chisel them. Or they'll replace them with a privacy wall without regard to the history that was behind them." Another person at the meeting concurred, "The newer stone walls, so square and so formal, belong in Greenwich and not Bedford. Bedford was an agricultural community. We should take stock of what we've inherited and try to preserve it." Yet another person added, "Greenwich walls are mansion walls. They're meant to keep people out. They're taller so you can't see over them and there's no oddball meandering quality. They're not hospitable" (Nardozzi 2000g). In response to resident concerns, the town zoning code specifies that walls at the property line cannot exceed four feet in height.

Some, like Ralph Lauren, have repaired their dry stone walls at a large expense. It is estimated that the cost of building a stone wall at present is $100 per running foot. A local woman told us about Lauren's attention to detail: "The walls along the front of the property were falling down a bit; you know the way they always looked in Bedford, so he of course had to make them perfect. He had a crew of men take them all apart and reassemble them. What really amazed me was that after they had rebuilt a hundred-foot section, they came and tore it down again and rebuilt it a second time. I guess he didn't like the style. Can you believe it?" We can believe it because Lauren is a master of the hyperreal, sparing no expense in making the fake look authentic. The hyperreal is a copy of a copy for which there was never an original. In this case, however, the original is historically and spatially diffuse—a set of floating signifiers reappropriated in various contexts. In this he is not fundamentally different from others in Bedford. The difference is that he is more self-conscious about what he is doing, has an eye for detail, and has nearly limitless resources.

The Dirt Roads

Many of Bedford's roads follow seventeenth-century Native American trails. With the spread around the country of the gridiron and the straight road, the curving road such as found in Bedford came to symbolize the pastoral and the bucolic, while the straight road symbolized the efficiency of the modern factory (Jackson 1985, 76). As such, the curving road became a synecdoche not only for the countryside, but also for the time before rationality was applied to the countryside (Jackson 1979). But if the curving road recalls history and nature, then the unpaved, curving road does so even more effectively. Roads were paved in large east coast American cities by the late nineteenth century and, by the late twentieth century, it was uncommon to find unpaved public roads within the suburbs of major cities. But dirt roads are, in the words of a recent article in the *New York Times* (November 7, 1993), "hallmarks of Bedford." Of Bedford's approximately 110 miles of roads, thirty-two remain unpaved, among them some of the most prestigious roads in town, such as Guard Hill, Hook Road, and The Narrows.

Anne Bermingham (1986, 167) points out that on the outskirts of early-nineteenth-century London, "The more rustic-looking a suburb, in fact, the more prestigious it was to live there." In Bedford, because unpaved roads increase the social prestige and property values of an area, residents react strongly to suggestions that any of these roads be paved. Over the years, town officials have occasionally suggested paving the roads on the grounds that dirt roads cost up to three times as much to maintain as paved roads (Brown 1979; *New York Times* November 7, 1993). When paving was attempted in the 1960s, women laid down in front of the bulldozers until the town relented and abandoned the project. In an early attempt to pave Guard Hill Road, one large landowner flew home from her vacation in Europe to join the protest. The town supervisor in the early 1980s said, "Here it's like death to suggest that they be paved. A lot of residents work in New York City, and after a pressure day, they like to come home and drive down their dirt roads, even though they're dusty" (*New York Times* March 27, 1983). The 1997 survey asked residents, "What is your favorite Bedford road?" The most popular roads are those with pastoral or lake views and most of these are dirt. Of the thirteen most often named roads, ten are dirt.[10]

Many residents we spoke to expressed intense feelings in favor of dirt roads. A former teacher said that the dirt roads were one of the things that made Bedford a special place for her. They "are very important because they add to the pastoral— the rural look of the town. They are one of the things that make it truly beautiful." For some, like a stockbroker who works in New York, "they are part of the history of Bedford. They're what gives that old-fashioned feeling to Bedford. It's part of the uniqueness of the place. It's wonderful for riding." A village merchant concurs, "It helps to keep in touch with the way things used to be." A number of others argue that dirt roads help them symbolically escape modern, urban life. One longtime resident says, "They are expensive to maintain, but they are important because they contribute to the rustic atmosphere of the town." A more recent arrival takes a more distanced, ironic stance: "People like the dirt roads. It makes them feel uncivilized. They are artificial but so are the [Bedford Village] green and the historic buildings. It's sort of our reverse snobbishness to have these rustic things here." One woman we interviewed spoke of the roads in terms of her own personal history: "Dirt roads are extremely important to me. I would be just heartbroken if they paved them over. I have such vivid memories of walking along the dirt roads when I was a child. It seemed like I spent hours and hours walking along dirt roads when I was little. They are good to ride horses along and they make Bedford seem unique." For some residents, the dirt roads evoke great outpourings of affection of the kind normally felt for living things. One woman who moved to Bedford a decade ago said, "I'm in love with the dirt roads," while another said. "I'd die without the dirt roads. Riding is the most important thing in my life." A man who has lived on one of the most prestigious dirt roads in town for nearly fifty years said,

> I love them. They are what keep Bedford rural. I have horses and it's much pleasanter to ride on dirt. Also it makes the cars go slower, which is important if you are riding. I realize that they are more expensive to maintain, but they're worth it. Maybe people who live on paved roads in town don't like paying higher taxes for dirt roads, but dirt roads are what Bedford's about. If people don't like dirt roads, they should go back to the Bronx where they belong.

Finally, a man who has lived in Bedford all his life said, "Dirt roads are the soul of the town. They are like the fine old floorboards in a house. They are the foundation for everything else."

Not everyone accepts that dirt roads are a source of aesthetic pleasure and distinction. One man who has recently moved to Bedford said, "We want the dirt roads paved. They are dirty and the gravel and potholes damage our car." For a Central American gardener that we interviewed, dirt roads are bad roads. He said, "I don't like the dirt roads because when it rains it gets your car dirty." A clerk who works in a shop in Bedford Village said, "I'm not from here and I'm used to the city look. I can't understand why people like muddy, dirty roads." A Central American cleaner said, "In my country, poor people live on dirt roads, not rich people." One woman who moved to Bedford recently felt she made a mistake buying on a dirt road:

> I live on a dirt road and want it paved. It does so much damage to the cars—it's ridiculous. It's like the Mississippi River sometimes. The potholes after [heavy rains] are unbelievable. You have to have a tank—or a Jeep Wagoneer. They think it will enhance the speeding situation, but it doesn't. They will speed anyway. It's just more dangerous on dirt roads. They want to preserve—fight against modernization—but you have to be practical.

However, the latter are definitely minority opinions in town. Beginning in the mid-1990s with the planning for the new Master Plan, residents have attempted to institutionalize their preference. An editorial in the local newspaper asks, "How can we protect the town's dirt roads" from development? (*Record Review* 1996). Increasingly, the call to reduce traffic and protect dirt roads has become part of the armory of those fighting development in Bedford. One woman wrote the following open letter to the newspaper as part of residents' fifteen-year fight to stop seventeen new houses being built on a hundred-acre parcel of land off the dirt road she lived on:[11]

> We have the pleasure of living on one of Bedford's rarest jewels—the prettiest *little dirt road* you can imagine—complete with twists and turns, flora and fauna—all

of which whisper a welcome to walkers, joggers, leaf collectors and bird watchers. But with the proposal of many houses by the Twin Lakes Farm Development, our beautiful bit of nature may disappear. The town commissioners fight to preserve and protect—the developer fights back to construct and destroy. And one by one, *little dirt roads* all over town are being eliminated. Well Mr. Developer, I will cry endless tears if you win your battle. You will permanently change the quality of my life and others who know and adore Twin Lakes for its beauty and quiet. [emphasis in the original] (Keiser 1996)

As the frequency of meetings to revise the Master Plan increased in 1999 and 2000, people persistently sought ways to protect dirt roads and reduce traffic. The Bedford Coalition, a recently formed umbrella group of organizations in town, coordinated many of these meetings.[12] The coalition in turn set up a Fragile and Scenic Roadway Subcommittee to develop policy on dirt roads. Some residents suggested that "traffic can be moderated by keeping the roads bad" (Lynch 1999a). Another wrote, "Bedford's unpaved roads are a source of delight and add immeasurably to the quality of life here." He continued, "Why not expand the dirt roads. Let the roads go to seed. Make sure they are pot-holed and overgrown, narrow, bumpy and treacherous, unlit and uninviting. If Bedford controls its roads, Bedford controls its habitat. If Bedford loses control of its habitat it will stop being country and turn into just another suburb" (Dungan 2000). Others felt dirt roads should be improved, or reduced in number. As one person wrote on the 1999 Master Plan questionnaire, "It might be nice to keep one fairly level dirt road in town just to remember the old Bedford." The local newspaper the *Record Review* ran an article in praise of dirt roads, quoting residents and town officials to the effect that the dirt roads are central to Bedford's identity. One resident is quoted as saying, "They're gorgeous. And it's something you can't find in Scarsdale or New Canaan." The chair of the Fragile and Scenic Roadway Subcommittee of the Bedford Coalition said, "They're so lovely. With trees on either side and a stone wall running along. It's the country. That's not bad for being only an hour north of New York City" (Nardozzi 2000d). In early 2001, as meetings preparing for the Master Plan continued, strategies were discussed to preserve dirt roads, such as designating them as "scenic" or environmentally "fragile,"[13] thereby opening them up to protection by town ordinance (Nardozzi 2001b). Even though they are extremely costly to maintain and, as we shall see in Chapter Five, they damage wetlands, most residents are so enamored with them that there is little question of the town paving them. Therefore, what members of the Bedford Coalition seem to be principally concerned about is preserving the verges of the dirt roads and not allowing further development along them. A town-planning consultant suggested designating dirt roads and getting residents to grant conservation easements to prevent the destruction of stone walls and trees within twenty-five feet of the roads (Nardozzi 2001d). Again, there is no reason at present to believe that there is any threat to these walls and trees; rather, controls are aimed at forestalling new development along them.

Conclusion

The residents of Bedford conceive of their town as a positional good. They construct Bedford discursively through what has been termed a "constitutive outside," just as they produce and maintain it physically through exclusionary zoning. The aesthetic appeal of Bedford is a highly political achievement. Underpinning the beauty of its landscape, including the village with its colonial common symbolizing New England community, is a highly exclusionary politics. In order to stop the transformation of Bedford's landscape, residents and officials stir up sentiment to mobilize support against the subdivision of land. This is not only because new houses decrease the pastoral nature of the town, but also because they are seen by many to be inauthentic, not truly historical, and thus not fully "Bedford." Although "old" Bedford itself is modeled on an imagined New England village and an imagined English countryside dating in many respects from the late nineteenth and early twentieth centuries, it has acquired the necessary "patina of age to be considered aesthetically pleasing," as one of our respondents put it. Many Bedford residents fear mimicry and become anxious about small differences. Keeping aesthetic differences subtle can be an effective strategy of social distinction. Over time the "inauthentic" becomes seen as authentic, which raises interesting questions about how long the process of becoming "authentic" takes and what exactly the nature of this authenticity is. As we can see from interviews, this is a matter of judgment over which there is little agreement. Historic preservation in Bedford, as in many places, can be described as the preservation of references to history. These references take the form of restorations and sometimes re-creations or reproductions. Skillful re-creations or re-creations that have, as another of our interviewees put it, "acquired dignity with age" are seen to be as good as authentic, and sometimes better. This is a game played by people with enormous resources and sense of commitment and thus must be taken seriously as much more than *merely* an aesthetic issue. The psychological and financial consequences of battles over issues of landscape taste for people in Bedford are very important, and as we shall see in the following chapters, so are the unacknowledged conditions and unintended social consequences of these struggles from a socially and spatially broader perspective.

CHAPTER 5

Legislating Beauty:
The Politics of Exclusion

We want to show that we have a twenty-first century civilization in the midst of an eighteenth-century landscape. Bedford still has the potential of maintaining that landscape, but time is running out.
—Bedford Conservation Board

Constance Perin (1977, 4) points out that "land-use planning, zoning, and development practices are a shorthand of the unstated rules governing what are widely regarded as correct social categories and relationships." Or as another commentator Richard Reeves (1974) put it, "Exclusionary laws are not completely explicit: there are no zoning maps divided into racially or economically restricted areas, so labeled. But there are thousands of zoning maps which say in effect: 'Upper-Income Here', 'Middle Income Here'; 'No Lower-Income Permitted Except as House-hold employees', 'No Blacks Permitted.' " We will argue that in an affluent community, such as Bedford, zoning not only reflects but also plays an active structuring role (instrumental, but over time increasingly naturalized) in grounding the practice of an aestheticized way of life in a place. It attempts to maintain sufficient social homogeneity within a territorially bounded and (relatively) defensible space in order to achieve a collective sense of place and landscape. We believe we are justified in placing a strong emphasis on sense of place and landscape here. We became convinced from our lengthy discussions with residents that they are relatively unconcerned about the personal characteristics (other than class-based taste) of people who might move into town. In part, this is because one finds over-the-back-fence type socializing in only a few areas of town. They are sorely afraid of the negative visual impact of new housing, however.[1]

Planning and land-use controls in Bedford as elsewhere in the United States are the responsibility of local government.[2] The legal right of municipalities to plan and control the use of land through zoning is derived from police powers over issues of health, safety, morals, and welfare granted by the states. Historically, police powers have been justified on the premise that one's use of one's own property must not injure others. The town law grants police powers specifically to lessen congestion, secure safety from fire and panic, promote health and general welfare, provide adequate light and air, prevent overcrowding, and facilitate provision of transportation, water, sewerage, schools, and parks. General welfare

85

is so vaguely defined and contestable that courts have usually been unwilling to interfere with local policy. A whole range of matters including stability of neighborhoods, racial segregation (still often the effect, but once actually the stated purpose, in some places), maintenance of the character of neighborhoods,[3] preservation of property values, general orderliness of development, and protection against nuisances caused by incompatible landuses have usually been considered acceptable uses of police power in the name of general welfare.

Although zoning was originally seen by many as a controversial invasion of property rights, it has been upheld in court numerous times beginning with the landmark case Village of Euclid v. Ambler Realty Co.[4] in 1926. By the beginning of the twenty-first century, zoning has become a largely unquestioned fact of life for most Americans. Few if any people in Bedford would not support zoning, although in a survey of approximately 150 people of all income groups living in and near Bedford conducted in the early 1980s we found a wide range of opinions as to the purpose of zoning. All supported it (apparently) without reservation (Duncan 1986). Four-acre residential zoning in places like Bedford allows individuals to forgo the sometimes (especially in the past) considerable economic benefit of subdividing their properties and yet retaining significant exchange value and (even more important) use value of a landscape relatively protected from development. It is a form of enforced collusion whereby no one is in danger of being left in the position of "sucker" by not dividing his or her property because one's neighbors may not do so either. Thus both property values and use values associated with relatively little housing development are maintained. In fact, it has been so effective that in the most desirable areas of town there has recently arisen a situation in which there is sometimes a premium for keeping large properties intact rather than subdividing them into the minimum-sized lots. This would not have occurred without a combination of factors coming together to place Bedford out of reach of all but a very few wealthy developers. These factors, as we shall see, include highly restrictive environmental legislation enforced by town boards, which use every possible means to greatly slow the process of making and reviewing development proposals.

Challenges to exclusionary zoning using the equal protection clause of the Fourteenth Amendment have usually been successful only in clear cases of *intended* racial discrimination. The action of a community is not held to be unconstitutional simply because the impact is racially disproportionate. A record of racial hostility must be proven. Wealth has been considered a "suspect category" under the equal protection clause, and a right to housing is not guaranteed constitutionally. Shifting of the burden of providing affordable housing onto adjoining towns or counties has usually been rejected as a ground for invalidating local autonomy in zoning. However, a regional fair share argument was successful in landmark cases in New Castle (Chappaqua) in Westchester County[5] and Mount Laurel, New Jersey.[6] In another case in 1977, the New Jersey Supreme Court ruled that "a municipality must not ignore housing needs, that is its fair proportion of the obligation to meet the housing needs of its own population and that of the region (the area from which in the view of available employment and transportation the population of the township would be drawn absent exclusionary zoning)."[7]

Most significant in protecting exclusionary zoning is the unshakable American ideology of local autonomy or home rule. Michael Danielson (1972, 164) says, "Given the nature of the local constituency and local government's dependency on the property tax, the suburban political system has few incentives to act in anything but the town's self interest." This is further reinforced by the courts' usual refusal to take an active role in preventing bias in access to good educational services and other advantages such as employment opportunities. As the suburbanization of employment opportunities steadily grows in Westchester County with the new business and financial service and construction jobs being created in central Westchester, especially White Plains, there has been more and more pressure for housing in the area (Westchester County Housing Opportunity Commission, 1997; Zukin 1991). The regional effect of Bedford's zoning might not be significant if so many other towns in the region did not also have highly exclusionary zoning codes compounding the effects of each others' codes. The invisible walls around towns such as Bedford become further and further strengthened as housing pressure builds. The autonomy of towns and the fact that schools are funded largely from within local tax bases creates an extremely uneven and inequitable geography of educational[8] and other opportunities. Mike Davis (1998) and Michael Orfield (1997) show how poor suburbs effectively subsidize wealthy ones. The poor are squeezed into small areas and pay more for housing than they would if those in richer areas did not pay artificially low prices per acre for land due to large lot zoning.

Finally, only those who already own land in town have standing in court to bring a suit against a town; thus potential residents are barred from challenging the town's zoning. Those who might potentially benefit from opening up exclusionary zoning are unlikely to know of each other's existence and therefore are unable to organize any effective resistance against the structure of zoning.[9] As Donald Kirp et al. (1995, 4) wrote of America in the mid-1990s, "providing housing that poor families can afford and setting aside a fair share of suburbia for the impoverished—are nowhere to be found on our national agenda."

Bedford's original zoning code, which dates back to 1928, was adopted when most American cities and towns were still unzoned. The most notable feature of Bedford's zoning law is its Residence Four-Acre District that includes 80% of the land in town. Few towns in the country have such large minimum lot size requirements, although some places such as in Marin County, California, have five-acre zoning. Another 15% of Bedford's land is zoned for one- and two-acre lots. Bedford's zoning code was put in place during the boom years of the 1920s when a number of large landowners worried that estates might be broken into small parcels of land for sale to newly affluent New Yorkers as weekend and summer places. They saw what had happened on the south shore of Nassau and Suffolk Counties on Long Island, where by 1928 large country estates had been "decimated" by subdivision (Teaford 1997, 13). From its inception, the purpose of Bedford's zoning was aesthetic—to protect the look of the land. But the development pressures that had been so strong during the 1920s disappeared with the Depression and World War II and it wasn't until the 1960s that twenty years of postwar affluence again raised widespread concern about development changing the look of Bedford. As the 1960 Town Plan reveals, planners assumed that Bedford would not in fact be developed to a density of four-acre lots, because a great deal of undeveloped land was thought to be too wet or steep to make building economical. But by the late 1960s and early 1970s, it became clear that people were willing to build on such "marginal" land and as a consequence the number of four-acre properties might increase dramatically. At first, it was unclear what to do about this. The threat of lawsuits over exclusionary zoning within the New York metropolitan region made it politically unthinkable to raise the minimum lot size. In fact, at that time, four-acre zoning itself was seen as susceptible to challenge on exclusionary grounds. It soon became apparent, however, that the new environmental movement might provide a politically acceptable rationale for retarding development. Consequently, a series of environmental codes were put in place in Bedford beginning in 1973 that greatly reduced the possibility of subdivision of large estates into the maximum number of four-acre lots allowed by the zoning. In this chapter, we will first examine the residential zoning code and then discuss the environmental legislation and the ambivalent reactions of Bedford residents.

The Residential Zoning Code

Minimum lot sizes are declared to be "necessary for the protection and promotion of health, safety and general welfare" (Town of Bedford 1989a, 1992). Of the thirteen stated goals of zoning that apply to residential districts, however, most are aesthetic. Among the goals are provision of privacy; avoidance of congestion of population; conservation of the value of land and buildings; protection against unsightly, obtrusive, and obnoxious land uses; the enhancement of the aesthetic aspect of the natural and man-made elements of the town; preservation of the existing historic character of the town; restrictions on the use of solar energy collectors (despite rhetoric of environmental protection); and the minimization of conflicts among uses of land and buildings. Privacy, congestion, and incompatible uses (among other things) are predominantly visual concepts about which residents hold strong opinions. Requirements first introduced in New York City's model zoning code of 1913 that were directly related to health and safety have become incorporated into zoning law in places like Bedford where circumstances are very different. It is not clear, for example, how the height of buildings on large properties is anything other than an aesthetic issue. Other laws regarding underground installation of utilities and buffer screening areas of evergreen planting to hide nonresidential activity are explicitly aesthetic in purpose.

Residents strongly believe that Bedford's four-acre zoning is essential for maintaining its rural atmosphere. One man stated flatly, "Four-acre zoning, made Bedford." Another said, "If you get rid of the zoning, you would get pocket handkerchief–sized pieces of land all over. The number of houses would explode by 50%." A real estate salesman emphasized, "It's important to everyone's real estate values." This latter remark reflects the above-mentioned complex enforced collusion whereby all property owners individually give up the opportunity to subdivide their own land and all benefit because the town as a whole retains a pastoral landscape that maintains high property values. This arrangement would be jeopardized if even some owners subdivided their properties into small lots.

Very few of those interviewed cited exclusion as a purpose of zoning.[10] Some people thought that while exclusion might possibly be a byproduct of zoning, it is a worthwhile and inevitable price to pay for retaining the town's rural atmosphere. One woman told us, "Zoning is important for creating spaciousness and privacy." A number of residents stressed the necessity of zoning for protecting ecology. As one person put it, "My primary concern is protecting the ecology of the town. I don't care about social composition." Someone else admitted that the zoning did have the effect of segregating the rich and the poor. She said, "Yes it's the *effect*, but the purpose is ecological. We are a watershed. Of course it excludes every Tom, Dick, and Harry." Another man said, "The most important thing that zoning can do is protect our natural environment. I have been very involved in getting the town to protect our land and water. It is irreplaceable and must take priority over more people wanting to live in Bedford."

However, more commonly people told us that they supported zoning primarily for aesthetic reasons:

> I think it's important to protect the green spaces. You can't build on less than four acres and that's good. Some people consider four-acre [zoning] exclusionary, but I think it's important to have it for aesthetic reasons. It's not to discriminate against any particular types of people, although it does exclude people without money. I don't care who my neighbors are as long as they don't build anything unattractive. Just about every house in Bedford has plenty of privacy so it's more a matter of aesthetics than a social thing.

Another man expressed a similar sentiment: "Our zoning is here to protect the look of Bedford. It's aesthetic more than it is environmental. I don't think that zoning should be used to keep a particular group out. If people can afford it, they should be able to buy here. I don't have any control over who lives next door and quite frankly I don't care, because I won't see them anyway." A man who has been active in local politics and has some experience with zoning and planning board meetings stated,

> I think it's aesthetic more than environmental and it isn't about who lives in these houses either. It's about how well they preserve the Bedford style. Money certainly isn't the question. In fact, having money can be considered a liability around here; if you have bad taste, it shows all the more, because you have more discretionary income to put into making over your property.

Although some people would not want to admit to exclusion even if it *were* a motivating factor, it is quite believable that aesthetics is the primary concern.[11] A man who lives on eight acres in a house hidden from the road and no neighbors in sight argued, "The origin of zoning was in Germany and England. It was to preserve amenities. Why should the land be ruined for the rest of us? The idea was not—as has been argued relentlessly by those who are interested in breaking zoning—to keep the poor out; I think it should be forty- or thirty-five-acre zoning."[12] Another said, "I personally feel that it is an attempt to keep it rural. We personally like to be surrounded by property. Some people say it is to keep out other people. You have to keep the population down to keep it rural or semi-rural. The purpose is for aesthetic reasons—to give beauty and privacy." One could argue that visual privacy is an aesthetic of individualism. One woman told us, "I remember that, from my childhood, family discussions were often about houses and land. Privacy seemed to be far more important than any other aspect. It was always the land and not so much the house. If a house didn't have enough land or trees to keep it private, you had to have a tall wooden fence or stone wall." Others stated it simply and boldly: "If you took away the zoning, Bedford would disappear" and "Four-acre zoning has done a really good job; it would look like any other suburb without the zoning." One can detect in the above comments a slight uneasiness about exclusion. Residents seem keen to make a distinction between consciously trying to exclude people, which they see as wrong, and excluding people as a consequence of the pursuit of beauty, which they see as laudable.

It appears to be a widely held view that the current zoning is not restrictive enough to prevent suburbanization. One of the people we interviewed said, "I'm worried about the subdivision of large properties. I'm not sure that four-acre zoning is large enough to preserve the look of the place." Almost everyone except those in the land development business and presumably a few property owners who would like to subdivide their own property are opposed to subdivisions of large properties into four-acre portions. Respondents to the 1997 Conservation Board survey felt strongly that there should be stricter regulations to keep large tracts of land intact. While all groups irrespective of length or residence support this strongly.[13]

Our own interviews reveal that loss of open space is the principal change that is feared in Bedford. A stockbroker from Bedford told us when we asked him if he approved of the subdivision of large properties:

> It's hard to say. I am tempted to say nothing [should be subdivided] under a hundred acres but then I think of the very small, original colonial houses on small lots and what would have happened to them if there were only large properties. I suppose in an ideal world I would want the vast majority of the land to be in large estates. Of course I am talking ideally because I couldn't afford either to buy or pay the taxes on one hundred acres. But I am sad to see properties being subdivided into four-acre parcels. Eight acres isn't that large you know. If you have a lot of lots that size, people can see each other's houses. I suppose a four-acre minimum is about as democratic as I would want to get in Bedford. If we start dividing the land into anything smaller than that, then we might as well pack our bags and move to Vermont because Bedford no longer exists.

A young woman is emphatic about the importance of keeping many of the large properties intact. She hopes that some of their owners will deed parcels of land to the town and told us about some friends who are intending to do so. As she put it, "A town full of four-acre properties makes a very nice suburb, but if it is to continue to be country, then many of the properties have to be larger than that. If the developers had their way, every property in Bedford would be four acres." Typical of the comments we heard was the following:

> Of course for aesthetic reasons I would prefer if there weren't ever any more subdivisions in Bedford. Most subdivisions are unattractive. Occasionally land is divided and from the roads you really don't see any difference. Like West Patent Elementary School—you drive by it and it looks like a small driveway into the woods. Although I must say their big new sign spoils the effect. Otherwise you'd never know a school was back there. But those subdivisions are usually [divided into] ten-acre [lots] or something like that. Then you just have to hope no one goes and puts any big gates in front of their property and destroys the look of the landscape.

Another says, "I don't have a problem with development as long as the land can support it ecologically and it is aesthetically pleasing."

It would appear the town government concurs with the view that subdividing land down to four-acre plots should be discouraged wherever possible. Certainly developers we spoke to believe this to be the town's position. One developer told us that the town usually made subdivision down to four acres impossible by invoking wetlands, steep slopes, and tree preservation laws. He stated, "People have to be realistic. They can't keep out all development. Otherwise you could get exclusion suits." The developers and real estate agents we talked to were understandably in favor of a certain amount of subdivision, but were also conscious that much of the value of the land comes from the fact that Bedford is not "overdeveloped." As one real estate broker put it, "Subdivision can be a problem. It has to be done to fit the character of the area or the subdivided land isn't worth as much as the original land." A developer who lives in town told us,

> I don't want subdivision if it's next door. No one wants it next door. Everyone wants to be the last person in town. People try to fight the development of land near them on their road. But if you ask them, why don't you buy that land to keep it open, they say they can't afford it. So then you say to them, do you think that the owner of that land can afford not to develop it just so you can have the privilege of not looking at a new building?

The same developer went on, "four-acre zoning should be retained by allowing all four-acre plots to be developed. If you fight every four-acre subdivision, the zoning will get broken. You will end up with them building an apartment." A real estate agent told us,

> Subdivision is fine if it's well done. I'm anti–cookie-cutter development. You have to work with the topography. It's not fair not to allow people to subdivide their land. Most of the time the components are worth more than the single piece. People have earned their due. They should reap the benefit of their property. At the same time, they do have to take into consideration the way it will look afterward. The placement of the house is very important, and you can't simply cut down all the trees.

One woman we interviewed stated, "Subdivision isn't a problem if it is four-acres. You can't keep people out. I like four-acre [zoning] because it keeps more land free. Cluster zoning is another way to conserve the landscape and nature." However, a real estate broker disagreed with her:

> Cluster zoning is unpopular. The value is not there. The preserved land doesn't increase the value of the lots. The members of the Conservation Board don't understand this because they are middle class. Most of them don't live in four-acre zoning. No matter how well it's done, people won't like it. People move to Bedford because they want privacy. They want their own land, not some middle-class cluster.

Another put it, "Cluster or conservation zoning isn't practical because the land at the back is worthless land. No one knows it's there. It could be fifty feet or 500 acres. You can't really tell. So it doesn't add value." It is very possible that they are correct. However, the 1997 survey revealed that a small majority of residents (56%) were in favor of cluster zoning as a way of allowing some development while maintaining rural character. What the survey does not reveal, however, is whether the respondents would themselves be interested in living in cluster housing. Finally, one retired man, who has lived in Bedford all his adult life and who was quite vocal about his dislike of new houses, nevertheless felt that property owners should not be prevented by the delaying tactics of the Planning and Conservation Boards from legally dividing their land: "Subdivision is a legal right. I don't see how you could object to anything that the town has zoned for. It [subdivision] is certainly people's right if it conforms to the zoning."

The subdivision of land has increased the importance of trees for many people in Bedford and shifted the balance between a pastoral and wooded landscape. Each property owner still wants their property to be private and to have visual separation from neighbors who may at times be less than a hundred yards away. Such privacy requires trees to shield properties from one another and, of course, the more properties there are, the more trees are needed.

The Environmental Protection Code

Beginning in the early 1970s in response to increasingly intense development pressures, the town instituted a number of environmental protection laws. Many residents see these laws as necessary to protect the environment of the town from further degradation. In fact, such measures are often considered an environmental duty of citizenship. For others, the environmental laws are largely an attempt to use a currently fashionable concern in order to maintain Bedford's green spaces by excluding future development in whatever ways possible. Most common of all is a view that the environmental ordinances are important not only because they protect the environment but also because they protect the visual character of Bedford by excluding development. The 1999 Master Plan survey reveals that over three-quarters of residents who responded believe that the environmental quality of the town would be threatened by uncontrolled growth of housing on undeveloped land.

The Bedford zoning code contains three chapters devoted to environmental law. The first, enacted in 1973 and revised in 1991, is concerned with wetlands (Town of Bedford 1991). The second, adopted in 1986 and revised in 1997, deals with tree preservation (Town of Bedford 1986), and the third, enacted in 1989, concerns steep slopes (Town of Bedford 1989c).[14] There is compelling evidence that these laws came into existence as a result of development pressures in the town. In this respect, it is instructive to examine the two town plans prior to the first 1973 wetlands legislation.

Table 5.1 Percent Agreeing That There Is a "Threat to Environmental Quality from Uncontrolled Growth as New Housing Replaces Undeveloped Land"

Net Difference = Agree − Disagree				
A. *By Length of Residence*				
<5 Years	5–9 Years	10–19 Years	20 Years+	
+72.4%	+75.3%	+83.0%	+72.8%	
B. *By Area*				
4 Acre+	Bedford Village	Bedford Hills	Katonah	Outside Hamlet 1–4 Acre
+77.3%	+75.8%	+ 63.6%	+75.5%	+76.5%
(649 = Total Number)				

Source: Town of Bedford 2000.

The 1960 town Development Plan stated that 69.6% of the town land was classified as vacant. This included privately owned wooded and open lands, farmland, and "public or private land not in any specific use" (Town of Bedford 1960, 13). The term "vacant" was applied to land that had not been developed as intensively as permitted by law. The owners of much of this land would not consider it vacant, however. The concept of a country estate, for example, requires that it include many more than four acres in order to afford the owners "unspoiled" views or complete privacy.

Of the vacant land, the plan considered 8.7% to be marginal land unsuitable for development. These marginal lands were either swampy or steep with slopes greater than 20%. It is interesting that in the 1960 Town Development Plan the term "wetlands" does not appear. The terms "swamp" and "wetlands" come from different political discourses. The anti-development activists found that by the 1970s their best arsenal came from the environmental movement and its vocabulary of wetlands and biodiversity. In the 1960 plan, there was a section titled "Flood Plain Areas," which dealt with areas that were wet or subject to periodic flooding. The plan stated that almost none of these areas had been developed and went on to say that intensive use of these areas should be prevented because of the potential public expenditures associated with protecting property in areas susceptible to flooding (Town of Bedford 1960, 32). The plan suggested ways of preventing the development of wet areas, among them public ownership: "The surest way to prevent intensive use of low and swampy areas is through public ownership. These areas are often suitable for parking or recreation purposes, and, in many cases, the keeping of these areas as open space can serve more than just flood control purposes" (Town of Bedford 1960, 33). The plan then recommended that certain of these areas could be developed if they were filled or dredged and it could be demonstrated that no flooding or pollution would be caused elsewhere by building (Town of Bedford 1960, 33). The concern of the planners for the flood plains was expressed differently from present-day concerns for wetlands. There is little sense of protecting the environment conveyed in these statements. Rather it was primarily life and property that was to be protected by forbidding unsound building practices that would cause flooding. Second, there was no concern expressed about protecting steep slopes or trees.

The 1972 town Development Plan introduced some significant changes. During this period, developed land increased from 30.4% to 44.2%, a rate that the planners found troublingly high. Still more troubling was the fact that 5% of the newly developed land previously had been considered unbuildable. The value of land had become sufficiently high to justify the cost of filling or excavating a building site on such land. The planners concluded that (Town of Bedford 1972, 16) "it seems apparent, then, that while most swamplands and steeply sloping areas in Bedford may be unsuitable for future development in terms of the despoliation of the natural environment which would result, such development can no longer be realistically regarded as infeasible or unlikely." Thus the planners revised the grounds of their opposition to such building. They now spoke not of property damage but of the more abstract "despoliation of the natural environment." Such concerns, it would appear, were driven in part by the rise of environmentalism as a popular movement in the late 1960s and by a desire to find new legally sound reasons to slow residential development. At root, the problem was that the zoning as it presently stood allowed for more development than the town boards and the majority of the residents wanted.

Not surprisingly, given the cultural history of Bedford, the environmentalism expressed in the 1972 town Development Plan was driven primarily by aesthetics. Take for example the following two planning recommendations (Town of Bedford 1972, 26): "1. Conservation of existing open space, particularly in areas of high visibility, should receive high priority in the overall planning of future development in Bedford. 2. Special attention should be given to preserving such features as streams, water bodies, forests, ridgelines, and other places of distinctive scenic and ecological value." Similarly, a recommendation that "a primary objective in the design of all new subdivisions and developments in the outlying areas of Bedford should be the preservation of the natural environment" (Town of Bedford 1972, 27) appeared under a section titled "Community Appearance." The plan went on to urge that rivers and streams be preserved "because of their extraordinary scenic value, and the essential role they play in maintaining natural water supplies and controlling storm water drainage" (Town of Bedford 1972, 54). Similarly, steep slopes, rock outcroppings, and hilltops are to be preserved because they are "scenic" or allow "panoramic views" (Town of Bedford 1972, 56). And yet the planners realize that passing laws to promote a particular aesthetic is problematic. Consider, for example, the following discussion of flood plain zoning:

> Flood plain zoning is a necessary water resource measure; it also preserves what are usually scenic parts of the countryside. But aesthetics is not the justification. A flood plain ordinance takes away the owner's right to build on such property, and the ordinance must clearly be based upon the necessity of protecting a resource that is vital to the health, safety and welfare of the public. (Town of Bedford 1972, 61–62).

The problem here and throughout is that the legislation of an aesthetic is difficult to justify under police powers. This is especially the case where individual rights to property are jeopardized. Picturesque landscapes can, however, be protected through legislation that is ostensibly put in place to protect property or the environment.

The Wetlands Code

A year after the 1972 town Development Plan raised concerns about the development of wetlands in Bedford, the town board passed the first wetlands law.

The law, which was revised in 1991, states as its purpose the promotion of the health and welfare of the citizens. It forbade *any* encroachment or elimination of wetlands. The law recognizes that wetlands have been progressively encroached upon throughout much of the eastern United States and that resisting such encroachment at the local level is at the heart of the environmentalist duty to "think globally and act locally." It has, however, been suggested by certain of the more cynical commentators that environmentalism is the self-serving radicalism of the elite, and that it should be read as protection of their own rural interests (Tucker 1982). We take this point, but might choose to temper it: environmentalism and aesthetic interests are both served by Bedford's legislation.

The law defines wetlands as a natural resource that serves not only the town, but also the surrounding region, by (1) controlling flooding and pollution, (2) providing recreation, (3) providing open space to satisfy "aesthetic and psychological needs," and (4) providing suitable environments for fish, birds, and animals (Town of Bedford 1991, 12202). Here, under the law, the traditional concern for flooding and the protection of property has been broadened to formally recognize both aesthetics and the rights of animals. The law goes on to recognize the problem of adopting an ecosystem approach: "Wetlands in Bedford and other areas form an ecosystem which is not confined to any one property owner or neighborhood" (Town of Bedford 1991, 12203). The code further addresses the issue of individual rights to property more directly: "These regulations are enacted with the intent of providing a reasonable balance between the rights of the individual property owner to the free use of his property and the rights of present and future generations" (Town of Bedford 1991, 12204).

An important deterrent to development is the cost of applying for a land development permit. Applicants have to produce plans at the scale of one inch to thirty feet certified by an engineer, architect, land surveyor, or landscape architect certified by the state. Such plans must show the location of wetlands as determined by an ecologist, botanist, or soil scientist, as well as the impact of any development both on and off the property. Such requirements not only greatly increase the cost of a project and slow down the permission process, but there is no certainty that at the end of the process the board will approve the proposed development. Several real estate brokers in town told us that the wetlands legislation is one of the primary ways in which the town deters potential land developers. As one real estate broker put it, "They want to try and completely control aesthetics and, more important, to bankrupt developers. Regulations keep them [developers] coming back to town so eventually it's too expensive for them to build."

The people we interviewed about the Wetlands Code were divided in their opinion of how successful they thought it was in retarding development. Predictably, those who were against it had themselves been stopped from developing their property in some way by the code. Those in favor of the code often felt that it needed to be strengthened to stop abuses. The 1997 survey by the Conservation

Table 5.2 Percent in Favor of Environmental Regulations of Wetlands

Net Difference = Stricter Regulations − Looser Regulations

A. *By Length of Residence*

	Total	10 Years or Less	11–20 Years	More Than 20 Years
Aquifer Protection	+66%	+69%	+71%	+61%
Restricting Building on or Near Wetlands	+62%	+69%	+70%	+53%
Wetlands Filling	+62%	+65%	+61%	+62%

B. *By Area*

	Total	Bedford Village	Bedford Hills	Katonah
Aquifer Protection	+66%	+67%	+69%	+58%
Restricting Building on or Near Wetlands	+62%	+56%	+79%	+54%
Wetlands Filling	+62%	+65%	+73%	+51%

(529 = Total Number)

Source: Town of Bedford 1998.

Board shows strong support for wetlands protection across all areas of town and length of residence.

Our own interviews also revealed strong support for the wetlands code. Many felt that the town's water supply and ecology needed protection from developers. As one man said, "We can't be naïve and think that because we live in the country our environment is safe. We need legislation with teeth to protect nature." Another said, "There are rivers in this town like the Mianus that flow into the Croton watershed. We have a responsibility to protect our own drinking water and that of tens of thousands who live down stream." Yet another said, "The animals who live in our wetlands can't protect themselves, so we must do it for them. We are their stewards." Some residents were in favor of the wetlands code but wanted better enforcement. A horse trainer said, "The law isn't strong enough. There's only 30% (of the wetlands) left." A real estate agent felt that developers had exploited a weak law: "They have gotten away with a lot. Environmental concerns will cut back on that. Watershed regulations will make it much tougher." A homemaker who grew up in Bedford thought that the problem was lax enforcement by town officials:

> I don't know much about wetlands. I don't think the term existed when I was a child. There are a tremendous number of laws about wetlands, but people seem to be able to get variances. I think the laws should be very strict. I don't understand about variances. What is the point of the law if they are given out? These wetland laws are important to preserve the look of the land.

It is interesting to note that she thinks that the purpose of the code is to preserve an aesthetic—"the look of the land"—rather than an ecology.

A number of people we interviewed strongly disagreed with the code. The owner of a small, local business said,

> The wetlands control is ridiculous. They wouldn't let me divert a stream under my property. They said it had to be active and uncovered because it had invertebrates in it. So that took away half my property. And yet they don't control the use of the stream. It is polluted. They only pay attention when you go for building permits and it's all a matter of who you are. How much money you have. If you are rich they'll let you do it, because you can give them support in their office.

This man also questioned the variance procedures. However, while the woman quoted above implied that variances were freely handed out, this man felt that they were reserved for those willing to pay. All evidence we are aware of does not support his view, at least not at present.[15] A developer with experience working in Bedford thought that the environmental regulations were just a pretext to keep out development:

> Most subdivisions take ten years to get permissions. A lot of the subdivision regulations are supposed to be about the environment, but really they are about aesthetics. You see other situations where there are environmental problems and the town doesn't care. It all depends who calls up and screams. If neighbors don't call up and scream, the town doesn't care what happens.

A long-term resident who had a request turned down thought that the code was unjust. He said, "Well I'm no expert on conservation, but it seems to be going overboard when you can't build a tennis court within a hundred feet of wetlands. That law should be replaced."

A number of people were ambivalent about the code. A real estate agent felt that "there are some serious issues like poisoning water. Dry cleaning fluid in the water that needs to be regulated. Most of the rest of the regulations are just a way of stopping development." Another interviewee said,

> I understand they [wetlands] are important for ecological reasons. They used to be called swamps and were considered unattractive. I actually think swamps are attractive. I understand that they are a good habitat for animals and birds. But people here use wetland regulations as an excuse sometimes to prevent new building. Whereas it's hard on the owners [of property], I can sympathize with that attitude.

Finally a banker understood wetlands purely in visual terms and his ambivalence toward them was framed by this: "Are wetlands important to me? I wouldn't say they are my favorite part of the landscape although sometimes they can be pretty."

In spite of some people's belief that variances are freely handed out, in fact the Wetlands Board is very hesitant to pass projects. They are also very much opposed to granting mitigations, which are permissions to build on wetlands in exchange for creating wetlands elsewhere.[16] Because of the difficulty of getting a variance, some of the people we spoke to had either resisted the wetland code or knew of neighbors who had. One man told us how he circumvented regulations that he disagreed with: "I have been filling mine in. First I cut out the skunk cabbage and cut holes in the canopy to let the sun in. It's amazing how some of the small ones can be filled in. Another thing I do is to put down soil a bit at a time and plant grass. I told a friend about this and he says it's working for him too." A homemaker told us in outraged terms about a neighbor who disregarded the code:

> We know this jerk with millions to spend on his house. He built it close to a pond and has had constant trouble with water. His wife puts in lots of plants but they all die. What do they expect? They built their house in a swamp. The wetland zoning says they are supposed to have pond grass near the pond but they have lawn right to the edge. When another neighbor asked him how he was able to have lawn down to the pond's edge, he answered, "I factor in the fine to the cost of the job." I can't believe the arrogance!

Bedford's residents are great supporters of wetlands when they are fighting potential development, but when not wearing their anti-development hats, they appear somewhat less interested. In spite of all the rhetoric of saving the environment, as Table 4.2 demonstrates, no portion of the sample in the 1997 survey ranked protecting the environment as the most important challenge facing Bedford. In fact, as we shall see, residents strongly support certain forms of behavior that greatly damage the town's wetlands. We will now consider two factors that have been particularly damaging to Bedford's wetlands: the town's beloved dirt roads and its decision not to build sewers. We suspect that it would never occur to many supporters of wetlands that dirt roads can harm them. These roads are defined by most as an unquestioned good; they are thought of as premodern, closer to nature, and, therefore, less damaging to the environment than modern roads. There are some residents who are aware of the negative impact of dirt roads, however. A banker with environmental concerns told us,

> Beautiful as they are, they are continually eroding after heavy rains. I have seen three-foot gullies form on the Narrows Road after a bad storm.[17] A lot of the dirt from the roads silts up the wetlands. And yet so many of these so-called environmentalists in town who are all for the wetlands if it means no new housing would fight tooth and nail to preserve the dirt roads.

Another man argued, "The town is the biggest offender in terms of wetlands. Every yard of item 4 [the aggregate of stone and sand put on dirt roads] ends up in the wetlands. Dirt roads are an environmental disaster and the Mianus River Road is one of the worst. It deposits a huge amount of silt in the Mianus River. What I want to know is why the people from the preserve never complain about that?" Interestingly, as we saw in Chapter Four, those helping to create Bedford's new Master Plan are strong supporters of dirt roads. For example, John Friedler, head of Bedford Coalition's Traffic, Roads, and Safety Committee, argued in a town meeting in July 2000 that "narrow, gravel surfaced roads [are] both environmentally and aesthetically advantageous to the hamlets" (Nardozzi 2000d). He and Ann McDuffie, chair of the Fragile and Scenic Roadways Subcommittee of the coalition, went on to argue at the same meeting that dirt roads are cheaper to maintain. However, a study by the Bedford superintendent of highways showed that dirt roads cost one-and-a-half to two times as much to maintain and that it costs two to three times more to operate vehicles on dirt roads because of wear and tear. More apposite is the fact that calcium and magnesium chloride are spread on the roads in summer to keep dust down that, along with the silt, goes directly into the wetlands.

In August 2000, the League of Women Voters of Westchester reported that "storm water runoff is the largest source of water pollution in the United States," and that fourteen of the fifty worst sites in the Croton watershed are located in Bedford, the largest number of any town. The Bedford town supervisor observed at the time that "this is the little known side of having dirt roads" (Nardozzi 2000e). In February 2001, a coalition of water quality groups identified "erosion emanating from its miles of dirt roads" as the principal source of water pollution in Bedford. The town supervisor told the environmental group that Bedford had been working to reduce this problem for the past ten years and was installing silt basins and drainage pipes. He further told them that the basins cost the town hundreds of thousands of dollars each year and that during the current year the town had set aside $250,000 for drainage and storm water improvement (Nardozzi 2001b). The federal Environmental Protection Agency is requiring municipalities nationwide to develop storm water management plans by March 2003 and to implement them by May 2008 (Eddings 2001). There is no question that Bedford's dirt roads will make compliance much more difficult. Nevertheless, the town's Master Plan remains committed to preserving dirt roads. This is another example of choosing aesthetic over environmental concerns.

Yet another example of Bedford residents' situational environmentalism occurred in 1991 when a proposal to build a sewer treatment facility in town was overwhelmingly defeated. It was opposed not only because such a system would be costly to install but, more important, because sewers would allow a greater density of housing in Bedford with less damage to ground water than occurs at present. Such a system had been urged on Bedford by the city of New York, which is anxious to preserve the quality of its drinking water supply.[18] From New York City's point of view, Bedford is culpable because waste water overflow, particularly in the business districts of Bedford Hills and Katonah, flow into the New York City reservoir wetlands. The septic systems in these hamlets were installed in the late nineteenth century and require extensive maintenance. The cost of replacing these systems in 1991 was estimated to be $12 million. In the 1997 survey, a slight majority of residents of Bedford Hills were in favor of sewers while the hamlet of Katonah was about evenly split for and against (Town of Bedford 1998). In Bedford Village, which, as we shall see in Chapter Seven, has a serious pollution problem, residents voted three to two against.

After years of applying pressure on Bedford to no avail, New York City threatened litigation in 1994 unless Bedford solved its waste water problems. The Bedford town supervisor at the time said, "We want to do this [clean up town water] as much as New York City does, but the issue is economics" (Carroll 1994a). The alternative that New York City faced was to build a filtration system at a cost of $4 billion to $6 billion.[19] In January 1994, Bedford joined five other Westchester towns in protesting these watershed protection measures. Town officials feared that individual homeowners might not be able to bring their antiquated septic systems up to code and that they would have to be replaced. Furthermore, New York City's interference was seen as a threat to "home rule." The town supervisor said, "Our argument relates to best available technology. If the best thing is to have a cesspool and pump more often, then we should be able to do that" (Sourby 1994a). Throughout 1994 and 1995, New York City's Department of Environmental Protection continued to pressure Bedford and other suburban towns to institute more stringent watershed protection measures.

In 1995, a compromise was worked out between New York City and the Westchester towns. The latter would provide more protection for New York City's drinking water while at the same time allowing towns like Bedford to continue to use antiquated septic systems. In March 1998, the New York office of the Environmental Protection Agency argued that a filtration system was needed for New York City. Such a system, however, was opposed by environmentalists in Westchester County on the grounds that it would undercut attempts to retard development (Carroll 1998). Two years later, the city faced the prospect of having by federal law to build a filtration system unless the safety of the water in its reservoirs could be improved (Nardozzi 2000f). At a public hearing held by the U.S. Environmental Protection Agency (USEPA) in June 2001, federal officials said that every reservoir serving Westchester County and New York City is threatened by pollution. But at the meeting, some regional and environmental groups once again argued against building a filtration system (Witherspoon 2001a). The upshot is that neither the city nor the towns in Westchester want the filtration system and consequently both have an interest in finding the least expensive way to have the water in the Croton reservoir system meet minimum federal standards. Anti-development interests in Bedford have found an unusual ally in the City of New York city as one might think that it would look to suburban towns to loosen their exclusionary zoning codes in order to help alleviate its low-income housing crisis. However, such housing issues have necessarily taken a back seat to the huge financial implications of bringing the city's water quality up to new federal standards. According to Gandy (2002, 64–65), New York City is facing huge costs, not only because of the declining quality of water in the Croton Watershed, but also from a tightening of the federal water quality standards. He argues that the scale of expenditure for the city to meet these higher

Table 5.3 Opinion Regarding Water Quality as a Percentage

Net Difference = Improving − Worse

A. *By Length of Residence*

	Total	10 Years or Less	11–20 Years	More Than 20 Years
Quality of Streams	−42%	−36%	−46%	−44%
Extent of Water Pollution	−39%	−36%	−39%	−42%
Quality of Ground Water	−39%	−38%	−38%	−41%
Quality of Reservoir Water	−35%	−28%	−33%	−42%

A. *By Area*

	Total	Bedford Village	Bedford Hills	Katonah
Quality of Streams	−42	−45	−43	−39
Extent of Water Pollution	−39	−40	−41	−37
Quality of Ground Water	−39	−37	−49	−37
Quality of Reservoir Water	−35	−31	−44	−32

(529 = Total Number)

Source: Town of Bedford 1998.

environmental standards not only threatens to undermine citizen support for environmental issues, but also negatively impacts other social programs. What is clear, however, is that there would be less tension between the housing and water needs of New York City if northern suburbs such as Bedford installed sewers throughout town.[20] Although there are undoubtedly real economic factors involved,[21] the principal reason that Bedford is unsewered today is that sewers would erode environmental arguments against highly restrictive overlay zoning.

The 1997 survey reveals that residents believe that water quality in town is either staying the same or decreasing in quality. Table 5.3 shows little variation of opinion by area or length of residence.

When a draft of the new Bedford Master Plan was presented to the town in late 2001, sewers for the hamlets of Bedford Hills, Katonah, and Mount Kisco were given high priority because of pressure from the Environmental Protection Agency. However the plan argued for "the need to *avoid* sewer construction in the rest of the town." The one-, two-, and four-acre zones of town, which is to say approximately 90% of the town, were identified as "sewer avoidance" areas for fear that sewers will allow more development (Nardozzi 2001g).[22] Foot dragging on building sewers and continuing support for dirt roads on the part of residents and officials in town hardly speaks of a fervent concern for water quality. Rather it suggests the issue of water quality is secondary to retarding development.

As part of its effort to improve water quality in the Croton reservoir system, the Department of Environmental Protection in 1999 placed four roadside signs in Bedford warning people not to pollute the watershed and providing a Department of Environmental Protection number to call if anyone is seen doing so. Although residents of the town have persistently argued that they wish to protect wetlands from pollution, they strongly oppose the presence of these signs in Bedford. The town supervisor said, "I think they are visually offensive" (Marx 1999c). A month later, a member of the Bedford Coalition wrote an open letter to the Department of Environmental Protection, saying, "I feel compelled to voice my disapproval of the unsightly signage your agency has placed in our community. While the concept of alerting potential polluters and possible informants to the existence of the watershed is sensible, I believe the large, bright blue signs introduce a new color into the roadway which clashes with our beautiful landscape" (Bianco 1999).

All of this might prompt the question, do the residents of Bedford truly support environmentalism or do they strategically use it to other ends? The answer, we believe, lies in the amalgamation of several different strands of environmentalism, some more ecological and others more spiritual or aesthetic. People often subscribe to multiple strands without being troubled by contradictions. They would put their emphasis on whatever aspect of the environment most concerns them at a given moment. One interviewee told us, "The people of this town have had to acquire a lot of knowledge of ecology in order to fight off development. We have organized meetings with environmental experts to help teach us about the environment and how to use our knowledge to help keep Bedford the way it is." A developer bitterly agreed, stating, "The people here don't care about the environment for its own sake. The environment for them is simply the means. 'No development' is the end they really care about."

Some of the residents of Bedford are like their Republican Congresswoman Sue Kelly. She was voted in as, among other things, a strong local environmentalist. Upon her arrival in Washington, however, she joined her Republican colleagues in their attack on environmental legislation and voted to revise the 1972 Clean Water Act to make it easier for businesses to pollute. After the vote, members of the New York League of Conservation Voters picketed her Mount Kisco office (Zink 1995a). Her opposition to clean water nationally has not affected her standing in Bedford, however, where in November 2000 she was voted in for a fourth term. The next year she voted to allow oil drilling in the Alaskan National Wildlife Refuge (Nardozzi 2001f). The congresswoman strongly supports an aesthetic environment for her constituents, but is indifferent or even hostile to environmental issues elsewhere when they conflict with the interests of business. In light of such limited support for scientific as opposed to aesthetic environmentalism, it is hardly surprising that Green Party presidential candidate Ralph Nader received only 4% of the vote in town in 2000.

The Tree Preservation Code

After much debate, a tree preservation ordinance was passed by the town in 1986. This particular ordinance remains controversial in that it forbids property owners from cutting trees over a certain size on their property without a permit. Those we interviewed were on the whole far more ambivalent and tentative about the tree ordinance than about any other aspect of land law, or any other question we posed. The justification for the law is put forward on two grounds. The first is the protection of "the town's ecological systems" (Town of Bedford 1986, 11202). Here the language of science is invoked: trees "control water pollution by preventing soil erosion and flooding . . . yield advantageous microclimatic effects, provide a natural habitat for the wildlife of the town . . ." (Town of Bedford 1986, 11201). We would argue that legislation based on size of trees rather than species and other forest characteristics, points much more toward anti-development and the English landscape taste for meadows with copses than to ecological health.[23] Furthermore, it is interesting to note that none of our informants mentioned the ecological importance of saving trees. The second justification is visual—to preserve "unusual, large and old trees that have unique aesthetic and historic values" and more generally the "rural character of the community which is reflected in the woodlands of the Town of Bedford" (Town of Bedford 1986, 11201–11202).

While there is no question that erosion, habitat preservation for animals, and microclimate effects are of concern to some people in Bedford, these concerns do not explain why this law came into existence. An initial proposal for the tree ordinance stated that a permit was required for cutting on all lots. Significantly, after a storm of protest, this was altered so that it applied to the cutting of trees of twelve inches or more in diameter *only* if that tree is on a "parcel of land of five acres or more or on any parcels of land without residence structure" (Town of Bedford 1986, 11203). Individuals with residences on standard four-acre lots can cut down all of their large trees so long as they are not "landmark" trees or on slopes of 25% or greater. Such a massive loophole demonstrates that the law is not so much to protect trees, as to slow the process of getting permission to develop. Although this legislation alone probably doesn't prevent development, it adds to the cost and the lengthy process of getting permission, which discourages developers who do not have sufficient resources or patience. The cost of obtaining a permit is very high. The permit application requires the following:

> A survey of that section to be disturbed showing the location of all trees regulated herein to an accuracy of one (1) foot, indicating those trees to be removed and those trees to be preserved, their species and their diameter. In the case of site plans and subdivisions, the tree survey shall be submitted to the Planning Board as a part of the site plan or subdivision construction plans. Where no subdivision or site plan is involved, the survey requirement may be eliminated and a simple sketch drawn by the applicant may be substituted. (Town of Bedford 1986, 11205)

It is telling that all of this costly counting and labeling of trees can be eliminated if one does not intend to develop. Even if a builder demonstrates that the removal of trees will have no deleterious effects on the ecosystem, the permit still may be denied, for listed under the conditions for granting a permit is a clause that allows the building inspector to deny the application if he judges that the removal of the trees has a negative effect upon "the property values and aesthetics of the neighborhood" (Town of Bedford 1986, 11204).

Although, as we shall see, residents are ambivalent about the very idea of a tree ordinance, complaints continually pour into the town about cutting. Apparently even more people would complain if they were informed about cutting, for three-quarters of those surveyed in 1997 answered that the town did not keep them sufficiently informed about nearby tree cutting (Town of Bedford 1998).

Those who have lived in town for ten years or less felt less informed than others. However, in the same survey, residents were divided between making tree-cutting regulations tougher and leaving it the same. Recent residents were most in favor of stricter controls as were residents of Bedford Village (Town of Bedford 1998).

There had been enough resident dissatisfaction that in 1997 the ordinance was strengthened by requiring a permit to cut more than ten trees on four-acre lots, protecting trees along certain scenic routes and increasing the fine to $350 per tree rather than per offence. Nevertheless, some residents at the hearing on the proposed change charged the town with depriving them of their property rights, while another accused the town of creating a "police state" (Zink 1997). Most were supportive, however, and the new ordinance was enacted in April 1997.

Very few of the people whom we interviewed supported the ordinance un-ambiguously. One informant told us,

> I think the law has gone too far. Certainly the truly grand old trees should be protected but the circumference of the trees that you are not allowed to cut should be increased. Also it depends if you are opening land to build new houses. I am not in favor of that. I think they should retain trees along the road and hide the houses behind the trees. But if anyone wants to open up views and make Bedford more pastoral looking, that's all to the good. It's so hard to enforce what would be best.

One man who supports the ordinance without reservation said, "The trees are what is special about Bedford. We need an anti-cutting law, otherwise people will cut everything." Much more common was qualified support such as that given by a long-term resident: "Basically it depends where the trees are. It may not make sense to keep all the trees. Remember it was all clear once. Buffers between properties are important. If people cut down trees on property lines and disturb neighbors, that would be bad." A venture capitalist agreed: "People shouldn't be allowed to cut very large trees, but certainly smaller ones. I guess really that I have sympathy for the law because it preserves privacy." Like the woman quoted above, this man favors the law because it maintains the rural aesthetic of the house surrounded by nature.

In our interviews, the question "Should people be allowed to cut down trees on their own property?" seemed to cause people more difficulty than any of the others that we asked. People were very ambivalent and unsure how to answer this. On the one hand, they subscribe to a liberal individualistic view and think that people should have the right to do what they want on their own property. On the other hand, they feel that while they themselves would make the right decision about which trees to cut, their neighbors might not. One woman argued that "regulation wouldn't be necessary if people had common sense. We have a lot of regulation already." Another woman put it more strongly, stating, "I favor legislation because people can't be trusted. They are ignorant." One longtime resident blames the need for legislation on newcomers: "When I first came to Bedford we didn't need all this legislation because Bedford was more homogeneous and people could agree on what the place should look like. Now with all the newcomers and development you have to legislate everything because these people don't share our taste."

Again and again, the issue seemed to be one of individual rights to property versus legislating an aesthetic. The importance of the latter to these people can be seen from the fact that for many it overrides the right to control uses of their own private property. This ambivalence was well represented by one woman who said, "I have mixed feelings about that. When I see trees like this ash tree that has been here forever, I don't want it ever to be harmed. I wonder if history counts anymore to many people. I do like the regulations to stop people from destroying something for nothing." One woman argues strongly against the tree ordinance on the grounds that it is an invasion of private property: "I have fought it tooth and nail. Basically it's not anybody's business what you do with your land. Adjacent neighbors shouldn't have the right to say, 'You can't cut this tree down.' It's often neighbors who put pressure on the town to stop tree cutting." As is so often the case in a place like Bedford, individualism and notions of privacy sit uneasily with notions of community control over aesthetics.[24] Consider what this man has to say: "I disagree with that law. It is an invasion of privacy. I don't think anyone in their right mind would cut down a beautiful tree on their property. But they should be entitled to cut out trees that they don't want. But people want to keep trees so they can protect their property." The protection he is referring to is protection against having to look at a neighbor's house. For some, however, such as one informant who had recently moved to Bedford, it simply has to do with control over property: "I'm very big on people's rights. They should be able to cut trees on their property if they are not landmarks. If you buy a property with a covenant, that's one thing, but if not, the perimeter process is fine."[25] Others feel that they are willing to trade off what they see as a loss of freedom for necessary legislation. One woman puts it this way: "I don't care if it's an invasion of private property. We need legislation to protect trees from these people who don't know a maple from an oak." One man pondered for a moment and then said, "It's a tough one. It curtails my freedom but I still want to keep the trees. What choice is there?"

The 1997 survey asked for opinions about whether town ordinances more generally should be more or less restrictive and whether developers and homeowners should be treated equally. The logic of supporting these ordinances generally is the same as for zoning. It creates an enforced collusion so that each individual will give up rights because the benefits to the individual of

Table 5.4 Percent Disagreeing with the Statement "All These Ordinances Infringe Too Much on the Rights of Individual Property Owners"

A. *By Length of Residence*			
Total	10 Years or Less	11–20 Years	More Than 20 Years
66%	70%	69%	61%
B. *By Area*			
Total	Bedford Village	Bedford Hills	Katonah
66%	68%	61%	65%
(529 = Total Number)			

Source: Town of Bedford 1998.

forcing everyone to do the same is greater than the cost. The survey revealed that two-thirds of residents did not believe that town ordinances infringed too much on their rights as property owners. While residents overwhelmingly agreed that developers should be more tightly restricted, they thought that homeowners didn't need tighter regulations.

Some oppose the tree code on the grounds that it destroys the pastoral nature of the landscape. One longtime resident put it this way: "Preservation of open spaces is absolutely central. I worry that with all this talk about tree preservation we may eventually lose some of the beautiful open fields." A man who recently bought property said, "Bedford is forested with second growth. A lot of what I would call weed trees. I wanted to restore my property to its 1890s condition and keep its bigger trees. Bedford was pastoral. I want it to return to that, but I'm not sure I will be allowed to." Another resident said, "If we want to preserve Bedford, the last thing we need is more trees. Instead we need to open more fields and make it more pastoral, like it was in the nineteenth century when it was all farmland. You can tell it was farmland because you find apple trees and stone walls in the woods." One woman who owns over 200 acres and is committed to an open pastoral landscape told us, "I can't tell you how strongly I feel against the tree ordinance. On our property we have always fought to keep the land open,

Table 5.5 Percent Agreeing with the Statement "We Should Work Hard to Restrict Conventional Tract Development as Much as Possible"

A. *By Length of Residence*			
Total	10 Years or Less	11–20 Years	More Than 20 Years
77%	81%	80%	74%
B. *By Area*			
Total	Bedford Village	Bedford Hills	Katonah
77%	80%	80%	71%
(529 = Total Number)			

Source: Town of Bedford 1998.

and keep back the trees. If you let a field go unmaintained for twenty years, then you become affected by the tree ordinance and you can't clear it." Some people oppose the ordinance by breaking the law. One woman told us how she did it:

> I wanted to open up a view on my land by taking down some trees. So I went to the town and they wanted me to draw a map of all the trees on my property and indicate the species. I couldn't believe it. I know now that this is a delaying tactic that raises the cost so maybe you won't do it. But I thought to myself, how can they enforce this? So I waited a few months and cut down the trees I wanted to. They can't check on every property. It's not like the Gestapo or something. I found out that the time to do it is on weekends. The tree companies do great work on Sundays because neighbors can't call the inspectors. Basically there is a lot of cutting on weekends. When they [inspectors] do come and look, they say it's beautiful because they like the look of open land. Of course I'm not talking about cutting beautiful trees like the Bedford oak, but second growth.

The strategy of cutting even second growth without permission is not always without consequences. In the mid-1990s, a couple who bought a fifty-acre property illegally clear cut a hillside on which they built a 22,000-square-foot house. The Planning Board objected to the felling on two grounds. The first was the erosion from this hillside into an adjacent nature preserve, and the second was the "view from 'Sunset Ledge,' a popular spot in the sanctuary where visitors once could look below at the rolling hillsides and trees, now looks directly upon the couple's new 22,000 square foot mansion atop a hillside cleared of trees" (Carroll 1995c). Consequently, the Planning Board objected and refused to grant them permission to build their tennis courts until they agreed to replant the hillside with 150 six- to eight-foot trees (Carroll 1995b). Having said this, being required to plant less than $20,000 worth of trees is a small penalty for people who are spending millions on a property.[26] In late 2001, the town discovered that another resident, identified in the local press as "a former Scarsdale resident," had clear cut seventy-four trees and filled and leveled wetlands on his six-and-a-half-acre property. He was required by the town to hire a wetlands consultant to study and reverse the damage he had done. The upshot was that he was required to replant 201 trees and over a hundred shrubs at a cost of $58,000. In addition, he had to post a bond with the town to assure that he watered and maintained the trees and shrubs for five years and that they be checked by a professional every six months (Nardozzi 2002d). Another strategy was told to us by a man who said that his neighbor wanted to greatly reduce the number of trees on his property:

> He knew he couldn't get permission to clear cut so he asked permission to thin the trees, and it was granted. He went back to the town three different times over a number of years until eventually he had opened up his property. Only the very large trees remained. This cost him a lot more than if he was able to go in and do it all at once, but he got around the restrictions and his property looks much better.

Because of the vigilance of residents, even legally cutting trees can be problematic. A man told us that he had a crew cutting trees under four inches in diameter on his property, which he was perfectly entitled to do. He said,

> Within half an hour of us starting, an inspector from town came to see what we were doing. He told me that they had received over thirty calls about the cutting. The property is on a pretty remote road and only a couple of cars had passed. Obviously one of them must have called their "network," and they all called in to get the town to stop it. Anyway, the inspector approved what we were doing and said he would come back later in the day to make sure we only cut small trees. When he came back, he told me that the department had received over twenty calls an hour throughout the day trying to get them to stop me . . . and I wasn't doing anything wrong. People in this town are completely out of control.

A real estate agent told us that in spite of the new ordinance the town is more relaxed about tree cutting than it used to be, simply because it is so difficult to police. He said,

> Unless you are clear cutting or taking down landmark trees, they don't enforce much. The people who work for the town get sick of all the complaining that goes on. The building department is really a huge complaints department. They are in favor of permits [to cut] because then they can tell neighbors who complain that the people have a permit.

Anti-Development Activists

There appears to be a general consensus in Bedford that the town's zoning regulations on their own will not stop development. Consequently, we have seen the proliferation in the past decade of citizen groups organizing to supplement the zoning code. Neighbors want to know when the town receives applications to build new houses so that they can attempt to block them at public hearings. As active as they are, residents still feel insufficiently informed.

Residents, either singly or as part of organized committees write letters and petitions and appear at public hearings to attempt to block any subdivisions of large properties or zoning variances. The power of advisory boards, organized resident groups, and individual neighbors, although always considerable, has grown over the years. Citizen participation in Bedford appears to be at an all-time high and it is focused on keeping the town looking rural. Residents either join neighborhood organizations, privately put pressure on neighbors, or put themselves forward for membership on advisory boards and thereafter try to stall development. One resident familiar with the structure of the boards told us, "There is a hierarchy of boards. At the top there is the Town Board, the Planning Board, and the Zoning Board. Beneath them there are a lot of advisory boards, such as wetlands, conservation, and historical. People who are ambitious work their way up through the advisory boards until they get to the big boards." We asked her if she thought that real power still lay with the town supervisor or with the three major boards. She replied,

> He is certainly very powerful in town, but nowhere near as much as he used to be ten or fifteen years ago. The supervisor has been losing control because of the proliferation of boards and the power of neighbors showing up and screaming at hearings. On development issues, a supervisor used to be able to say, "grant this one and jerk this guy around for ten years." But it's not his call anymore. Now everyone gets jerked around for years.

Newcomers as well as old-timers are represented on the advisory boards. There are more long-term residents on the town Planning and Zoning Boards, only because to get on these boards, one normally must have served on the advisory boards. Longtime residents have told us that in the past power in town lay in the hands of a local establishment referred to as the "Holy Trinity" (St. Matthew's Episcopal Church, the Bedford Golf and Tennis Club, and Cisqua-Rippowam School). Today, however, of the thirty-one members of the major town boards (the Town Board, Planning Board, Zoning Board of Appeals, Wetlands Control Commission, Conservation Board, and Bedford Historic District Review Commission), only five are members of the Bedford Golf and Tennis Club and none are members of the "Holy Trinity." They point to this as a measure of how much the power of the old elite has been reduced.

In addition to the boards, citizen groups form around specific development issues. One of the oldest active groups is the 250-member-strong Regional Review League, formed in the mid-1960s to oppose interstate 684 cutting through Bedford. It failed to stop the highway, but only because the alternate route would have cut through New York State Governor Rockefeller's family estate in Pocantico Hills. Members of the Regional Review League sit on the Town Board, Planning Board, and Wetland's Control Commission. The league has been in the forefront of the fight against development not only on various boards, but also by bringing in expert guest speakers to argue against development. The league led the fight against sewers in Bedford and its members have lain down in front of bulldozers to prevent the paving of dirt roads in town. A spokesperson for the group summed up the league's position when she said, "What people have found is that their zoning is their destiny" (Carroll 1996c, 5). Citizen groups proliferate in response to the perceived threat of development. Some are ephemeral, such as groups of neighbors who come together to combat change on their road, while others are broader based such as the Bedford Coalition.

The Bedford Coalition is of particular interest in that its goal has been to organize the other special-interest groups in town. It arose in early 1999 out of a growing sense that Bedford's zoning laws had to be made more effective if development was to be kept at bay. The specific catalyst for its foundation was the drafting of a new town Master Plan, Bedford 2000. There was a concerted effort on the part of the coalition to rally residents around a strengthened anti-development movement. A series of town meetings were held in late 1995 and 1996 to canvas resident opinion on the future direction of the town.

Table 5.6 Percent in Favor of Increasing Zoning to Ten Acres or More in Rural Areas

A. *By Length of Residence*

Total	10 years or Less	11–20 years	More Than 20 Years
68%	76%	71%	62%

B. *By Area*

Total	Bedford Village	Bedford Hills	Katonah
68%	72%	69%	64%

(529 = Total Number)

Source: Town of Bedford 1998.

Although members of the various boards strategically steered discussion along desired paths, in fact citizen support was overwhelmingly behind the boards' anti-development position. At one of these meetings, more than a hundred residents were briefed by town officials and then asked to discuss "ways to preserve Bedford's small-town character." As Donald Coe, the chair of the Bedford Planning Board told the residents, "We aren't able simply to outlaw development. If we tried to do so, a judge would jump on us in two weeks and slap us with a fine, but we can limit it" (Luman 1995). The town clearly attempts to evade the spirit, but not the letter, of the law by blocking or stalling development in ways that are difficult to challenge legally, making litigation prohibitively expensive for developers. At a second town meeting a few weeks later, an environmental planner was brought in to argue that zoning in some parts of town should be raised to a ten-acre minimum (Cappa 1995). The 1997 survey revealed that over two-thirds of residents favored increasing the zoning to ten acres or more.

Newspaper editorials and letters to the editor have taken up the anti-development struggle as a major theme. In a letter to the editor of a local newspaper, one man claimed that development was denying his "fundamental right to the pursuit of happiness." He stated, "A certain level of development can be supported, but then traffic becomes unbearable, taxes become unbearable, and open woods and fields disappear. The lifestyle that the town once presented and that each of us chose to live in ends" (Barnett 1995). Throughout the late 1990s, town meetings and editorial coverage in the newspaper continued to build support for the notion that there was a crisis of threatened rurality in Bedford. This effort was greatly aided by the launching in 1995 of a new local newspaper, the Bedford *Record Review*. This paper is specifically oriented toward the towns of Bedford and Pound Ridge, while the other local papers, the *Patent Trader* and the *Journal News,* are more regional in focus. The *Record Review* has become a mouthpiece for anti-development sentiment in Bedford and neighboring towns. Members of its editorial board are also on the Conservation Board and other town boards. It is probably not going too far to say that the *Record Review* has gone a long way toward creating a sense among residents that Bedford's rural atmosphere is in steep decline. The paper publicizes the alarmist views of the various town boards and provides extensive negative coverage of development projects, a weekly report naming residents who are in violation of local land law, and editorials voicing fears that Bedford is on the verge of being irrevocably changed. We couldn't help but notice that the language and turns of phrase of some of the residents we interviewed about change in Bedford often mirrored the language of the newspaper coverage.

In February 1997, the Conservation Board sent a questionnaire to 6,200 households in town seeking to canvass their opinion on the direction the town should take. The survey made its intentions clear: to "better understand your perceptions of what contributes to Bedford's unusual mix of villages and rural landscape. Further, we need to hear from you about any concerns and ideas you may have about how the town can act to maintain its character" (Town of Bedford 1997). The questionnaire itself was divided into four main sections. The first asked about "quality of life," which was defined as rural character, quality of trees, views, and so on. The second asked if the town was exercising sufficient control over a whole range of issues from tree cutting, to wetlands, to keeping large tracts intact. The third section raised a series of questions proposed during the three town meetings in 1996 for Bedford 2000. It asked residents about their preferred ways of controlling development. The fourth section again asked residents their opinion about different facets of development and what their favorite views in Bedford are. We can summarize the 550 residents' responses thus. The majority feel that the rural nature of Bedford is in decline. More specifically, "traffic," "open space," "rural character," and "scenic vistas" are seen to be getting worse and residents are overwhelmingly in favor of further controls on development.

In January 1998, the Conservation Board published its findings (Town of Bedford 1998). It concluded that "the rural character and beauty of Bedford are of paramount concern to these respondents" and recommended to the Town Board that, among other things, ways be sought to preserve large tracts of land from development, scenic roads be listed and preserved, developers be made "to pay their own way," and neighbors be warned of land use changes near them. The *Record Review* disseminated the findings to the town in a front-page article titled "Bedford supports rural character" (Marx 1998).

The following year, in a rare attempt at regional action, the Bedford Conservation Board met with the conservation boards of neighboring North Castle, Pound Ridge, and North Salem to join in a common goal of "protecting open space" and "using environmental law to the towns' advantage" (Bladen 1998). While most residents seem to have been persuaded that rural Bedford was in decline due to development, some residents saw development in more catastrophic terms: "Why is it so impossible in the town of Bedford and surrounding areas to 'JUST SAY NO' to developers and builders? It works for drug abuse!! The developers come in, rape the land, add more houses/commercial buildings than the roads, traffic, historical area, and schools (overcrowding) can accommodate" (Bradsell 1998). In fact, the United States would be fortunate indeed if the various campaigns against drug abuse were half as effective as Bedford's campaign against development.

In early January 1999, the newly founded Bedford Coalition organized a town meeting to help shape the Bedford 2000 Master Plan. John Feingold of the Westchester Land Trust said that the various organizations came together as the coalition because they had "a common set of concerns, all having to do with community character, and open space and trails, as well as the way growth and development was occurring in the town and affecting the quality of the town." Carol Niemcyzk, also of the Westchester Land Trust, told the audience that Bedford's current zoning in and of itself was insufficient to restrict development. But, as she put it, "you don't have to rework your whole zoning arrangement" (Marx 1999a). The answer, she said, in addition to vigilance on the part of residents, is "overlay zoning" for special areas; this is the designation of special areas to be given extra layers of protection. John Feingold was explicit about the multiple purposes of public forums; not only are they to inform residents about the threat to the town and elicit residents' opinions about how to respond, but, he added, they will provide useful documentation of a public mandate should any new legislation be challenged in court. Town meetings and surveys are clearly part of an ongoing legal strategy for dealing with developers. More town meetings sponsored by the Bedford Coalition were held in 1999. In a meeting in early February, "loss of rural character" was stated as the major problem facing Bedford and the "tactical use of environmental law to protect [the town's] character" was again reaffirmed (Carroll 1999).

In December of the same year, the town of Bedford sent out a Master Plan questionnaire to 1,000 households. An astonishingly high number (649) were returned, indicating a strong interest in protection of Bedford's landscapes. Respondents indicated that the most important challenge facing the town was the "loss of community character as new homes replace undeveloped land," and three-quarters of the respondents wanted the town to find ways to preserve open space.

Table 5.7 Percent Agreeing with the Statement "As Bedford Continues to Grow, the Town Should Encourage More Preservation of Open Space"

Net Difference = Agree − Disagree			
A. *By Length of Residence*			
<5 Years	5–9 Years	10–19 Years	20 Years+
+75.8%	+74.0%	+71.1%	+70.7%

B. *By Area*				
4 Acre+	Bedford Village	Bedford Hills	Katonah	Outside Hamlet 1–4 Acre
+76.1%	+80.6%	+62.7%	+74.5%	+71.8%

(649 = Total Number)

Source: Town of Bedford 2000.

In March 2000, the *Record Review* gave the survey results front-page coverage under the headline "Survey says: let's keep Bedford green" (Nardozzi 2000a) and ran an editorial titled "Survey results are call to action" (*Record Review* 2000). The combined results of the 1997 and 1999 surveys were justifiably interpreted by the town as a mandate to acquire undeveloped land.

But just how real is the threat of development in Bedford? The town Planning Office estimates that of the 25,182 acres in Bedford, one-third is undeveloped. But not all of this land is even potentially developable. According to Jeff Osterman, the director of planning, undeveloped land includes that which is legally undevelopable, in addition to that which *appears* to be potentially developable to a four-acre minimum. The former includes a large amount of land held by the nature preserves, New York City–owned reservoir and watershed land, and state and federally owned lands. It also includes the increasing number of conservation easements that residents have attached to their land.[27] The potentially developable portion includes the town's golf courses and other privately held blocks of land larger than four acres. However, Osterman points out that the golf courses and most of the large estates can never be developed down to their legal four-acre lot size because of "overlay zoning." He argues that while in theory 1,138 lots remain undeveloped, it's impossible to say how much of that could actually be developed into four-acre lots. As he says, "It's a moving target, but it's always being reduced" (personal interview with Jeff Osterman). A real estate broker with long experience working in town told us, "Effectively, we now have seven- or eight-acre zoning on most of the remaining land in town." In his opinion, it was unlikely that much of the remaining land would be subdivided into lots of even this size. As he put it, "Much of the potential development pressure that we have had over the past ten years has been decreased by large properties now being worth more as a whole than they are subdivided. People aren't going to subdivide their land if they can make more money by keeping it intact." This is reinforced by a desire on most owner's part to keep the land undivided for reasons of emotional attachment to the landscape and feelings of obligation to the community.

Tactics by the town to make development prohibitively expensive, coupled with the fact that large properties have recently become worth more than their component parts, have resulted in a situation that Bedford's doomsayers had never imagined. Bedford will undoubtedly gain some new housing, but its rural character will remain intact. There is nothing in the foreseeable future to change Bedford's landscape significantly. Nevertheless, the rhetoric of struggle and loss continues unabated. New citizen groups continue to be spun off older ones to fight specific issues. In June 2000, the newly formed Open Space Coalition, a subgroup of the Bedford Coalition, sought a referendum on a special tax to help the town acquire open land (Nardozzi 2000b). This was followed in October by a series of town meetings to drum up support for a referendum on a special tax break for open land. Concurrently, a spin off of the Open Space Coalition, the Citizens for the Open Space Fund, mailed 10,000 copies of a four-page brochure urging residents to vote yes on November 7 for the special tax. The brochure urged residents to "'Think globally, act locally.' If you believe rampant over-development is ruining the American landscape, now is your chance to vote locally on this issue." This tax, it was argued, was a way to protect the look of the land, for "when large acreages come on the market, there is no assurance that the owner will not build on a field or hillside that offered our community a long-cherished view."

The brochure points out that the 3% increase in town tax only represents a mere six-tenths of 1% of total property taxes, and that for two-thirds of the town, the increase would be less than $46 per property, per year. This increased cost, it was argued, was in fact a good investment as open space would "increase your own residence's value." It further explained that the tax would raise $325,000 in the first year, which would be used to pay interest and principal on a bond to acquire land (Citizens for the Open Space Fund 2000). Not everyone in town supported the proposed tax. At one of the October meetings, a resident questioned the idea that unless Bedford purchased undeveloped land it was at risk of experiencing urban sprawl. He asked, "Aren't most of these undeveloped lots zoned for four acres? Who's deciding this development would constitute urban sprawl? People who live on ten acres?" The director of planning, who was in attendance, replied that "an endless series of housing lots, even on four acres, would meet the definition of urban sprawl" (Nardozzi 2000c). Another man wrote in the *Record Review* that when he built a home in Bedford in the 1950s, "We never dreamed of ever closing off the land in the town to newcomers and or family members and preventing them from attaining a homestead and enjoying all that the town has to offer as we have done" (Bartels 2000). He went on to urge a no vote on the open-space proposition. In the weeks leading up to the vote, articles in the *Record Review* were used to help turn out the vote. The chair of the Conservation Board argued in a letter to the editor, "Bedford is defined by its vistas and giving the town the ability to set them aside for future generations is a worthy cause to champion" (Skolnik 2000). On November 7, the residents voted for the special tax for open land by a margin of 70%. In March 2001, the town supervisor named seven members to the newly formed Bedford Open Space Acquisition Committee. Its task is to designate potential properties for purchase with the new tax money and to encourage conservation easements on privately owned property.

This was followed by other Master Plan meetings. At an April meeting, members of the committee again worried that the town was losing its rural character and asked a consultant to review the town's "menu of controls" on development to see if any more controls could be added (Nardozzi 2001i). In June, the Master Plan Committee suggested that an additional form of control might be developed to protect ridgelines and wildlife corridors. They asked the Conservation Board to identify important ridgelines to target. Those attending the meeting then proceeded to strategize how these new controls might be accomplished.

The consultant argued that the town could regulate ridgelines as it did steep slopes, but that it had to allow discretion on whether or not to grant a permit. Joel Sachs, the town attorney, concurred: "You should avoid giving an absolute no. You need to consider what the courts will uphold as being an unjust taking." He recommended a case-by-case approach by local boards as the best strategy. While aware that adding more controls ran the risk of residents suing over the loss of development rights, another member of the committee argued that the committee "take the risk in favor of controls, the same as we did with steep slopes." The consultant cautioned the committee that "clear environmental reasons for increasing buffers or construction setbacks must be given." He suggested that both Lewisboro and Pound Ridge had used biodiversity studies to justify new controls (Nardozzi 2001m).

In November 2001, the Conservation Board submitted in draft form two amendments to the town zoning laws. The first was a ridgeline protection ordinance that would forbid new construction on ridgelines. The stated purpose of this ordinance was to "maintain the semi-rural character and beauty of the Town of Bedford by preserving its open and uncluttered topographic features." Exceptions could be granted if the proposed development "would not have a substantial visual impact when viewed from lower elevations, or not interfere with a ridgeline trail corridor or compromise open space and scenic character." The second amendment picked up on the strategy suggested at the June meeting of playing the biodiversity card to control development. The Conservation Board argued that Bedford's protected areas constitute "a mosaic of ecologically dysfunctional wetlands and woodland areas," and that wildlife corridors were needed to serve as "avenues along which wide-ranging animals can travel, plants can propagate, genetic interchange can occur, populations can move in response to environmental changes, and threatened species can be replenished from other areas." Applicants wanting to build in "sensitive areas" will be required to survey all wildlife species on the property and the habitat they require to remain viable (Nardozzi 2001n). While the ridgeline ordinance appears to be sufficiently vague to allow discretion by local boards, the wildlife corridor is a brilliant new anti-development strategy. It will be extremely costly for a developer to provide the type of environmental impact statement required. Furthermore, rather than depending on separated patches of wetland and particular steep slopes to limit development, now buildable land in between which is judged to be a corridor can for the first time be restricted on environmental grounds.

The Affordable Housing Debate

The Westchester County Housing Opportunity Commission (1997) argues that there is a huge imbalance between household incomes and housing costs in the county. In 1992, the County Board of Legislators proposed an Affordable Housing Plan that called for 5,000 units of affordable housing within five years. In fact the number of units added to the housing stock during that time from any source amounted to only 1,890 units. This rate would only deliver 54% of the number needed just to supply the *increased* need for the growth in the number of income eligible households. It ignores both those units lost from the housing stock and does not account sufficiently for the needs of tens of thousands of poor households living in overcrowded and deteriorated housing. Affordable housing is defined by the county as that which is available at a price or rent not exceeding 30% of the gross income of income-eligible households. Income eligibility means having a gross income below 80% of the county's median. The median house price in Westchester in 2000 was $365,000, and the median income for a family of four was $83,100. Using the government's formula of 30% of a family's gross income, an income of $110,000 would be needed to buy the typical home in the county. A family of four presently earning $66,480 qualifies for assistance. If affordable housing becomes available at the maximum price to be considered affordable, it would be helpful for some, but not for many others whose income falls below $66,000 per year. The housing problem is exacerbated by the lack of rental apartments. During the 1980s, 40,000 apartments were converted to condominiums and today only 10,000 rental units remain, which is 16% of the housing stock.

Of the forty-three municipalities in Westchester, nineteen failed to respond with a statement of good intentions to the goals set for them by the Housing Opportunity Commission. Yonkers and Cortland are presently under court order to produce low-income housing and Harrison and Port Chester passed resolutions opposing county goals. The town of North Salem by the mid-1990s had spent over a million dollars fighting the introduction of 184 units of affordable housing in town (McCabe 1995e, 1996; Rieser 1990). In comparison to these towns, Mount Kisco has a lot of affordable housing, and Bedford escapes a court order because of pockets of affordable housing in the hamlets.[28] Resistance to affordable housing in Westchester is driven by a combination of aesthetic and economic concerns, including preserving open land, keeping out inexpensive-looking housing, sustaining property values, and holding down school enrollments. The upshot, in the words of political scientist Robert Siedelman, is the creation of "a gated community without gates" (Gross 2000c).

In January 1999, George Raymond,[29] chairman of the Westchester Housing Opportunity Commission, wrote a letter to the editor of the *Patent Trader* arguing that "one by one, the Northern Westchester municipalities are using the zoning laws . . . as the means of economic discrimination which excludes 80% of the population from the area" (Raymond 1999). There no longer exists, he says, a free market in land in the area.

> A market in land, which also largely determines the housing market, is hardly "free" when it is constrained by carefully man-crafted laws and regulations that exclude from the municipality all but the well heeled. Further, the long-sustained campaign for the preservation of every square inch of semi-rural character in each municipality cumulatively results in the exclusion of all but large lot single family development from an area covering some 40% of Westchester County. The latest tactic aimed at excluding moderate and middle-income families from

locating in northern Westchester is based on the allegation, unsupported by hard
environmental science or available engineering alternatives, that water quality
in the Croton watershed can be protected only by stopping development. Even
if all these factors that negate market freedom are the result of independent
actions, they undeniably result in a coordinated exclusionary program.

In May 2000, County Executive Andrew Spano, a Democrat, named the lack
of affordable housing Westchester's number one problem and began a $250,000
campaign to convince communities to build more of it. He argued, "when we talk
about improving the quality of life for all our residents, we must attack the lack
of affordable housing" (Gross 2000c). This will prove a very tough sell in northern Westchester, where, as we shall see, "quality of life" refers not to improving
the economic lot of the middle and lower classes, but rather to a set of aesthetic
concerns. The debate over affordable housing versus preserving Bedford's rural
character is a long-standing one. In the early 1980s, the town was preparing a new
Master Plan. At one town board meeting in 1984 the issue came to a head. The
majority of the board thought that keeping Bedford rural should be the highest
priority. One man argued, however, that it was in the interest of the town to
provide affordable housing, as the rising cost of housing in Bedford was driving
less affluent residents out: "This town *had* all kinds of people. You didn't have to
go beyond your town to shop or find people to work" (Schult 1984). The issue of
social responsibility for this man appears to be one of convenience for affluent
residents. Missing is any sense of regional responsibility. But even convenience
or paternalism did not convince others, one of whom argued that "Bedford is not
an island in the middle of the ocean. We have surrounding towns with higher-
density housing available." The same person argued that Bedford's green space
"is a social obligation too. The time could easily come when Bedford could be
to Westchester County what Central Park is to New York." Board members were
aware, however, that such a policy had potential legal ramifications. As one member said, we "don't want to be accused of exclusionary zoning" or restrict new
housing to such a degree that it "could be insupportable in court" (Schult 1984).

In the late 1990s, similar debates took place as the town prepared its 2000
Master Plan. In early 1999, the Bedford Coalition organized a number of meetings to encourage resident participation in formulating the new Master Plan.
All agreed that the town's goal should be to preserve Bedford's "quality of life."
Among the suggestions were stricter measures to protect the town's rural character and to build affordable housing for town employees and senior citizens.
At the late January meeting, the following exchange took place. One older man
observed that "Bedford does have a certain lack of housing opportunities." Another resident was quick to reply, "you wouldn't want it on your street, would
you?" The older man remained silent. Another woman offered, "there is no
housing for senior citizens." A lively discussion ensued about where affordable
housing might be located. The first proposed site was Adams Street in Bedford
Hills, which is zoned commercial and for decades has been the street where

poor blacks lived and now increasingly where Latino day laborers find relatively inexpensive rentals. The second was behind a movie theater in Bedford Village. Both areas are, from the point of view of locals, marginal, out-of-sight locations. We interviewed a large landowner who told us that she had two possible solutions to the town's lack of affordable housing. Her plan was to make affordable housing disappear into the landscape. She said,

> I am in favor of having greater density in the three hamlets. It makes more sense to have them dense and keep outlying areas open. I believe in accessory apartments. I don't believe the town has been liberal enough with them. They are the answer for big places. This is a way to make more affordable housing, increase density, and leave large properties intact. There always were a lot of people—hired help—living on these places that were not family members.

Several residents took a harder line, stating that the topic didn't need to be discussed at all because "there is no place to build the housing" (Lynch 1999a). At a meeting the following month, the same issues were discussed, prompting one person to suggest that residents have a "schizophrenic mentality" in wanting simultaneously to block the construction of new housing, thereby driving up the cost of housing in town and to provide affordable housing (Marx 1999b). The 1997 survey reveals that 68% of residents wish to increase zoning to ten acres or more in rural areas of town, and nearly three-quarters of those surveyed in 1999 agreed that the town should encourage more preservation of open space (see Tables 5.6 and 5.7). The 1997 survey also reveals that only 34% want to "encourage denser residential growth inside hamlet centers" (Town of Bedford 1997).

This latter result is consistent across the town. Taken together these results clearly indicate that over two-thirds of the residents do not want to provide more housing in town. While the 1997 survey did not ask specifically about affordable housing, the 1999 survey did. When asked if "loss of diverse population as property values rise and homes get bigger and more expensive is an important issue for the town," residents were divided. Approximately one-third of the respondents had no opinion on the issue. Of the remainder, only residents of Katonah scored strongly positive. Once again, Katonah hamlet residents appear out of step with other residents of Bedford. One is tempted to conclude that the reason for this is that Katonah is more densely populated and more uniformly middle class than other parts of Bedford. It comes as little surprise that the residents of 4 acre+ zoning have the lowest score. There is a dramatically higher score for those who have lived longest in town because this group includes many who anticipate not being able to afford to remain in town themselves.

When residents were asked what the single most important challenge facing Bedford is, "loss of diverse population as property values rise and homes get bigger and more expensive" was rated second from last in order of importance (see Table 4.2).

When the question of affordable housing was stated as a general principle about diversity, as in Table 5.8, more residents agreed than disagreed. However,

Table 5.8 Response to the Question, "Is Loss of Diverse Population as Property Values Rise and Homes Get Bigger and More Expensive an Important Issue for the Town?"

Net Difference = Agree − Disagree			
A. *By Length of Residence*			
<5 Years	5–9 Years	10–19 Years	20 Years+
+7.2%	+7.9%	+20.6%	+30.5%

B. *By Area*				
4 Acre+	1–4 Acre	Bedford Village	Bedford Hills	Katonah
+2.1%	+16.0%	+21.2%	+19.8%	+52.1%

(649 = Total Number)

Source: Town of Bedford 2000.

in the same survey when the question was phrased, "As Bedford continues to grow, should the town encourage more diversity of housing size and type serving a more diverse population," the response was much more negative. It appears that while a small majority agree in principle with diversity, they don't support it if it entails building more houses. As Table 5.9 shows, only long-term residents and residents of Katonah agreed that the town should encourage a diversity of housing.

Since the late 1990s, town officials have been generally sympathetic to the idea of allowing the continued growth of very small amounts of affordable housing. Although lip service is paid to regional needs, it is clear that in practice such housing will go only to town employees. Town officials have been extremely sensitive to the location of such housing. Proposed projects are encouraged only when they can be located in marginal, or already densely settled, parts of town. For example, twenty-eight apartments and fourteen middle-income homes were built near the center of Bedford Hills. In order to qualify to rent an affordable one-bedroom apartment, the applicant must be fifty-five or over and earn less

Table 5.9 Response to the Question, "As Bedford Continues to Grow, Should the Town Encourage More Diversity of Housing Size and Type Serving a More Diverse Population?"

Net Difference = Agree − Disagree			
A. *By Length of Residence*			
<5 Years	5–9 Years	10–19 Years	20 Years+
−26.6%	−35.4%	−6.4%	+5.8%

B. *By Area*				Outside Hamlet
4 Acre+	Bedford Village	Bedford Hills	Katonah	1–4 Acre
−24.6%	−3.1%	−4.0%	+15.3%	−15.4%

(649 = Total Number)

Source: Town of Bedford 2000.

that $55,450. To buy one of the fourteen town houses, the maximum income eligibility is $77,000. In addition, applicants are prioritized in the following fashion: 1. Town employees (fire, ambulance), 2. School district employees, 3. Town residents, 4. Other persons employed in town, 5. Relatives of residents, 6. Residents of Westchester, 7. Persons employed in Westchester, 8. Others (Record Review 1999). Vacancies are infrequent and the waiting list is long. The chance of anyone not in the first three categories getting a place is, therefore, very slight.

Although marginal locations are favored by town officials and residents of other parts of town, residents in those areas often fight the introduction of affordable housing. For example, in 1999, neighbors in a mixed residential-commercial area of Bedford Hills vigorously, but unsuccessfully, opposed the addition of two cottages on a one-acre site that already contained a two-family house and a small cottage (Chitwood 1999f).

Another affordable housing project was approved by the town in late 2001 (Nardozzi 2001h). A nineteen-unit two-story brick apartment building is planned on a five-and-a-half-acre site behind a Pier One store on the main arterial connecting Bedford Hills and Mount Kisco. Because it is located on this strip at the border with Mount Kisco, many residents of Bedford assume it is in Mount Kisco. We found that people in most parts of Bedford had no interest in this strip except to use it for shopping. Councilwoman Lee Roberts said of this project, "We want to find housing for people we want to remain in town" (Schleifer 2000). Another resident stated the affordable housing issue more candidly: "We are just trying to keep volunteer firemen living in town. God forbid we have a fire in the middle of the night." With the support of the town and little neighbor opposition because of its location on a main arterial, it looks sure to pass.

The 1997 and 1999 surveys reveal that Bedford residents do not support building affordable or any other kind of housing either in rural parts of town or in the three hamlets. It appears, however, that by instituting a strict priority system favoring the sort of town workers that they want to encourage to remain, Bedford may be able to create "sufficient" affordable housing to meet what it perceives to be its needs. Because relatively little will be built, it can be located in the marginal spaces of town and as such will be hardly noticed by those who live in the estate areas. It is precisely this "spatial solution" that allowed the Republican town Supervisor John Dinin and County Legislator Ursula LaMotte to run on a platform of preservation of open space *and* the creation of affordable housing in Bedford (Gorman 2001d, 2001e).

Illustrative Development Cases

We will now turn to a brief examination of other recent development cases in Bedford that illustrate the manner in which residents and officials mobilize to fight not just affordable housing, but any change to the look of the land. We have chosen three cases that give an idea of the range of different types of development cases: a seventeen-house development, a new campus for a private school, and a resident who wants to build a stable for her personal use.

Twin Lakes

A proposal to build seventeen houses on a ninety-nine-acre parcel of land that was zoned four-acre residential was initially brought to the Planning Board in 1987. As this allowed an average of over five acres per house, one might assume it would be possible to secure permission. But as one developer unconnected with this project told us,

> The town's strategy is to drag everything out as long as possible to tie up your money. So they will ask for certain tests and when you have done those, they will ask for others and after you have done those, they want more. It's endless. They hope you will just give up and go away. Or if you don't, that you will be so fed up that you will never do another project in town.

After four years of facing what it considered to be a deliberate strategy of stalling, the developer of the Twin Lakes parcel sued the Bedford Planning Board for taking too long to review the plan. The New York State Supreme Court ruled in favor of the developer in 1992 and ordered the Planning Board to grant preliminary approval of the plan. The town subsequently stalled the development for a further three years by appealing the decision. That appeal was rejected by the Appellate Division of the State Supreme Court in May 1995. The developer was granted until March 27, 1996, to satisfy the Planning Board for final approval. On February 12, 1996, the Wetlands Control Commission stated that the developer's new plan did not meet its standards for wetland approval. Four days later, the developer with his court-ordered preliminary acceptance of the plan in hand came before a public hearing. The lawyers for the developer, the town officials, and thirty-five other people were at the hearing. The developer claimed that he had answered the town's concerns about the threat posed to the Mianus River by the new houses and argued that he had already agreed not to place any houses on thirty-eight acres near the river. The director of the Mianus River Gorge Preserve, who attends all such hearings with the intention of opposing any new housing, argued that even in their new position the houses would pose a threat to the river. In a letter to the Planning Board presented at the hearing, the Conservation Board expressed concern that seventeen houses would pose a threat to the "fragile dirt road" they were to be built along, and wanted the developer to reduce the number of houses to six or seven on the ninety-nine-acre property (Carroll 1996b). This would have meant that the average lot was fifteen acres. On March 27, the board voted to deny the application on environmental grounds. In the summer of 1997, after another year and a half of sparring with the town, the developer obtained a hearing with the Wetlands Control Commission to secure approval for its plan. The commission voted not to grant a permit. With the application for wetlands permits denied and the time frame for the court-ordered preliminary acceptance expired, the developer was told by the town that he had to return to the preliminary planning stages (Marx 1997a).

A lawyer we interviewed told us, "I told the Twin Lakes people that the court-ordered temporary permit wasn't worth anything, because the town would just continue to stall them. It's the final approval they need. The temporary one isn't worth the paper it's written on." The attorney for the developer said that he would continue to try to work with the town on getting the project through, but if that was not possible, that he would once again consider litigation. The development plans continued to be held up as the developer negotiated with the town over the number of houses to be built and what their environmental impact would be. In September 1999, the Wetlands Control Commission finally accepted the plan (Chitwood 1999a). However, by the spring of 2002, nearly fifteen years after the project was initiated, construction had not yet begun. It is unlikely that this developer will ever try to build in Bedford again.

Rippowam-Cisqua School

On Route 22 near Bedford Village lies a 113-acre property that used to have a sand and gravel quarry in the days before residents gave much thought to environmental issues. It had never been considered an eyesore, as it could not be seen from the road. Years ago the pits were flooded to create seven ponds. In 1959, it was rezoned for research-office use and in the early 1980s, plans were submitted to build an office complex employing, 1,670 people. In 1982, residents began organizing to block this development, forming the Committee to Save Bedford and raising an $80,000 war chest. During the summer of 1984, the proposal was turned down by the town on environmental grounds and the application was withdrawn. The property, which lies across the road from a small shopping center, was subsequently purchased by a development company that proposed building fifty-nine luxury town houses. The negotiations with the town resulted in the development company agreeing to site the proposed houses on twenty-three acres and to leave the remaining eighty-five acres undeveloped (Vizard 1993). By spring 1996, after twelve years of negotiating with the town, the Planning Board finally granted the developer a permit. However, there was still no indication as to when they might get approval from the town board for the construction of a special water and sewage district (Carroll 1996c). It was at that point that the developer threw in the towel and decided to cut his losses and sell the land undeveloped.

The purchaser was Dort Cameron, a member of the board of trustees of Rippowam-Cisqua School, which already has two campuses in Bedford but wished to expand by adding grades ten through twelve, for which they needed a large, new campus. Cameron, through his family trust, purchased the land in July 1996 for $6 million with the intention of giving it to the school if the town approved the campus (Foderaro 1999). The site required a Special Use Permit and, given the antipathy to any development in town, the school should have realized that approval was far from a foregone conclusion. However, because the private school, along with St. Matthew's Episcopal Church and the Bedford

Golf and Tennis Club, forms part of what has for decades been termed the "Holy Trinity" in town, it was unimaginable to the trustees that they would be turned down. In February 1997, the Wetlands Control Commission held a meeting to discuss the school's preliminary plans. The school had hoped to piggyback its plan onto the prior wetlands approval granted to the developer a year before. In fact, they thought they could get the Wetlands Control Commission to be more lenient with them because they wouldn't be building houses. They hoped to build six of the school's fourteen proposed new playing fields within a portion of the prior development's proposed eighty-five acre "conservation area." However, the director of planning informed them that not only should they not think of going beyond the prior Wetlands Control Commission approved area, but that even that was no longer valid. He said, "If you measure water quality, for example, the standards over time get stricter and stricter" (Gallagher 1997). The director of the Mianus River Gorge Preserve who attended the meeting added that she objected to the fact that the proposed playing fields were encroaching on the Mianus River flood plain. By the summer of 1997, the school realized that it was in for a long battle and began to make strategic concessions to the town. Primary among them was the removal from the plan of two proposed fields that were in the wetland zone. The various town boards became involved as the school sought to comply with the mandatory State Environmental Quality Review Act (SEQRA). The chair of the Bedford Planning Board said ominously, "We are at the beginning of a long process" (Lombardi 1997). The board of trustees of the school didn't realize just how long it would be.

In February 1998, the draft environmental impact statement was accepted by the town pending "minor" revisions. These revisions as it turned out were far from minor. For example, the Wetlands Control Commission wanted the school to eliminate four of the proposed fields and shift another away from the wetlands buffer area. The attorney representing the school refused to reduce their number. Presuming that the town would prefer a school campus to houses, he threatened to withdraw the application for the school unless the fields were retained (Lynch 1998). Other concerns raised by the Planning Board chairman were the environmental impact of traffic and the impact of building on wetlands, and it was on these two fronts that opposition to the school's plans coalesced.

Over the next two years a series of public hearings on the project were scheduled. At these meetings and through organized letter-writing campaigns, neighbors and environmental groups tried vigorously to stop the school from being built. The opposition to the school was well organized even by local standards. It called itself the Concerned Citizens of Bedford. Many of its members live in a 1950s housing development known as the Farms located between Bedford Village and the proposed new campus. This development, which looks like a classic middle-class suburb, is composed of what, by local standards, are modest houses on quarter-acre lots that now sell for more than half a million dollars. Led by a husband and wife team who were respectively former chairperson of the New York State Democratic Party and ombudsman for former governor Mario Cuomo, members of the group attended public hearings and vociferously opposed the school's plans. One of the organizers, who is a partner in a New York public relations firm, used his firm's resources to commission a survey of 200 Bedford residents. This "push poll" was used to persuade officials that the town's residents were opposed to the new campus. The school dismissed the questionnaire as biased and sent out two mass mailings to residents putting forward their position on the benefits of the new campus.

At a public hearing in May 1999 to assess resident reaction for the Final Environmental Impact Statement, the opposition came out in force. Residents of the Farms argued that the campus was a threat to local history and rural character. As one resident of the Farms put it, "What is the impact of this, of the development of this property on our historic district? To me, Bedford Village is the Village Green and the historical district. And anything that negatively impacts the Village Green I think should not be accepted" (Kovacic 1999). It is important to note that this site is not actually close enough to have an visual impact on the green. Another wrote a letter to the hearing arguing that "the school simply is oversized for the site and will create a disruptive influence in the town. The rural character of Bedford would be ruined forever" (O'Shea 1999). Another person worried about the environmental impact of the playing fields: "This is a massive impact, this project, on the environment there. And let us just stop pulling the wool over anyone else's eyes about it. It's a very big project that will have a dramatic impact on the site and perhaps on the watershed" (N. Shoumatoff 1999). Another person at the hearing questioned the need for a private high school in town: "Why must we cede the best part of our town to a private school serving but a handful of families who might live in Bedford Village?" (unidentified speaker 1999). In the weeks following the hearing, residents in favor of the school realizing that their opponents had dominated the public hearing sent letters to the town in order to have their support for the school recorded in the Final Environmental Impact Statement. The letter writing was coordinated to address various concerns raised by the opposition. Some argued that a school was preferable to a housing development: "Realizing that the property is destined for development, an attractive college preparatory program designed in such a way as to leave 100 of 113 acres open space, is infinitely preferable to a large cluster of town homes and 59 different approaches to lawn care" (Lovejoy 1999). Another stated,

> The proposed school will clearly be an asset to the community as a whole, not just those families who have children enrolled. It will also give families who choose to send their children to Rippowam-Cisqua a reason to be rooted in this community for a longer period of time. A higher percentage of talented local students will remain at home during their formative high school years. They will be more likely to develop a deep attachment to their community than if they go elsewhere to school, and this bond to their community will strengthen Bedford in the future. (Brouder 1999)

Another letter writer dismissed the opposition as a NIMBY group, "while neighboring property owners always like to keep unoccupied land undeveloped indefinitely, that is neither a reasonable nor realistic expectation" (Blinken 1999).

In August 1999, much to the annoyance of the supporters of the school, an article in the *New York Times* cast the controversy over the new campus as a conflict between those who live in a "modest neighborhood where . . . Toyotas and Hondas fill the driveways," the children attending "well-regarded public schools," and those who "live in the 'estate area' where mansions sell in the millions, Jaguars and Range Rovers punctuate long driveways, and properties (not yards) are measured in multiple acres" (Foderaro 1999). The article quoted Dort Cameron who purchased the property as saying, "If they [the town] come back and say you have to cut the fields by half, sorry, then, well, I guess we'll build some low-income housing or something." We spoke to a parent from the school who said the article "wasn't helpful" in its emphasis on class difference. She went on to say that some of the school's supporters had been arrogant and that this attitude had counted against them. For example, she said that the school officials had "got people's backs up" by arguing in a rather patronizing manner that an elite school like Rippowam needed twelve playing fields because of the importance of sports to the (originally English) private school philosophy of producing future leaders who are sound of body as well as mind.[30] Another longtime resident acidly observed at a public hearing that she remembered forty years ago speaking against the plan to build the Farms. The implication was that people who live in a development such as the Farms, which itself represented dreaded development to an older Bedford, have no business complaining about another development, especially one proposed by the Rippowam-Cisqua school. Yet another long-term resident who is an alumnus of the school told us, "I can't believe the people from the Farms are complaining about Ripp moving in. It won't even be seen from the road. They should be pleased because it raises the tone of the area. In fact, my parent's generation chose that part of Bedford to put in a middle-class housing development [the Farms] and besides there's already a shopping center just down the road from it. It's not exactly Guard Hill, is it?"

Two years later in October 2001, the school agreed to withdraw their request to build three playing fields in wetlands and to move their proposed athletic buildings to the rear of the property where they would not be visible from Route 172, in the hope of securing approval of their environmental impact statement (Nardozzi 2001i, 2002b). In April 2002, the Wetlands Control Commission and the Bedford Planning Board deemed the environmental review complete and a public hearing was held (Nardozzi 2002c). But in spite of this, the town continued over the next five months to insist upon further changes to the school's design plans. In light of this, by the end of September 2002, the school decided that they could no longer afford to continue to fight the town. Six years after purchasing the land, and after spending another $6 million trying to meet the building criteria set by the town, the school withdrew its application.

Martha Stewart's Stable

In 2000, writer, publisher, and television celebrity Martha Stewart, the doyennne of fine country living, purchased a 150-acre farm in Bedford for $15.2 million. In early 2001, she presented the town with plans for a new 2,500-foot stable, which was to be clad in stone, with a slate roof and mahogany trim. Because of the proposed building's size, a special permit from the Planning Board was needed. A dozen of her neighbors came to the Planning Board meeting in an attempt to block the proposal. One neighbor said at the meeting, "We can't tolerate this as it would block the 'viewshed' that all the neighbors have come to know." Another said, "Everybody who comes to walk there treasures that view and have for generations and generations. This is a terrible place for a barn and it's a modern barn. It's out of character with the road and the whole view and vista of the area." It's important to note here that the proposed stable only blocks a small portion of the view on that stretch of road, and that furthermore the view is of Martha Stewart's own property. Typically in development conflicts, neighbors argue that traffic will increase. In this case, neighbors argued that traffic had already increased because a celebrity lived there and somehow it would increase further if the stable were built. One person complained, "I can hear people walking and talking on Maple Avenue when I'm sitting in my pool." A neighbor who lives across from the proposed site of the barn said, "I have a house and barn and two paddocks. People are stopping to take a look at that property. Sometimes they try and interact with my horses and they often leave debris behind. *It's changed my whole life*" (Nardozzi 2001a). Just before the Planning Board meeting in May, Stewart stated that she was considering burying the power lines in front of her property on Maple Avenue at an estimated cost of over $100,000 and replanting the maple trees that had died over the years along the picturesque dirt road. The latter is one of the Bedford Conservation Board's pet projects. At the meeting, she appeared with homemade cookies for the board and made an hour-long presentation on why her barn should be approved. In the end, the board voted three to two in favor of letting her build the barn (Nardozzi 2001j, 2001k). One neighbor who had been opposed to her plan before her offer to beautify Maple Avenue said, "the people with deep pockets" are needed to preserve Bedford's beauty (Nardozzi 2001j).

Conclusion

The anti-development sentiment set in motion by the old Bedford elite in the 1920s has become so successful that it is difficult to build anything in Bedford at present. What these development cases reveal is just how emboldened the anti-development movement has become during the past decade. The various boards in the town filled by anti-development activists have quickly learned the formulae for slowing to a crawl any building project, whether it be a high- or low-income housing development, a private school, or a homeowner's plans to construct an auxiliary building on their own property. Time after time, neighbors argue that any new building in town will rob them of a view, increase traffic congestion to dangerous levels, irreparably damage the environment, or destroy the town's rural character and its history. We have argued in this chapter and in others that these are seen as quality-of-life issues in Bedford and that they are considered crucial to those who live the aestheticized life. It is interesting to note the concentration of power in the hands of residents. They have gained more and more control through the proliferation of town committees, thereby reducing the power of the town supervisor. Through highly organized opposition, they are able to take on not only their neighbors but also large development companies and extraordinarily wealthy individuals.[31] The high level of activism and diffusion of power to residents more generally has escaped the control of the "Holy Trinity" in town who used to have more influence on major decisions. As one long-term resident of the town told us, "The old Bedford types still can't believe that people from a place like the Farms are able to block the school. It's beginning to dawn on them that all this anti-development stuff is out of control."

CHAPTER 6

The Taxman Cometh: The Gift of Nature in Suburbia

To the extent that we live in an urban-industrial civilization but at the same time pretend to ourselves that our real home is in the wilderness, to just that extent we give ourselves permission to evade responsibility for the lives we actually lead.
—William Cronon, *Uncommon Ground* (1995, 82)

Introduction

This chapter examines the production of nature in Bedford. In particular we look at nature preserves, focusing on the romantic ideas of wilderness that have been institutionalized in Bedford and the role these play in the politics of exclusion. First, we critically examine the actions and attitudes of our respondents toward nature preserves, focusing particular attention on the claims made by the officials of the preserves. Second, we explore the offering of land or conservation easements on land through the Westchester Land Trust. Donating land to an environmental organization in exchange for tax relief is an anti-development strategy that has been used with great success. It was first adopted in Bedford a half century ago when wealthy landowners donated land to form nature preserves that would be forever untouched by development. More recently, this strategy has been supplemented by the granting of conservation easements on a property owner's land. The latter is proving even more popular than the outright gift of land, as the property owner retains the right to use and sell the land and yet secures a tax break for agreeing not to develop the portion under easement. We argue that the underlying philosophy of these practices is a fundamental separation between nature and culture with pristine wilderness seen as endangered and in need of cordoning off. Natural processes encountered by the administrators of the preserves are resistant to the preservation discourse, however. Dynamic ecological relationships must be controlled if the nature of these preserves is to conform to the dominant view of what wilderness should look like. This produces contradictions in the literature produced by the administrators of the preserves and ambiguity in the self-conception of the preserves' stewardship committees.

Appreciation of Nature as Cultural Capital

Contemporary models of wilderness in Bedford can perhaps best be interpreted as late-twentieth-century environmentalism set within a framework of eighteenth- and nineteenth-century romantic views of nature (Marx 1964; Nash 1982). Although these traditions have sometimes conflicting histories (Pepper 1984), the romantic with its emphasis on the aesthetic appears to remain the dominant view in Bedford and has been successfully assimilated to and camouflaged (not always conspiratorially) with modern scientific rhetoric.[1] The latter is thought to have more legal legitimacy and it is emphasized at strategic moments. The romantic model of nature, however, supports quests for elite social status through reference to earlier aristocratic models of distinction. As we saw in Chapter Three, two principal strands of the romantic model have been used to construct nature in Bedford: pastoral, tamed nature and wild nature known since the sixteenth century as the picturesque and the sublime. The latter is the focus of this chapter. William Cronon (1995, 69) says, "[wilderness] is a profoundly human creation," and because it refers to the natural, it is "particularly beguiling." He adds, however, that "the non-human world we encounter in wilderness is far from being merely our own invention" (Cronon 1995, 69–70). We too see the idea of wilderness itself as very real and as having material effects on very real and very resilient and recalcitrant material landscapes.[2]

As we saw in Chapter Four, Bedford's residents cherish the pastoral scene, while also looking to the wilderness as a uniquely American landscape ideal. This view of the wilderness frontier as productive of American culture has a long emotional history going back at least to the War of Independence (Schmitt 1990, xvii). Before the mid-twentieth century, there was only a relatively small, urbanized elite who had an aestheticized romantic appreciation for nature in its wildest state (Bunce 1994; Nash 1982; Stilgoe 1988, 22–23). Michael Williams (1989, 15) writes that for the nineteenth-century (English) elite, "increasingly, primitivism and romanticism became a slightly decadent cult, the hallmark of the well-educated gentleman." And in the American context, Cronon (1995, 42) notes,

> Wilderness came to embody the frontier myth . . . The irony of course, was that in the process wilderness came to reflect the very civilization its devotees sought to escape. Ever since the 19th century, celebrating wilderness has been an activity mainly for well-to-do city folks. Country people generally know far too much about working the land to regard unworked land as their ideal.

Cronon continues, "Only people whose relation to the land was already alienated could hold up wilderness as a model for human life in nature, for the romantic ideology of nature leaves no place in which human beings can actually make their living from the land" (1995, 42). While Cronon may unwittingly buy into an elitist distinction between the cultivated taste of the educated and the embodied, unreflective "getting by" of those who work with their hands, he nevertheless captures the idea of an aesthetic of detachment from nature underlying the preservationist movement. Today wilderness is widely considered the quintessential embodiment of nature, while the visual consumption of nature is seen as culturally enriching. Taste that constructs wilderness as appropriate for aesthetic appropriation can be considered cultural capital and such taste is being cultivated by increasing numbers.

Early in the twentieth century, members of an American upper class and educated elite decided that they had a duty to help assimilate children, especially those from immigrant families and city backgrounds, into an appreciation of nature and the old, rural, republican way of life. Forests were seen as a fragile inheritance that Americans had a patriotic duty to protect from the devastating effects of modern civilization. This nature movement played a role in the production of a class-based, anti-modern aesthetic with nationalistic, sometimes nativist, overtones. In 1913, a group of local nature lovers organized the Bedford Audubon Society. Their job was to study and educate the citizenry about nature and its stewardship. In 1950, the society raised a small amount of money, which they gave to the Bedford Garden Club to set up markers on a nature trail in a nearby county park (*Northern Westchester Times* 1950). By supporting nature in such ways, the members of these societies helped to establish or secure their place among Bedford's elite. This is not to say that their love of nature or their patriotism was not genuine, but that motivations and outcomes are multidimensional.

The sense of social purpose of these early stewards still prevails as the nature preserves actively involve school children in their various conservation projects. Many of the parents we interviewed were enthusiastic about nature education, speaking of the importance of raising children in the country and taking them into the woods to learn from nature. One man described the preserves as follows: "They are one of the biggest draws of Bedford for me. Even with Lyme disease, it's so important for kids to be exposed to nature. It teaches them values they can't learn in the city." Another woman told us that her mother had encouraged her to spend time in the town's woods contemplating the personal essay she would write for her application to university. Her mother had suggested that she focus it around the fact that long hours spent in the woods as a child had given her strength of body and character. Another told us she had given up a good job in Manhattan because she refused to raise a "city boy" who didn't know the "ways of the woods and wildlife." She strongly believed that a rural, wooded setting was a psychologically and physically healthier location for a child. Yet another interviewee told us that when he was a child his parents had taught him that it was cruel to raise children in cities because they were polluted and because there were moral lessons to be learned from nature that one could never gain as an adult. In response, he felt sorry for city boys and had urged his family to take in "fresh air" children in the summers so that poor children could be exposed to nature.[3]

As we have seen, despite the strict zoning code and the fact that in the last several centuries there have never been more trees in Bedford (Shoumatoff 1979), there is a fear that the rural, wooded nature of Bedford will be lost. It was decided

Fig. 6.1 Old Stone Walls in the Wilderness.

that one way to combat this was to remove land from the market by creating nature preserves. In 1953, five wealthy people decided to found the Mianus River Gorge Wildlife Refuge and Botanical Preserve. It became a pioneer land acquisition project of the Nature Conservancy, a national, nonprofit conservation organization. In 1964, only eleven years after its founding, the preserve became the first registered Natural History Landmark in the United States. At present, the preserve is composed of 616 acres of forest, wetlands, and abandoned agricultural fields. It might at first seem surprising that this small and relatively undistinguished gorge in the outer suburbs of New York City should have been registered by the conservancy before any of the much larger and nationally known sites elsewhere in the country. However, its designation undoubtedly had much more to do with the elite status and landscape tastes of its proponents than with the natural wonders or ecological significance of the site itself.

Invisible to the viewers' gaze and contrary to popular romantic perceptions, property relations are constitutive of wilderness in places like Bedford. The town's environmental history, as it is told locally, is the story of a pastoral, agricultural landscape valiantly carved out of a hostile wilderness by white settlers. In a largely unremarked reversal, a few small tracts of wilderness are portrayed as having been saved from encroaching human occupation. As we have said in Chapter Two, contrary to local myth history, Bedford's agricultural landscape long preceded the English settlers. The nature preserves are not pristine wilderness, but land carved out of a very old agricultural landscape. They also include some land that had always been marginal to agriculture such as wetlands and steep ravines. This primordial wilderness is not only the historical product of human physical, ideological, and organizational labor; it is a hybrid product of topography, inherited ecosystems, fragmented political jurisdictions, government tax structures, and institutionalized systems of property relations first of Native Americans,[4] later of Anglo-American farmers, and, more recently, of wealthy urbanites who impose strict limitations on the sale of land through highly restrictive zoning regulations and covenants. If this particular land had not been controlled by wealthy people, it is safe to say that none of it would have been turned over to nature preserves, for none but the rich can afford to give away land or would sufficiently benefit from the tax advantages of doing so.[5]

Bedford's wilderness, like its pastoral landscape, has been produced out of a class-based aesthetic that itself is the product of wealth generated in an urban industrial and financial realm. Alienated sentiments that fail to acknowledge this interdependence are enabled by the spatial separation of the suburban private home realm from urban centers. Spatial productions such as these are not new. Keith Thomas (1983, 286–87) writing about the educated tastes of late-eighteenth-century English aesthetes who saw industrial production as ugly and distasteful, says, however, that:

> such men seldom allowed their aesthetic sensibilities to get in the way of the productive process. In the ensuing century and a half these private sensibilities would have to be gratified by the creation of special reservations, landscape gardens, greenbelts, and animal sanctuaries: artificial oases or peepshows into an idealized world whose very existence underlined their essential opposition to the fundamental values of ordinary society.

Over the years, the Mianus River Gorge Preserve has received numerous small gifts of land, much of which is very steep or marshy and parcels that have historically been of very little economic value. We say this not to denigrate the gift of land, but simply to point out that "wilderness" often results from the low economic value of land. In this case, the value has been further depressed by recent local legislation forbidding the building of houses or roads near wetlands or on steep slopes.[6] This local legislation, as we have seen, is a more stringent overlay on top of state environmental legislation. It is rigorously enforced decreasing the amount of land that can potentially be built upon. Due to the very high value placed on visual consumption of land and the desire for green space and views, undeveloped land held in a preserve adds value to an adjacent property, especially if it is not heavily screened by trees. If one can get a tax benefit from not owning but have all the visual advantages of owning, then it makes sense to give away land.

Another way that property relations are incorporated into this new wilderness in Bedford is through naming. At the Mianus River Gorge Preserve, there are numerous plaques celebrating those who gave land or other forms of support. At the entrance to the preserve, the five founders' names appear on a bronze plaque set in a stone. Other plaques tell visitors that they are walking in the Terry Lawrence Memorial Forest or the James and Alice de Pester Todd Woodlands, viewing the Sanford Cascade, crossing the Edith Faile Foot Bridge, or sitting on the Lucy D. S. Adams Memorial Bench. Nature is converted into prestigious "cultural capital" whereby people can celebrate themselves or members of their family by having their name displayed on the valued object. Given the symbolic importance of wilderness to elites, this permanent linking of a person's name to treasured "islands of nature" resonates with spiritual and moral power. As we shall see in Chapter Seven, there are plaques on the historic courthouse in the village informing people that "history" is provided for them through the benevolence of named citizens. In the same way, members of the local elite provide the town with "nature" in exchange for recognition by all who visit the preserve. Clearly there is something more than wilderness being preserved here.

At the entrance to the preserve is a sign reading, "You are guests in a private reserve not a public park. Our only purpose is preservation of biotic diversity not public recreation." There are a number of issues raised here. The first is that, as the sign points out, this is private land, communal property held in trust that people are allowed to walk on if they obey the rules of the preserve's owners. The second is that this is not called a park, with all of the connotations of middle-class recreation. This preserve encourages an aesthetic way of seeing that treats wilderness with great respect, reverence, and learned appreciation. The preserve lists twelve activities that are prohibited including everything other than walking along the precut trails. The value of places such as this preserve is predicated on the fundamental separation of humans from the environment. Nature in this managed world is an exhibit to be visually consumed. The preserves are like exhibits in a museum, offering huge outdoor dioramas that one can walk through, places where one can look or quietly contemplate. However, a class-based aesthetic is encoded into the environment, the same aesthetic that is wielded as a political weapon securing and maintaining the town's exclusivity. Property relations are encoded in the nature preserves through the conception of nature as capital. Nature, we were told in these and similar words, "is our most precious inheritance, we must save it for future generations." The conception of nature is permeated by the language of capitalism, of economic rationality, and of the passing of wealth from one generation to the next: "We have been entrusted with this land to pass on to our children and grandchildren." Signs at the entrance to the preserve assure people that here "nature is being preserved intact" and urge visitors to "help save these twenty-seven species of songbird for your grandchildren." It is a rationality that converts all things including nature and spirituality into capital. This rhetorical linking of cultural and economic capital obscured by romanticism has become a powerful idea in the politics of conservation.[7]

Aesthetic Environmentalism

The nature preserves claim to protect a particular ecosystem as it existed at one specific point in time 300 years ago, before the founding of Bedford as an English settlement. Wilderness in Bedford is a type of ecosystem that looks to the untrained eye as if it has been little influenced by human activity. The value of this wilderness is underpinned by the long-held Western dichotomy between the human and the nonhuman. Many residents of Bedford also subscribe to another popular environmental perspective that sees humans and the rest of nature as belonging in a fundamental sense to one interacting whole. Such ecological perspectives contradict the possibility of pristine nature. However, this contradiction is unnoticed or at least not troublesome to those whose aesthetic environmentalism tends to outweigh their ecological concerns. Wilderness in Bedford is a human creation in the sense that it is an invented category based on a dualism that is scientifically indefensible.

One could similarly say that Bedford's wilderness is thoroughly cultivated. It is both the wilderness of "cultivated" people who have developed the aesthetic sensibility to appreciate virginal nature, and it is cultivated in the sense that it is, to a very large extent, humanly produced and maintained as a garden is. This untroubled contradictory double meaning can be seen in the organization's literature. The "Mianus River Gorge Trail Guide" (n.d.) claims to preserve untouched nature while calling for volunteers to work on the land to maintain it in its present untouched state. The guide states the following as the preserve's policy: "The Mianus Gorge area is being maintained as a 'wilderness island' on which nature, including all plants and animals, may live so far as possible free from any interference by man directly or indirectly while the tract develops along wholly natural lines, regardless of what these may prove to be." One would think from this statement that it is an "island" removed from human control. But a report from the Stewardship Committee in the 1993 news bulletin reveals a tension between the stated policy and the program of management to fashion nature according to culturally specific aestheticized views of wilderness. The report begins,

> The first and foremost duty of the Preserve's Stewardship Committee is to see that the natural and unique state of the Gorge is maintained and protected. Because so many natural elements have been removed from our landscape in the past 300 years, we now must manage many of our ecosystems in order to improve or even to maintain the Preserve's biodiversity. How do we replicate the effect of the fast moving fires that for 8,000 years were set by Native Americans in these woods? How can we re-establish meadows, those critical habitats for insects and birds? . . . What can we do about the uncontrolled growth of the white tailed deer herds that are destroying the forest's understory? (The Mianus River Gorge Preserve 1993)

The first sentence of the report refers to "the natural and unique state of the Gorge." The problem, it explains in the second sentence, is that "so many natural elements have been removed from our landscapes in the past 300 years." Here, in a rhetorical move, the arrival of the Europeans marks the beginning of culture's threat to nature. There is, of course, some truth to this view. The Indian patterns of agriculture were less harmful to the environment than later settlers' methods of farming and permanent settlement, if only because of low population density. The identification of the first of the "natural elements" removed from the landscape as "the effect of the fast moving fires . . . set by Native Americans in these woods" reveals a particular romantic ideology that separates nature from culture seeing the fires as "natural" because Native Americans are seen as belonging to nature. The myth of the noble savage, although intended as a critique of Western civilization, nevertheless is predicated upon a tacit hierarchy of races with some closer to nature and those of European descent at the apex of civilization (Anderson 2001; Willems-Braun 1997). In singling out the burning of the forests, the committee recognizes the role that the Native Americans played in maintaining a certain type of forest. However, in calling it natural, they fail to see it as a product of Native American economy, assuming instead that it is God's or Nature's economy.

The purpose of the Mianus River Gorge Preserve is said to be the preservation of biotic diversity through the creation of a wilderness island. Its publications do not give evidence to support these claims. The rest of Bedford is heavily wooded and full of protected wetlands. These areas also support biodiversity. Furthermore, the preserve (just over 600 acres) is too small to constitute an island for many species.[8] Some of the animals could not maintain a viable breeding population if they were restricted to the area. The preserve, therefore, is not a wilderness island in any valid scientific sense of the term. Cindy Katz (1998) states that the preservation of "pristine" nature where biodiversity can be "locked up" is often based on what she calls an "elegiac exercise" rather than on valid principles of ecology, and tends to be arbitrary or nonscientific in terms of scale. She states, "As such preservation is quite unecological, defying natural history and the vibrancy of the borders—physical, temporal, spatial—where evolution, change, and challenge are negotiated and worked out in culture."[9] The preserve is marked as an island, not because of the quality of the nature, as much as by the institutionalization of it. The preserve is marked as an island because it is a different sort of private property, given over to a cultural ideal of the separation of nature and culture, born of nineteenth-century romanticism, twentieth-century popular ecological rhetoric, and the federal tax structure.[10]

In order to maintain their preferred style of wilderness, the preserve's Stewardship Committee commissioned a study of the gorge by "an international expert" who produced a 220-page report titled "Management Survey and Recommendations" (Mianus Gorge Preserve 1993). The title reveals an Enlightenment rationality that attempts to ensure that nature in no way escapes human control. Even when people support the idea of letting nature have its own way, it ends up being dominated by culture in the form of stewardship, as is evident in the very name of the committee. The apparent contradiction here can be understood if one makes a distinction between certain scientific understand-ings of the natural environment that recognize nature as dynamic and in need of management in conjunction with aestheticized notions that depend on an artistic illusion, but not necessarily the actuality, of a complete separation of the natural from the cultural.

James Proctor and Steven Pincetl (1996) argue that while nature and culture are highly entangled, biodiversity-oriented conservation efforts often proceed with purification and separation as goals. They believe that a more thorough understanding of biophysical-human networks might lead to a revision of such romantic ideals. One could say that nature as an active agent in the preserve un-settles the nature/culture dichotomy, which the administrators try to maintain in the face of contradictory evidence.

Thus despite romantic claims of undisturbed wilderness, one can see the application of bureaucratic rationality and management techniques. Twenty-seven types of songbirds found in the gorge are listed at the entrance to the trail. A list of the trees, shrubs, and wildflowers found there are provided in the trail guide. Identifying signs are placed on selected trees in the Westmoreland Sanctuary. The committee calls for volunteers: "We hope many of you will be joining us in clearing sections of second growth woods, monitoring birds and plants, recreating vanished habitats, collecting water samples and photograph-ing the ever-changing landscapes of our 615 acres throughout the seasons" (Mianus Gorge Preserve 1994, 3). Applying technologies of control and surveil-lance, the committee urges that nature be monitored and photographed (Evernden 1992; Wright 1992).

Is this wilderness very different from a garden? Symbolically the garden in the nineteenth century was seen as not radically different from the forest, but as a pale version of it (Bermingham 1986, 182–83). In the Arcadian myth, as in the Garden of Eden, idealized nature is seen as a garden. This picturesque "wild" gar-den aesthetic is supplemented in America today by an interest in ecology.[11] The increasingly popular "new American garden" uses "native plants" to create an "ecosystem in miniature in one's own back yard" (Druse 1994, 27). This move-ment is spreading in Bedford.[12] Those newly arrived in Bedford, as we have seen, often learn through friends and garden clubs to reject the suburban aesthetic of a manicured lawn with ornamental trees. There are close connections between those who sponsor or run the nature preserves and gardening associations. For example, Mrs. Butler and Miss Frick, who were the major donors for two of the nature preserves, were members of the exclusive Bedford Garden Club. Mrs. Lockwood, who recently donated nearly thirty acres to the Mianus River Gorge Preserve, was described in the article announcing her gift as "a nation-ally known horticulturist and member of the Garden Club of America" (*Patent Trader* 1992, 12). Anne French, past administrator of the Mianus River Gorge Preserve, was presented a medal "for notable service to the cause of conservation education" by the Garden Club of America. Finally, the Butler Memorial Sanctuary is administered by two of Bedford's garden clubs and the Bedford Audubon Society. This is not to suggest that there is anything misguided about belonging to a gardening club and also sponsoring a preserve, or having a garden club manage a preserve, but instead to suggest that conceptually the preserves could be considered wild gardens at a larger scale, subject to a similar mindset and technologies.

It is easier to give romantic rather than ecological reasons as to why nature in Bedford today should look as it did 300 years ago. Ecologically the periodization may be somewhat arbitrary. In terms of the history of white settlement, however, it is significant. In fact, a case could be made that the major ecological changes occurred later in the nineteenth century when agriculture became market driven (Cronon 1983, 76; also see Kearns 1998 on this). Again the naturalization of a particular landscape aesthetic tends to obscure the ideological basis of its support. While the idea that such a small-scale wilderness island supports a significant degree of biodiversity may be questionable, from the point of view of aesthetic environmentalism, the scale of a preserve (as far as the eye can see) makes a lot of sense, although, as we have indicated above, areas, especially small marshes and bogs, do provide valuable habitat for certain species as well as help purify water. Nevertheless, we think the spatial scale of environmental concern in Bedford is dictated far more by aesthetics and pragmatic issues to do with the average size of private properties than ecosystem requirements. The latter are best planned for at a broader spatial scale. Bedford's idea of wildlife corridors discussed in Chapter Five may go some distance toward extending the scale of protected land. Furthermore, the idea of the separation of the natural from the built environment should be unsettled so that the protection of cordoned-off nature does not provide an excuse to neglect environmental issues elsewhere.[13]

A prominent local biologist, Michael Klemens, has made a plea, which is unlikely to be heeded, that planners in Bedford and other towns restructure controls on development to be more compatible with the environmental and social needs of the metropolitan area. He suggests that it is very costly in both environmental and social terms to impose low-density zoning uniformly across the region. Development should be concentrated so that the preservation of much larger-scale, ecologically healthy, areas of significant biodiversity can be planned by a regional-level organization (Anderson 1997). If this suggestion for effective regional scale planning were taken seriously, it might lead the way toward greater social as well as ecological justice. However, it clearly would threaten the localized pattern of decision-making that supports aesthetic environmentalism. Unlike in many other countries, in the United States, the idea of local autonomy in matters of planning is considered virtually sacred.[14]

In effect, wilderness in Bedford is privatized. It is intended for the visual enjoyment and edification of the residents. Although outsiders are not excluded from them, the preserves are difficult to find; only a few small signs lead to some and none to others. As a consequence, not many of the residents and only a few outsiders and school classes visit them. It is the landowners in town who benefit most from the advantages of having forests and open meadows within sight or an easy walking or driving distance of their homes.

The nature preserves are also products of transcendentalism, a discourse that originally arose as a reaction against scientific rationality, but now appears to be incorporated into a diffuse set of mutually reinforcing discourses. For example, it is argued that species should be preserved not only on scientific grounds, but also on the grounds of "God's great chain of being" (Lovejoy 1974; Pepper 1984). Nineteenth-century transcendentalists, such as Ralph Waldo Emerson, saw forests as God's first temples and as "plantations of God." For them, a walk in the woods was a religious rite, and we can see a degree of continuity in contemporary attitudes (Schmitt 1990, 141; Thomas 1983, 216, 269). The Nature Museum in the Westmoreland Sanctuary is a reconstructed Presbyterian Church built in 1783 and moved to the preserve by a neighbor and benefactor in 1973. Here, a powerful blending of religion, nature, and history attests to the morality of the place. A sign on a tree in the preserve puts forward a classic statement of transcendentalism:

> The kiss of the sun for pardon.
> The song of the birds for mirth.
> One is nearer God's heart in a forest
> Than anywhere else on earth.[15]

One finds strong elements of transcendentalism in the Mianus River Gorge Preserve as well. At the entrance to the preserve there is a sign with a number of aphorisms about nature. Among them are quotations from psalms, Henry David Thoreau, John Muir, and John Burroughs. The centerpiece of the preserve is the "Hemlock Cathedral," a stand of very tall trees, the oldest of which is reputed to be over 325 years old. At the center of this "cathedral" is a sign reading, "Monte Gloria," in honor of one of the original founders. This echoes Charles Eliot who in 1896 referred to the wilderness as the "cathedrals of the modern world" (Eliot 1902, 655; quoted in Thomas 1983, 269). The name Monte Gloria, the glorious mount, likewise has a religious ring to it, transforming a gift of property into a quasi-religious act. The discourse of aestheticized romanticism has become materialized in the physical landscape (Schein 1997). One can see this aesthetic transforming nature in the desire to keep woodland clear of heavy underbrush and in the paths cut through the woods to afford walkers glimpses of the most picturesque scenes; it can also be seen in the construction of a viewing spot in the Mianus River Gorge Preserve, where a bench is positioned for contemplating a stream through a frame of foliage. We are reminded of Alexander Wilson's (1997) words: "nature appreciation is an offshoot of art appreciation from nineteenth century England." The importance of the aesthetic in wilderness preservation is signalled by the sign at the entrance to the Westmoreland

Fig. 6.2   A Place for Quiet Contemplation.

Sanctuary. It reads, "Nature sanctuary dedicated to the protection of all forms of nature within its boundaries, for the appreciation and inspiration of those who love natural beauty." The founder of one of Bedford's nature preserves states, "An appreciation of nature is more than aesthetic; it is essential to any real understanding of ourselves." Her romantic understanding of nature was echoed in many of our interviews.

We asked residents of Bedford what they thought of the nature preserves. Interestingly, only a few, those most closely involved with the preserves or conservation organizations, mentioned ecology or biodiversity. The most common response was that they are valuable because they can't be developed. One man told us, "Nature preserves are very important because they concentrate land. They mean no houses. They keep the place rural looking." A real estate broker said, "The nature preserves are great. Permanently preserved open space is a major asset to the town. My customers don't want to move here to see houses on small lots. They want nature, beautiful open land." These respondents are typical of those we interviewed in seeing the preserves as aesthetically valuable in themselves and as instrumental in maintaining the picturesque beauty of the whole town by restricting development. Others see the preserves not as places to visit but as visual barriers between properties. Although most prefer the pastoral landscapes of the town's many horse farms, the preserved forests are considered Bedford's second best landscape type. Although neither of the

Table 6.1 Response to the Question, "Is the Town of Bedford Doing Enough to Protect Our Forests?"

Net Difference = %Stricter − %Looser [Need for Stricter or Looser Regulations]

A. *By Length of Residence*

Total	10 Years or Less	11–20 years	More Than 20 Years
+61	+70	+65	+54

B. *By Area*

Total	Bedford Village	Bedford Hills	Katonah
+61	+70	+67	+49

(529 = Total Number)

Source: Town of Bedford 1998.

town's surveys asked any questions specifically about the preserves, one can infer something of the value of the preserves by examining the answers to the question, "Is the town of Bedford doing enough to protect our forests?"

There is a fair degree of variation within the sample on attitudes toward forests. Newcomers are much keener on preserving them than are old-timers. It is unclear why. Perhaps longer-term residents are more committed to a remembered pastoral landscape in Bedford, which they see being encroached upon by forests, while newcomers think of Bedford as a largely wooded landscape to be protected. Or possibly the longer-term residents know more about Bedford's anti-development history and have come to trust the vigilance and activism of boards, organizations, newspapers, officials, and ordinary individuals to effectively counter forces for development. Once again, Katonah residents part company with other residents of Bedford. They may be more focused on their own hamlet and have relatively less interest in what are known locally as "the estate areas" where the larger preserves are located.

It is interesting in this regard to compare responses to the questions, "What is your favorite Bedford view?" and "What place in Bedford should be kept intact at all costs?" (see Table 4.3). Only thirteen of 447 respondents chose any of the nature preserves as their favorite view while the preserves collectively were far down on residents' lists. This may either be because they are largely wooded and thus do not afford a view or because they are seen as already protected and thus not vulnerable. That the preserves are primarily valued on aesthetic grounds, however, can be inferred from the second question where the preserves rank even further down residents' lists. At the very least, the latter suggests that the preserves' rhetoric of the crucial importance of biodiversity is not on the minds of most residents. This is not to say that residents don't value the nature preserves, as they clearly do. Some of our respondents argued that Bedford needs more preserves. One woman said, "[Nature preserves] are important because they keep the land open. The more land we have in preserves, the fewer houses we will have." Another said, "They are good. It would be nice if more people gave land to the town so it would never be built on." A developer stated, "They [the boards of the preserves] are trying to get everyone to give them land. Certainly anyone who wants to subdivide a sizeable piece of land has to give land to the town to protect nature. But let's face it: what people of this town really want to do is to protect views." A real estate broker had a similar point of view: "The nature preserves are a racket. They [the town's residents] just want them for aesthetic reasons."

Others approached the preserves less instrumentally as things of beauty in and of themselves. One woman loved them for their trees: "The preserves are great. There are beautiful stands of conifers in them." A horse rider told us, "The nature preserves are my favorite place. We can ride through some of them. They are magical." A man who commutes to New York sees the preserves in transcendental terms. He says, "You get a sense of privacy and inner peace in the woods that you don't get anywhere else. Nature is the most important thing to me. It's worth two hours on the train. We need zoning and environmental protection to preserve this. Development pressure must be resisted."

Wilderness in the nature preserves has reacquired some of its earlier active, frightening qualities. Lyme disease, which can have serious long-term health effects if not treated quickly, has become prevalent in the area, with Westchester having one of the highest rates in the country.[16] A few people told us that they have acquired a new perspective on forests and fields. One said, "I've gone a number of times to the preserves. They are very beautiful. But I worry about getting Lyme disease." Another said, "We used to do a lot of hiking. We don't go to the nature preserves anymore because I have had Lyme disease. I really have no interest in going into the woods anymore." Nature rather than being a threat to humans had until recently been seen as something wholly good, itself threatened by humans. The spread of Lyme disease in the area has brought back a much older sense of fear into people's interaction with nature. However, this fear may cause people to aestheticize nature even further, and see it as something to be consumed visually at a distance, as undeveloped land seen from the road or from one's own property.

The Westchester Land Trust

The Westchester Land Trust, which is headquartered in Bedford, was founded in the late 1930s and at present has over 700 members. The trust's stated mission is to protect land from development and preserve scenic sites within the county. It accepts gifts of land, either in the form of outright donations or easements, that the Nature Conservancy, a national organization, cannot accept because they are highly fragmented or not considered ecologically important enough to spend their limited resources on. A woman who works for the trust explained to us quite candidly that local values are different: "In a place like Bedford, sometimes it is principally the 'look of the land' that needs to be maintained."

The trust's activities are reported on a regular basis in its newsletter, on its website, and also on the front page of the town newspaper, the *Record Review,* whose board members and editors are either on, or closely connected to, the town's Conservation and Planning Boards. Since 1988, the trust has accumulated sixty properties totaling over 1,500 acres in Westchester. Of these, approximately two-thirds are conservation easements. The trust is able to accumulate land because the Internal Revenue Service not only allows a charitable tax deduction for gifts of land, but in 1996, reaffirmed that a deduction would be granted for conservation easements as well. Under an easement that is granted to the trust, property owners usually agree not to develop a portion of their property. Such a restriction in theory reduces the value of the property and consequently the owner can take a tax deduction on the difference between the value before and after the easement. The attraction of an easement over an outright gift to the trust is that the property owner continues to own the land and can sell it at a later date, albeit with the easement attached. The trust has used such tax incentives as the principal way of accumulating land. Such a strategy works best, however, if property owners are convinced that there is a financial advantage to giving up their development rights. For years, very few people in Bedford were willing to donate land because it was more valuable in four-acre parcels than in larger blocks. As recently as September 1999, when an expert on preserving open space was brought to a town meeting, the town supervisor told him,

> Don't waste time talking about transferring development rights. It doesn't work. You're not going to get anyone in Bedford to sell an acre's worth of development rights for $10,000. A lot of people talk the talk, but when it comes to stepping up to the plate as private citizens, putting their property into conservation or deed restriction or something like that, they won't do it. (Chitwood 1999b)

But over the past several years, that has changed. Now there can sometimes be a premium paid for large properties over their value if subdivided. In addition, because it is now so difficult to subdivide property in Bedford, as we saw in Chapter Five, development is a risky and exorbitantly expensive option. As one real estate broker told us,

> I'm advising more and more people about the economic advantages of conservation easements. You get a write-off on property you can continue to use and, given that properties are often worth more whole than divided, you aren't doing yourself any harm. The only potential problem will be if the IRS realizes that the easements aren't necessarily decreasing the value of the properties.

The changing nature of the land market has resulted in the Westchester Land Trust's receiving a number of large donations in Bedford in 2000 and 2001. Included among them is a 110-acre easement on a farm, an eighty-three-acre piece of land owned by a riding school, thirty-one- and sixty-four-acre portions of two large estates, a fifty-eight-acres plot, and, in December 2001 at the end of the tax year, four further donations totaling sixty-four- acres (Westchester Land Trust 2001b, 2002; Gorman 2001a, 2001f). To give an idea of the potential tax savings to large property owners, the thirty-one-acre piece alone is estimated to be worth $3 million (Westchester Land Trust 2001b). The gift of nature, whether it be to a nature preserve or the Westchester Land Trust, not only helps to keep Bedford relatively undeveloped, but financially benefits individual landowners. But it would be a mistake to believe that landowners only give easements to save money. To think so would seriously underplay the very real emotional attachment that many have to rural Bedford. As one of the larger landowners said upon giving an easement on sixty-four-acres of her estate, "the preservation of Tanrackin Farm has been one of my dearest wishes for years. Bedford remains such a beautiful place because parts of it still have the feel of farm country. A portion of Tanrackin will now remain an important part of that forever" (Westchester Land Trust 2001b). Several people who have known the owner of Tanrackin Farm for many years told us of the depth of her emotional attachment to her land. Protecting her land against development has been "a lifelong passion" for her because she truly loves the landscapes of Bedford where she has spent a lifetime raising horses, riding through her woods, and working on committees to preserve the natural and agrarian landscapes of the town and Westchester County. Her identity is intimately tied to her land. Her actions will be widely appreciated because Tanrackin Farm, which is largely open pastureland bordering on Guard Hill Road, is considered by Bedford residents to provide one of their favorite views on their favorite road (see Table 4.3).[17]

A lead article in one of Bedford's papers (Carroll 1995) portrayed the decline of the large landowner and the redistribution of land in Bedford as a tragedy. The president of the Westchester Land Trust called the possible breakup of a number of great estates "a potential time bomb." He explained that "the heirs, tragically, can't afford to support the land, to hold it and pay taxes on it." He added that land taxes are a form of "financial oppression for the owners who want to keep it [an estate] in the family." We found little recognition of any tension between valuing Bedford's history of small, independent farmers and the love of great estates. This is probably because only large landholders can provide the visual scenes that the residents associate with Bedford's sparsely populated agrarian past. Until the 1980s, almost all of the largest landowners belonged to the exclusive Farmer's Club, a century-and-a-half-old club now devoted to the history of farming and methods (including tax planning) of preserving the rural landscape and the memory of farming in Bedford.[18] The landowners whom we interviewed clearly see themselves as living the simple, good life and as preserving agrarian values in Bedford for themselves and future generations. The natural and agrarian histories in Bedford are thus appealed to in the quest to have one's lifestyle and landscape taste for open land subsidized. Financial planning here is seen as consistent with an act of civic virtue.

The Westchester Land Trust's website (http://www.westchesterlandtrust.org, April 2002) tries to allay any fears that the local tax base will be eroded through the gift of such conservation easements. It states, "In any area, a small reduction in the taxable valuation of eased property would be more than offset by enhanced taxable value of the surrounding properties. It is common knowledge that property surrounding parks and preserves commands premium prices." It would appear that residents of Bedford cannot lose.

In answer to the question, "Won't conservation easements limit the availability of needed housing?, "the website (April 2002) states;

> No. Good planning dictates that new housing should be concentrated in those areas best able to service it with roads, water and sewer facilities (infrastructure), and employment and shopping opportunities. Conservation organizations usually do not accept easements on land that should more appropriately be developed for housing. In those areas of the County where development is appropriate, conservation easements will only be accepted in connection with open space set aside as part of planned cluster developments, or to preserve scenic or ecologically sensitive areas such as wetlands, stream corridors and riverbanks, steep hillsides, etc. A conservation easement strategy goes hand-in-hand with capital improvements to infrastructure in order to concentrate development in those areas best able to service it. In this way, an adequate supply of housing at high enough densities to be affordable can be created.

Quite possibly the above makes sense in terms of regional scale environmental planning. Unquestionably it makes aesthetic sense to many residents of Bedford who wish to protect their open spaces, views, woods, and wetlands. However, it will be difficult to implement given the "fair share of regional need" view of the courts (Berenson v. New Castle and Southern Burlington NAACP v. Mount Laurel) and towns such as Mount Kisco whose residents and officials feel they already have their fair share of development and affordable housing (workshop for Westchester planners and town officials, Katonah Library, April 2002; interview with Mayor Reilly of Mount Kisco). Questions of environmental justice may also be raised if new development is directed principally toward areas considered "already spoilt." There are hopeful signs, however, of a trend toward regional organizations such as the Westchester Land Trust and Westchester County Housing Opportunity Commission meeting to discuss issues that are usually seen as separate rather than highly interdependent: affordable housing and the preservation of nature.

The elites who maintain large estates or who take tax breaks on portions of their land by giving them to land trusts and nature preserves are seen as performing a type of community service by most of the people we interviewed. A banker argued that estate owners shouldn't have to lose title to their land in order to get tax breaks. He said, "No one does more for Bedford than the people who keep open land. I don't know if the town gives a tax break, but they

Table 6.2 Percent in Favor of Tax Incentives to Large Landowners to Keep Large Tracts Intact

A. *By Length of Residence*

Total	10 Years or Less	11–20 years	More Than 20 Years
75%	77%	79%	74%

B. *By Area*

Total	Bedford Village	Bedford Hills	Katonah
75%	80%	78%	68%

(529 = Total Number)

Source: Town of Bedford 1998.

should because they are doing a huge amount for the rest of us by keeping the land beautiful." Another informant went even further, saying, "They [the large landowners] should be given a tax break to keep them here. I would be willing to pay more taxes to help because they add to the charm of the town." Table 6.2 demonstrates that such a view has strong support in Bedford.

While there is some variation within the sample, support is broad. This level of support is striking, given the real concern in town with rising property taxes and the fact that residents realize that if large landowners pay less, the rest will have to pay more.

As it turns out, the town decided not to pursue the option of reducing town taxes on the large estates. Instead, for the moment they encourage conservation easements. The advantage of this option from the point of view of the town is that the cost of preserving open space is born principally by the federal and state governments in the form of lost tax revenues, rather than by the town.

The horse farms with their pastoral views were singled out as being particularly important. A resident says, "I would hate to see Sunnyfield go. Everyone can enjoy it while driving by." Another woman remarks, "The horse farms are what have saved the Bedford ambience." A man who lives on eight acres argues,

Table 6.3 Response to the Statement "Rising Property Taxes Are an Important Problem"

Net Difference = Agree − Disagree

A. *By Length of Residence*

<5 Years	5–9 Years	10–19 years	20 Years+	
+73.5	+ 55.2	+65.4	+78.2	

B. *By Area*

4 Acre +	Bedford Village	Bedford Hills	Katonah	Outside Hamlet 1–4 Acre
+65.4	+ 65.0	+79.5	+76.3	+71.9

(649 = Total Number)

Source: Town of Bedford 1998.

"Of course the large landowners are a good thing. Why wouldn't I want someone to own a hundred acres and pay taxes on it and let me look at it." It is difficult to argue against this logic, for it is based upon an assumption of the primacy of the visual. If someone else will pay to maintain the desired aesthetic on a hundred acres of land, then they are subsidizing the landowner on eight acres who can look at the land. As most landowners in Bedford tend to use their land as visual space rather than for activities, a neighbor may derive virtually the same use value as an owner, but without the expense.

Conclusion: The Illusion of Disconnection

The past director of the Mianus River Gorge Preserve had the following to say in an interview published in a local newspaper under the title "Couple Donates 30 Acres to Mianus Gorge Preserve": "To go out there and walk the road in the moonlight and to think 400 years ago the moonlight shone down on that rock, and it looks just the same today. There are not too many other places 42 miles from New York City where you can look at the moonlight on a whole landscape and it looks just the same [as it did then]" (*Patent Trader* 1992). The first sentence demonstrates a romantic desire, found in American and European cultures since the Enlightenment, to return to a state of nature, before people were "civilized." Precontact North America is a principal site of this fantasy. The second sentence is virtually identical in its structure to the way in which history in Bedford is portrayed. Local people often make the point that there are not too many places forty-two miles from New York City where you can look at a picture-perfect colonial New England village. Both historic buildings and historic nature are conceived of as scarce positional goods that the town claims to have more of than other towns. But the key to the director's last sentence is "42 miles from New York City." This situates the whole statement and captures perfectly nature as seen by an elite that is both highly urbane and yet anti-urban. It is its proximity to New York City that gives this piece of nature its particular value—pristine nature easily accessible to but visually separated from New York City with its high culture, sophistication, and intense global interconnections. Having cultural and economic links are considered essential, as life relatively more isolated from these connections would be unbearable culturally as well as financially for most of Bedford's residents.

The aesthetic attitude toward wilderness with its complex and ambiguous history in rational and anti-rational schools of thought has become a hegemonic ideology in Bedford. It is an ideology that tends to mystify because it is based in a poorly articulated, immediate, sensuous, naturalized pleasure in wilderness. It is taken for granted as spontaneously shared with others. It is seen as democratically arrived at and as having roots deep in the American psyche. The aesthetic and ecological value of providing green spaces within the metropolitan area of New York City is seen as uncontroversial, albeit dispensable by a few who are more interested in land development for housing than in the preservation of the wilderness. Thus the wilderness aesthetic may become the object of a politics of exclusion or anti-development, but it is assumed that the aesthetic itself is innocent.

What we have found in Bedford is a reembedding in place, the celebration of the aesthetic (but not the reality) of intimate, premodern community relations, and the illusion of disconnection from a wider world of global interconnections. As Cronon (1995, 81) suggests, this retreat often entails a celebration of the natural in the form of wilderness. He states,

> to the extent that we live in an urban-industrial civilization but at the same time pretend to ourselves that our *real* home is in the wilderness, to just that extent we give ourselves permission to evade responsibility for the lives we actually lead. We inhabit civilization while holding some part of ourselves—what we imagine to be the most precious part—aloof from its entanglements.

Wilderness in Bedford can thus be seen in part as the alienated product of urban-industrial and financial market–generated wealth that banishes from view the modern economic landscape sustaining it. This includes importantly a very uneven and inequitable geography of housing and related resources. We say alienated because the connections between aesthetics and negative geographical externalities remain obscure to the many who sincerely believe that their efforts to make a lovely place will contribute to a wider society through environmental conservation and that these efforts have little or no negative consequences for that wider society.

CHAPTER 7

Fabricating History: The Production of Heritage in Bedford Village

> The word for Bedford Village is colonial. It was founded in 1680 and hasn't changed much since. The older folks managed to unite and convince the others that they didn't want modernization. That makes the town unique—a welcome break from everything else around here.
>
> —local policeman

> Towns across the nation are seeking somehow to recover a sense of place that they have lost. Bedford never lost that sense of place . . . but now it is clearly threatened [by a traffic light].
>
> —Bedford Village Green Traffic Study, 1992

Introduction

We use the term "fabricate" not to suggest that Bedford's history is somehow false, but rather that history isn't simply a telling of the facts. History is a "making," a "doing," and an interpreting of those facts with performative or causative power. We also use the term "fabricate" to refer to the fact that history for people in Bedford is quite literally built into the physical fabric of the village. In a brochure for a recent membership drive, the president of the Bedford Historical Society wrote, "Realize that you really do take pride in your village and that Bedford is unique among towns, because it has made its history a part of our everyday life" (Bedford Historical Society 1993, 1). Living in history is a powerful nostalgic desire that suggests that the essence of the past can in some sense be recaptured through the landscape. Feelings of historical authenticity are, in the words of Dydia DeLyser (1999, 602), "triggered by landscape." Bedford is a self-consciously historical place. In this chapter, we explore the social practices of history, and how it is made visible and enacted in the museum and the historic village tour.[1] A few residents read the volumes of the history of Bedford produced by the Bedford Historical Society. Many more have read the society's pamphlets giving a short account of the town's history, and most are familiar with the central foundation story of the town, that it was purchased by twenty-two settlers from native Americans in 1680. It is safe to say that for most residents, Bedford's history is the story of a democratic New England village surrounding a large village green that symbolizes community and continuity with its rural, republican past. As we pointed out in Chapter Three, this archetypal New England village had in fact been reconstructed in the late nineteenth and early twentieth centuries by wealthy New Yorkers to more closely resemble their romantic ideal. The village is the principal site in which residents encounter and reproduce their history. This landscape has been "museumized" since the early 1970s as an historic district, which is seen by some residents in reverential terms and by others as somewhat hyperreal—as beautiful, but perhaps overly precious and museum-like. Some complain, for example, that there are too many antique shops and real estate offices. They bemoan the loss of what they term more "real" or "useful" stores. We then examine the way in which people are encouraged by the Historical Society to experience the village through the historic tour and finally we focus on a telling controversy over the placement of a traffic light near the village green.

The Rise of Historic Preservation

Contemporary Americans live in an age enchanted with the past. There are at present thousands of local historical societies in the United States and hundreds of historical museums visited by millions of people yearly (Wallace 1986, 137). In this respect, the United States is becoming like Britain where heritage has evolved into a major industry and one of the country's greatest tourist attractions (Lowenthal 1985, 1989). Whereas many commentators welcome this interest in the past, for others, it is symptomatic of a society in economic and cultural decline. Robert Hewison (1987), for example, sees the rise of the heritage industry in Britain as a sign of decline, not only in the British economy, but in national self-confidence. Patrick Wright (1985) takes an even stronger view, "A society which understands itself through a preservationist perspective is in a morbid state." Marshall Berman (1982) sees nostalgia for the past as loss of confidence in the modernizing impulse. While Frederic Jameson (1984) theorizes the historicizing impulse as an integral aspect of the postmodern condition, David Harvey (1989, 303) makes the more general point that the aestheticization of local history tends to be conservative. He says, "At best, tradition is reorganized as a museum culture . . . of local history, of local production, of how things once upon a time were made, sold, consumed, and integrated into a long-lost, often romanticized daily life (one from which all trace of oppressive social relations may be expunged)." He argues that with the confusion and uncertainty of time-space compression, globalization, and the disembedding of institutions, the "turn to aesthetics . . . becomes more pronounced . . . Aesthetics has triumphed over ethics as a prime focus of social and intellectual concern (1989, 327–28). We would add to this that ethics and specific values such as community, integrity, coherence, historical continuity and wholesome country life have become aestheticized.

The interest in history and historic preservation itself has a fascinating history (Samuel 1995, 259–73). Antebellum Americans showed little interest in historic preservation. In fact, during the War of 1812, the state of Pennsylvania began demolishing Independence Hall in which the Declaration of Independence had been signed in order to sell the land to a developer. Two wings were demolished before protests halted the project. This cavalier attitude toward preservation began to change with the approach of the Civil War in the 1850s as a segment of the patriciate became convinced that a memorialization of the nation's founders might help to preserve the Republic. In 1850, Hamilton Fish, governor of New York, convinced the legislature to save George Washington's revolutionary headquarters from impending demolition. Three years later, Washington's home, Mount Vernon, was threatened by speculators who wished to purchase it and convert it into a hotel. Although the governor requested that the Virginia legislature purchase the estate, they balked at the $200,000 asking price and the project was left to private initiatives. Ann Pamela Cunningham, a wealthy Southerner organized a group of socially prominent women to create the Mount Vernon Ladies Association whose immediate task was to save Mount Vernon but whose broader goal was to preserve the Union and combat a commercialism that overrode the traditional values of her class. The association's campaign attracted the support of the middle and upper classes in both the North and South who wished to preserve the Union, and in 1859, Mount Vernon was saved. Although these early preservation movements did not usher in a widespread preservationist attitude, they marked the beginnings of an interest in preserving the past and "a certification that it was proper for upper-class women to preserve and present history to the public" (Wallace 1986, 139).

The final two decades of the nineteenth century saw the flowering of corporate capitalism in the United States. A new order became evident—one in which financiers, industrialists, and managers competed socially with the patrician elite. It also produced dissatisfaction among other remnants of the old order, such as artisans and small farmers and added a large, potentially destabilizing, new group of immigrant workers. The battles between these groups were waged across political, economic, and cultural terrains.[2] Patricians formed the leadership of historical societies while the rank and file began to include middle-class professionals, small businessmen, and politicians. These groups constructed memorials for past wars and preserved seventeenth- and eighteenth-century architecture. By doing so, the elite not only sought to symbolically align itself with past heroes, but also with a preimmigrant social order. They created a taste for the "authentic" by which they sought to demarcate themselves from both immigrants and those whom they viewed as nouveaux riches—the railway barons, mine owners, and streetcar magnates who were at the time transporting dismantled European castles to the United States in order to live in "simulated feudal grandeur" (Wallace 1986, 141). Local historical societies organized by the patrician elite in the early twentieth century turned houses into museums and initiated many preservation projects to celebrate the past within their localities. These museums preserved preindustrial crafts and rural traditions in various regions of the country and commemorated the life of the folk, visualized as a population of farmers and craft workers living a life of hard work, frugality, and self-reliance in harmony with a small landed patriciate. Living amid history, an appreciation of generational connections and the citation of hegemonic ideals would arise naturally. Local museums, histories, and preserved buildings and whole museum villages like Sturbridge Village in Massachusetts and colonial Williamsburg in Virginia were thought to serve a didactic function in the patrician cultural offensive against newcomers—the "vulgar" rich and especially the immigrant poor (Bunce 1994; Pregill and Volkman 1993). These historical institutions, it was thought, could inculcate in the children of the lower classes, and in particular in the children of immigrants, a respect for the old social order and its class hierarchies.[3]

Unlike commentators such as Hewison (1987) and Wright (1985), Raphael Samuel (1995, 307) argues that to look to the past is not necessarily to shrink from the future.[4] Rather, he believes that if one looks in particular at postcolonial countries, heritage is used as a way to produce a desired future. We would argue that the attitude toward the past that is reflected in Bedford's historical preservation movement is, in fact, quite complex and includes elements of both. In many respects historical preservation is a worthy project. However, here, as throughout this volume, we do not assume that aesthetics is an innocent realm set apart from the everyday struggle for class distinction, individual advancement, or nativist reaction to immigrant "impurity." Historic preservation tends to be based on an exclusivist aesthetic that no longer recognizes itself as such.

The Practices of History in Bedford

There have been five short histories of Bedford written by local amateur historians (Barrett 1955; Barrett 1886; Bolton 1848, 1881; Marshall 1980; Wood 1925). Robert Bolton's history marks the beginning of an interest in writing the history of Bedford. The next two histories attempt to establish the status claims of an old elite, which had become increasingly insecure as a new elite began to move into town. And the final two histories restake these claims as part of the official celebrations marking the 275th and 300th anniversaries of the founding of the town. These histories provide a form of social memory for the town. The tellers of Bedford's history have 300 years' worth of events from which to fashion a usable or inspiring account of the town. Typically the founding moment when the white settlers purchased land from the Indians is given a large amount of space in the official histories. In fact, in the brief narratives that appear in town brochures, newpaper stories, and merchant advertising, the history of the town is reduced to this founding moment. Later arrivals, such as the wealthy "Hilltoppers" from New York in the 1880s, who are largely responsible for refashioning Bedford from a poor farming community into an estate landscape, receive little attention. The working-class Italians who in the late nineteenth and early twentieth centuries constructed the mansions and picturesque reservoirs that dot the landscape rate only a mention. A small nineteenth-century mountain-top community of escaped slaves or the twentieth-century African-American community is rarely mentioned. Bedford as we see it today owes far more to late-nineteenth-century urban businessmen and immigrant and black labor than to the founding fathers,[5] but the narratives of self-made industrialists, immigrants, or the suburban dream are not those that have inspired the writers of Bedford's histories. Such narratives would not provide the moral distinction and social homogeneity Bedford's historians wished to promote. Instead, they chose narratives that emphasized age rather than newness and inheritance rather than self-fashioning. These nineteenth-century histories of the town devote extensive coverage to accounts of the history of the local Protestant churches and a few socially prominent families, such as the Jays or the Woods, who preceded the other "Hilltoppers." Bedford's history is written as "the New England past," which can be considered a code word for WASP history. The appeal to local genealogy and the culturally prestigious New England landscape strengthens local claims to distinction over any claims that might be made by newcomers, some of whom were wealthier or more prominent nationally, but whose presence does not add historical depth to the Anglo establishment image of Bedford.

The writing of Bedford's history simplifies a wealth of detail into a few major concepts. It proceeds not so much by accumulating empirical materials as by linking culturally resonant concepts into edifying narratives. Folklorists have noted that there exist local variants of standard stories (Fentress and Wickham 1992, 75). And Bedford's history can be seen as a typical example of the regional narrative or moral tale of brave settlers, sturdy farmers, and the New England village. Such stories have been transformed locally by specific events that put flesh on the narrative structures. Where local detail was missing, such as information about the character of the first settlers, necessary if history is to serve as a moral tale, it was filled in with standard accounts of "the New England personality type."

Because official histories, and more broadly social memory, are both partial and selective, they work in the interests of some more than others. It is not unreasonable, therefore, to pose the question, in whose interest is Bedford's history celebrated. The Bedford Historical Society in its histories and celebrations such as the commemoration of the 300th anniversary of the founding of the town retells and reenacts the story of the twenty-two founding fathers of Bedford. Because the Bedford Historical Society has been virtually a franchise of the descendants of these families, it chooses to celebrate above all else this founding moment to privilege this particular set of genealogies. By continually urging a reverence for the town history, the society promotes a reverence for the founding families. There are other elites in Bedford, but this group depends upon birth and a lineage that is traceable through its association with the town rather than through wealth or fame for its status.

David Lowenthal (1989, 26) has written that in the United States heritage in all its guises, whether it be historical preservation, genealogy, or antiques, has until recently been a conservative white, Anglo-Saxon, Protestant preserve. And George Lipsitz (1990) has characterized most local history as an uncritical glorification of the past. The local histories of Bedford are public histories and yet the line between telling the history of a place and celebrating the genealogies of certain prominent local families is fine. Lipsitz (1998, 27) writes, "One might call this history a kind of ancestor worship, but its bias towards a certain kind of experience—white, male, upper-class experience—means that most of us are being called upon to worship not our own, but someone else's ancestors." This veneration of other people's ancestors appears rational to those who practice it, because they accept a kind of fictive kinship that comes with placed-based identity.

The descendants of the original twenty-two proprietors of the town who are identified in the tricentennial history as still living in the town were prominent participants in the tricentennial celebrations in 1980. In fact, at the town pageant associated with the 300th anniversary of the founding of Bedford, the ninety descendants were given their own seating area and at one point in the proceedings were asked to stand so that the rest of the 10,000 people at the pageant could see them. The residents of Bedford are asked by the town historian (Marshall 1980, v) to appreciate "our history" and "our ancestors." The people we spoke to accepted the idea that Bedford's history, as it has been told, is their history. Perhaps this is because local history has been so thoroughly conflated in the popular imagination with ideas of heritage, genealogy, and distinction. As one man told us, "Bedford's history is important to me because it's the history of our town. I guess you could say it's our history. We have our Bedford Historical Society and town historian. Not every town can trace its history like this." This quotation captures what we have termed fictive kinship because this man has only recently moved to Bedford. Here heritage is a positional good, which one acquires with ownership of property and identification with a place.

We were struck by the fact that although Bedford residents are very interested in history, they tend to see it as something to be consumed visually and experienced artifactually. Consider the remarks of a woman who grew up in Bedford: "Bedford's history is important to me and I think to most people in Bedford. It's not that I know a lot about the history of the town. It's the historical *look* I like." Here history is refigured in the language of fashion advertising as a "look," a style that is visually appealing and that is different from other "looks," modern or postmodern. Another woman put it this way: "History is very important to me. I was a history major in college. I love the history of houses and people." History then, as conceived of by Bedford residents, is a complex phenomenon. It is a source of distinction, a condition of belonging, a moral tale, an aesthetic, and a possession that connects oneself to the founding myths of America through the idea of the New England village.

The Historic District Code

The Historic District Zoning Code for Bedford Village was adopted in 1972, as part of a town plan to create a Bedford Village Historic District. The proposal for an historic district originated with members of the Bedford Historical Society, notably the president of the society and the town historian. The document begins by stating that the purpose of the zoning ordinance is "to protect and perpetuate places and buildings having a special historic *or* aesthetic interest or value. Such special regulations are adopted in the exercise of the police power to promote the general welfare and with particular regard to the character of the district hereinafter designated, to conserve the property values therein" (Town of Bedford 1989b, 71-1). The wording of the code suggests that there are buildings that are of historic interest and others that are of purely aesthetic interest.

The intent of the zoning is to preserve the appearance of a New England colonial village. However, there are no buildings remaining from the colonial period, in part because Bedford was burned by the British during the Revolution. There are a few late-eighteenth and many more nineteenth-century buildings in colonial, Greek revival, and other historic styles. These, together with an early-twentieth-century copy of a nineteenth-century Greek revival building, are what officially constitute the historic buildings in the district. What is important is not so much historical correctness, but a kind of generic historical reference and an aesthetic judgment, which dictates that the buildings should have acquired a patina of age. The village, which is largely a nineteenth- and twentieth-century creation, has become a metaphor for history, or, as Joe Wood (1991, 36–37) puts it, "New England-as-tradition becomes New England village-as-tradition."

The reason why the framers of the Bedford Village Historical District zoning distinguished between the historic and the aesthetic is that the village has a few good-looking early-twentieth-century buildings that are seen to be in keeping with the historical character of the village. In order for the village to look authentic, nonhistoric buildings must blend with the historic buildings by referencing history; but unlike with postmodern buildings that reference history, they must not call attention to themselves. They must naturalize rather than denaturalize as postmodern buildings are often thought to do. In this way, the colonial New England village is created through a blending of the historic and the aesthetically pleasing.

The Bedford Village Historic District zoning states that "police power" will be used to promote the "general welfare . . . with particular regard to the character of the district . . . [and] to conserve the property values therein." As important as it may be to distinction, Americans tend to have difficulty accepting the notion that an aesthetic should be legislated, except within private associations. Protection of aesthetic values must, therefore, be included under general welfare and property values. The conservation of both the aesthetic and local history is justified, then, on the grounds that it conserves property values, which is of course to confirm that the dominant aesthetic confers value.

History and private property in Bedford are closely intertwined. To the extent that history in Bedford is artifactual, it can be considered property. For example, the properties adjacent to the village green are very expensive, not only because the houses are large and handsome, but also because they are designated as historic houses. Similarly, businesses in the village benefit economically from the Bedford Village Historic District designation and more broadly from the historicized aesthetic enforced by the town that gives the village its "charming New England character."

> The code specifies the areas over which the Committee exerts control within the district: to maintain the character of the Bedford Village Historic District and to regulate the construction of new buildings and the reconstruction, alteration and demolition of existing buildings, including outbuildings, walls, fences, steps and signs, to ensure that such construction and alterations are compatible with the character. In maintaining the existing character of the Bedford Village Historic District, the Review Commission shall consider architectural style, materials, color and detail. (Town of Bedford 1989b, 7104)

In the interest of this aestheticized re-creation of a New England village, every object is to be controlled—buildings, fences, and signs on shops. Although many objects such as signs are modern, they must be "in keeping." A subsequent paragraph in the code goes on to extend the control to such things as paving, topographical features, and landscaping (Town of Bedford 1989b, 7106–7106.1).

Although this local control over the aesthetics of the village works to the advantage of property owners, it nevertheless exists in tension with individualism. It is articulated in terms of civic responsibility and class-inflected stewardship, and the threat to the autonomy of property owners is tempered by a requirement that one of the five members of the committee be a representative of the property owners within the Bedford Village Historic District. In other words, as the code is legally enforceable, someone could in theory be sent to jail for violating the official aesthetic on his or her own property (Town of Bedford 1989b, 7106.1). For many, this goes against the grain of American values of private property and undermines democratic notions of the aesthetic that taste is arbitrary, the property of individuals all equal in the fact of having their own taste.

The puritan aesthetic and democratic philosophy signified by the New England village aesthetic also underlie the ambivalence residents feel about admitting the importance of aesthetics or the existence of an American class system. Thus although the commission employs a class-based aesthetic criterion, it uses the language of historical preservation, which works as history is seen largely in aesthetic terms. While minority groups within larger towns and cities challenge elite interpretations of history, campaigning for previously hidden histories to be reconstructed, Bedford has yet to experience any such challenge to its history, which remains generally taken for granted as uncontested and uncontestable. Few, if any, residents of the town would argue that the village landscape should not be preserved, or that it does not symbolize whole community.

In the case of the Bedford Village Historic District, 95% of the property owners within the district petitioned that it be established (Kurdell 1972). Such was the support for Bedford's history and the perceived economic advantages in terms of property values that that history would bring. The 1997 town survey revealed that the historic look of Bedford Village is of great importance to residents. As Table 4.3 demonstrates, in response to the question, "What is your favorite Bedford view?," Bedford Village was the third most valued view. The same table reveals that in response to the question, "What place in Bedford should be kept intact at all costs?," Bedford Village was judged to be the most important such place, receiving seventy-six out of 393 votes. Of these, the Bedford Village Historic District received all but one of the votes, within it the village green received sixty-one votes, and historic buildings received fourteen.

We asked residents of Bedford about their reactions to the Bedford Village Historic District. As one said, "We must preserve historic buildings because they are part of our heritage and because they are beautiful. We have something unique here, a colonial New England town within commuting distance of New York." A woman who recently moved to town stated that Bedford's attraction for her is "its historic buildings and the green—the fact that it looks like it's been there a long time. Bedford must do everything to preserve this." A local clerk stated that "Bedford Village has a very effective watchdog committee and Architectural Review Board. They see that the wrong thing doesn't come in. People don't want any more parking in the village. There was a meeting at Historical Hall. People I have never seen in the village were there to oppose it. They shot it [the parking proposal] down." Residents are largely satisfied with the degree of regulation over historic areas and landmarks in town. Fifty-five percent of those surveyed in 1997 thought the level of regulation at present was appropriate. A significant percentage, however, as we can see in Table 7.1, felt that regulations should be strengthened.

Table 7.1 Percent Favoring Stricter Regulation on Historic Areas and Landmarks

Net Difference = Stricter − Looser			
A. *By Length of Residence*			
Total	10 Years or Less	11–20 Years	More Than 20 Years
+39%	+44%	+43%	+35%
B. *By Area*			
Total	Bedford Village	Bedford Hills	Katonah
+39%	+44%	+49%	+30%
(529 = Total Number)			

Source: Town of Bedford 1998.

The Historic Village Tour

The Bedford Historical Society is seen not merely as a guardian of the past, but also as an enricher of the everyday lives of contemporary citizens. The village guidebooks (Bedford Historical Society 1971, n.d.) and plaques on the buildings "textualize" the village, instructing the visitor and resident alike on how to read the landscape.

> "What a pretty little New England town!" Visitors to Bedford Village, in Westchester County, New York, often make some remark such as this. And they are not far wrong, because one of the little known historical facts about Bedford is that it actually was a Connecticut town when it was founded in 1680 and did not finally become part of New York until 1700.

So begins the tour. This opening quotation conveys the preferred reading of the landscape as a New England village symbolizing "stability," "quiet prosperity," and "an intimate, family centered, God-fearing, morally conscious, industrious, thrifty, democratic *community*" (italics in original) (Meinig 1979), while suggesting a mood of visual pleasure. This "pretty little New England town" look is one among many examples of a key symbolic American landscape type analyzed by Meining. Other such symbolic types include Victorian Main Street, as

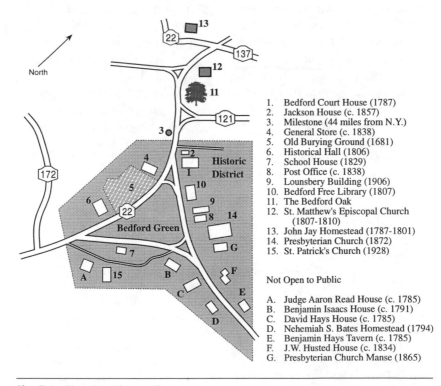

1. Bedford Court House (1787)
2. Jackson House (c. 1857)
3. Milestone (44 miles from N.Y.)
4. General Store (c. 1838)
5. Old Burying Ground (1681)
6. Historical Hall (1806)
7. School House (1829)
8. Post Office (c. 1838)
9. Lounsbery Building (1906)
10. Bedford Free Library (1807)
11. The Bedford Oak
12. St. Matthew's Episcopal Church (1807-1810)
13. John Jay Homestead (1787-1801)
14. Presbyterian Church (1872)
15. St. Patrick's Church (1928)

Not Open to Public

A. Judge Aaron Read House (c. 1785)
B. Benjamin Isaacs House (c. 1791)
C. David Hays House (c. 1785)
D. Nehemiah S. Bates Homestead (1794)
E. Benjamin Hays Tavern (c. 1785)
F. J.W. Husted House (c. 1834)
G. Presbyterian Church Manse (1865)

Fig. 7.1 Map of the Historical Tour.

Fig. 7.2 The Court House Museum.

exemplified by Katonah. However, Bedford Village's well-preserved New England landscape is sufficiently rare as it is within commuting distance of New York City to have acquired an aura of uniqueness for its residents and its other admirers.

The self-guided tour of the Village begins at the late-eighteenth-century courthouse that contains the village museum. As the oldest public building in Westchester County, it occupies pride of place among the historic buildings in the village. It no longer serves a function other than to stand as a signifier and container of history. Small local museums, such as this, limited in funds for acquisition and research, depend upon amateur historians whose notions of local history tend to range from the sentimental and nostalgic to the purely aesthetic, from a fascination with salvaging local curiosities and the honoring of elite families to an anti-modern reverence for the simplicity of the everyday lives of ordinary people of the past. The result is a loosely organized, unsystematic collection of disparate objects.[6]

The goal of the museum is ambitious given the paucity of artifacts, for it seeks "to depict the whole range of 300 years of Bedford life and history" (Bedford Historical Society n.d.). Nevertheless, an illusion of completeness (a reality effect) is achieved by the mixing of an extraordinarily eclectic collection of objects from various time periods and (despite the presumed self-sufficiency of its past inhabitants) from different places.[7] There are many significant omissions although these are unlikely to be missed by those who expect local history to be celebratory. One would never guess from the museum tour, for example, that there were ever slaves in Bedford and that after their emancipation a small colony of freed slaves and their descendants lived on Aspetong Mountain in Bedford well into the twentieth century. Their erasure is not accidental, for there is no place for them in a museum that celebrates the mythic history of Bedford as a New England village inhabited by independent yeoman farmers. There is certainly no room for slavery in a town that insists that its history is one of "democracy in its purest form" (Barrett 1955).

Few of our informants have been inside the Bedford museum. One who has told us, "I have been to the museum a couple of times with my kids. I think it's particularly important that school children go so they can come to appreciate the history of their town." Another said, "I have been to the museum once. I didn't find it particularly interesting. That's good. It means that local school children will go, but tourists probably won't bother, and we don't want tourists in Bedford."[8]

Armed with a pamphlet offered by the museum, the visitor is invited to go outside to "see the points of historical interest," which includes a building with a small white plaque that reads, "JACKSON HOUSE, 1857. BEDFORD HISTORICAL SOCIETY."

The pamphlet explains that Jackson House was purchased by the Bedford Historical Society in order to "protect the Court House" aesthetically. Although it looks like a colonial New England building, it is a mid-nineteenth-century reproduction. As a former livery stable whose owner operated a stagecoach connecting the village to the train station in Bedford Hills, this building might be celebrated as a symbol of the mid-nineteenth-century transformation of Bedford, but this is clearly not what the history of Bedford is based around. Ironically, while Jackson House aesthetically supports the old order, it undermines it by housing a real estate office whose business thrives on the collapse of the old order that was stable, insular, and rooted in place. Furthermore, over and over again informants told us that the real estate offices in the village have displaced more useful stores, thus spoiling it as a living village.

The visitor walks past a long twentieth-century brick building housing an antique shop and other stores. Beyond that is the site of a former gas station

Fig. 7.3 Village Green and Cemetery Beyond.

with a cupola on its roof, mirroring the cupola on the roof of the courthouse. At present, plans are being drawn up for a redesigned colonial-style office building. Next to this building sits yet another colonial, housing a bank and a real estate firm, this one owned by a past president of the Bedford Historical Society.

The next historic building is a white wooden building with a front porch and a sign that reads, "OLD GENERAL STORE, c. 1838, Originally on Pound Ridge Road, also Village Post Office, Moved Here in 1890s. Acquired 1968, BEDFORD HISTORICAL SOCIETY." In addition to serving as a general store and post office, the building had also been used as an antique shop for years until its owner retired and sold the property to the Bedford Historical Society in 1968. Once associated with history in the commodified form of antiques, now the store itself has become designated as "history." Adjacent to the Old General Store is the Old Burying Ground, established in 1681. It was last used as a cemetery in 1885 and in the twentieth century fell into ruin as the old tombstones decayed and toppled while weeds and grasses turned it into a rough field. There has been sporadic interest in the Old Burying Ground in the twentieth century. In 1917, the year after the founding of the Bedford Historical Society, Miss Sarah Williamson and Mrs. James Day transcribed many of the epitaphs on the tombstones. In 1933, detailed maps were made of the cemetery under the Federal Works Projects Administration (Riso 1972). By the year 1972, when the Bedford Village Historic District was set up by town ordinance, the Old Burying Ground had become

Fig. 7.4 Historical Hall.

completely overgrown. In that year, with the help of nineteen other boy scouts, David Riso undertook as his eagle scout project the clearing of the brush and the mapping of the grave sites. Since then, as the town has become increasingly concerned with its history, the graveyard has been well kept.

Adjacent to the Old Burial Ground is the sixth point of historical interest on the tour, a large white nineteenth-century colonial-style building. The plaque on it reads, HISTORICAL HALL, 1806. Formerly a Methodist Church. Moved here 1837 from Bedford Four Corners by 20 yoke of oxen. Acquired 1916. BEDFORD HISTORICAL SOCIETY." This building is of particular significance to the history of Bedford, although this is left unremarked upon in the pamphlet. It was centrally involved in bringing about the formation of the Bedford Historical Society in 1916, in response to what the society (Bedford Historical Society 1993) calls "its first preservation crisis, to save the building from being turned into a tenement." The fact that this building was purchased from the Methodist Church by a Polish immigrant to be used for apartments for working-class people constituted what was perceived by the patrician class as a "crisis." By purchasing it, the fledgling Bedford Historical Society asserted WASP control over the symbolic heart of the village, the green. In choosing the name "Historical Hall," the society proclaimed its manifesto through this building.

On the southern edge of the village green is the School House, a small stone building. Inside is a re-creation of a nineteenth-century one-room school. The

Fig. 7.5 Schoolhouse and Catholic Church.

sign notes that the Bedford Historical Society took over the town's Historical Society in 1918. The sign calls attention to the history of the building after it was acquired by the Bedford Historical Society, placing the emphasis on the process of historic preservation and the preservers. After fifty-eight years as the principal museum in Bedford, in 1970, it was reconstructed as a schoolroom, with rows of wooden desks, old blackboards, and a wood burning stove. The pamphlet points out that it has been restored to its original condition (Bedford Historical Society, n.d.), but none of its present contents were there between 1829 and 1912. The School House, like the Court House Museum, reveals the importance of representing the aura of the past, even when historical correctness is considered unobtainable or unnecessary.

To the south of the village green stand five late-eighteenth-century and one early-nineteenth-century white wooden houses of colonial and Greek revival style. These houses each have a small plaque identifying it by the name of its original owner—for example, the "Judge Aaron Read House (c. 1785)," "Nehemiah S. Bates Homestead (1794)," and "Benjamin Hays Tavern (c. 1785)." Here we have history privately owned. Nearby is Saint Patrick's Roman Catholic Church built in 1928 in a simple New England Protestant style designed to be compatible with the local Anglo aesthetic. The Italian and Irish Catholic presence in the town is thus aesthetically and symbolically overshadowed by the Protestant English management of the landscape.

Fig. 7.6 Post Office.

The village green is a large triangle of grass flanked by tall trees. It was laid out when the town was founded in 1680, and is the most ceremonial space in the village. The village green is treasured by the residents of the town and visitors alike, not only because of its symbolic association with the historical New England village community, but because its large expanse of grass is aesthetically pleasing. In the late 1980s, one of the local garden clubs planted hop vines as a reminder that the town was originally known as the Hopp Ground. The chair of Bedford's Historic District Review Commission argued that these vines are symbolic, because hop plants "have very strong roots and once they get firmly established, they're hard to dislodge. They're like people in Bedford. It's appropriate" (*New York Times* 1987, 31). One can see here history being converted into heritage. Local history buffs in the late nineteenth century decided to retell the story of the Hopp Ground and incorporate the hop vine into the town seal. While the early settlers had worked hard to clear the stubborn hop vines from the village green, we now see the celebration of the vine through the ideology of heritage and then the imagining of a shared psychological character extending over the centuries reaffirming the value of rootedness in the community.

Across the road from the southeast corner of the village green stands the white wooden Presbyterian Manse, built in 1865, and the Presbyterian Church, a tall white Victorian Gothic structure erected in 1872. This church was built during the first wave of new affluent settlers in Bedford from New York City. As such, it is a late-nineteenth-century imposition that is seen to refer to history generally rather than to the old agrarian order specifically. The aura of history represented by authentically old buildings and others that are considered "in keeping" is enough to satisfy the taste for the historical. Adjacent to the church is the Post Office, a white wooden Greek revival building. The sign outside the building reads, "POST OFFICE, c. 1838." Although it was originally a harness shop in a different location and did not become the village post office until the 1930s, again it is the historical look or aura rather than correctness that is valued.

The next point of historical interest is the Lounsbery Building, built in the Greek revival style in 1906. This housed the local A&P supermarket for many years. It was the first A&P store in the United States not to have the trademark red front. It was leased to the chain on condition that it not be painted red. The aesthetic restrictions on the lease inspired a *New Yorker* cartoon showing a local matron and visitor to the village gazing across the Bedford village green. The caption reads, "We're terribly proud of our little town. I defy you to spot the A&P." This cartoon points to an aesthetics of disappearance. The obscuring of the A&P reflects the same mentality as the "hiding" of the Catholic Church making it resemble a New England Congregational Church. In 1972, the A&P building was purchased by the Bedford Historical Society and leased to what it termed "a more suitable type of business," first a fine antiques shop and now a shop selling riding equipment.

Adjacent to the Lounsbery Building is a colonial-style red brick firehouse with a white cupola on the roof, built in 1930. Next to it stands the Bedford Free Library, a small white two-story building also with a cupola on the roof. The plaque in front of the building reads, "Bedford Academy Building. Erected 1807. Bedford Free Library. Since 1908. Given by Corporation of Bedford Academy to Bedford Historical Society 1972." The pamphlet tells the visitor that this school building was erected "with funds contributed by John Jay and other leading citizens." It goes on to say that this was "one of Westchester's first classical schools" and that "many well known men received their schooling here, including the first United States Cardinal, John McCloskey, Jay's grandson, John Jay II, and William H. Vanderbilt." This two-story private school existed cheek by jowl throughout the nineteenth century with the one-room public schoolhouse. The former was to prepare the children of the local elite for "college and the professions" while the latter was for the rest of the town folk. As such, the Bedford Academy and the School House facing each other diagonally across the village green could well be seen as symbols of old class divisions within Bedford, but these are masked in the official histories by a discourse of the oneness of community. Flanking the entrance to the library's front garden are two huge sycamore trees beside which are bronze plaques that read, "The International Society of Arboriculture and the National Arborist Association jointly recognize this significant tree in this bicentennial year as having lived here during the American Revolutionary Period 1776–1976." The plaques announce that these trees are symbolic of both nature and history. The trees are not only old, large, and beautiful, partaking of romantic nature, but are associated with one of the greatest events in American ideology, the War of Independence.

Next to the library is another white wooden building, a colonial with large Greek revival columns, built in 1970. It replaced a small, ramshackle variety store beloved as a village eccentric—old and scruffy, but nevertheless an essential part of the local color. The building that replaced this store houses another real estate office. Although no expense was spared to make the new building blend into the streetscape, interviews showed that some old-timers missed the variety store of their youth and were critical of the design of its replacement, arguing that it looked "too new."

Next to the real estate office is a long, brick, two-story, twentieth-century building with shops on the ground floor, a delicatessen, a dry cleaner, yet another real estate office, and two antique shops. As with all the other stores in the village, the names of the businesses are painted in the discrete black lettering required by the Bedford Village Historic District code above the entrances to the shops. Fire-blackened oak barrels containing flowers decorate the fronts of the shops enhancing the historic look of the village. New, old-looking pink brick has recently replaced the cement sidewalks in the village and traditional-style street lighting has been installed. We might add here that one person we interviewed wondered if Bedford is " a real colonial town" trying to look like the new reproduction [neotraditional] colonial towns and shopping centers that are "sprouting up all over the place" in the United States.

We return now to the Court House where our tour began. At the entrance to the Court House garden stands a small cannon. Its plaque reads, "English Merchant Ship's Cannon. Early 1800. Piece Found in a Swamp near Guard Hill Road about 1888 by a Mr. Earnest L. P. Hockley and Given by Him to Bedford Historical Society." This cannon raises further doubts about the practices of history in Bedford. Why was a ship's cannon found in a swamp placed in front of the courthouse? Certainly it was not there in the late eighteenth or nineteenth centuries. Perhaps because symbolically it stands for the Revolution, independence, self-reliance, and the constitutional right to bear arms. Once again, the Bedford Historical Society can be seen to be improving upon history by filling gaps with the hyperreal.[9]

The brick path leading to the Court House is bordered by a small garden built in memory of the wife of an ex-president of the Bedford Historical Society. The garden, a plaque tells the visitor, was donated by the Bedford Historical Society, the real estate office owned by the ex-president of the society, and by one of the town's garden clubs. On the front of the building is a bronze plaque describing the building's history: "COURT HOUSE, 1787. Built when Bedford was a half shire county seat. County Courts held here 1788–1870. Board of Supervisors 1789–1829. Town Meetings until 1879. Now a Museum. BEDFORD HISTORICAL SOCIETY." Another plaque next to the entrance reads,

"BEDFORD COURT HOUSE. Erected 1787 by Westchester County. Given to Town of Bedford 1878. Restored 1966–1970. Bedford Historical Society. New York State Historic Trust." This second, equally prominent plaque celebrates the management and restoration of the building and the "practices of history." A final plaque on the building marks the creation of the Bedford Village Historic District. It reads, "The Bedford Historic District. Comprising the original village laid out in 1681 was created in 1972. By an ordinance adopted by The Bedford Town Board through the efforts of HALSTED PARK, JR., President Bedford Historical Society. DONALD W. MARSHALL, Town Historian Bedford. ROGER S. COOLEDGE, President The Bedford Association. The district was placed on the National Register of Historic Places in 1973. Erected by the Town of Bedford, New York in Observance of the Bicentennial year of Independence 1976." This last plaque, we would argue, is revealing of the Bedford Historical Society's attitude toward history and the contemporary uses to which history is often put. Only three of the eighteen lines of text on the plaque speak of the history of the village, pointing out that it was laid out in 1681. The other fifteen lines speak of the contemporary individuals and institutions wishing to associate their names with this history. The individualism expressed in the wording of this plaque is quite striking. Fully one-third of the space is devoted to the names and titles of three local officials, and their names are inscribed in large block letters while their institutional titles appear in small letters. But who is it that is celebrating these people who have "created history" in the village? They are in effect celebrating themselves, linking their own identity to that of the village, becoming a part of the historic landscape that they have brought into being.

One of the things that strike us as remarkable about the Bedford Village Historic District is the number of plaques there—not only on the buildings (the Court House alone has three) but, as we have seen, there are even plaques identifying the two historic trees. Why are there so many signs announcing the historic? What other functions do these signs serve? First, the Bedford Historical Society conceives of the Bedford Village Historic District as a museum and as such the practices of museology (cataloguing and labeling) pertain. Second, the late-eighteenth- and nineteenth-century buildings are simple, wooden structures, not very different from many of the more recent surrounding buildings. To most people the old buildings and later copies are indistinguishable. Thus the plaques are necessary for they say in effect, this one is historic, even though it might not look any different from the other. These plaques, then, partake of the discourses of authenticity, of individualism, of genealogy, and of corporate-style philanthropy where giving and public service, although genuine and generous, constitute advertising that draws on the fact that local history is valued.

History, to use the terminology of Fred Hirsch (1976), is a "positional good." Were it not for the aura of the original, then there could be hundreds of Bedford Villages. Although the originals are necessary for the aura of that which is scarce, copies help to support these originals.[10] Having said this, we hasten to add that the relationship between the copy and the original is very complex. Jean Baudrillard (1988) and Judith Butler (1990) argue that the fetish of the original is based in the ideology of romanticism but that the distinction between an original and a copy is problematic. While we take their point, we would counter that the refusal to accept the idea of an original only makes sense at the level of ontology. In sociological terms, the distinction between an original and a copy is often extremely important to people and a whole series of status and economic differences flow from it. In order to understand the practices of history and historical preservation, we recognize the distinction as both socially constructed and real because it is consequential. To the residents of Bedford, having a courthouse built in the late eighteenth century is fundamentally different from having a late-twentieth-century copy of such a building.

Certainly our informants think of Bedford as a historic place. As one woman said, "Bedford is a New England colonial village. The fact that they have kept the green and original buildings means that basically it's the same as it was in colonial times." Another woman concurred, "What's good is they have preserved the buildings, but they haven't added historical reproductions, which give it a fake look. It looks like a living museum, rather than a museum for tourists. In Bedford, we want to discourage tourists." One woman was quite explicit that the historic is an aesthetic style: "The historic buildings in Bedford Village are charming and picturesque. It's not that the authenticity is so important. I don't care if they are exactly historically correct. To be attractive, they have to look real, not overly renovated or reproduced. Reproductions are fine, but they must be extraordinarily well done and most reproductions you see aren't."

However, a number of people felt that historic preservation was in part to blame for what they saw as the decline of Bedford as a so called "real" village. One woman said, "Bedford Village as a village has changed. There is no new building, and the buildings that are there are in better shape than when I was a child. But in so carefully regulating the historic character of the village, they seem to have driven all the real businesses out. I guess it's a trade-off that just had to be made." Another woman concurred, "Maybe Bedford Village is a little too cute; a mini-Williamsburg, but it reflects the care of people who appreciate the historical past. The downside is you don't have a self-sufficient town . . . But I'd rather have that than have it all built up." These women were willing to exchange what they saw as functionality for aesthetics. One of our informants who grew up in Bedford was not happy about this exchange, however. She said bitterly, "It used to be a typical New England village, a community. But now it's lost its character and has become a suburban village. There's no community left, just antique shops and real estate offices. Now it's a museum; it's dead; it just thinks of itself as a New England village."

The official Bedford Historical Society view is expressed by its past president, himself a descendant of a first settler and real estate broker:

> When we look at these old buildings here, we are reminded of our ancestors who toiled day after day to make a living for their families and keep the town alive. To not take care of these buildings and ignore what they mean to those of us who live and work here would be a crime. Preserving these landmarks gives our grandchildren a chance to see and appreciate what was and ensure that there will always be something around to remind them where we came from. (Wolfson 1995)

There is a blurring here typical of Bedford Historical Society pronouncements. Residents are being asked to remember this man's ancestors (not their own, for most residents' families, as we have pointed out, were not here before the twentieth century). For most residents in Bedford, there is nothing here to remind them of where they came from. Perhaps for some, this is why a place like Bedford is appealing. For most, however, claiming Bedford is more an appropriation of a heritage as a class-based positional good than a rejection of their own ancestry. People's historical attachments are multifaceted. Commodified heritage gives them more scope to create new hybrid place-based identities that incorporate, among other things, an old New England WASP veneer, not as an ethnicity so much as a class signifier. For others still, their imagined link is a new "imagined community" in which the old WASP establishment is increasingly irrelevant. Possession of land like possession of citizenship may or may not reflect heritage. It is something more akin to appreciation of a work of art or a set of values that is ever evolving and continually reappropriated in subtle ways.

The Traffic Light Controversy

Perhaps nothing better illustrates the importance of an aestheticized notion of history to Bedford than the five-year battle between the state and the town over whether to place a traffic light near the southwestern corner of the village green. With the increase in population in Westchester during the 1980s, towns like Bedford have experienced greatly increased automobile traffic. During the early 1980s, the New York State Department of Transportation (DOT) became concerned about congestion around the Bedford village green where Routes 22 and 172 intersect. A number of merchants in Bedford Village were also concerned that there was no longer sufficient parking in the village. In 1987, the DOT proposed a plan to eliminate a small portion of the village green adjacent to Route 22, place a traffic light near it, and encroach upon another part of it for parking. This, they argued, would improve traffic flow and safety and be good for village merchants.

The outcry from residents of Bedford was immediate and intense. The Bedford Historic District Review Commission spearheaded the resistance to the plan. The battle was scripted by the commission and the media as a struggle between history, aesthetics, and local self-determination on the one hand and modernization, utilitarianism, and state intervention or invasion on the other. A local newspaper *The Ledger* (1988a, 1988b) ran two articles on February 10, 1988, the first titled "Too precious to lose," which urged citizens to "stop the massacre of the Bedford Village Green," and the second titled "History, traffic square off at Bedford's Village Green." A member of the Bedford Historic District Review Commission claimed that "we'd have very little trouble getting people to lie down in front of steamrollers if the state decided to push something we don't agree with." The commission contacted the state Senator Mary Goodhue who lives in Bedford. On February 11, 1988, the senator wrote the following letter to A. E. Dickson, regional director of the New York State DOT (Goodhue to Dickson, Bedford Historical Society Library, February 11, 1988):

> I have been hearing from many residents of Bedford that the DOT plans to invade the Bedford Village Green in a manner which is offensive to our historians and others who are deeply concerned with maintaining the character of this unique and living testament to the lifestyles of our ancestors. I feel strongly that the Bedford Village Green is "off limits" to any modern traffic designs. I urge that no plan be adopted by the DOT without the consent of the Bedford Supervisor and the Bedford Planning and Town Boards, with some notice to myself before any plan is adopted. I really feel *strongly* about this. You are tinkering with our history, which must be given priority in this case.

On March 13, 1988, the *New York Times* ran an article titled "Traffic and history cross at Bedford's Village Green." They, like the Bedford Historic District Review Commission, presented the case as history versus utilitarian concerns. The DOT, which was on the defensive by this point, argued that their concern was the safety of local people. The chair of the Bedford Historic District Review Commission argued, "The green is still the center of the town and it's the symbolic heart of the whole community." A spokesperson for a group of local merchants argued for community over history, saying, "If we do nothing [to improve business], then I think the hamlet will die . . . you have to deal with both change and tradition." On April 5, 1988, the Bedford Historic District Review Commission wrote a letter to the Town Board with copies to the Planning Board, Senator Goodhue, and Assemblyman Henry Barnett, objecting to a plan submitted to the DOT by the Planning Board that would have encroached upon the village green (Bedford Historic Review Commission to Town Board, Bedford Historical Society Library, April 5, 1988). The letter went on to say that the Planning Board appeared to be forgetting "the importance to Bedford of its historical heritage." This was followed on April 11 by a letter from the chair of the Bedford Historic District Review Commission to the regional construction engineer of the DOT stating that this is "still another lessening of the aesthetic value of this historic district" (Carlebach to Bauman, Bedford Historical Society Library, April 11, 1988).

The DOT finally backed down on their plans to change the look of the village green. However, the commission's victory was short-lived, for in 1989 a young driver was seriously injured at the intersection of Routes 22 and 172 at the southern edge of the village green, when she failed to halt at a stop sign. The driver's attorney argued that "it didn't look like an intersection. People couldn't see the stop sign" (Cole 1995). The driver subsequently charged the DOT with negligence for failing to install a traffic light. Pressure on the DOT and Bedford Village mounted further when a local woman was killed crossing the road near the village green in 1990. In 1991, a judge of the Court of Claims ruled that the DOT was negligent and awarded the driver injured in the 1989 accident $350,000. (Cole 1995) In his judgment, he wrote,

> Clearly the parochial concerns of the residents of this Town placed the safety of out-of-town drivers a distant second to the ability to take a walk on the Village Green without having their field of vision cluttered by such a distraction as a traffic signal. It is, in my opinion, absolutely inexcusable for the State officials charged with keeping our highways safe for the travelling public to capitulate to local concerns. (Cole 1995)

The state attorney general's office immediately appealed the case, but the DOT responded by putting renewed pressure on Bedford Village to accept a traffic light. They argued that an average of 2,000 cars used these roads during peak hours and that there were about ten serious accidents a year in this area (*New York Times*, 1992).

In order to argue its case to the state, Bedford commissioned its own traffic study and presented its findings in January 1992 (Bedford Village Green Traffic Study 1992). It argued that a traffic light near the village green would destroy the "sense of place" of the community and proposed a one-way traffic flow around the green:

> Of all the elements that knit a community together, perhaps the most important is a sense of place. A sense of place is an ephemeral, almost indefinable quality, but it is composed of definable elements, most of them seemingly unimportant in and of themselves, but vital in their totality. Bedford is blessed with a "sacred place"... a focus of village life... whose importance is clearly recognizable to its citizens.
>
> But the Green's sacredness is fragile. True, much of its importance lies in the memory of its age and historical significance; but it is also composed of physical elements... its shape, contours, trees and plants, memorials and monuments... that can be too easily violated or destroyed. Towns across the nation are seeking somehow to recover a sense of place that they have lost. Bedford never lost that sense of place... but now it is clearly threatened. (Bedford Village Green Traffic Study 1992)

The report continues that the village green derives its sense of place from the,

> *totality* of the environment experienced by the individual... The experience of being in a special, historic place can be enhanced when that place contains cohesive and historically appropriate furnishings and materials. By the same token,

> inconsistent or inappropriately placed elements...even seemingly innocuous
> features such as lights and curbs...can rob an historic area of that sense of
> history and specialness. (Bedford Green Traffic Study 1992)

The choice to highlight sense of place as the crux of the issue in their case
against the DOT's plan to install a traffic light was astute. The romantic notion
of sense of place shifts what residents see as politically weak aesthetic criteria
into politically and legally more acceptable criteria such as historic and community preservation. Articles in a local newspaper drummed up support for the
fight against the traffic light by arguing that local self-determination was being
undermined—for example, "the State has an obligation to respect the residential character" of Bedford (Schwartz 1992a), and the "traffic light will urbanize
Bedford" (Schwartz 1992b). The latter resonates with the committee's claim
that the rural community would be shattered and replaced by placelessness or
an urban sense of alienation.

In March 1992, sixty people gathered in the town hall to rally behind the
town's opposition to the traffic light. A petition against the DOT's plan was
circulated. The petition read, "We have a very unique thing. We have a Green
and for some magical reason, it was never changed" (Schwartz 1992c). By April,
it appeared that the DOT plan would be put into effect, but the town continued
to fight. A spokesperson for a residents' group was quoted as saying, "People will
do what they do best—rise up" (Schwartz 1992d). In May, the town supervisor
appealed to the DOT to "demonstrate their sensitivity to the Green." He also
lobbied Andrew Cuomo, the son of the governor, to use his influence to oppose
the traffic lights (Gordon 1992a).

At the beginning of July, in response to a town lawsuit to stop the traffic
light, a New York State Supreme Court judge halted the DOT project until a
comprehensive study of traffic patterns and an environmental impact study on
the Bedford Village Historic District was conducted (Gordon 1992b). In mid-
July, an article appeared in the *New York Times* (1992) casting the controversy
as a clash between "past and present." Once again, Bedford was represented
as an island of rural history fighting off modern, urban America. On July 28,
the DOT submitted papers to the appellate division of the New York State
Supreme Court attesting to the fact that the "Green is currently unsafe" and
resumed construction on the traffic light (Gordon 1992c). In spite of protests
by residents against the work crews, the traffic light was in place by the end of
the summer. However, it was not placed right next to the village green but down
the road a little way away from the center of the village. (Cole 1995).

Knowing that this was an emotionally charged issue, we asked our informants
what they thought of the traffic light. For some, the issue of safety was paramount
and therefore they favored the light. Interestingly, while the DOT was primarily
concerned about the driver who was suing them, residents always mentioned
the local woman who was killed when citing their concerns about safety. One

woman said, "The light is great. I didn't want it at first, but it really is necessary to slow down traffic. All of the hub-bub wasn't necessary." One man thought that the light was necessary because of the types of people who had moved into town recently: "The new people race all over the place. They needed a light in the village. It's a shame that a lady had to die for it to happen." A village merchant had this to say:

> This is the best thing that ever happened. Now even the most outspoken people against it are happy. There was so much opposition. It [the light] could have been done better. They could have had a better-looking light, more hidden. There was animosity between the state and the town. The state won out and they didn't compromise very much. We were worried about the historic character of the town.

In fact, not everyone was happy about the light. Some people were distinctly ambivalent. One woman felt an unresolved tension between aesthetics and safety: "The problem is that they needed a light there, but the plans would have significantly changed the green. They wanted to take part of the green away. It would have spoiled the aspect of the village. I suppose it's all right." Another woman saw the traffic light as part of inevitable change:

> What the DOT wanted to do to the green was wrong, awful. Andrew Cuomo came to town. This is an example of the clout the town has. He was persuaded that it would be wrong to destroy the green. They were going to perform this abortion on it. I don't find the light offensive now. It's just an indication of the unstoppable urbanization of Bedford.

Those respondents who saw the issue primarily in aesthetic terms were still critical of the light. One longtime resident said shaking her head, "If they really do need the light in Bedford, it seems a shame. It doesn't really look like Bedford anymore with a traffic light near the green, which is so much a symbol of Bedford." Another woman put it even more strongly, "Bedford Village used to be a little sentimental country New England village with a lovely green. Then they put in that red light. I hate the village now. I avoid it." Yet another woman who grew up in Bedford said, "They've spoiled the village. It looks like Yonkers[11] now." We leave the final word to a policeman who observed the protests over the light in the village:

> The light in Bedford says it all. People actually tried to run over the DOT men who were hired to install the light. They went wild. I could tell you a bundle, but I'm not at liberty to. Of the people who were angry, very few had lived in Bedford more than twenty years. They feel that Bedford is their status reward. The biggest issue was that it would interfere with the historic look [of the village]. I don't mind the light at all. I thought they needed it [even] before that woman got killed.

CHAPTER 8

Another Country: Latino Labor and the Politics of Disappearance

Can't live with them, can't landscape without them.
—Purdy, 2001

Introduction

The political struggles in Mount Kisco are intimately linked to the rural aesthetic in Bedford. In Mount Kisco[1] there is a politics of the aesthetic as well, but it is openly inflected by race in a way that is masked in Bedford. Over the past decade the burning political issue in the village of Mount Kisco has been what is perceived to be an invasion of Hispanics[2] or "Guatemalans," as they are often called locally.[3] In this regard, the village and many suburban towns across the United States are at the leading edge of contemporary cultural change, for, as Michael Suarez-Orozco (1998, 5) points out, "Immigration is the driving force behind a significant transformation of American society.... Few other social phenomena are likely to affect the future character of American culture and society as much as the ongoing wave of the 'new immigration.'"[4] Mike Davis (2000, 5) speaks of a "far reaching 'Latin Americanization'" of New York and other metropolitan areas of the United States. He (2000, 15) states that U.S. Latinos are already the fourth largest "nation" in "Latin America" and in a half century will be second only to Mexico.[5] According to the U.S. Census of 2000, Latinos have become 25% of the population of Mount Kisco, but this figure is a minimal estimate. We argue that the perception of an invasion can be explained in large part by conflicting cultural conventions of public space based in an ethnocentric and class-based aesthetic.[6] It also points to a paradoxical situation in which those whose labor maintains Bedford's landscape aesthetic are themselves considered an unaesthetic element of the streetscape of Mount Kisco where Bedford residents habitually go for shopping and services.[7] Many residents of Mount Kisco and other nearby towns resent their towns becoming what they describe as "dumping grounds" or "servant's quarters" for places like Bedford.

Although smaller in population (9,983 people), it is much smaller in area than Bedford and therefore much more densely populated. It bills itself as the "commercial hub of northern Westchester" whose population swells to 20,000

Fig. 8.1   The Main Shopping Street of Mount Kisco.

daily (Mount Kisco Chamber of Commerce 1995). The village was described by one author in the mid-1970s as a "bustling market town, a heterogeneous blue collar community, a medical, automotive and shopping center" and a "beehive of business and industrial activity," "slightly more than two square miles replete with Elks, Lions, Masons, Rotarians, Kiwanis and an active Chamber of Commerce" (Shoumatoff 1977). While the village retains these elements, it has increasingly attracted younger, more highly educated residents. Off its three main avenues are peaceful village streets lined with trees and large Victorian houses lending it an air of a country town removed from urban problems. The majority of the population of Mount Kisco, although comfortable, is on average less well educated, less affluent, and less WASPY than Bedford. Fifteen years ago, Latino day laborers began to come to the village to find work. They rented the cheapest housing they could find and stood in groups on street corners, looking for work and socializing with friends. To local, non-Latinos, this represented a fundamental change in the look of the village.

The Latino day workers' housing situation is generally appalling. Local landlords can exploit Latinos because there are few low-rent apartments available in northern Westchester. A 1993 article in the *New York Times* (Berger 1993) quotes Luis Penichet of Westchester County's Hispanic Advisory Board as stating that exploitative landlords illegally rent basements, attics, and rooms to laborers who pay $150 per person to sleep in shifts, ten to a room.

A Mount Kisco village official told us in 1996, "A big problem in this area right now is that the housing inventory just isn't there. If it is available, the landlord charges $1,500 to $2,000 a month for an apartment. If you're a laborer, it forces overcrowding. Two hundred dollars a head is what most pay per month. That's seven to ten people in a one- or two-bedroom apartment." He continued,

> We couldn't allow this to go on. There are regulations and zoning ordinances that limit the number of people that can live in a housing unit. This is for the safety and health of the community. When the influx [of Latinos] began in '87 and '88, there was a fire in an apartment complex. The fire started in a unit where there were twenty-seven people living in three apartments. Some were living in closets. This is clearly not safe or healthy.

What he neglected to say was that the village's zoning code limits the amount of multi-family housing that can legally be built. The village's new development plan in 1999 suggests a need for more affordable (not necessarily low-income) housing, while arguing the need to keep the present balance between single and multi-family housing in order to retain the village's small-town character. Many of the federal and state government incentives for developers to build affordable housing disappeared during the Reagan era.[8] Although the village has more multi-family housing than surrounding towns (51% as compared to 22% in Bedford, and 7%, 11%, 21%, and 29% in the other neighboring towns), the trend has been sharply away from building affordable housing. The numbers of new units of multi-family housing built fell from 924 in the 1960s, to 395 in the 1970s, to forty-nine in the 1980s, and down to only eleven in the 1990s. Mount Kisco's willingness to welcome low-income residents has clearly declined. It has a significant percentage of overcrowded housing units (180 or 4.8%) and exploitative rents due to a severe shortage of affordable apartments. Forty percent of the village's renters are cost burdened, or pay more than 30% of their income for rent (Clark 2000).

The village's development plan suggests that a preference list for affordable housing be introduced, which would favor local residents, village employees, relatives of local residents, and people who work in the village. Such a policy clearly discriminates against newly arriving Latinos who wish to work in Bedford and other affluent towns that have even fewer rentals and higher rents. Liliana Keith, the site manager of Neighbor's Link, a recently opened job and social services center for low-income residents in the village, told us that three-bedroom houses, if one is lucky enough to find one, go for $1,300 to $1,700 a month, and one bedroom for four male occupants goes for $1,000 to $1,200 or $250 to $300 per person per month. She said that the landlords do not comply with regulations. Often there are leaking roofs, no working toilets, and no leases. There are also problems of lead paint poisoning children, but when tenants or advocates for tenants complain, the tenant often gets evicted. One landlord was fined for having over fifteen people in a single room.

Mount Kisco in Context

In order to understand why Latinos are part of a story that ties Bedford to Mount Kisco, Westchester County, New York City, and poor villages of Latin America, we will briefly place the Latinos in Mount Kisco within the context of the material circumstances and wider patterns of immigration from Latin America to Westchester County, which in turn are closely tied to American foreign policy over the past twenty years.[9] The 1980 U.S. Census records the number of Latinos living in Westchester County as 45,566. By the 1990 U.S. Census, the numbers had increased to 86,194. Ten years later, they had increased a further 67.2% to 144,124 (see Table 2.2). The actual numbers are unquestionably higher as recent immigrants, especially those without green cards living in overcrowded houses or apartments, are often afraid to fill out census forms.[10] In Mount Kisco, the number of Latinos counted by the U.S. Census rose from 401 (4.97% of the population) in 1980, to 1,108 (12.15%) in 1990. By 2000, the number had increased to 2,450 or 24.54% of the village's population (see Table 2.1). At the time of writing, the 2000 U.S. Census breakdown by nationality is not available, but according to the 1990 U.S. Census, of the 1,108 Latinos in Mount Kisco, 240 were Colombian, 165 were Salvadorian, 165 were Puerto Rican, 105 were Guatemalan, ninety-four were Peruvian, fifty-seven were Honduran, and ten were Ecuadorian. But this doesn't give a true picture of the Latino mix in Mount Kisco in the 1990s because of the impact of illegal immigration. Betty Urrutia, president of Organizacion Hispana, estimated that in 1994 50% of all Latino residents of Mount Kisco were undocumented.[11] At that time, she estimated that approximately 60% of the Latinos in the village were Guatemalan, 35% were Ecuadorian, and the other 5% were from elsewhere in Latin America (Lombardi 1994).[12] The numbers of Guatemalans in Mount Kisco have also increased during the last decade. A representative of the Neighbors' Link in Mount Kisco estimated that in 2002 about 90% of the day laborers living in Mount Kisco and/or waiting there to be picked up for work are Guatemalan.[13] Most are from the highland district of Chiquimula. In fact, some people call Mount Kisco "Chiquimula North" and say they meet fellow residents of Mount Kisco when they visit their home village.[14]

The dramatic increase in Central Americans in Westchester County is part of a wider trend toward the suburbanization of poor minority groups that began on a large scale in the 1980s. Minorities experienced a higher percentage growth in the nation's suburbs than in central cities, according to the 1990 U.S. Census.[15] Latino immigrants have been drawn to places like Westchester County because they are able to fill a growing niche in the local service economy. The New York metropolitan area has over the past 30 years developed an hourglass economy with many high- and many low-skilled jobs, but too few ways of moving from the latter into the middle class (Julca 2001; Sassen 1989, 1995). The metropolitan region was notable in the 1980s for the growth of sweatshops (Sassen 1989) and an informal and unregulated service industry

(Fernandez-Kelly and Garcia 1989) employing immigrant labor. The growth of an informal service industry in places like northern Westchester depends on a steady flow of undocumented workers to fill what Lisa Catanzarite (2000) has called "brown-collar" jobs.[16] Many of these are seasonal, nonunion, jobs with few benefits and little security (Zavella 2000). As authors such as Chris Martin (1999) and M. Patricia Fernandez-Kelly and Anna Garcia (1989) point out, the increase in wealth generated by Wall Street has produced an increased demand for status-creating personal services, which Latino workers are helping to provide. Such services are provided in a place like northern Westchester, however, under what as we shall see are often exploitative conditions. Immigrants are well aware of this, and because they have little prospect of advancement in such menial service jobs, they tend to see them as temporary forms of employment, either hoping to return to their home country or to find better, more permanent employment after a period of time (Roberts 1995; Sassen 1995).

In April 1997, the U.S. Congress placed a worldwide cap of 4,000 on the number of suspensions of deportation. Hardship to immigrants was no longer a consideration, and much of the time accrued in the United States was no longer to count toward permanent residence. Margie McHugh, executive director of the New York Immigrant Coalition, which serves about 150 immigrant groups attributed a shift in public sentiment toward immigrants to three pivotal events: the 1993 bombing of the World Trade Center in New York by Middle Eastern terrorists; the discovery off New York of the *Golden Venture*, an immigrant smuggling ship from China; and the passage of Proposition 187 in California, which ended government benefits to undocumented aliens. McHugh said, "These events served as a signal to politicians that immigrant issues would be easy pickings, one to exploit." She added that this is "the ugliest form of politics that lays blame for the country's problems on people who are seeking freedom and opportunity and are trying to build a better life" (Brenner 1996, 1–2). In April 2002, we asked Peggie Arriaza of Neighbors' Link if the events of September 11, 2001, had had any impact on the day laborers locally. She told us that there appeared to be no hardening of attitudes on the part of non-Latino residents against the laborers, but the ensuing economic downturn meant that work was harder to find and she had heard that it was tougher to get across the border now.

The twists and turns in immigration law, as well as some tightening and some loosening restrictions, have had less impact on undocumented Guatemalans in Mount Kisco than one might presume because the Immigration and Naturalization Service (INS) does not consider the scale of illegal immigration there worth prosecuting. This is consistent with the findings of Heather Muldoon (1999) who notes that there are increasing numbers of undocumented immigrants moving to small towns in the United States because the INS does not consider the levels of undocumented workers there to be sufficiently high to warrant spending resources on pursuing them. It is possible, however, that small suburban towns may soon begin to look somewhat less attractive to undocumented workers. In April 2002, the House of Representatives voted 405 to nine to abolish the INS and create two services, one concerned with entry and the other with enforcement of immigration laws (Schmitt 2002a, 2002b).[17] At that time, U.S. Attorney General John Ashcroft indicated that he is considering changing a Justice Department policy so that state and local law enforcement officers could enforce immigration laws. While the INS has 1,800 agents assigned to internal enforcement, a change in policy would increase the number of arresting officers to 300,000. Because many Latino immigrants to the United States work as exploited, seasonal day laborers [18] in an unregulated, informal sector, they tend not to compete with other groups for jobs (Fernandez-Kelly, Portes, and Zhou 1992). As we will argue, they are a cause for worry, resentment, and aversion more for social and aesthetic than economic reasons. This is certainly not to deny that deep structural, economic, and political inequalities explain why the Central Americans find themselves in such a hostile North American environment, nor to deny that their poverty contributes to the racialization of many Latin Americans. Rather, it is to say that economic factors alone are insufficient as an explanation of the unarticulated, deep-seated psychological insecurities that shape social relations between immigrants and nonimmigrants.

Getting by in Mount Kisco

Since the mid-1980s, every morning except Sunday from 6:30 on groups of men (often a hundred or more) have waited to be picked up by contractors and householders on the main streets of Mount Kisco and at Kirby Plaza next to the train station.[19] Often while having breakfast in a local diner, we overheard groups of older men grumbling about all the "Guatemalans" in town. "They can't even speak English" is a frequent complaint. Another said with obvious resentment, "When I came to this country from Italy years ago, no one cared if I had housing or a job. The Guatemalans are given a community hall. We had to make our own way." We met a local businessman who pointed out that "Earlier in the century, it was the Italians who came here and did what the Guatemalans are doing. Everyone in Bedford wants to be the last ones in. So soon they forget."[20]

In 1996, we briefly employed a research assistant, Luis Lujan, to conduct interviews with day laborers. He spoke in Spanish with six men in a group of twenty aged seventeen to thirty-five while they were waiting for work on a street corner in Mount Kisco. The men who were all from Chiquimula in the highlands of Guatemala said that although they had no family members in Mount Kisco, they each had come to town because they knew someone there. One man said, "You need to know someone who will help support you in the beginning." Another said, "We work here doing gardening and small jobs during the summer. We wait here every morning to be picked up by someone who needs workers. On a good day we can make $70 or $80, but sometimes the boss doesn't pay us.[21] We argue with him, but what can we do? There is

Fig. 8.2 Latinos Gardening in Bedford.

no one to complain to."[22] Village officials say the workers should complain to them. The workers rarely do, however, because of their limited ability to speak English, a fear on the part of some of being deported if they are seen to make trouble, and because local officials have often been unsympathetic. A village official said to Luis at the time, "They have a distrust of authority that makes it difficult to help them." They have had good grounds for being wary of the help that local officials offer, although as we show below, the current village administration has found that cooperation and more active involvement with the day laborers has improved the situation for everyone. Graciela Heymann of the Westchester Hispanic Coalition, the largest social service organization for Latino immigrants in the United States, says of the day laborers' unwillingness to pursue bad employers, "In Guatemala or in these dictatorships, it doesn't do a lot of good to confront the authorities. There's a very rigid class system—the employers belong to the upper class" (Rae 1998a).

Some Latino workers have steady work and rarely or never stand out waiting for work. We talked to a man from Honduras who came to the United States seven years ago and hasn't been back since, although he has a green card and plans to go next year.[23] He says he is treated well by shopkeepers and feels welcome in Mount Kisco even though he still speaks very little English. He can't attend English classes because he doesn't finish his gardening work early enough. After the first few years, he managed to find a "patron" who gave him part-time work and helped him to find work with other people. In the summer, he tries to work until dark every chance he gets. He says that unlike some other towns, Mount Kisco has a lot of Hondurans and he knows lots of people there from other Latin American countries.

We interviewed one man who has worked in Bedford since 1990. He doesn't have a green card, but is beginning the process of getting one by declaring all his income and refusing off-the-books jobs:

> When I came here from Colombia, I got a job with a man who hired lots of us to do gardening. He paid us very little, maybe $5 an hour. After a year, I found I could get work for myself, so why pay him? But you have to speak some English if you work for yourself. That's why many don't. They only speak Spanish. Now I charge $12 an hour and keep it all for myself. I work at five different houses— some for a day, some for two each week. I start at seven or eight in the morning and work until six. Sometimes I go and work at another place until it is dark. I do gardening and handyman work. I work every day but Sunday all summer. I make in a day here the same as I made in a month in Colombia. I am saving money and sending it home. I go home in the winter. There is no work here and it's too cold. I don't have to work at home. I just live.

We spoke to a woman in her late twenties from Guatemala who works each week in several houses in Bedford. She has obtained these jobs through a cleaning service that she has worked for ever since she arrived in the United States.[24] She also has no green card. She told us,

> I don't speak any English so I have to do work like this. I have been here two years and you are the first Americano I have spoken to because you speak Spanish. I like it here because of the money but I miss my family and friends at home. I have got to know lots of other people here in Mount Kisco so it's not too lonely. But I miss home. I am sending money back and I hope to visit next year.

A Salvadoran woman in her forties runs a housecleaning service based largely in Bedford that hires Latinas. Her English is fluent. She has a green card and has lived in Westchester for ten years.

> Most of the girls [that I hire] don't speak English. I can help them because I know what it's like when you come here first. I am making good money with this business. I charge about $20 to $25 an hour and pay the girls $7 an hour. I do about three houses at a time. We are making good money here. Last year my husband and I bought a house in El Salvador. It cost over $100,000 and we are renting it out. Someday when we have more money, we will go back to El Salvador to live.

When we asked some Guatemalan day laborers about their housing, they looked uncomfortable and fell silent. Finally one man said without conviction, "There are eight of us who share a four-bedroom apartment." Another man, a Honduran, told us that he pays $250 per month and sleeps in a living room with three other men. He sublets from Mexicans whom he doesn't like. He says it is typical for different nationality groups to resent being forced to live together because of lack of choice in housing. A woman who works as a cleaner told us, "I rent a room in Mount Kisco with some friends. It is small with only one little window, and expensive. There is no proper place to cook or to entertain my friends. I feel that I am not really living here, just working. I would like to find a nicer and cheaper place to live."

The extent of the housing crisis was brought to the attention of area residents in February 1999 when four Latino men were found living in wetlands near the village. In December of that year, a man, who had been evicted from his residence, was found living in a tent in the woods. In another incident, two Latino men were found living in an abandoned house in the village. In Bedford, two men were found living in cardboard boxes. While residents of the village were shocked to find homelessness there, Pastor Frank Vega whose Iglesia Hispana-Fuente de Vida in Mount Kisco has 300 Latino congregants, said they shouldn't be, because rents are so high (Driscoll 1999b). In 2001, thirty homeless day laborers were found living in the woods in Mount Kisco. Representatives of the Westchester Hispanic Coalition managed to find them jobs and housing (Driscoll 2002b).

Brownout: The Spaces of White Privilege

The number of Latinos spending many hours either waiting for offers of day-laboring jobs or socializing on the streets has, in the past five to ten years, reached what many non-Latinos consider to be an unacceptable critical mass. This highly visible nonwhite presence has become a constant topic of conversation, not only in Mount Kisco but to a lesser degree in Bedford as well. Those who are noticed as being Latinos are those whose visible, physiological characteristics of skin color, stature, and features mark them as indigenous (pre-Columbian or Amerindian), moreno (African or West Indian), mestizo, or mulatto looking. It is this racialized,[25] bodily difference as well as certain highly visible practices, especially among males—for example, socializing in public and walking or bicycle riding on roads designed for cars and trucks—that differentiates and racializes them, marking them as poor.

Local opinion ranges from what might be termed "moral panic"[26] to paternalistic "tolerance," including a desire to help the newly immigrated assimilate to "proper American middle-class" ways of behaving in public space. The most extreme of the many nativist reactions recorded in the 1999 public opinion survey for the new Mount Kisco Development Plan accuse immigrants of undermining the integrity of national space and of threatening the United States through various means including terrorism. One respondent went so far as to say that, since the bombing of the World Trade Center in 1993, he feels he cannot trust any immigrants, any one of whom he sees as a potential terrorist. How and why he should distinguish among them is of no consequence to him. Most of the remarks about Latinos made in the public opinion survey mentioned above reveal an implicit, unreflexive form of nativism. Among many local non-Latinos, there is a strong, visceral distaste for what are seen as the foreign looking, indigenous American features and skin color of poor Latino men whom they accuse of loitering. Loitering here is a racialized, gendered, and class-based concept in that it is the difference in appearance and ways of being male of those socializing on street corners that makes their behavior so offensive and sometimes threatening to middle- and upper-middle-class non-Latinos.[27] The same behavior by unmarked middle-class whites, including middle-class, light-skinned Latinos, might not be so immediately defined as loitering.[28] An interesting example of the way race is crosscut by class[29] is provided by Edward Chacon, a Guatemalan immigrant who in thirteen years progressed in Mount Kisco from a dishwasher to landscaper to financial analyst at Citibank. He said he found that acceptance was largely based on appearance: "When I wear my name tag from work in the street, I'm treated with respect. If I dress casual, they treat me like garbage" (Gross 2000a). Graciela Heyman of the Westchester Hispanic Coalition also argues that discrimination is not just about race: "It's a class thing. Because the men are skuzzy, they're short, and they're brown" (Gross 2000a).

Identity in the United States, on the part of nonimmigrants, is defined in large part against and in contrast to an outside world beyond its borders (a constitutive outside). To many, the very bodies of undocumented immigrants can be said to act as a metaphor for insecure national boundaries. As Susan Mains (2000, 151) says, immigrant bodies are marked as "separate, marginal, [and] different." The idea of insecure borders is aggravating or alarming to many nonimmigrants (Price 2000). Furthermore, many residents feel that the visibility of racialized difference, the phenotypic differences, act as daily reminders of the vulnerability of Mount Kisco to the negative externalities of more affluent towns: "Our town is a dumping ground." "We want our town back!" people said in the village survey. Furthermore, in the United States, the visible presence of males congregating in public spaces is often seen as signifying a challenge to the individualistic public order. Nevertheless, nonimmigrant attitudes toward immigration are ambivalent (Nevins 2002, 95–122). The historical narrative of the successful assimilation of immigrants into a vast melting pot is widely celebrated. Contemporary immigration, however, is often viewed with suspicion. Although diversity and multiculturalism are sometimes successfully embraced as enriching aesthetic and commercial themes, as political values, they are too often associated with a political correctness foisted on the nonimmigrant population.

As Etienne Balibar (1991, 40) points out, "[T]here is not merely a single invariant racism but a number of racisms."[30] Iris Marion Young (1990, 141–42), following Joel Kovel (1984), distinguishes between "dominative" and "aversive" racism. The former is an openly admitted and practiced racism while the latter is a racism of avoidance and separation. While dominative racism has characterized much of nineteenth- and early-twentieth-century race relations, especially in the American South, since then the most common form in the United

States has been aversive racism. The shift is one from racism at the level of discursive to practical consciousness. Explicit theories of white or Anglo-Saxon supremacism, although present in Bedford and Mount Kisco as elsewhere in the United States, are marginalized today. At present few people would admit to being racist; however, Young claims that aversive racism is widespread. The problem, Young says, is that reactions of aversion to people of another race, though profound, is largely unacknowledged as racism. Such reactions are primarily bodily, material, and unconscious. They include nervousness, avoidance, disgust, and distancing. Local examples of aversive racism would be negative aesthetic reactions to the bodily presence of Latinos in Mount Kisco and the sounds of their speech, music, and consumption styles.

Because places, especially homeplaces, are so closely associated with one's sense of identity, the presence of cultural Others attempting to share one's residential space can be deeply threatening. As Patricia Price (2000, 104) argues, the blurring of insider and outsider undermines place identity and leads to its rupture. The impact of this rupture can be profound as it can shatter the illusion of a stable identity.[31] People may feel aversive racism for different reasons either because their place-based identity is undermined by being spatially and economically close to members of a disdained group or because they have been taught to reject discursive racism. Julia Kristeva's (1982) concept of the "abject" introduces the idea of ambiguity as threatening or loathsome, adding a visceral and psychological dimension to our understanding of aversive racism. When one's social relations to Others are not clear or agreed upon, if they seem uncontrolled, illegal, or disrespectful of norms, these relations become difficult to tolerate. Many of those who object to Latino presence are Italian Americans, whose ancestors suffered hatred and spatial exclusion in the late nineteenth century (when Italian immigrants rioted in Mount Kisco protesting against unfair working conditions, and the whole village of Katonah was deed restricted against selling or renting property to Italian immigrants). They are as quick as anyone else to urge the village to solve the Hispanic problem.[32]

While some may indeed enjoy the color and enrichment of ethnic restaurants, world music, foreign travel, and multiculturalism in their urban experiences, they choose a more familiar, culturally homogeneous, safer aesthetic at home precisely because their liberal ideology requires them to embrace a narrative of equality that disallows overt racism.[33] Because of affluent Americans' aesthetic mode of treating foreign subjects, setting becomes important. Foreigners appreciated as romantic and colorful in their proper foreign place can become a repugnant and intrusive presence in American homespaces where a secure and stable retreat from the challenges of a globalizing world is sought. Many such people expect their homespace to provide continuity with either the real or imagined landscapes of childhood, to provide them with a mirror of their social selves and perhaps, more important, their memories or fantasies of the good life. In order to achieve this, their homespace must be purified.

To Young's notions of dominative and aversive racism can be added white privilege. Laura Pulido (2000, 13) defines "white privilege" as an unconscious form of racism resulting from a lifelong inculcation that takes as natural "the privileges and benefits that accrue to white people by virtue of their whiteness" (Devine 1989; Lawrence 1987).[34] It "thrives in highly racialized societies that espouse racial equality, but in which whites will not tolerate either being inconvenienced in order to achieve racial equality—or denied the full benefits of their whiteness" (Pulido 2000, 15). White privilege is such a powerful force, Pulido argues, precisely because most whites are unconscious of it and thus, unlike in the case of dominative or even aversive racism, they can exonerate themselves from racism.[35] She (Pulido 2000, 16) argues, "The full exploitation of white privilege requires the production of places with a very high proportion of white people. 'Too many' people of color might reduce a neighborhood's status, property value, or general level of comfort for white people." Pulido says that white privilege underlies institutional racism. We would add that as well as underlying institutional racism, white privilege is also greatly enabled by institutional racism. We have discussed the institutional basis for the relative homogeneity of towns like Bedford. Residents need not be racists, or at least not confront any racism they may harbor in order to enjoy their privilege because of institutional racism such as the Federal Housing Authority's mobilization of bias against nonwhite homeowners.

The immigrants who stand on the streets of Mount Kisco are there in large part because of the increasing demand for their labor on Bedford's great estates and smaller would-be estates. They help to sustain the narrative structure of Bedford's landscape by re-creating and maintaining its walls, gardens, lawns, and country houses. And yet they don't quite look the part. Furthermore, because their presence is seen as a manifestation of the suburbanization of urban and global problems, they are thought to be a very mixed blessing by residents of Bedford.

Many of Mount Kisco's Central Americans have inadequate private space in which to entertain, and furthermore they have a culture of socializing in large groups in public; this is especially true of the men (Low 2000). As we pointed out earlier, this use of space deeply troubles many non-Latinos for it challenges key tenets of privatism and individualism that have become extended to the level of community. A suburban community for many Anglo Americans is an exclusive, semiprivate space where people of like minds and similar tastes do not so much interact, as maintain similar aestheticized, private lifestyles. The presence of racially marked outsiders offends the aesthetic of homogeneity necessary to the maintenance of such a community. It is not so much the actuality of the presence of poor Latinos in the area as their visibility that disrupts the spatial/moral order of white suburban society. To put it bluntly, as many of our informants did, the presence of the Latino day laborers on village streets is thought to spoil the look of the landscape. Such concerns are far from unique to Mount Kisco.

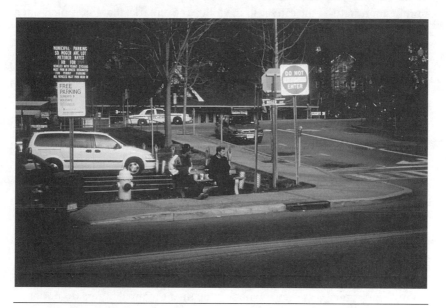

Fig. 8.3   Latinos on Moger Avenue.

Don Mitchell (1997) argues that underpinning the growing number of anti-homeless laws in the United States is a concern for landscape aesthetics.

Even though the village public opinion survey did not specifically ask about loitering, a large number of the respondents (118) offered optional written comments stating loitering as the major problem facing Mount Kisco.[36] In response after response, loitering or hanging-out is mentioned, and in others, it is alluded to through the use of code words such as "quality of life." In many of the questionnaires, the issue of loitering is slipped in wherever possible in answer to many different types of questions. The naturalized concept of loitering is culturally and historically specific in ways often unacknowledged by most who complain. In Latin America, far more than in the United States, civic and social life takes place in plazas and other public places. On moving to the United States, Latinos are expected to abandon their normal modes of interacting and reproducing their community spatially. This expectation is communicated to Latinos as a helpful part of what non-Latinos see as a necessary assimilation process.

In response to a survey question about what detracts from the quality of life in Mount Kisco, a large number of answers referred to loitering—for example, "Groups of day laborers grouping downtown and sitting around the town on park benches," "Loitering takes away from the village. Many people will not come to town," "Loitering detracts from the quality of life in Mount Kisco," "The men that are illegal and stand around Main Street," and "Too many illegal people standing around." The term "illegal people" spoken thoughtlessly is revealing of the attitude that the Latinos of Mount Kisco have come to embody their immigration status. One can see in the following remarks that loitering is often seen in aesthetic terms as visually offensive bodily behavior—for example, "The loitering problem on Maple Avenue and along Lexington is getting to be an eyesore," "The beautiful benches are occupied by day workers," "Young men perched on the benches [are] unsightly," and "Illegal aliens [are] cluttering up the Kirby Plaza." A large number of comments made about noise and the sounds of Spanish being spoken in the village shows that people object to what they see as aural as well as visual pollution—for example, "The new immigrants take away from the beauty of the village by hanging around and not learning the language." Others remarked that they "despised the Latinos who hang out in the town on the street corners and gazebo." They argued that "day laborers shouldn't be in Kirby Plaza." Presumably such comments are made unreflexively without irony and with little thought about what plazas, gazebos, and benches are designed for or what the definition and cultural history of the plaza is (Low 2000). Ironically the village stopped the day laborers from using Leonard Park, the one outdoor space where people are expected to come together in groups. Citing the residency requirement for using the park, the village asked for driver's licenses and signed leases, two types of document many laborers do not have, but did not regularly check non-Latinos for proof of residence.

The fact that Hispanic men make comments to women and are sometimes perceived as leering and eyeballing women adds to the intimidating appearance of the day workers. Residents made comments such as, "You can't walk around town at certain times without comments from people hanging out on the streets," "Loitering detracts—way too many men roaming, too many groups hanging around the town is very intimidating," "The look is disturbing sometimes for a single woman," "There are too many people hanging out on the village streets, day workers without proper police presence," "There are too many Hispanics hanging out on the street corners and a lack of police presence," and "There is loitering of rough types at Kirby Plaza and the train station."[37] Many respondents specifically mentioned Kirby Plaza[38] in front of the village train station as the main hangout of Latinos. The thrust of these comments about loitering is that the quality of life of residents is threatened; quality of life, in this sense, as Don Mitchell (1997, 326) points out, prioritizes the aesthetic values of the middle class over the survival of the poor.

While some of the residents call for more police presence, in fact the same survey reveals that residents of Mount Kisco are overwhelmingly satisfied with the quality of their police protection; 369 were satisfied, sixty-one were not, and fifty-one had no opinion (Clark 2000).[39] In their written comments, many respondents admitted that Mount Kisco has a relatively low rate of crime compared to many parts of the metropolitan area; in fact some stated that they moved to Mount Kisco precisely because of its low crime rate. Our interviews show that Mount Kisco is desirable to Latinos for such qualities as "its small

Table 8.1 Response to the Question, "Which of the Following are the Most Important Housing Problems in the Village?"

Illegal apartments	605
Not enough housing in moderate price ranges	549
Property maintenance	483
High purchase price of housing	406
Not enough housing for young families	179
Not enough housing for single people	162
Not enough senior housing	153
High property taxes	122
Not enough rental housing	115
High rents	110
(710 = Total Number) (Respondents could choose more than one problem.)	

Source: Clark 2000.

village feel," "good sense of community," "the fact that people are kind and the community is multiracial," "nice people and clean streets," "low crime rate," and "safe environment," all of which reinforces our belief that crime is not at issue but that complaints are about behavior that differs from white middle-class norms.

Some unarticulated racist practices take the form of calls for the enforcement of housing codes and other safety measures on the part of residents who normally take no special interest in the health and safety of renters. In fact, the word "renters" along with other words and phrases such as "quality of life issues"[40] have become codes for complaints about the increasing visual presence of poor Latinos in Mount Kisco and other towns in Westchester County. The 1999 village survey showed residents to be extremely concerned about the issues of illegal apartments, deterioration of neighborhoods, dirt and decay, which, along with loitering, come under the euphemistic category "quality of life." The survey quite clearly reveals residents' attitudes toward low-income renters such as the

Table 8.2 Response to the Question, "What Type of New Development Do You Favor?"

None	346
Retail shopping	274
Single family residential	243
Office buildings	121
Light industry	106
Multi-family residential	102
Warehousing	35
(710 = Total Number) (Respondents could choose more than one problem.)	

Source: Clark 2000.

day laborers. In response to the question, "Which of the following are the most important housing problems in the village?," illegal apartments, which provide inexpensive housing, were seen as the most important problem and "not enough rental housing" and "high rents" were seen as the least important (Table 8.1).

The residents' view that there is not a serious shortage of low-income rental properties is confirmed by their answers to the question, "What type of new development do you favor?" "Multi-family residential" was second from the bottom, between "light industry" and "warehousing" (Table 8.2).

And yet in response to the oddly worded question, "Should housing opportunities (e.g. overcrowded housing) be given special attention in developing the Village Comprehensive Development Plan?," the residents are strongly in favor (538 to 172) (Clark 2000). Housing opportunities for whom, one wonders? And what kind of "special attention?" One suspects that the village administration wanted to know if residents supported more village action to deal with overcrowded housing, but sought to package it as "housing opportunities." Clearly as we can see from Tables 8.1 and 8.2, the "special attention" to overcrowded housing the residents have in mind does not include providing more rental housing. The residents overwhelmingly want the village to crack down on illegal housing and evict the poor who are living there (134 versus eleven, with forty-four having no opinion) (Clark 2000). This perhaps helps answer the question we posed in regard to the question about housing opportunities. The opportunities that the residents support are opportunities for low-income people to find rental housing in some other town!

At the end of the questionnaire, respondents were invited to write additional comments; many respondents chose to complain about illegal apartments and declining quality of life—not of poor Latinos in overcrowded buildings, but the white privilege of the rest of the village residents not to have to see day laborers in the center of the village. Concern about deterioration and pollution becoming out of control was revealed in 115 written comments, which referred to housing code enforcement and neighborhood deterioration. The thrust of all these comments was that people who do not belong here are spoiling this place. It is about the "contamination" of a place that represents achievement and the good life for those non-Latinos and some middle-class Latinos who think they do belong and thus it is about their own identities. Reactions range from sympathetic concern to rage, from shrewd manipulation of an issue to moral panic over the invasion of urban and third world problems into the heart of the first. David Sibley (1995), Tim Cresswell (1996), and Steve Pile (1994) in their psychoanalytic analyses of geographies of exclusion draw on Mary Douglas's (1966) definition of "dirt as matter out of place" in order to emphasize the spatial dimension to the relation between defilement and group boundary maintenance. Sibley says exclusionary discourse often comes back to dirt as a signifier of imperfection and inferiority (1995,14).

One can see how place-based identity is linked to anxieties over border maintenance and vigilance over dirt and decay in the resident's responses to the village survey. The following remarks were made: "The town looks like a big garbage dump," "At this time, there is nothing but garbage and crowds of people on street corners and this makes the town look terrible," "The sidewalks are dirty and littered, especially near the train station," "Visitors arrive by train and see dirt and litter. It creates a bad first impression of us," and "People moving into the village are bringing lower or no standards; they are not cognizant of this."

On the question of quality of life, dirt and filth is mentioned over and over again—for example, there is "an increase in filth and general ugliness" and "graffiti and dirty streets." It is suggested that the town "resolve the litter problem in Kirby Plaza" and "initiate a summons program for litter in and around the gazebo." Our own observations of Mount Kisco do not confirm this picture of the village or its train station as either dirty or rundown. The village by most standards, and we have known it for decades, has steadily improved aesthetically over the years. We can only ascribe the nervousness about decline to aversion or fear of uncontrolled Others.

The decline of neighborhoods ("inability to preserve neighborhoods" and "neighborhood decay") seems to respondents to be attributable to such factors as "nonenforcement of housing codes," "too many rental families," "lack of enforcement of housing violations," "overcrowding, illegal apartments with illegal aliens," "too much illegal housing," the "conversion of single family to two-, three-, and four-family houses," and "overcrowding with illegal immigrants." One person says, "Transient workers (are) making the downtown a seedy place," and another says, "Mount Kisco is becoming too urban, with a bad element." An irony in the popular association of immigrants with the urban is that the Guatemalan immigrants in Mount Kisco are largely from rural areas and have told us how they appreciate the rurality of Westchester because they too find urban environments alienating (also see Muldoon 1999).

It would appear that the existence of undocumented workers is a license for disguised racism. Because some of the Latinos are undocumented and are unmarked as such, many of Mount Kisco's other residents act as if the whole Latino population has forfeited the right to be treated as belonging in the village. To many residents of towns such as Mount Kisco and Bedford, every Latino's bodily presence attests to the weakness of the government of the United States in the face of illegal immigration. Those whose racist reactions are more straightforwardly discursive resent the fact that Spanish-speaking children are taught in the same public schools as their own. As one wrote in response to the village survey, "I greatly resent paying almost $10,000 in taxes to have Mount Kisco Elementary School so full of Spanish students, many of whom speak little English (their parents speak none) when many of these kids and their families don't even belong in this country or are here illegally. Classes are getting too overcrowded."

Such people display white privilege when they say that they resent Latinos using the schools or Village Park and Kirby Plaza outside the train station where they are thought to give the wrong first impression of the village to commuters and visitors arriving from New York City. Many Mount Kisco residents also worry about what they perceive as the village government's lack of control over the immigrants. One respondent to the village survey complained that "there is a lack of control over 'diversity' issues. The Hispanic population seems uncontrolled." Such a perception of the Other out of control is precisely how Kristeva describes abjection. Here we see white privilege under threat through the presence of too many people of color. The presence of Latinos is unsetting because parents worry that the high quality of education and other privileges they believe their families as middle-class whites deserve are threatened. We do not address the question here of whether they are right or wrong about their children's education being negatively affected, we merely call attention to their assumptions about their own privilege. However, as a counterpoint, one non-Latino mother explained that her children benefit from being in the Mount Kisco Elementary School because when Spanish-speaking children are taken out of the classroom for ESL (English as a Second Language) classes, her children get more personal attention due to the resulting smaller class sizes. An informant who grew up in Bedford and had attended private school there praised the Mount Kisco Elementary School for its high standards. She felt that the ethnic diversity of the school was an invaluable part of her own children's education.

The Politics of Exclusion

In 1993, Mount Kisco began a concerted effort to crack down on rental housing violations. In response, the *Patent Trader* (1993) published an editorial on over-crowded houses charging that "Mount Kisco and all its legal residents can be held responsible for a philosophy that looks uncomfortably like banging the door in the face of the unfortunate." In a letter published the following week, the deputy mayor of Mount Kisco replied that this charge was "total nonsense": "If you and others want to be critical of our efforts to clear these horribly unsafe, over-crowded homes and apartments, what will you say when 20 people lose their lives in a fire or are exposed to serious public health threats? What then?" The deputy mayor pointed out that Mount Kisco had more than 500 units of assisted housing while Bedford only had seventy-one (Vigliotti 1993). While the 1993 housing concerns did not specifically mention day laborers, they were its intended target.

In October 1994, two local women wrote a letter to the editor of the *Patent Trader* specifically mentioning the day laborers as a problem (Lombardi 1994; Skiba and Vetare Civitello 1994):

> The influx of illegal aliens is astounding. The problem of loitering in and around the downtown area has generated a feeling of discomfort so strong amongst tax-paying citizens that local businesses are suffering. The overwhelming amount of incidents that involve intoxicated persons should be alerting us to a major problem. Check the police records concerning arrests made involving Hispanics (for lack of a better term); undocumented or legal, either driving while intoxicated or throwing beer bottles or tearing street signs out of the ground or knifing one another.

They concluded, "We want our town back!"

This letter ignited a public outcry in Mount Kisco over what was termed "the deteriorating 'quality of life' in the town due to an influx of a high number of illegal aliens" (Skiba and Vetare Civitello 1994). The mayor reacted immediately to what he perceived as a political crisis over the day laborers creating a Committee on Community Relations to find a solution to the problem (McCabe 1995a). The village's Subcommittee on Employment Practices issued a report on April 7, 1995, in which they noted that members had met with representatives of the INS, the Criminal Activities Division of the Internal Revenue Service (IRS), and the Department of Labor, Standards and Practices Division, in an effort to convince the federal government to remove the undocumented workers by deporting them or fining them and their employers. The IRS told the subcommittee that the typical local case of someone hiring one to four laborers "is too small for the IRS division to concern itself with." The INS told them that Mount Kisco is low priority because "most of these transients are Guatemalan and can claim political asylum" (McCabe 1995a). In effect, the village was told that if they wanted to get rid of the Latinos, they had to do it themselves.

One of the goals of the Committee on Community Relations was "to help ensure that all members of our community—Hispanic, Anglo and the rest—respect the rules of our village and the customs of our culture." One can see here how the American ideologies of individualism and privacy are crosscut by a powerful desire for conformity that often surprises immigrants who repeatedly state that the United States is a free country.[41] Expressions of individualism are encouraged only as long as the broader cultural frameworks such as the public-private space dichotomy remain undisturbed. The committee's report stated that there is a concern "about the effect of enclaves of workers on the public image and quality of life in the village" (Town of Mount Kisco 1995). Here again we see quality of life referring to Latino street life.[42] In a telling comment, a Mount Kisco official said to us at the time, "Mount Kisco to my knowledge has no homeless people. But you do see people who look transient." It is this look that lowers the quality of life for area residents.

Local resident and university professor Pedro Laureano who teaches at Marist College in neighboring Poughkeepsie said he was "shocked by some of the statements being made by a variety of educated people" (Lombardi 1994). He stated,

> No one seems to be frightened by a large number of Latinos congregating in the kitchens of diners, or when five or six Latinos come to their house to mow their lawn or paint their house. But now it's a problem when they become part of your daily life, when they want to have a cappuccino in the mall. As a Latino foremost, hearing some of this was frightening.

The village's solution to loitering was to pass laws to supposedly protect the day laborers from exploitation thereby significantly reducing their numbers, because they can only survive in a place as expensive as Mount Kisco if officials turn a blind eye to their exploitation. This same protection strategy has been used increasingly in other states to counter the movement of Latinos into suburban areas (Cooper 1999; Muldoon 1999). In their April 1995 report, the Committee on Community Relations recommended that the exploitation of workers and the erosion of taxes through off-the-books jobs could be stopped if the village made it illegal for workers standing on a street or sidewalk to solicit employers or for employers in a vehicle to hire workers standing on the street.[43] Furthermore, people who employ casual workers were henceforth to have licenses guaranteeing that they would abide by national and local laws. When put into law, this had a predictably chilling effect on employment, as employers feared the financial and legal implications of hiring those they assumed were undocumented aliens. Predictably, the response from contractors and laborers was negative. As one contractor said, "You have to have a license to hire them? That's ridiculous. You should be able to hire anyone you want" (Andersen 1995a). Robin Bikkal, chair of the Hispanic Democrats of Westchester, said that the proposed $25 hiring license would drive contractors to other villages, and one of the day laborers said, "This [law] was done by Americans, for Americans" (Andersen 1995b).

The second part of the village's plan to protect the Latinos was to designate the back of a commuter parking lot next to the railway tracks as the only place where workers could be picked up for work. The plan temporarily improved the appearance of the village from the point of view of non-Latinos by removing many of the day laborers from the streets; however, it soon became apparent that the workers were reluctant to go to the new site because as they said, "We are no longer visible to employers." An interesting and telling exception to the law is the "employment of full-time students under the age of 22 engaged in seasonal or part-time employment." Employers need not register in order to hire them, and they could solicit work wherever they wish. Apparently middle-class teenagers are not considered in need of the same degree of protection as foreign adults. As the law effectively only applies to Latinos, it is, de facto, a race law to make poor Latinos disappear from public view.

On August 7, 1995, the first day of the new legislation, police forced the Latinos to go to the back of the parking lot. One hundred laborers assembled there, but only one contractor came and hired three laborers. One of the laborers said, "We feel we're really abandoned" (Andersen 1995c). A week later, nearly 200 day laborers met with village officials to express concern about the new law. Officials agreed to issue temporary permits to employers free of charge and post signs directing them to the parking lot (McCabe 1995c). Several days later, in response to the unsatisfactory nature of the meeting from the point of view of the Latino workers, an ad hoc committee was formed that included representatives of the Center of Immigrant Rights in New York City, the Westchester Hispanic Coalition in White Plains, the national and local Civil Liberties Union, and the

Hispanic Democrats of Westchester. By the end of the month, as few as twenty-five laborers were showing up at the parking lot and few of them found work. Many left Mount Kisco in the weeks after the new law was enacted (Andersen 1995d). In September 1995, the committee met with Mount Kisco officials to urge them to change the law.

A member of the Center for Immigrant Rights pronounced the meeting "a waste of my time," while a representative of Mount Kisco said, "I don't understand what their [the ad hoc committee's] priority is, it's certainly not the day workers of Mount Kisco." Workers said that because of the licensing requirement, employers feared an IRS sting. This requirement and a heavy police presence in the parking lot kept employers away (McCabe 1995d). Just as we have seen in Bedford, enforcement is usually driven by citizen complaints to the town, so it appears that citizens played a key role in making sure public space in Mount Kisco was kept clear of day laborers. In April 1996, police lieutenant Jack Wade said that he realized that the police deterred contractors at the hiring site. He added, "We're stuck in the middle on this one. If we're not there and there's five or six guys [looking for work] on the corner, somebody's going to call and the feathers start to fly" (Andersen 1996). In 1996, Luis Lujan talked to a Mount Kisco official who defensively stated that rather than trying to get rid of people, the village was welcoming:

> Mount Kisco has always been a very nice middle-class village. It's a nice environment...all-American. We welcome anyone who wants to come here to live and we want them to prosper. Since the 1980s, there has been an influx of mostly seasonal laborers wanting to generate money. Many stay and we want these people to become an integrated part of the community. We want them to learn English and their children to come to our after-school programs.

The official defended the village's policy on employment, referring to it as an anti-panhandling ordinance. He said, "We don't want residents of Mount Kisco to be abused. That's why we have passed a no-panhandling ordinance. It is not safe for people to stand on the street asking for money or jobs. Sometimes these people are not paid for their services if they are picked up on the street to work." He is correct to say that sometimes the workers are not paid; this has been confirmed to us by many of the workers, newspaper reports, and the site manager of Neighbors' Link. However, it is disingenuous to label this an anti-panhandling law, as the Latinos are waiting for work, not begging. Such language is best interpreted as official spin intended to enforce a normative geography by delegitimizing the Latinos' behavior in public spaces while professing to represent their interests.

In August 1995, shortly after the first hiring law (Local Law 6) was enacted, the mayor's Committee on Community Relations proposed a new housing law. Because of violations of zoning codes concerning numbers of tenants per unit, it was suggested that all rental units be licensed and inspected to conform to proper safety standards. The village hoped to drive them out of town, for as a village official had admitted to us, most day laborers can only afford to live in overcrowded accommodations. This is a common strategy used by suburban communities. Muldoon (1999, 117) quotes the director of the American Friends Service Committee, located in Newark, New Jersey: "Under the guise of health and safety standards, many small towns in New Jersey are passing stricter occupancy codes as a means of getting rid of minorities who can only afford rent if they split it with a number of people." This strategy has a further advantage of satisfying aversive racists by reassuring them that they are in fact tolerant and liberal.

The vote on the new housing law was preceded by a strategically timed raid, which found fifty-two men identified as Latinos living in a house with a maximum legal occupancy of seventeen. Photographers accompanied the raid to take photographs for the press. A housing official was quoted as saying that "people were found sleeping on porches and in closets—every square foot of the premises had bodies except for the kitchen and bathroom floors." He added that there was a severe cockroach problem. He went on to add that these were "severe life-threatening conditions" (McCabe 1995b). While such overcrowding is deplorable, the politically induced hyperbole about life-threatening conditions was clearly aimed at the upcoming village vote. The age-old specter of foreign-bred disease and urban problems of overcrowding spreading out to the suburbs had its predictable effect on the Village Board. It was noted that the landlord was collecting $8,000 per month rent for the house. What was left unremarked, however, is the fact that the village zoning codes and planning policies severely restrict the possibility of building new affordable housing, which, compounded by even more stringent policies in surrounding towns, creates a structural situation that enables landlords to extract such exorbitant rents.

In November 1995, the Republican village administration was voted out of office, in large part because of its clumsy handling of the quality of life issue. Although Mount Kisco's new Democratic administration in late 1995 stated that it would not enact the proposed housing laws (*Patent Trader* 1995), in fact it was tougher on the Latino workers than its Republican predecessor. Beginning in 1996, the new administration conducted a series of late-night raids on overcrowded dwellings. What was most unusual about these raids was that tenants as well as landlords were charged with violating the housing laws.

And yet, the village's action was not decisive enough for some. One Planning Board member who resigned because the village was not tough enough on Latinos said,

> The more you move into the village proper, you see people sitting on benches. You see them walking around the village. You know they're not Mount Kisco people. They're Hispanic. Remember one thing. We're all in good faith. We have

our Christian image. Everyone's a human being. But I don't see that that gives them the right to overburden our facilities: water, sewage, garbage. (Dugger 1996)

We asked a businessman from Bedford what he thought of the ordinance. He replied,

> Mount Kisco has certainly solved the problem of all the Guatemalans hanging out on the street. They did it in the proper liberal way by saying that they were protecting them from exploitation. They made them all go to a specific place to be picked up for work. Then they made the people who want to hire them register. The people who hire them wanted to be anonymous so they stopped coming to pick them up. Now these illegals have moved to Brewster. People still have gardeners but these are the more Americanized ones. The town has gotten smart about how to get rid of these people and make it seem like they are protecting them. Now it's Brewster's problem.

While he was correct that many workers left Mount Kisco immediately after the ruling, some returned when it became clear that, although the new law made life more difficult for them, they could still survive in Mount Kisco. A few Guatemalans we spoke to at the time were willing to speak about their resentment against Mount Kisco. One man said, "Guatemala is in Central America. We are Americans too." Another added, "Yes, we're all Guatemalans here in Mount Kisco. Guatemala is in America, so we are Americans. We have a right to be here, and they can't make us leave. We have a right to make money here." While towns can try to deny them access to public space, Central Americans have made a social and potentially political network for themselves that extends up and down the railroad line connecting cities and towns such as White Plains, Brewster, and Bedford Hills with Mount Kisco as an important central meeting point for friendship, essential information about housing, immigration and acculturation problems, and, most important, jobs.

Don Mitchell (1995) claims that public space is crucial to what Jurgen Habermas (1989) calls the "public sphere," the universal, abstract realm in which democracy occurs.[44] Following Nancy Fraser (1990), Mitchell (1995, 115) argues that "public spaces are absolutely essential to the functioning of a democratic politics." For only by being granted legitimate access to public space can marginalized groups like the homeless and day laborers "represent themselves as a legitimate part of the public."[45] The village's plan to remove the day laborers from sight to a marginalized space on the outskirts of the village can thus be interpreted simultaneously as a move to marginalize them socially, economically, and politically.[46] As such, we can clearly see that public space is "a legal entity, a political theory and a material space" (Mitchell 1996b, 155). Such public civic life is often seen as threatening in such a highly individualistic society as the United States.

Setha Low's study of a Central American plaza provides an interesting parallel to our observations in Mount Kisco. She (2000, 240) says that plazas,

> are one of the last democratic forums for public dissent in a civil society. They are places where disagreements can be marked symbolically and politically or personally worked out. Without these significant central public spaces, social and cultural conflicts are not clearly visible, and individuals can not directly participate in their resolution. Insofar as they [individuals] remain invisible to society, they fail to be counted as legitimate members of the polity.

Low describes how Costa Ricans have redesigned the central plaza in the capital city of San Jose, hoping to make it safer and more attractive. They have removed the stone benches in hope of discouraging Nicaraguan refugees who use the park as a place to hang out and meet others who may have essential information about loved ones and the political situation at home or about strategies of coping in a new environment. She quotes one middle-class user of the plaza who said the problem was the Nicaraguans: "Costa Rica is not the same place with all the foreigners" (Low 2000, 193).

In November 1996, the Westchester branch of the Immigrants' Rights Project of the American Civil Liberties Union filed a class action suit against the village of Mount Kisco in the Federal District Court in White Plains on behalf of the Westchester Hispanic Coalition and four immigrants. One of three principal issues in the suit was the right to free assembly denied by Local Law 6, which banished workers to the back of the parking lot. Another involved the raid on a house where the tenants were prosecuted for overcrowding, and the third charged the village with excluding many of the Latino families from the town park.[47] The heart of the issue was whether day laborers were to be allowed to live in the village and use public space there. The *New York Times* published several critical articles on the case. In one, it quoted a past village attorney who noted that prior administrations had not generally prosecuted tenants. "We felt tenants were victims," he said (Dugger 1996). In another article, Graciela Heymann, executive director of the Westchester Hispanic Coalition, is quoted as saying, "Everyone else gets a building inspector who knocks on their door, but these people get awakened at 12:30 in the morning" (Brenner 1996).

As the American Civil Liberties suit was about to go to Federal District Court, Heymann increased the pressure on the village by arguing the coalition's side of the case in the *New York Times* (Greene 1997). She pointed out that Local Law 6, rather than protecting laborers, as its advocates claimed, simply drives the employment "underground." She stated,

> What I see is a violation of a very basic human right to be able to make a living. So there have been struggles with the police telling them to move back to the site. When they obey the police, they get no work because the employers don't

go there. So there is a struggle every morning. And also anyone who is around that area in the early morning and looks Hispanic the cops stop and tell them to move on, that they have to go to the site. It's pretty tense.

Heymann went on to say that the coalition had formed the Mount Kisco Worker's Project "to educate day laborers about their rights and their responsibilities." In that way, they can become strong, and once a bad employer is known, others can know not to work for him.[48] She added, "We're trying to organize the day laborers. We're trying to listen to their needs, to enlighten them a little. We managed to establish a minimum wage, which wasn't too hard, because the workers themselves won't go for less than about $10 an hour. We've advised them of their rights and we talk to them about housing." In response to the question, "Were the village's intentions decent, looking to make their community safe?," she replied, "The lawsuit we filed charges the village with discrimination. There is a systematic pattern of behavior here." Of Mount Kisco she said, "It's a very polarized community. It's a class thing. These people who are coming here working six or seven days a week in the jobs that nobody else wants to do . . . cutting lawns, watching the children, cleaning houses. It's really a great American tradition. They come here hoping that their children will be educated and have a better life." While Heymann is correct that "it's a class thing," it is clearly racialized and cultural as well; the conflict in Mount Kisco isn't explainable in terms of class, race, or culture alone, but rather as an explosive mix of the three. This is perhaps especially true given the close correlation between race and class among Latin Americans.

Celeste Calvitto and Mel Berger (1997), two members of the mayor's Committee on Community Relations, replied to Heymann's charges by saying that she was "slander[ing] an entire community." They claimed that the village was "sensitive to the needs of all ethnic groups while trying to provide education about village laws." The needs of the other ethnic groups presumably include most importantly the need not to be exposed to Latino "loitering." They then went on to suggest that Heymann ask "her own community—Chappaqua—to help Mount Kisco's efforts by providing a hiring area and housing for Hispanic day workers since many employers of day workers live in Chappaqua." While the intention is to deflect criticism away from Mount Kisco's handling of the day labor issue, the point about the neighboring communities' failure to help the situation is well taken.

Two weeks before the discrimination suit against Mount Kisco was due to go to court, a similar case was settled in Addison, Illinois, a suburb of Chicago. The *New York Times* gave it front-page coverage under the headline "Landmark settlement ends Hispanic housing bias suit" (Belluck 1997).[49] In the three previous years, three towns had reached settlements with the Justice Department in housing discrimination suits against Hispanic residents. Wildwood, New Jersey, paid $75,000 damages for selectively enforcing an ordinance of one person per bedroom. Hatch, New Mexico, paid $260,000 for banning mobile homes, and Waukegan, Illinois, paid $200,000 damages for limiting the number of people living in a house to immediate family and two relatives. Justice officials said that these cases represent a "recent and troubling trend in which Latino residents have become the target of the kind of bias that blacks once faced." They went on to point out that increasingly "zoning laws are being used as discriminatory tools" (Belluck 1997).

The parallels to the upcoming case in Mount Kisco were disturbing to village officials. Within a few days of the Addison, Illinois, settlement, the Mount Kisco village attorney received a telephone call from the village's insurance company whose head office is in Chicago. The attorney was told that unless the village settled, "all costs . . . would be borne exclusively by the village" (McCabe 1997). The village decided that it could not afford to risk a trial. In August 1997, Mount Kisco reached an out-of-court settlement on the class action suits. While not admitting liability, the village agreed to the key demands of the lawsuit and agreed to pay the plaintiffs court costs of $393,000. As a result of this case, Local Law 6 was no longer enforced and attendance at the hiring area became voluntary. Contractors no longer had to register with the village or purchase a license. The village also agreed to post notices in Spanish and contribute toward funding for a Westchester Hispanic Coalition site coordinator (Brandt 1997; Dugger 1997; Farrell 1997; Gonzalez 1997).

Henceforth, the village also had to give notice of inspections and allow landlords and tenants to fix problems. Furthermore, the village was required to replace its own code with the less restrictive New York State Uniform Fire Prevention and Building Code.

Resident Latinos were also to be given access to Leonard Park (Brandt 1997; Dugger 1997; Gonzalez 1997). The issue of a good spot for day laborers to congregate in the mornings to be picked up by employers continued, however. The residents and merchants still wanted the workers out of sight, and the village now claimed to be worried about workers impeding traffic flow. Heymann of the Westchester Hispanic Coalition reacted to the decision by saying, "We really need to move toward some racial healing. I think the hard work is ahead of us." Celeste Calvitto, the chair of the mayor's Committee on Community Relations that drafted the overturned laws, tried to put a good face on the village's defeat by saying that the "agreement gives many opportunities for the Mayor's Committee to continue with education and outreach efforts on behalf of the Town." She added, "It's apparent that both sides gave a little and gained a little. That's what getting along is all about" (Brandt 1997). Jonathan Lovetl, a specialist in federal civil rights cases against municipalities, said that the village "decided to cut their losses rather than get massacred at trial." He added that had the village lost at trial, it would have "set up 'slam dunk' wins by any Hispanics seeking compensation for civil rights violations" (Klein 1997).

In 1999, the village of Mount Kisco settled a further lawsuit out of court involving the midnight housing raids of 1996. This time the village had to pay $480,000 to twenty-two defendants who claimed that Building Department officials and police officers who executed a search warrant shortly after midnight had violated their constitutional rights. The attorney for the plaintiffs charged the village with "targeting and oppressing members of the Latino community." The raids he claimed "were to send a message directly into the homes of the Latino residents." It was further determined that the law that was invoked had been invalid since 1985 (Driscoll 1999g).

Life has improved for the workers since they forced the village to back down on its harassment of Latinos and discriminatory laws. The housing situation is still unsatisfactory, however. Whereas the village has been barred from engaging in discriminatory inspection tactics, rents are still unreasonably high in many cases and day laborers do not have security of tenure. Harold Lasso, then of the Westchester Hispanic Coalition, said that after the settlement of the court case a great many landlords evicted Latino tenants for fear of continuing problems with the village. As a result, many left Mount Kisco for Ossining, Brewster, and White Plains. There are still landlords who won't rent to Latinos and most of those who do are unwilling to give leases. They know that there are many day laborers ready to move in as soon as they evict anyone. Consequently the workers live on a month-by-month basis with rents often increasing. The only way that they can afford the ever-increasing rents is by subletting to others, thereby increasing overcrowding (Driscoll 1999a).

The negative attitudes of merchants in Mount Kisco toward the Latinos were also revealed in the case of the Ah Fun restaurant. Angela Stern, the Chinese owner of this take-out restaurant, which had been open for twenty-three years, faced a dwindling business. Therefore, in 1996 she added Guatemalan food to her menu, and her restaurant soon became a popular place for Guatemalans to eat and drink beer in the evenings. Stern admitted that at times her customers drank too much and that she sometimes had to call the police to take them home. In the late summer of 1999, she received an eviction notice. Her landlord said that he had received complaints about her clientele from neighboring merchants and had been told by the mayor to "get rid of your problem tenant." In September 1999, she filed a $1.5 million civil rights suit in Federal District Court against her landlord and the mayor. Judge McMahon, who would be hearing the case when it came to trial, granted a preliminary injunction against the eviction. The judge said in the ruling, "No one wanted to talk about race at the hearing but the court must, because race is really the issue at hand." The judge concluded that the reason the restaurant lost most of its American customers when it began to serve Guatemalan food was because of "considerable hostility" toward Latinos in Mount Kisco. Such hostility she assumed was because Latinos are "culturally alien to American suburban residents." She pointed out that only under cross-examination did the witnesses for the defense mention race. Instead they used terms like "those people" and "not a nice element." She concluded, "Everybody in town managed to convey in word or in substance, that they hated Ms. Stern's customers" (Gross 1999).

In her affidavit, Stern states, "The ongoing efforts to remove the visibility of Latinos from the greater Mount Kisco area is deplorable and unconscionable. Latinos have every right to eat and recreate downtown and to publicly enjoy the benefits available to all others. To deny my right to serve them is tantamount to denying them their rights of association as guaranteed by the constitution." Stern's attorney stated that the landlord closed Ah Fun because Mount Kisco officials want "a Latino-free downtown in response to residents' complaints about 'quality of life'" (Driscoll 1999d). The judge wrote, "The real problem in the eyes of all was not that Ah Fun sold so much alcohol . . . but rather that it attracted Hispanics to the downtown area . . . It thus appears that Mrs. Stern's lease is not being renewed because of her willingness to cater to and do business with Mount Kisco's Hispanic population, and (the landlord's) basing his complaints on people who exhibit racial animus." The judge continued, "I am not a dope. I have been reading the newspapers for a long time and I realize that there is a hostility in that part of the county because of the presence of day workers. I know that." The judge found no evidence of the claimed negative behavior of the customers. The judge also said that she believed Stern's testimony that "efforts were made to get her to relocate to a less desirable (more rundown) area of town where her customer base resided" (Driscoll 1999e). The case, which drew national attention, was eventually settled out of court and the restaurant remained open.

Quality of life remains a code word in the village for ethnic homogeneity. At a village board meeting in the summer of 1999, a couple complained that young men "disturbed them" as they walked down Moger Avenue (a place where Latino workers and young African Americans often congregate after work). They suggested to the Town Board that a policeman be assigned to this area "and make a few 'quality of life' arrests, perhaps acting as a deterrent to future activity [there]." At the time, the mayor said that he supported an increased police presence to deal with "quality of life issues downtown" (Driscoll 1999c). In November 1999, the Democrats were turned out of office, the second administration in a row to fall over their handling of the quality-of-life issue. A letter to local papers just before the election captured the frustration that many non-Latino residents felt. The writer stated, "It upsets me to see large groups of people congregating on streets in Mount Kisco, especially near the railroad station and North Moger Avenue parking lot waiting to be picked up for a job. This daily 'hanging around' detracts from the beauty of our village and demeans the workers who are trying to earn a living." The writer goes on to say that as a result of the lawsuits the town has lost $640,000 and that "Mount Kisco has never since been able to enforce any housing code violations of a similar nature. The decision made by the majority on the Mount Kisco Village Board was a total disgrace. They gave Mount Kisco away and we must reclaim it" (Benanti 1999).

The fact that two administrations in a row fell for not being able to solve the day laborer problem suggests that any administration that could not respond to the demands to remove the day laborer presence from the center of the village would not survive. The present Republican Mayor Pat Reilly campaigned on a platform of housing "code enforcement and police presence in the Village center [to control loitering]," which the survey revealed were two of the most pressing issues for the voters (Driscoll 1999f). She has been rewarded for managing the day laborer problem better than her predecessors by being reelected for a second term in 2001.

In spite of repeated setbacks in court, village officials have continued to try to move the Latinos out of the village. Although in the 1997 settlement to the discrimination suit the village agreed to abide by the state housing standards, in March 2000, the village tested the Latinos once again by adopting a housing ordinance that defined a family as one, two, or three people who occupy a house, or four or more people who live together as "the functional equivalent of a traditional family." The Mount Kisco Workers Project charged that the village had deliberately modified the ordinance to force workers out and filed a motion in U.S. District Court in October 2000. The village once again settled out of court and agreed to rewrite the ordinance. The settlement also required that the village pay the Westchester Hispanic Coalition $10,000 for the social services that it provides (Archibold 2001).

In May 2000, the pickup zone for the day laborers who had come back to Kirby Plaza was again in the headlines (Driscoll 2000). Yet another spot had been suggested and rejected because of complaints from residents of the proposed area, who said they didn't want their families "subjected" to comments and "inappropriate public behavior," potential noise, and traffic. Merchants near Kirby Plaza continued to complain that the day laborers adversely affected their businesses. One business owner we spoke to, himself a Latin-American immigrant long settled and successful in Mount Kisco, suggested that the day laborers be moved to Bedford, which he saw as the root of Mount Kisco's problems. A Community Relations Committee member, who was sympathetic to the day laborers, reacted in frustration to attempts to block a pickup zone: "I keep hearing 'these people, these people'; it seems like they don't want people (nearby) because of their race. That's what I'm hearing. I don't think that (race) should play a part in this whole situation." The head of the Mount Kisco branch of the Westchester Hispanic Coalition at the time said, "You are afraid of them. Why? Because they don't speak English? You're talking about children. They have children. They have wives, too" (Driscoll 2000).[50]

Finally after these various alternative sites in the village had been explored, a community center and hiring site was opened in April 2001 in a warehousing district on the outskirts of the village.[51] Even in that marginal district, several dozen residents and businesses signed a petition against the proposed center (Worth 2001). The center is run by Neighbor's Link, an amalgam of community

Fig. 8.4   Neighbor's Link in the Warehouse District.

organizations with the backing of the Presbyterian Church and the Westchester Hispanic Coalition. Bilingual fliers announcing the center's opening were distributed at Kirby Plaza to contractors and day laborers announcing the new location and promising no fees, registration, or questions. The fliers asked that day laborers only be picked up at the site and nowhere else. It assured workers and employers that there would be a site coordinator, and a translator to help with labor needs. The center has been supported by $100,000 in donations, 60% from two local families and a $25,000 start-up grant from the village.[52] The center provides coffee, donuts, prearranged jobs, classes in English language and American culture, vocational skills and citizenship, immigration counseling, housing and health care advise, a Buddies group,[53] Head Start, a wide-screen television for watching soccer, and space for socializing (Driscoll 2001, 2002b; Gross 2000a). We interviewed Liliana Keith, the site coordinator, just before the center was due to open. She was enthusiastic and optimistic about attracting both the day laborers and contractors. She said that she expected approximately 150 day laborers in the summer and forty in the winter. The village board also voted to prohibit any vehicles except passenger cars from using Kirby Plaza from 6 A.M. to 10 A.M. Monday to Saturday in order to get employers used to the idea of a new pickup spot. On the first day, about 120 workers and twenty-five contractors used the site. The center instituted a registration system for day laborers noting their job qualifications. A contractor can request a specific laborer or set of skills; otherwise a lottery system is used to assign jobs. The site coordinator also negotiates the wage with the contractor and notes his name. Some day laborers try and jump ahead of the lottery by rushing out to arriving cars while the site coordinator is inside the center; others feel they can secure more work by remaining at Kirby Plaza than by joining the lottery system at the center. This choice was made possible by the fact that the village was not enforcing its no-pickup law at Kirby Plaza.

When we returned to Mount Kisco in March and April 2002 we visited the center, which appeared to be popular with the day laborers and has been reasonably effective in reducing the visibility of Latino men in the village center. Nevertheless we were told by the mayor that she had been personally visiting Kirby Plaza and the train station to try to convince a remaining forty or so workers who hoped to find work without having to join a lottery system to go to the center. She also told us how she had solicited a donation from a local school bus company to provide a bus to transport workers from the station to the hiring center a mile away. In April 2002, the village with the support of the Westchester Hispanic Coalition and Neighbor's Link began to enforce a no-pickup zone at Kirby Plaza to encourage the remaining day laborers to go to the Neighbor's Link hiring center on the outskirts of the village. From the point of view of the village and Neighbor's Link, it was a win-win situation. The village didn't want the day laborers in the center of the village and the Neighbor's Link believed they could help them more if they came to the hiring center. Only some of the day laborers who had not chosen to throw in their lot with Neighbor's Link were unhappy with the turn of events. "We prefer to find jobs for ourselves," one man we spoke to at Kirby Plaza said. "But I guess now we have no choice but to go to Neighbor's Link. This *parada* [hiring site] is dead." Another man said, "We came here for work, not entertainment."

The village continues to argue that the reason they wanted the day laborers to leave Kirby Plaza is because of the traffic problems that they cause. However, a recent newspaper article in a local paper reveals once again that the day laborer problem is not as much a matter of traffic, safety, or numbers of people in Kirby Plaza as the village has claimed, as it is a matter of aesthetics, the day laborers' ethnicity, visible poverty, and their use of public space. The article states, "A sign hanging between the trees in Kirby Plaza at the train station announces the Village's entry into a warm weather tradition—farmers selling their locally grown products at an outdoor market." The president of the Mount Kisco Chamber of Commerce is hopeful that the market will become a fixture. In fact 300 to 500 customers have begun to shop there on Saturdays (Gorman 2001e). On Saturdays, Kirby Plaza is to become a festive space, what Jon Goss (1996) terms a "nostalgic, festival marketplace for the middle class." Such festival marketplaces are springing up all over the United States. In order to purify and aestheticize such spaces, the poor and homeless must either be removed or greatly outnumbered so that the middle class can feel comfortable.

While, as we have seen, the village has specifically targeted day laborers, other Latinos have also felt pressure from the village. Pastor Frank Vega of the Iglesia Hispana-Fuente de Vida in Mount Kisco told us that he has 300 Latino members in his congregation and 98% of them are not day laborers. He says most day laborers either go to the Catholic Church or no church at all. We asked him about a public hearing concerning the relocation of his church to a former Elks Club. He said that he had not "even dignified some of the questions [asked at the hearing] with answers. One man asked if there would be prostitutes hanging around and another asked if there would be drive-by shootings." He shook his head and said, "We have a very settled, respectable congregation." In March 2001, the Mount Kisco Zoning Board of Appeals approved the church's request to occupy the site but set limits on how the site could be used. In particular, the decision outlined buffers preventing such things as weddings or a church picnic being held within 150 feet of the back or sides of the 8.3-acre property. In July 2001, the church filed a lawsuit in State Supreme Court seeking to strike down the property restrictions. Pastor Vega said, "We can't do anything outside, like something as simple as an Easter egg hunt for the kids. We don't know why they imposed these restrictions...no other church in Mount Kisco has that restriction. So why is it imposed on us?" (Gorman 2001g). Six months later, the village at the urging of State Supreme Court Justice Peter Leavitt agreed to drop the property restrictions (Driscoll 2002b).

We Are Not Racist

Because the dominant form of racism in places like Bedford and Mount Kisco is aversive based on the implicit notion of white privilege, many residents fail to see their attitudes as racist. Consequently, as the lawsuits began, some residents were dismayed that Mount Kisco was getting what they considered unfair coverage in the *New York Times*. One letter to the *New York Times* (Karsch and Karsch 1996) said,

> As residents of Mount Kisco, N.Y., we take issue with your Dec.1 news article on the American Civil Liberties Union's lawsuit that accuses the town of selectively enforcing its housing code and violating the constitutional rights of its Hispanic residents. You paint Mount Kisco as a reactionary town ... [it] is a middle-class town; few would call it affluent, as you do. Many of the Hispanics who live here work for homeowners in truly affluent towns like Chappaqua, Armonk and Bedford. As far as we know, these towns have not made any real effort to deal with the issues Mount Kisco is grappling with.

It is hard to disagree with their observation that communities such as Bedford want to employ the day laborers but are unwilling to house them.[54]

In 1997, a resident replied to Heymann's charge in the *New York Times* that the village discriminates against Latinos: "I have to question why the town of Mount Kisco is being unfairly depicted as a racist town and how the rights of workers have anything to do with racism. It is unethical for employers to exploit the day workers and it is an issue that must be dealt with." She continues, "As a resident of Mount Kisco for nine years, I love Mount Kisco for its cultural diversity, which is absent in some of the neighboring communities. To have suggested that racism is the root of the day worker problem is insulting and unfair to the residents of Mount Kisco" (Maroti 1997). It might appear that the thrust of this letter is to deflect the problem from one of racial discrimination by the village to one of economic exploitation by people from other towns, but perhaps this woman really does fail to recognize the village's unarticulated racist actions taken on behalf of its citizens (at least its more vocal citizens).

This sense of hurt flared up again with the negative publicity the town received in the press over the Ah Fun restaurant. A letter to the editor reflects this (Matts 1999):

> It is deeply disturbing to me that many of the quality of life issues facing the Village have been twisted into race and political animosities. All residents have the right to feel comfortable and safe in their town and have the right to speak up when behaviors that adversely affect their quality of life occur. The issue is not race, creed, color or age related. It is behavior related. Why the Hispanic Coalition takes these issues and makes the Village or its officials the bad guys instead of assisting in stopping unsanitary and dangerous behaviors is beyond me.

As we have seen, it is not uncommon for people to feel that Bedford is to blame for the Latino presence in Mount Kisco and that the residents of the village are unfairly taking the heat for trying to deal with Bedford's problems. In response to the survey question of what detracts from the quality of life in Mount Kisco, one person writes, "Abrasive and abusive loitering teenagers and young adults. We moved here over thirty years ago. The quality of life has diminished over the past five years. Why can't the surrounding towns house their day laborers?" Such a resentment toward Bedford and other towns has overtones of class resentment. For example, one man we spoke to said,

> We are portrayed in the press as the bad guys. Now that's unfair. In Bedford they aren't called racist. They don't have to be—they have exported their problem to us. We're the one's offering affordable housing and social services—they're the one's with the big houses and gardens they don't want to take care of themselves so they get Jose and Pedro to do all the work. Then they send their kids to private school so they aren't held back by being in a school full of kids who don't know English.

In 2001 when we asked an official of the village if we could see the results of the public opinion survey, we were given a summary of answers compiled in a binder. The next day when we went back to ask if the original questionnaires were available, we were given what looked like the same bound volume. We asked if this was the same one we had seen yesterday and were told, "Oh no, these are all the nasty, bigoted things that people had to say." When we went back a year later in April 2002, the village manager's office was reluctant to let us see them again. "Relations are so improved now we would rather not let this out," we were told. The official added, "The village has had a bad experience with law suits." In fact, day laborers have been quoted in the newspapers saying that they don't need to read the papers to find out that many of the other residents dislike them. One man said, "A lot of people would tell us to leave. They make us feel worse. We don't like it" (Driscoll 2002b).[55]

Comparing the summary with the transcription of the original answers that we examined in 2001, we could see that although the village had quoted some of the racist remarks in their summary, they tried to present the results in a positive a light. We noted, for example, that the village interpreted some remarks as positive that we would describe as intolerant. The summary specifically says that "The majority of comments [about Latinos] were positive and focused on the need to assimilate new residents into the community; encourage them to be more involved." The village officials tried to present the residents' responses about building a community center where Latinos can wait for jobs, find toilets, socialize, and learn English in the best light by suggesting that such concerns were positive. Certainly these comments were more constructive and less offensive to Latinos than the more overtly racist remarks; however, as Hage (1998) says in a different context, the discourse of toleration implies that there is something negative to be tolerated by those who believe they are dominant and thus have the power and the responsibility to be tolerant.

While the village planners try to play down the discursive racism of some of the villagers, they fail to see the aversive racism (albeit less obvious) of wanting the Latinos to blend in better and not stand about on street corners. Examples of the remarks the village planners found to be positive are as follows: "Find a place for the day workers to go during the day if they don't get work. That way, they don't have to hang out at the train station" and "Find another place for day laborers to congregate." In one sense, the village is right; those with solutions rather than simply complaints are more positive. However, the logic of the sentiment is the same: all are unwilling to embrace visual difference. When we interviewed the mayor in April 2002, she mentioned her dismay at the idea of a judge calling the town racist. Her feeling of hurt appeared quite genuine. As a former educator, she thinks of herself as a mother hen with her arms open to everyone. But for her, only discursive racism constitutes racism; in her opinion, it does not characterize the views of the village administration, but rather, in the words of one of her colleagues, a "nasty, bigoted" minority of vocal residents. Alan Pred (2000, xii) is especially concerned to understand good-hearted views such as those expressed by the mayor. He refers to "that host of countless voices that are possessed of little or no malice, that are more or less innocent of the cultural racism they proclaim."

The intolerance of some of Mount Kisco's residents is disturbing not only to Latinos, but to some others as well. One journalist (Potter 2001) who lives in Mount Kisco is appalled by her fellow citizens attitudes toward Latinos. She makes the point when speaking of a Latino friend's father: "He came here for the same reason as all those hungry-looking men standing on Kirby Plaza: to make a better life, just like the fathers and grandfathers of many Mount Kisco residents who are now so offended by the sight of Central Americans walking on their streets. Some people make the connection though." She said a neighbor told her that her parents came from Ireland. "My parents came here from Ireland," the neighbor in her building said. "My mother was a maid and my father dug ditches. So who am I to look down on the day workers?"

In fact, those who themselves immigrated or whose family members immigrated earlier in the twentieth century display a range of reactions to immigration, some distancing themselves from what they see as inferior versions of their former,[56] unacculturated selves and others showing more empathy. Many of the latter are ambivalent, however. They see their tolerance coming at a cost.

A few of the respondents to the public opinion survey mention racism. When asked, "Are there new or improved services that you think the village should provide for residents?," one respondent answered, "Programs about bigotry are needed for local residents." Another suggested, "The quality of life [issues] are the scary voices in letters to the editor railing about unfounded and racist fears regarding the future of Mount Kisco." Another mentioned racial prejudice as something that detracts from the quality of life in Mount Kisco and another named "intolerance toward immigrants." It is impossible to know whether these people are Latino or not. It is quite likely that there were very few Latinos among those who answered the questions. We were surprised to find that the village was not interested enough in the opinions of Latinos to have the questionnaire translated into Spanish, thereby reducing the number of Latinos who could potentially answer. However, we would not be surprised if the respondents were not Latino, given the fact that many non-Latinos in Mount Kisco maintain an anti-racist stance and welcome what they term "diversity." Some in their answers on the survey celebrated the diversity and heterogeneity of the village. One suggested that "the sense of community could be stronger; (the village should) establish a pride day celebrating our diversity."

Out of the Fire and into the Melting Pot

In the mid-1990s, towns in southern Westchester composed a flier to familiarize immigrants with what one journalist termed the "tacit codes of the suburbs" (Berger 1993).[57] These leaflets outline what types of behavior are considered unacceptable in suburbia. The fliers explain cultural differences between Anglicized Americans and newly arrived Latinos in the proper use of public space. At the forefront of the drive for cultural assimilation desired by non-Latinos and many Latinos as well is the Neighbor's Link center. The Reverend Douglas Phillips of the Presbyterian Church in Mount Kisco argues that outdoor socializing is a principal problem. "Anglos don't do that, so we assume they're up to no good," he said (Gross 2000a). Middle-class locals assume that public spaces are to be used for walking and that socializing is to be done in private, either in the home or in a bar or restaurant. In Mount Kisco, Latino advocacy groups, such as the Neighbor's Link, provide this kind of cultural information to day laborers and hold workshops in which they explain how they should behave in public spaces. Peggie Arriaza, office supervisor of the Westchester Hispanic Coalition center at Neighbor's Link, told us that she specifically tells day laborers not to stare at women, drink in public, or hang around in large groups on the sidewalk. Some day laborers, she said, are resistant to her advice, saying, "It's a free country, we are free to do as we please." She said, "I tell them, 'then you have to deal with the consequences and it will reflect badly on all of you. It will make life here tougher.'"

Harold Lasso of the Westchester Hispanic Coalition is an advocate for Latinos, but he holds to an assimilationist ideal and hopes that Latinos will do the work necessary to find acceptance. The problem of racism as he sees it is one that Latinos themselves can play a large part in solving. He says that there is a feeling among Latinos that they have to prove something to the other residents (Driscoll 1999a). He continues,

> They know they are being watched. They want to present themselves in a good light. They're always on the lookout. When you know you have to strive to get people's respect, it ends up being good. There's pressure to be normal. The young want to go to school and prove they can make the America dream [come true]. Then they say that their kids won't have accents when they get older. They'll be "pure Kisco."

In a similar vein, Pastor Vega of the Iglesia Hispana-Fuente de Vida told us the local dislike of Latinos is a visual thing: "People don't like the look of these poor people." He adds, "We need to assimilate to prosper. In private we can have our own culture, but in public we must fit in." We can see from his words that invisibility is considered the ideal among some Latinos who have adopted the dominant culture's view of themselves—if they don't like to look at us we will obligingly disappear into whiteness. The urge to teach a minority population to conform to dominant ways and help them assimilate is an example of toleration in the sense that the Other is incorporated on terms set by the dominant population. According to Paula Moya (2000), the assimilationist ideal is based on a false universality. Although this universality is in reality white, affluent, European American, and, to a degree, male dominated, it is not perceived as a racialized, class-structured, gendered, or historically particular ideal (Gracia and De Greiff 2000, 6).

There is an ambiguous in-betweenness, or liminality, to the Latino population from the other residents' viewpoint. Race relations in the United States have been predominantly interpreted within a dichotomous framework that cannot accommodate the brownness of the Latino day laborers.[58] The confusion among non-Latinos about the legal status of the immigrants produces a profound uneasiness. Their diasporic identities, their continuing strong transnational familial ties, their remittances home,[59] their continued use of their native language, and the incompleteness of their families (wives, children, parents left behind) make it difficult for other residents of Mount Kisco to imagine them ever becoming equal, fully participating members of the community. As one of our interviewees said,

> I can't imagine the Gualemalans ever becoming volunteer fireman, for example. They seem inwardly focused as a community—or maybe I should say outwardly focused on Central America. Other immigrant groups in the past couldn't maintain the same links; they had to become Americans to survive. They couldn't make weekly phone calls or buy cheap airlines tickets home and stay all winter living well on their hundred dollars a day they get here in the summer.

Alejandro Portes, Luis Guarnizo, and Patricia Landholt (1999, 228–29) argue that the popular American assumption that immigrants will remain and slowly assimilate to American culture is increasingly thrown into doubt. Now they argue that not only are there increasing transnational movements of people and goods, but, whereas previously economic success and social status depended exclusively on rapid acculturation, now there is also more of a dependence on cultivating strong social networks across national borders. For those who choose a more transnational identity, acculturation is less important (Goldring 1996; Guarnizo 1997).[60]

We should note here that the housing director for the Westchester Hispanic Coalition says that there is a popular misconception that most day laborers go home in the winter. Many actually go to the Carolinas or Florida to work on plantations (Schleifer 2000a). In April 2002, Peggie Arriaza of the Westchester Hispanic Coalition in Mount Kisco told us that of the 120 day laborers that she normally sees at Neighbor's Link, only about 2% go home for the winter. She said that about 50% stay in the area working in restaurants, or working as cleaners or cashiers in stores. Another 25% work as housecleaners in Hartford, Connecticut, and another 15% go to Florida to work on farms. These winter jobs have been arranged though the center. There is a confusion between day laborers, many of whom do not have green cards, and Latinos more generally. The day laborers are in many ways a quite separate group. A higher percentage of those with permanent jobs go back to Central America for vacations.

The attitudes about allegiance to the community, such as that expressed above, upset some of the Latinos in Mount Kisco. One man who immigrated from Guatemala fifteen years ago says he is permanently settled in Mount Kisco with his whole family. He has a secure job with a bank and is studying for a business degree and "really enjoys being part of the community." He says more and more Latinos are establishing permanent roots in the village. The president of the board of Neighbor's Link says, "I think the issue of day laborers has kept us from respecting and caring about the larger Latino population who are invisible. We all keep looking at the day laborer population because it's easy to see them. It's visible. But they're only the tip of the iceberg" (Gorman 2001b). This was confirmed by Arriaza who told us that there are several types of Latinos: day laborers (some transient), families with children trying to establish themselves, and those who are well established (mainly Hondurans and Peruvians). It is also confirmed by the fact that Neighbor's Link estimates that there are approximately 160 day laborers in Mount Kisco who seek jobs every morning, plus an unspecified number of day laborers who have steady seasonal employment with a patron. This constitutes a relatively small percentage of the 2,450 Latinos enumerated in the 2000 U.S. Census.

The View from Bedford

As we have noted, from the point of view of the residents of Mount Kisco, Bedford is one of the affluent towns that profits from the labor of the Latinos but doesn't have to suffer what they see as the negative externalities of their presence. Unsurprisingly, that isn't the way that Bedford residents see it. They are deeply ambivalent about the Latinos living in Mount Kisco. Displaying what we have described as aversive racism and white privilege, they would like them to live and spend their leisure time even further away, completely out of sight. Bedford residents tend to use Mount Kisco for shopping and services and hence are concerned with its appearance. One resident of Bedford told us, "When you step across the border into Mount Kisco, it's like a frontier, like crossing into a different country." In fact, as Price (2000, 101) points out, in contemporary America "wholly new borders are irrupting at multiple scales and in unlikely places." To this Davis (2000) adds that in numerous instances variously reinforced borders are appearing between residential communities of affluent Anglos and working-class Latinos.

One interviewee stated, "I don't go to Mount Kisco anymore because of all the Guatemalans hanging around on the streets. It's like going to the Bronx to shop. It looks dangerous." Some of the large stores on the strip, which runs between Bedford Hills and Mount Kisco, hire Latinos. A woman from Bedford told us, "I have a problem with all the development toward Mount Kisco. It is horrific to walk into a supermarket and no one speaks English." And a man said, "I went to the store and I think that I was the only English-speaking person there. I never went back." One woman who grew up in Bedford said, "I went to the bank machine and I couldn't believe it—the instructions were in English *and* Spanish. In Bedford!" For this woman, anything that is not Anglo is out of place in Bedford, a transgression against her memories and sense of aesthetic and moral order. She feels deeply angry and defeated by outsiders who she considers to have spoiled Bedford: "I looked up the hill to McClain Street. I was down in the Guatemalan section of Mount Kisco. Bedford nowadays is Jewish and Spanish. I don't recognize it anymore." For her, the old Anglo border of Bedford has been breached and in its place has sprung up what Rouse (1997, 17) has termed "a proliferation of border zones."

One of our interviewees asked us,

> Where have all the blacks gone? On Maple Avenue where the blacks used to live, there are all Guatemalans now. They have moved on and dispersed, I guess, into the middle-class parts of Mount Kisco and other towns. They were sometimes intimidating, and yet somehow their faces seemed more familiar. They didn't hang around so much, there weren't so many, and also they speak English. Somehow, they didn't seem so out of place. I suppose it's the sheer number of Guatemalans here; it no longer feels like my hometown.

And here as Tim Cresswell (1996, 11) says, "When an expression such as 'out of place' is used it is impossible to clearly demarcate whether social or geographical place is denoted—place always means both." Paul Cloke and Jo Little (1997) argue that residents of rural areas often think of things like homelessness, crime, and racial Others as being urban phenomena and, therefore, fundamentally out of place in the country, which they associate with idealized images of nature, close-knit community, and white privilege.[61]

A number of people we spoke to also mentioned a concern about the number of Latino children coming to the public school that Bedford shares with Mount Kisco. In their opinion, the fact that these children speak little English disrupts the classroom and lowers the quality of education. A real estate agent told us that he thought that the perception that the public school was "full of Hispanics" was beginning to hurt sales in the lower end of the market in town (houses in the $300,000 to $500,000 range). Above that he said it has little impact because people in this price range tend to send their children to private schools. In June 2000, voters in the Bedford-Mount Kisco School District voted down a controversial school budget. Although Mount Kisco voted for the budget, Bedford voted against it. The controversy was largely over new teaching positions in ESL (English as a Second Language) favored by many Latinos and other residents of Mount Kisco concerned about the assimilation of the "foreign element" in their midst. At present, 8% of the students in the district are non-English speaking and 80% of those are Latino (Rosenberg 2000). Only when the budget was modified by removing some of these ESL teachers was it finally passed (Schleifer 2000).

Others claim the Latinos have made the area unsafe. One long-term resident said, "My sister has been away in Europe for eight years. She has noted a tremendous change in Bedford Hills and Mount Kisco—the ethnic change—so many Latinos. My kids used to walk home from the movies; now I think it is too dangerous with all those people on the streets." Another spoke in strongly nativist terms of Mount Kisco as an extension of New York City, which to him represents a disfigured landscape of civil strife and illegal aliens:

> Mount Kisco is a dump filled with foreigners. Some of the big stores [along the strip between Bedford Hills and Mount Kisco] hire Guatemalans and bus incompetent people in from the Bronx because they will only pay $5 an hour. Local kids won't work for that. Most of them don't even speak English. You go in there and ask to buy a radio and they bring out a toaster. The manager of one place told me that the clerks were all stealing, so the store hired security people, also from the Bronx, and now they are all stealing too.

A woman we spoke to was sure that people standing on the streets must be up to no good: "Mount Kisco is saturated with illegal aliens. They hang around the streets with nothing to do day and night. I am sure they are very drug oriented." As we pointed out earlier, resident opinion as recorded on the Mount Kisco survey and police records do not support the view that Mount Kisco has experienced any significant increase in crime.

People in Bedford are clearly ambivalent about the Latinos. They know that some are in the United States illegally, but they want gardeners and cleaners. Landscaping and house-cleaning services have in fact become a big business in Bedford and other towns of Westchester since the mid-1980s. Only a few of Bedford's wealthiest residents have full-time cooks, cleaners, and gardeners. The most common exceptions are au pairs, usually hired for a few years by families with young children. The rest of those living in multimillion dollar houses hire Latinas to clean their houses and Latinos to tend the grounds. One resident, unhappy about the increase in Latinos in the area, told us he blames the new wealthy people who have bought houses in Bedford:

> Before the 1980s people did most of their own gardening, and if you wanted some work done at your house, you hired a kid. I worked for people when I was growing up. But [now] teenagers can't compete with the Guatemalans. Some of them work for as little as $4 to $5 an hour. You can't even talk to these people. They don't speak English.

We asked a local businessman about the workers:

> Probably most of them are illegal. At first people were nervous about hiring them because of the $10,000 a day fine if you get caught with them working for you. But people soon realized that the fine is a joke. It just isn't enforced around here. Now everyone is hiring them because they work hard and they are cheap.

One Bedford man we talked to was angry about illegal immigrants. He asked us,

> What is this country coming to when thousands of Hispanics are allowed to come into the country illegally every day? Pregnant women swim over the border and have babies at public expense and then their children become citizens. And nice Irish people have quotas. They have to wait years to get in. It just isn't right.

When we asked him what he thought of the Latinos who worked in Bedford, he looked slightly uncomfortable: "It's still not right that they come here, but I have to admit that I'm guilty of hiring them. I have a woman who cleans my house and I haven't seen her papers. I know it's not right, but she works hard and she is very reasonable."

Some feel that they themselves are part of the problem of illegal immigration that they do not fully understand but reluctantly take advantage of. They would rather not ask too many questions about either the legal status or housing situations of those they employ. As one respondent told us,

> We hire one man from Guatemala and in the past we hired others. We worry sometimes about where he stays especially in the winter because he has no work then. He seems to move around a lot, sometimes staying with friends. I know that he often shares a room with many other laborers. I have to contact him through his friend because he has no phone or permanent place to live. I guess I don't really want to know too much about his situation or whether he has a green card yet. Of course it's hard for me to communicate anyway. He speaks so little English and I have virtually no Spanish. I don't know if I am hiring him legally, but I guess I'm not because I pay cash. Although he once said he was paying taxes so he could get a green card. He says he goes home to see his family sometimes so maybe that means he is legal; otherwise how could he get back in? I really don't understand the whole illegal immigration thing. They say some travel here in rubber rafts across the Rio Grande risking their lives and others just seem to go back and forth by flying. I've seen the Latino travel agencies in Mount Kisco. All I know is that I can't be exploiting him because I pay $10 an hour and that is much more than minimum wage. But on the other hand I know housing is a struggle for him and I only hire him part time. I just don't ask too many questions about how he manages. Gardening services are so much more expensive and he is willing to do any odd jobs—painting and repairing and basically whatever I want. I really depend on him.

An article in the *New York Times,* titled "For Latino workers, dual lives: Welcomed at work, but shunned at home in the suburbs" (Gross 2000a), quotes a local minister who says, "Its easier to be generous with people and situations not close to us. It's like our reaction to a hungry child from another country versus a hungry family down the street who could diminish our property values." At the root of such tensions between the towns is a political structure supported by a deep attachment to the American individualistic idea of home-rule that spatially fragments social problems and discourages regional-level solutions. Anthony Cupaiuolo, professor of public administration who lives in Bedford, says, "I can't come up with a legal argument, but there is a moral argument for a regional solution" (Gross 2000a).

We did find on our most recent visit in the spring of 2002 less of a sense of panic about Latino day laborers. A heightened sense of panic by definition tends to die down. People begin to become more used to seeing Latino faces and they see that crime does not increase. But it is clear from newspaper reports that what has appeared to make the most noticeable difference in attitudes not only in Mount Kisco and Bedford, but in many similar places across the United States, is indoor hiring centers that greatly reduce the bodily presence of Latino men (Llorente 1998). As one activist for day laborers in Mesa City, Arizona, put it, "[A job center] is a way to give the workers some dignity and refuge from angry residents who don't want them on the street. But that won't stop the racism, but it might keep them out of sight. If we can help them become invisible, maybe people will stop complaining" (Ortiz 2000, 1).

Conclusion

Our concern in this chapter has been the active constitution of places through cultural struggle (Cresswell 1996, 13). It is about the relative success of Bedford in keeping its landscape unspoiled by the labor that maintains it's aesthetic. It is about the frustrated short-term failure of the non-Latino residents of Mount Kisco to enforce their normative geography of proper behavior in public places. It is also about the miserable conditions under which day laborers live and how the beautiful gardens in Bedford are internally related to the slum housing in Mount Kisco. As Mitchell (2000, 140) points out, "Each sort of landscape depends on the other: Our ability to consume is predicated on 'their' low wages and the miserable conditions that exist elsewhere." This chapter also hints at Mount Kisco's longer-term success in integrating some of the people from different cultural backgrounds on their own (largely) unilateral terms. This is due to not so much conscious strategizing, but to the overwhelming hegemony of the receiving culture that establishes the measures of success—for example, a good job at the bank, a bachelor's degree, and a nice house and car to keep one invisible. This is not to say, however, that the Latino Pastor Vega's vision of "having our own culture at home" is a trivial form of resistance (hooks 1990) to the dominant culture. There will be many ways that Latinos "temper and vary the effects of cultural hegemony" (Grewal and Kaplan 1994, 14) while at the same time "getting ahead" in terms of the material conditions of their lives. With growing numbers of Latinos in Westchester, there may be a degree of "multidirectional cross-cultural acculturation" (Moya 2000) as notions of who and what patterns of interacting belong in suburbia change due to the restructuring of suburban economies.

We have argued that global political and economic structures as well as the local structure of zoning supported by a socio-spatial ideology of local autonomy and home-rule lie beneath Bedford's successful exclusion of its day laborers and Mount Kisco's failure to keep out what they see as Latin America's and Bedford's "negative externalities." We have also attempted to show how aesthetic concerns dominate social relations between Latino immigrants and the receiving communities. Racism in the form of feelings of aversion and abjection and nervousness and disgust, as well as anxieties over maintaining social distance and containing pollution are manifested most clearly in the closer confines and integrated spaces of Mount Kisco and less obviously so in the exclusivist residential spaces of Bedford where laborers are seen primarily in clearly marked service roles. While residents of Bedford react to poor Latinos on the streets of Mount Kisco with aversion, their presence as servants in Bedford is naturalized as white privilege. One could even go so far as to say that the Latino day laborers, through their labor in the landscape, form a constitutive part of the status claims and by extension the identity of Bedford's residents. Put slightly differently, it is the Latino labor that reproduces Anglo Bedford.

CHAPTER **9**

Epilogue

Bedford Pastoral

At the center of the estate area of Bedford, across the road from the Bedford Golf and Tennis Club, at the corner of the Hook Road, and on one of the most loved and prestigious dirt roads in town stands the Bedford Oak, whose branches spread nearly 130 feet from tip to tip and whose age is estimated to be between 300 and 500 years old. The view from the road is a classic pastoral scene: a dry stone wall overhung by the boughs of the great oak and beyond a field framed by forest. It is little wonder that this scene, which so resonates of the cultural codes of the town, has been made iconic, for the view from the road is remarkable for its purity. One sees nothing modern, nothing that one could not imagine being in that view when the first white settlers cleared that field 300 years ago. The only thing that betrays the scene's modernity is a carved granite plaque attached to the wall by the Bedford Historical Society announcing to viewers that they are in the presence of history.

Just as residents of Bedford use this scene to stand for the town, so we will employ it to draw together the main themes of our book. Nowhere in the town is the line between nature and history so blurred as it is at the Bedford Oak, and nowhere is the interlinkage between aesthetics, affection, and place-based identity made so clear. The oak draws its symbolic power not because it stands out as different from the rest of the town, but precisely because it is a quintessential site of all that is valued in rural Bedford.

The Creation of a Town Symbol

The first mention of the Bedford Oak in the town records appeared in "Squire" James Wood's 1916 history of Bedford (Wood 1925), where he calls it "the pride of the town." But in his day it was called the Woodcock Oak after the family that owned the land in the 1860s. In 1936, the Bedford Farmers' Club, by then already an elite social club dedicated to the memory of farming, held their annual meeting under the tree. A local worthy, Colonel Thatcher T. P. Luquer, suggested that the tree's name be changed to the Bedford Oak. Symbolically, if not legally, it belonged to the town. L. Hollingsworth Wood, the son of "Squire" Wood, said in a speech to the Bedford Garden Club (Wood 1952),

> My father taught me to take my hat off whenever I passed what he used to call "our most venerable citizen." I do it to this day, as does my son and I commend

219

Fig. 9.1 The Bedford Oak.

it to you. Long may the old oak's proud crest stand in Bedford, a challenge to stability and generosity, so that its qualities may be found always in the character of Bedford citizens.

In 1947, Harold Whitman, whose family owned the estate on which the tree was located, deeded a small plot of land around the tree to the town in memory of his first wife. This was one of the first gifts of land by a wealthy individual in town to protect land from future development. Whitman's civic mindedness and love of nature have been celebrated in the town ever since. Wood (1952) said of this property transfer, "The tree became the Bedford Oak in truth as well as sentiment." The oak became further entrenched as the symbol of the town in Robert Barrett's 1955 history of Bedford whose frontispiece is a photograph of the tree and whose foreword is titled, "As it might be spoken by the Bedford Oak." The tree speaks as a witness to local history: "I am the symbol of that vital force that has breathed through all that has been best in Bedford and in what it is today or may hope to become. I am a continuing reminder that it is the indwelling spirit of a community that makes its history worth recording and its anniversaries worth observing."

The Bedford Oak is thought by residents to be a unique local tradition. However, we would argue that the oak resonates as a cultural symbol for the people of Bedford precisely because great oaks have an extra-local cultural history. Put slightly differently, the Bedford Oak illustrates what Pierre Bourdieu (1984) terms "enchantment," a process whereby people forget the cultural history of an object or idea, coming to see it as either natural and universal or, conversely, unique to them alone. In fact, the history of great oaks is neither universal nor unique to Bedford. The veneration of old oaks arose at a specific time and place and diffused to certain other places. The adoption of the idea of the great oak in Bedford was not a chance occurrence.

Keith Thomas (1983, 213–20) points out that the oak has been a symbol of strength in Britain since the sixteenth century and is an emblem of the British people. In the latter part of the eighteenth-century portraits of trees became popular and at the same time books on famous trees were produced in increasing numbers. Great trees, especially oaks, have been cherished not only for their beauty but also as symbols of continuity with the past. William Cowper wrote that to worship a venerable oak might be idolatry, but it was "idolatry with some excuse" (Cowper, cited in Thomas 1983, 216). Many English parishes had a famous tree and a few were known nationally, such as Greendale Oak at Welbeck, which was thought to be over 700 years old, and the Great Oak in Salcey Forest reputed to be 1,500 years old. The famous parish oaks, because of their great age, symbolized the continuity of the community for its residents. They were also a symbol of the family and in particular the aristocracy whom Edmund Burke called "the great oaks that shade a country." Eighteenth-century family portraits were often centered on a "family tree" symbolizing continuity (Thomas 1983, 218). The tradition of a great oak or town oak also became fashionable in the late nineteenth and early twentieth century in certain Anglophile towns on the east coast of the United States (Stilgoe 1988).

The Bedford Oak is in one sense a local phenomenon; there are no other great trees widely known and revered in the immediate surrounding towns. In another sense it is clearly derivative of an English tradition transplanted to the United States. The symbolism of the Bedford Oak is part and parcel of the Anglophilia that pervades Bedford. The late nineteenth century, as Eric Hobsbawm and Terrence Ranger (1983) show, was a fertile time for the "inventions of tradition" and it appears that the invention of the oak as a symbol of Bedford dates back to then and is probably a byproduct of the country house tradition adopted by wealthy New Yorkers who built estates in Bedford after the 1870s. Perhaps the myth of the oak in Bedford was consciously created by the locally famous Anglophile "Squire" Wood, who wrote it into the 1916 town history.

While all of the people we interviewed were aware of the local symbolism of the Bedford Oak, it is safe to say that none knew that this local tradition originated in Britain or that it was a regional tradition in the eastern United States in the late nineteenth century. One man told us, "I find this rather deflating. It makes it seem less special." Nevertheless the oak's aura of uniqueness, along with that of the village green, remain two of the positional goods that differentiate Bedford from neighboring towns.

Saving the Bedford Oak

In 1977, the Whitmans sold a thirty-acre parcel of land to a developer who proposed a subdivision of new houses. Controversially, he planned to site one house near the oak. Arguing that a new house would spoil the scene, the town exerted great pressure on the developer not to build near the tree, and in February of 1977, a compromise was reached, whereby the developer would give a gift of one acre of land around the tree to the town in exchange for a permit to build on a lot adjacent to the one-acre parcel. This was one of the early instances in Bedford of what has become the standard practice of developers trading land for permission to build. The town board was ambivalent about the developer's offer but in the end agreed to the proposal. Little did they anticipate the outraged reaction of residents who felt that a key landscape and Bedford's heritage would be desecrated. One letter to the editor said,

> Tuesday's town board meeting marked the death of one of Bedford's greatest scenic values. This spring, the backdrop for the Oak will most certainly not be the pastoral scene so familiar to Bedford residents and beautifully pictured postcards, but will be another house and a gaping garage . . . It is too bad the citizens of Bedford were not aware that the owner of the property would force the issue and threaten to withdraw his "gift" Tuesday night if his building site was not approved immediately. If he had agreed to the town board's request for a ten day postponement, the town and its residents could possibly have gotten the money together to buy the pasture to save the scene. But now it is gone. I doubt if we will be sending our friends the new picture postcards of the Bedford Oak. (Hencyey 1977)

The town board assured residents that the tree had been protected by the one-acre gift, while for their part the residents, faced with what they thought was a fait accompli, reluctantly accepted the decision. In May, however, the appearance of a bulldozer in the meadow behind the tree ignited the controversy once again, this time with increased ferocity. At this point the Bedford Historical Society joined the fray and began its campaign to save the tree in the name of heritage. The president of the society conceived of a plan to buy a two-acre plot of land around the tree, for which the developer was asking $38,000. The "Committee to Save the Oak," hastily formed for the purpose, enrolled the local newspapers, radio station, the four local garden clubs, civic groups, and merchants to help mobilize the population (Bedford Historical Society 1980). The committee developed a two-pronged argument to raise funds. The first of these was based on science. The committee argued that any house built anywhere near the tree would kill it, as runoff from a septic tank might poison it or a creek might be diverted that could deprive it of water. Given the zoning controls on the placement of septic tanks, this is highly unlikely. However, people wanted to believe it. This was an early instance in Bedford of scientific ecology being used to achieve an aesthetic end.

The second argument scripted the tree as the embodiment of history: "The great tree has thus been part of the life of Bedford from the Town's earliest days" (Bedford Historical Society 1980). Failure to support the tree was a rejection of history and the community itself, for "the Oak stands as witness that the people of Bedford understand and cherish their heritage" (Bedford Historical Society 1980). Poems were written about the tree and paintings were made of it. L. Hollingsworth Wood was quoted as proclaiming the oak "our most venerable citizen" (*Patent Trader* 1980). The campaign skillfully drew upon symbols of history and community to "save the scene," and effectively cast the developer in the role of the dreaded figure who intented to "pierce the very heart of the town."

The committee collected 426 tax-deductible contributions (Ploss 1977). As one organizer proudly told us, "It was a community endeavor. People wrote from way off. It was quite a united effort." The most sadly ironic effort was the contribution from a class of school children in the city of Yonkers, forty miles away in southern Westchester, who organized a bake sale and sent $30. As Yonkers has one of the poorest populations in Westchester, this contribution attests to the hegemony of elite views of nature and the idea that the landscapes of the wealthy are a resource for all and for this reason are justly subsidized.[1] Within the six weeks, $55,000 had been collected, and on June 20, 1977, the two-acre plot was conveyed to the Bedford Historical Society. Six years later, the town drafted an ordinance to protect all trees in town "of exceptional dimension, and community value." As one reporter noted at the time, "In a town where the Bedford Oak has an endowment fund, it is not surprising that Town officials are considering a resolution to protect trees on private lands from being destroyed" (Satkowski 1983). The fight to save this particular oak from a developer led inexorably to the fight to save all large trees from developers throughout Bedford.

A quarter of a century after the tree was saved from a developer, the scene remains the same. The Bedford Oak is a hybrid figure of local lore, part nature, part history. Children learn about it in the local schools and they take field trips to visit it, measuring its girth and calculating its height. In doing so, they are educated into the patterns and values of living the aestheticized life. Articles still appear in the local paper extolling its importance to the town. The Bedford Historical Society uses it as a symbol for fund-raising campaigns. It is tended by the town using all of the skill that modern arboriculture has at its disposal. The field in which it stands is kept mowed, and if perchance you should drive slowly down Hook Road on a summer day with your car window open, you might just hear the sound of Latin music coming from the cassette player of the Latino day laborers who tend this scene in the heart of rural Bedford.

Notes

Chapter 1

1. Benedict Anderson (1990) defines "imagined community" as a shared identity that can only be imagined, for the collectivity to which individuals feel attachment is too large for any individual to know all the other people who share that collective identity.
2. However, see Massey (1992).
3. An "edge city" is defined by Joel Garreau (1988, 4) as new urban complexes that have more than five million square feet of office space, more than 600,000 square feet of retail space, and more jobs than bedrooms. He describes their history in the following words:

> First we moved our homes out past the traditional idea of what constituted a city... (the suburbanization of America)... Then we wearied of returning downtown for the necessities of life, so we moved our marketplaces out to where we lived (the malling of America)... Today we have moved our means of creating wealth, the essence of urbanism—our jobs—out to where most of us have lived and shopped for two generations (the edge cities).

4. A sense of placelessness is said to be caused by overhomogeneity across space that diminishes national, regional, and local differences (Duncan 1999b). The term is associated with Relph (1976). Popular critiques of the placelessness of twentieth century American, middle-class consumer society include *The Lonely Crowd* (Riesman et al. 1950) and *The Organization Man* (Whyte 1956).
5. On the unevenness of the benefits and oppressions resulting from global restructuring, see Warf (2000) and Marchand and Runyan (2000). Cox (1993, 254) speaks of those who benefit most from globalization as a class of cosmopolitans who form a cross-national, cross-cultural set of elites with "common criteria of interpretation... and common goals anchored in the idea of an open world economy." But Harvey (1989, 350) argues that even those who benefit most from globalization sometimes exhibit a degree of withdrawal "into a kind of shell-shocked, blasé, or exhausted silence," and that they may be tempted to "bow down before the overwhelming sense of how vast, intractable, and outside any individual or even collective control everything is." Temporary retreats into a privatized world of country houses have long been a response of those tied into the operations of imperial and global cities. Bedford's elite's resistance to the negative impact of globalization through their retreat to the countryside is distinguishable from "resistance identities" posited by Castells (1997, 62–63) in his analysis of defensive community formations. Castells sees such defensiveness

225

as resistance to global capitalism. Bedford's localism, on the other hand, entails an aesthetic withdrawal that operates *within* a broad support for global capitalism.

6. Duany and Plater-Zyberk (1992) state that American suburbanites are "happy with the private realm they have won for themselves, but desperately anxious about the public realm around them . . . the late-20th century suburbanite's chief ideology is not conservativism or liberalism but NIMBYism: Not in My Back Yard."

7. For a discussion of differences between the uses of performative by Austin and Butler, see Butler (1997) and Lloyd (1999).

Chapter 2

1. Davis (1998, 400–3) describes similar "first ring" suburban decline in southern California where Latino suburbs have fallen into an "abyss of disinvestment and social destabilization" through loss of jobs and the tax base. Also see Valle and Torres (2000) for a more in-depth and nuanced analysis of Latino suburbs on the greater east side of Los Angeles.

2. "White privilege" is the "privileges and benefits that (are seen to) accrue to white people by virtue of their whiteness" (Pulido 2000, 13).

3. On fragmentation, see Danielson (1972, 1976) for a classic work on the political effects of fragmentation and Valle and Torres (2000), Weiher (1991), Cox and Jonas (1993), Brown (1994), and Jonas (2002) for more updated work on the subject. Zukin (1991, 165) also adds, "A far-sighted landed elite . . . tended to develop and control town-planning institutions. But in the suburbs they also relied on the traditional political fragmentation of towns and villages to provide space for action."

4. As we shall see in Chapter Eight, such institutions as the American Civil Liberties Union have made some slight inroads. This power pales in relation to the interests of those who can best benefit from the fragmented jurisdictional pattern of residential suburban regions.

5. We are grateful to the staff of the Museum in Pound Ridge Reservation for sharing their knowledge of local tribes with us.

6. Bedford Village, Bedford Hills, and Katonah are incorporated villages, often referred to as hamlets.

7. Just as Katz (1998) and Luke (1995) show how nature preserves tend to be located on economically less viable land, so well-preserved historical landscapes, such as Bedford Village, are often found in places that were never subjected to "disfiguring" modernisation projects. Bedford Village is still less exposed to the unwanted visual changes in the form of day laborers who arrive by train to work and find rental housing.

8. An excellent study of the nineteenth-century re-creation of this romantic idea is Wood's (1997) *The New England Village.*

9. Berenson v. New Castle (1975) 38 NY 2nd, 378 NYS 2d 672, 341 NE 2nd 235.

10. Totals add up to more than 100% because Hispanics can classify themselves as either black or white.

11. It should be noted that primarily because of the presence of illegal immigrants, but also because of the presence of unrelated people often occupying the same apartment, the number of Hispanics may be undercalculated.

12. National origin here means where one's ancestors came from.

13. See Baxandall and Ewen (2000) and Mattingly (2001).

14. An early example of a privately planned community is Gramercy Park in New York, formed as an exclusionary association with restrictive covenants in 1844. Later, in the beginning of the twentieth century, suburbs called garden cities with parkland appeared. These were privately planned developments with restrictive covenants (Howard 1902). McKenzie states that by 1928 "scores of luxury subdivisions across the country were using deed restrictions—including racially restrictive covenants—as their legal architecture" (McKenzie 1994, 9; Stern and Massengale 1981).

15. Lewis Mumford and the Regional Planning Association of America, of which he was a member, encouraged the early movement toward restrictive covenants run by homeowner's associations that came to be called CIDs. Today more than 12% of the American population lives in CIDs (McKenzie 1994). CIDs attempt to maximize the number of units in a development by offering open amenity space held in common rather than in private gardens or yards.

16. There are also many large developer-planned communities (MPCs, or master planned communities) that include public spaces to encourage a sense of community as well as residential space. Some of these communities have what are referred to as CC&Rs (covenants, conditions, and restrictions on the deeds), a relatively new form of private residential government that sets limits on many aesthetic aspects of individual properties such as exterior colors and types of planting (McKenzie 1994). Increasingly such planned communities are gated (Davis 1990, 1998; Ellen, 1996; McKenzie 1994).

17. The aesthetic can, however, in some instances heighten class awareness. For example, in England, "posh" accents and clothing of upper-class "toffs" accentuate class-based antagonisms for many middle- and working-class people.

18. In everyday speech and often in academic writing, class is used as a descriptive term referring to status, occupation, or lifestyle and consumption patterns. Despite the recent increased interest in issues of identity, class remains the one relatively neglected of the list of variables that Butler refers to as the "agonizing etceteras"—race, gender, sexuality, and class. Smith (2000) and others have argued that it is in fact *because* of this recent interest in identity formation that class as production relations is neglected. We take this point and see in places like Bedford an aestheticization of class relations whereby class is seen to be based largely on taste, aesthetic values, consumption patterns, and lifestyle. With the weakening of trade unions and the globalizing of class relations (Smith 2000), class in the United States today tends to be most consciously articulated and most fully elaborated in the homeplace rather than the workplace; the emphasis in most people's minds is on consumption rather than production relations. Cultural analysis can enrich our understanding of this aestheticization process as well as the lived reality and material conditions of the class relations that are aestheticized. Although class, gender, race, and sexuality should be understood as fragmented and fluid practices and performances, it should also be recognized that they are structured by relations of exclusion and exploitation. In fact, an overemphasis on fluidity and performance in this context can lead toward a confirmation of liberal individualism. On the concept of class in cultural geography, see Duncan and Legg (2003).

19. See Featherstone (1991) on the function of sign values in the aestheticization of contemporary everyday life. On the aestheticization of history and community as illusion see Boyer (1992); Featherstone (1992); Harvey (1989); Jameson (1984); Sorkin (1992); and Zukin (1992), but see Jacobs (1998) for a cautionary note and critique of any automatic assumption of the depoliticizing effects of aestheticization.

20. In Chapter Eight we do, however, point to a potential form of regional organization that might help Latino immigrants come together from across Westchester to improve their chances of finding affordable housing. On this, also see Valle and Torres (2000, 40–43).

21. For an elaboration of the idea of complicity in cultural geography, see Duncan and Duncan (forthcoming).

22. We agree with Bourdieu (1987) when he says it is important to transcend the opposition between the objectivist or structuralist and constructivist or subjectivist accounts. He says, "Any theory of the social universe must include the representation that agents have of the social world and, more precisely, the contribution they make to the construction of the vision and consequently, to the very construction of that world."

23. See Atkinson and Laurier (1998), Philo (1998), and Sibley (1998), on aversion and the abject in relation to place.

24. Perhaps this is because we have chosen to study mainly elite communities. Using standpoint theory (Harding 1991; Hartsock 1987), it might be possible to show that the place-based experiences of the more oppressed members of society might provide a more "objective" basis for a critical and progressive view of social and political structures. On the other hand, interviews in Bedford and adjoining towns have convinced us that, in this case at least, members of all classes share aestheticized views and alienation from the structures of inequality (N. Duncan 1986; Duncan and Duncan 1997). For a discussion of both the reactionary and progressive aesthetic attachments to place, see Jacobs (1998) and Penrose (1993).

25. In Nancy Duncan's Ph.D. dissertation (1986) and our previous work on the area (Duncan and Duncan 1997), we used 150 interviews conducted in the early 1980s that have been largely left out of the present work (except as they gave us a longer term perspective than we would otherwise have achieved) because we wanted to focus (principally) on recent Bedford.

26. We interviewed twenty-two men and twenty-nine women from Bedford and seventeen men and eight women from Mount Kisco. Included were ten homemakers, thirteen day

laborers, eight local business owners, people in the entertainment business, students, lawyers, stockbrokers, bankers, venture capitalists, cleaners, shop clerks, a designer, a taxi driver, an electrician, a plumber, a policeman, and a horse trainer. We also interviewed people with special knowledge about the issues raised in our study. These included six town officials, three real estate agents, two developers, two social workers, an environmental activist, a landscaper, and a pastor.

27. The number of years spent in Bedford was quite evenly spread: <5 yrs. (9), 5–10 yrs. (8), 10–20 yrs. (10), 20–40 yrs. (9), 30–40 yrs. (7), and 40+ yrs. (8). The question was not asked of the respondents from Mount Kisco.

28. On methodological issues in studying elites, see (Cormode 1999; Hughes and Cormode 1998a; McDowell 1998).

29. Well-known academic and popular studies of elites include Aldrich (1988), Baltzell (1958, 1964), Fussell (1983), and Lapham (1988), and of affluent places include, Birmingham (1987), Breen (1989), Dorst (1990), and Shoumatoff (1979).

30. Woods (1998) makes some useful observations that apply in the case of Westchester. He argues that elite status is context specific. In a given town, there are usually multiple elites drawing on a range of sources of power and prestige. Elite status is fluid, permeable, and nonhomogeneous and varies according to the scale at which it is recognized and can be mobilized. Woods (1998, 2106) points out that an individual actor does not need to control all types of resources but simply needs to be able to enroll them into a network of action when necessary. We found this to be true of the various types of elites we studied. Despite the varying bases of their status, they tend to come together over issues of landscape preservation, if not over the finer details of this process.

31. Although it is sometimes thought that elites are more inaccessible than others, we found in Bedford a willingness to be interviewed regardless of status. While we had known some informants for a long time and had interviewed them for earlier studies, the great majority we had not met before we interviewed them. We think the excellent response rate is explained in part because we contacted them in person or by telephone rather than by letter. A few we contacted through friends. Respondents found the topic nonthreatening, as it had to do with their home community rather than their business (with the exception of some whose work relates to the local landscape and its development). They assumed that we would be sympathetic to their efforts to preserve the landscape. Most seemed keenly interested in talking about their town as evidenced also by the high response rate to the town's mailed questionnaires.

32. For a discussion of some of the ethical issues surrounding our research, see Duncan and Duncan (2001a).

Chapter 3

1. Arcadian ecology can be traced back to the seventeenth and eighteenth centuries. Worster (1977) describes it as the nostalgic ideal of a simple rural life in close harmony with nature. It evolved into the contemporary ecological view of coexistence with, rather than domination over, nature by humans; also see Oelschlaeger (1991) and Pepper (1984). And for the popular reception of the idea, see Schmitt (1990). On the romantic vision of wilderness, see Nash (1982), Oelschlaeger (1991), Thomas (1983), and Williams (1989). See Bunce (1994), Jackson (1985) and Marx (1964) on the pastoral basis of American values. On the nineteenth-century politics and popularization of the picturesque, see Bermingham (1986). On aristocratic ideas of stewardship, see Tucker (1982). See Wood (1991, 1997) on early historic preservation. On Jeffersonian agrarianism and yeoman democracy, see Cosgrove (1984), Schmitt (1990), and Stilgoe (1988).

2. In his work on landscape and power, W. J. T. Mitchell (1994) uses the term "landscape" to mean both a scene "out there" in the world and a genre of painting associated with an histori-cally specific way of seeing. We use him, however, in the context of our own work to mean the former. The landscape "out there," so to speak, can of course only be seen through historically and culturally filtered lenses constructed in large part through a practical familiarity with paintings. These lenses are by no means to be interpreted as providing a unified or necessarily uncritical perspective.

3. Moscovici (2000, 243) writes, "many people talk about and use notions pertaining to Darwinian theory or psychoanalysis without even knowing the names Darwinism or

psychoanalysis, Darwin or Freud." We would add that a great number of other people have heard of these thinkers, but often subscribe to their ideas as part of common sense not making a connection to the scholarly texts.

4. Shoumatoff wrote this in the 1970s; since then, even more fields have succumbed to the regrowth of forest.

5. Gandy's (2002, 136) comments on Long Island parkways also applies to Westchester's "roads to nature"; they "could only be experienced in cars: their underpasses were purposely built too low for busses to clear them, so that public transit could not bring the masses of people out from the city . . ."

6. It is worth noting here that while wilderness is traditionally associated with transcendental-ism, pastoralism has religious connotations as well, as the cognate term "pastor" suggests.

7. Pregill and Volman (1993, 394) say that the works of such romantic landscape theo-rists as Repton, Price, and Chambers "were required reading for all cultured New World residents . . . who were conversant with the general principles of landscape gardening and picturesque theories of design."

8. Some of those who perform the labor necessary to maintain these landscapes come from other traditions or understandings of landscapes. While many value rurality, the origins of their attitudes toward landscapes differ. For example, Latino day laborers recently arrived from rural Guatemala told us they love Bedford for its rurality but find some of the choices of "los ricos" [wealthy Anglos], such as dirt roads, bizarre.

9. Butler (2000, 37) expresses such appropriation as a kind of mimesis that causes any claim to originality to lose some of its credibility. As she says, "Mimesis can effect a displacement . . . or, indeed reveal that [the original] . . . is nothing other than a series of displacements that diminish any claim to primary or authentic meaning." Sharp (1999, 199) argues that one of the benefits of Butler's dynamic understanding of identity performance as pattern of repetition is that it "allows a possibility for politics and for transformation, for if there is always a compulsion to repeat, 'repetition never fully accomplishes identity' (Butler 1990, 24). Furthermore, identity is only secure when performed 'correctly,' and, as Butler's work has demonstrated, this offers a great potential for subversion."

10. This style of image advertising, which is still uncommon in real estate advertising else-where, began early in Bedford. In 1951, one advertisement read, "Picture Book Land. Lakes! Waterfall! Secluded, attractive. 3 bths, 3 fireplaces, 15 acres, pastures, evergreens, swimming, fishing."

11. As late as 1979, Shoumatoff wrote, "The days of big houses ended with the Second World War. Maids disappeared and they never appeared again . . . I can think of a dozen (estates) right now that are vacant on the hill tops of Bedford. Some of them have been on the market for years and haven't drawn so much as a nibble."

12. Currier and Ives were nineteenth-century printmaker of rural scenes. The prints were origi-nally cheap mass-produced pictures that have gained dignity with age and are now collectors items. Being so familiar, they help to conjure up pictures of rurality in the minds of home buyers in Bedford.

Chapter 4

1. Houses in the Hamptons are generally even more expensive than in Bedford.

2. We believe that most of our informants felt comfortable about expressing opinions, even "politically incorrect" ones. In reference to Mount Kisco, disparaging comments about Lati-nos were openly expressed. Those in the minimum four-acre zones of Bedford often do not socialize with neighbors and some told us that they don't often ever see them.

3. In addition to providing tax relief, state and federal funds are made available to the county or a land trust to purchase conservation easements so that it will remain open space. Funds are also available for historic preservation of farms and farm houses (Witherspoon 2001a).

4. Seventy-two percent more people think the rural character is being lost than think it is improving. Seventy-eight percent more people think open space is being lost (town of Bedford 1998).

5. There were 57% more who favored stricter regulation than who favored looser controls. Length of residence and part of town were not significant.

6. It might be added that the term "view" is more often associated with long-distance viewpoints. The preserves have few such viewpoints. Most of the views that people chose are available from a car window.

7. Some others have very high wire fencing to keep out deer who not only damage plants and small trees, but also bring ticks carrying Lyme disease. This type of fencing is seen as purely functional and serves no aesthetic purpose.

8. As we have noted, it is clear from looking at the landscape of Bedford that there was obviously a fashion for gates in the 1920s.

9. Serious crime is rare in Bedford. Four people were murdered one night in 1978 by some men who drove up from New York City with the intention of killing one young man. Unfortunately, they were misdirected and ended up in the wrong house. After killing the occupants, they drove on and found and killed their intended victim and his parents' housekeeper.

10. Guard Hill, the most popular road (133 votes) is dirt and has pastoral views.

11. We discuss this battle in detail in Chapter Five.

12. The coalition is composed of seventeen organizations: Beaver Dam Sanctuary, Bedford Association, Bedford Audubon Society, Bedford Farmer's Club, Bedford Garden Club, Bedford Historical Society, Bedford Riding Lanes Association, Chowder and Marching Society, Cross River Reservoir Association, Marsh Sanctuary, Mianus River Preserve, Northeast Katonah Community League, Nature Conservancy, Regional Review League, Rusticus Garden Club, Westchester Land Trust, and Westmoreland Sanctuary.

13. The irony of designating dirt roads as environmentally fragile will be explored in the next chapter.

Chapter 5

1. Ley and Mercer (1980, 100) surveyed ninety-eight land-use conflicts in Vancouver, Canada. The leading single argument raised against a land use was failure to reach a "required level of visual attractiveness," and the silence over economic impacts was remarkable. Of the ninety-eight conflicts, on only one occasion was an allusion to potential tax revenues made.

2. For an overview of land-use planning, development, and regulation in the United States, see Platt (1995).

3. For example, a New York court upheld a two-acre minimum lot zone by stating that protecting the "appearance and environment of this rural high-class community" is included under general welfare. Elbert v. Village of North Hills, 28 N.Y.S. 2d 317, 318 (Sup. Ct.) (1941).

4. Village of Euclid v. Ambler Realty Company, 272 U.S. 365, 386–87 (1926).

5. Berenson v. New Castle 38 N.Y. 2nd 378 N.Y.S. 2d 672, 341 NE 2nd 235 (1975).

6. Southern Burlington NAACP v. Township of Mount Laurel, 67 N.J. 151, 423 U.S. 808 (1975).

7. Oakwood at Madison, Inc. v. Township of Madison.

8. Some school districts in Westchester spend nearly three times as much per pupil as other districts.

9. As we will see in Chapter Eight, for certain groups, namely the Latinos of Westchester, there are new organizations that may provide a model for low-income people to organize politically to challenge the local rather than regional orientation of zoning and planning in American suburbs. On this, see Valle and Torres (2000).

10. In an earlier survey of 130 respondents from a broad range of socio-economic backgrounds, 14% of respondents from Bedford cited exclusion as the reason for zoning (Duncan 1986). In New Castle, 4% of respondents and in Mount Kisco, 17% of respondents thought exclusion was the purpose. More common reasons were the following: "keep it rural" (Bedford 65.5% and Mount Kisco 43.5%) and "privacy" (Bedford 14% and Mount Kisco 26%). Only a few of Mount Kisco residents were more cynical about the exclusionary aspect of zoning. For example, respondents made comments such as, "a form of protection against 'them out there,'" and "'keep Bedford green' is a euphemism used by those who inherited money." However, the majority of Mount Kisco's residents defended Bedford's zoning and did not think it had any adverse effects on them. Typical remarks were the following: "To give people elbow room," "I think it's alright . . . to each his own. People must want it," "To keep it the way it is . . . forever green," and "That's the way the people who own the land want it. There's no reason to change it." See also Duncan and Duncan (1997).

11. This is also not to say that in a more confined space, these same people might not show more intolerance. The social factor is simply less of an issue in their situation, especially for those who use the private schools and clubs.

12. When we asked him who it is who argues so relentlessly against zoning, he could only cite one person, Stuart Shamburg, a local lawyer who represented the developer in the Berenson v. New Castle case and was known locally, especially in the 1970s and early 1980s for his stance against exclusionary zoning.

13. Sixty-seven percent more people favored stricter rather than looser regulations. There was very little difference between the areas of town or based on length of residence (Town of Bedford 1998).

14. As the structure of this legislation and citizen reaction is virtually identical to the other environmental legislation, it is not discussed in any detail here.

15. One old-timer hinted at corruption in the past (forty or more years ago) in regard to the granting of variances more generally. At present, some informants claim that celebrities in town find it easier to get variances, although there are a significant number of instances where celebrities have had their plans thwarted.

16. For a discussion of the politics of wetlands mitigations, see Robertson (2000).

17. In the summer of 1994 this road had to be rebuilt four times (Sourby 1994b).

18. See Gandy (2002) for an excellent discussion of the history and contemporary politics of New York City's water supply.

19. New York City is the largest city in the country without a filtration system.

20. While Gandy's (2002, 263–64) general point that sewering in poor upstate towns would improve water quality is undoubtedly correct, the particular towns he names do not fit his description. He writes, "many small low-income towns in the Catskill-Delaware system, such as Bedford and Katanah [sic] have no sewers." Bedford also does not fit his description (2002, 65) of upstate towns that are pro-development and against stringent environmental controls.

21. Bedford would have a higher tax base if it allowed more commercial and industrial development in town.

22. In early 2002, the state agreed to allow Bedford Hills and Katonah to tap into the sewer system of the Bedford Hills Correctional Facility, thereby cheaply solving the sewage problems of these two hamlets. It appears, however, that the town will have to find a way to deal with waste from Bedford Village (Nardozzi 2002a).

23. See Demeritt (1998, 182–85) on tree cutting and forestry management.

24. For a fascinating discussion of the conflict between tree legislation, private property, and differing conceptions of individualism in Vancouver, Canada, see Ley (1995).

25. Here we assume he means that people's right to cut trees should extend to the perimeter of their properties.

26. A case for more extreme sanctions was recently reported in neighboring Greenwich, Connecticut. A doctor moved into town, bought a heavily treed property, and knocked down the house and ninety-five trees, some of which were on wetlands and some on public land. The building permit for his nearly completed house was held up until he replaced the trees at a cost of $100,000. His new patients abandoned him, and he subsequently sold his property and moved to New York (Schembari 1996).

27. Conservation easements will be discussed in Chapter Six.

28. The Bedford town planner stated that in 2000 Bedford had 1,200 rental units, most of which are located in the three hamlets (Nardozzi 2000h). Some of these units are large houses, and it is unclear what percentage of the 1,200 units would be classed as affordable, given the town's formula.

29. George Raymond was formerly the chief planning consultant to Mount Kisco in the days when it was adding affordable housing to its stock. In the last decade, Mount Kisco's middle-class constituency has grown more anti-development in orientation and the village now hires the same firm as Bedford.

30. Rippowam-Cisqua proposed to have 12 fields for 400 students while the public schools in town have four fields for 1500 students.

31. Another case of an individual who has battled the town of Bedford and two adjoining towns is Donald Trump who has been attempting to build an exclusive golf club and having great difficulty getting his plans passed.

Chapter 6

1.   We say rhetoric because science is *used* rhetorically, not because we see it as *merely* rhetoric or somehow wrong. We should perhaps make it clear here where we stand vis-à-vis certain interdisciplinary debates that have been ongoing in geography and other fields for some time. Demeritt (1998) distinguishes among various types of realism and social constructivism showing which are compatible and which mutually opposed. Although there are many such discussions in science studies, philosophy, and social science, we have chosen Demeritt's because he uses examples that are relevant to the environmental issues discussed in this chapter. We subscribe to a similar position, one that might be called ontological realism and epistemological falliblism. His article is useful for its emphasis on nonhuman nature as having a type of agency that actively resists erroneous scientific understandings. Although such resistance or nonvalidation may or may not be recognized, it is not without consequence due to the active nature of "nature." While we emphasize institutions, historical and cultural discourses, and political-economic and emotional biases in the production, circulation, and use of scientific knowledge, we do not intend to signal a strong social constructivism that is incompatible with a realist ontology or empirical methodology.

2.   As evident from continuing debates in the geographic literature (see Braun and Castree 1998; Castree and Braun 2001; Demeritt 1994a, 1994b, 1998, 2001; Gandy 1996; Harrison and Burgess 1994; Livingstone 1995; Proctor 1998; Walton 1995; and Willems-Braun 1997), positions that focus attention on ideas, discourses, texts, myths, and imaginings are commonly misunderstood (sometimes disingenuously) as idealist, relativist, or social constructivist in a strong anti-foundational sense. For example, the statement that wilderness is a human creation is not an ontological assertion. It certainly does not mean that the nonhumanized landscape to which the word refers (the reality "out there," so to speak) would not or could not exist independently of human knowledge of it; but in actuality, it is not entirely independent in that knowledge practices do impinge on it. Wilderness as a *concept* is humanly imposed and has a particular geography and history. Like the concept of race, which refers to *real* people who are categorized as belonging to one race or another based usually on skin color, the categorizing *really* happens. The concept (race) has *real,* very material effects on peoples' lives. But it is a humanly created category, one that happens not to have a sound scientific basis. Nevertheless, it has a very real, very violent history.

3.   The "fresh air" program offers children from poor urban families an opportunity to spend a week or more with a family that lives in the country.

4.   What Demeritt (2001, 24) says of the native peoples of northern New England applied in Westchester as well: "Access to game resources was controlled by strict property rights, which allocated hunting territories to particular family groups. Hunting practices were regulated by a complex belief system of myth and origin stories that ensured game species were not over-exploited. None of these made any sense to English settlers." Demeritt quotes Cronon (1983, 57) who says that the English settlers "both trivialized the ecology of Indian life and paved the way for destroying it."

5.   One could argue that if it is the rich who can afford to protect nature and they have a culture of responsible stewardship, then the society benefits. (A similar argument was made in Vancouver by wealthy homeowners. They argued that because they could afford to maintain large properties with beautiful gardens for all passersby to enjoy, then they should be subsidized through lower taxes [See Duncan 1999]) Such an argument in the case of Bedford is most persuasive if one naturalizes the whole idea of individual houses on large lots dotted across a landscape protected from further development by various means including the use of septic tanks, which puts water quality limits on density of development. An alternative pattern of more concentrated development possible through the use of sewer systems would allow for regional preserves or parks large enough to effectively support biodiversity across a wide range of plants and animals. The idea of suburban sprawl with small individual houses on small lots so abhorrent to many Bedford residents can be seen as a naturalized aesthetic reaction. However, what may not have occurred to many people in Bedford is that large houses dotted across fields and hills could be considered sprawl from an ecological point of view. Aesthetic scale, or the scale of landscape as view, is naturalized within romantic discourses.

6.   See Katz (1998, 49) on the fact that until a recent trend toward seeing preserves as biodiversity

banks, much of the land selected for preservation was available because it had little economic value.

7. See Demeritt (1998, 82–83). Katz (1998, 48) writes about "problematic tropes of wild and wilderness." She points to the increasing tendency within capitalism to think of nature as an investment or "biodiversity reserve." In fact, she (1998, 48) says that "the environmentalist literature is so full of metaphors of investment saving and future gain that it often reads like a boardroom script." She also points out that the nature conservancy now operates on a global scale and has links with corporate capitalism, which encourages the creation of preserves to be saved for future biotechnical and other potential uses. Although this level of corporate environmentalism and "bio-accumulation" strategies are new, we can see in Bedford a similar, more romantic, less commercial interest in nature preserves as an investment for the future. Katz (1998, 53) provides an interesting parallel example: "The Ordway family, heirs to the notoriously polluting Minnesota Mining and Manufacturing Company (3M) is one of the darlings of the Nature Conservancy. They and their well-heeled neighbors along the Brule River in an exclusive neck of northern Wisconsin formed a property association in the 1950's to protect 'their' river and its environs, their estates of thousands of acres each." She says they enlisted the nature conservancy to protect their properties (from their own heirs) and prevent future development.

8. We are aware that these preserves like other relatively small areas including even suburban lawns or small urban gardens or parks can provide a viable habitat for some species to thrive and thus we are not opposed to preserves. We simply question some of the claims made in their support.

9. Katz (1998) argues that restoration ecology, which is also based on a nature/human dichotomy, tends to be local in scale and romantic in orientation. Nevertheless, she says it is based on more ecologically sound principles and is not so apt to fix nature at one point in time. We agree with her general point but might be less strong in condemning preserves. The management principles applied at individual preserves change and respond to new scientific knowledge, even as they continue to be traditional in their rhetoric. Managers may employ romantic rhetoric for purposes of public consumption—some no doubt believe their own rhetoric. Furthermore, we have found that it is possible for people to hold contradictory sets of beliefs, especially when these beliefs work toward the same end.

10. Luke (1995) considers that much of the land preserved by the nature conservancy in the United States and elsewhere does not support viable ecologies. He claims instead that preserves tend to serve as memorials to what once was. "Nature cemeteries" is his perhaps overly disparaging term. It is clear, however, that nature in the Mianus River Gorge Preserve, for example, is seen not so much as an historical process, but as a remnant of a past time. However, it is important to note that Luke's view neglects the active agency of "nature," which changes and survives despite efforts at preservation.

11. On the concept of nature in twentieth-century natural garden design, see Wolschke-Bulmahn (1997).

12. But see N. Duncan (2003).

13. The naturalized separation of private homeplaces from "already spoilt" workplaces reinforces this excuse because people can believe they are good environmentalists despite complicity with environmental irresponsibility in their workplace or in the distant places where their workplace decisions may have negative environmental and social impacts.

14. In an earlier survey conducted in four northern Westchester towns (Duncan 1986, 282–322; Duncan and Duncan 1997), respondents were asked, "What would you think of regional planning and zoning as opposed to each town having autonomy in these matters?" An overwhelming majority (103 versus five) said each town should decide for itself. "Home rule" was taken for granted as central to the American way of life. Typical comments were as follows: "That would be striking at the heart of the American way of life," "Each town must decide for itself," "You have to have home rule," "Each town has its own personality," "If I wanted a different approach, I would move there," "Each town knows its own problems; the county could care less," "I would hate that. I would move away. I'm a great one for home rule," "It's unfair for people from elsewhere to dictate changes. Regional planning would be a gross infringement," "It's a disaster," "It's a gross infringement," and "Maybe if I was a twenty-five-year-old sociologist, but at sixty-five I wouldn't like that." We argued in these earlier studies that the extraordinary degree of agreement is particularly amazing

because local control is not actually in the interests of many of the poorer respondents from towns such as Mount Kisco who suffer the effects of exclusionary zoning in northern Westchester.

15. The preserve has substituted the word "forest" for the word "garden," which appeared in the original version of this poem (Gurney 1979, 237), reminding us once again of the close connection between gardens and nature preserves.

16. For a geographical perspective on Lyme disease, see Duncan (2003).

17. In her study of the love of nature, anthropologist Kay Milton (2002, 93) says, "The (social scientific) emphasis has been on 'values' as guides to decision making rather than on 'valuing' as part of the process of living in and engaging with the world." Surveys, such as the one we draw on here, record preferences and to a certain extent values. We have found, however, that it is useful to conduct in-depth interviews to discover the depth of emotional attachment.

18. The Bedford Farmer's Club was founded by local elites in the mid-nineteenth century in order to introduce agricultural innovations into Bedford to make it more competitive in the New York market. It also served as a social club from its inception, and while some poor farmers in town were invited to its meetings, they often felt intimidated by the lavish displays of food and drink. Increasingly, by the late nineteenth century as farming declined in Bedford, the club became a social gathering for reminiscing about farming and "old Bedford." It continues to serve this purpose today although to dwindling numbers of Bedford families. Twenty years ago most of the large landowners in town were members; because there are many wealthy newcomers, this is no longer the case.

Chapter 7

1. On the concretization of history as social memory in the landscape, see Johnson (1995) and Withers (1996). On landscape and social memory, see Till (1999, 254–55).

2. As Wallace (1986, 140) points out,

> The Haymarket affair and the great strikes of the 1880s appear to have been the events that galvanized the bourgeoisie into reconsidering its disregard for tradition. Convinced that immigrant aliens with subversive ideologies were destroying the Republic, elites fashioned a new collective identity for themselves that had at its core the belief that there was such a thing as the American inheritance, and that they were its legitimate custodians. Class struggle was transmuted into defense of "American values" against outside agitators.

In the vanguard of this movement were the patrician elites who "discovered in their historical pedigrees a source of cultural and psychic self confidence" (Wallace 1986, 140). Historical societies and preservation groups were also formed at this time and family genealogies and biographies of American heroes increased in popularity.

3. Mrs. J. V. R. Townsend, colonial dame, vice-regent of the Mount Vernon Ladies Association, explained in 1900 that the "Americanizing of the children—by enlisting their interest in historical sites and characters has a great significance to any thinking mind—and making of good citizens of these many foreign youths" (Wallace 1986, 141).

4. For critical approaches to heritage, see Tunbridge and Ashworth (1996); Uzzell and Ballantyne (1998); Landzelius (1999); and Graham, Ashworth, and Tunbridge (2000).

5. In the foundation myth of town, they *are* "fathers," for it is always twenty-two *men* who are mentioned.

6. See Dorst (1990, 182) who describes another such museum as a "vehicle of traditionalization and the selective reduction of a complex history to a simple readily comprehensible set of images that establish legitimizing connections between present institutions and an imagined past." Also see Jordanova (1989).

7. On reality effects, see Barthes (1973).

8. For an interesting contrast to Bedford in this regard, see Hoelscher (1998).

9. See Eco (1983) on the hyperreal.

10. Johnson (1996) reminds us that not all heritage sites are sanitized. Some may in fact be a source of new critical insight about the past.

11. Yonkers is a declining industrial city in southern Westchester with a population in 2000 of 196,086 people!

Chapter 8

1.   The Village/Town of Mount Kisco is its official name. Some of those we quote call it the village, others the town. For the sake of simplicity, we refer to it as the village.
2.   We use the terms Latino or Latina except in quotations and where the official term Hispanic is normally used. The 2000 U.S. Census for the first time lists Spanish/Hispanic/Latino as a category broken down by national origin or ancestry, eliminating the official sanctioning of the homogenizing term Hispanic, allowing for the diversity of nationalities, ethnicities, and racial identifications to be somewhat better represented, while also allowing the various groups to gain representation as a whole in terms of social and economic indicators. The U.S. Census also asks respondents to list one or more races they consider themselves to be, allowing Latinos to list, for example, white *and/or* black, African American or Negro *and/or* American Indian where appropriate. Although official organizations and newspaper reports tend to use the term Hispanic, most Latinos we met identify themselves either as Latinos or by their national origin—for example, Salvadoran. Latino and Latina appear to be the preferred self-applied terms to distinguish themselves as a group (although amorphous) for political or social reasons. We also use the locally self-applied term Latino when men and women are referred to collectively.
3.   For a striking parallel on Long Island, see Baxandall and Ewen (2000, chapter 17). Local newspapers have been reporting similar anxieties about the growing visibility of Latinos on the streets of towns across the United States. Task forces are being set up in many towns and cities to find solutions to the problem of (as one newspaper puts it) how to "satisfy businesses and residents who don't want to *see* men on sidewalks waiting for work" [emphasis added] (*Arizona Republican* 2000, B3).
4.   Prior to 1965, the vast majority of new immigrants to the United States were European. After 1965, Afro Caribbeans, Asians, and Latin Americans became the largest groups.
5.   Here he excludes Brazil as not having a Spanish surname population. New York City, Davis (2000, 16) says, vies with Los Angeles and Miami for the distinction "capital of Latin America." Latin America is defined in this context as a "usable" set of nations or hybrid identities negotiated within what Davis calls a "contemporary force-field of the majority culture and its 'others'."
6.   On the connection between the use of public space and aesthetics, see Mitchell (1997).
7.   For other examples of the aesthetic attitude that wishes to erase the signs of labor from the landscape, see Williams (1973), Cosgrove (1984), Daniels (1993), and Mitchell (1996a).
8.   The Westchester County Department of Planning Division of Housing and Community Development (DHCD) receives federal funds (CDBG, HOME, and HOPWA) to help them provide grants to developers. However, these were never adequate and have been dwindling (Westchester County Housing Opportunity Commission 1997).
9.   The increase in the number of Central Americans in Westchester County since 1980 is in part a result of U.S. foreign policy and its shifting approaches to immigration. Since Castro came to power in the late 1950s, the United States has had a policy of combating what it sees as leftist influence in Latin America. In Central America this has taken the form of arming and financing national armies and right-wing paramilitary groups to combat leftist insurgencies. In countries such as El Salvador and Guatemala, the result has been long-term civil war. In Guatemala the civil war came to an end in December 1996 after thirty-six years of fighting. During this time it is estimated that 100,000 people were killed and a million displaced. Some were able to make their way to the United States to seek work and send their earnings to families still living in Guatemala. On the similar experience of Salvadorians in Long Island, see Mahler (1995, 1996, 2001).
10. Mahler (1993) in an alternate enumeration in a neighborhood in Long Island found an 80% undercount of Salvadorians.
11. Except in quotations, we use the term "undocumented" instead of "illegal," which is commonly used by non-Latinos. Nevins (2002, 93–122) traces the ideological roots of the "illegal." He writes (2002, 95–96), "The manner in which American society talks and writes about unauthorized immigration has changed significantly over the last several decades, entailing a growing emphasis on the legality of migrants ... A database search of judicial decisions, for example, found no reference to the term *illegal* in regards to immigrants prior to 1950 (Newman 1993, 1899)." Nevins says the preoccupation with the illegality of immigrants is recent. In the late 1970s, the Carter administration forbade official use of the term "illegal alien," but since

then it has become increasingly common in government and media language. He points out (2002, 113) that "the mass media clearly helped to construct the image of an immigration and boundary enforcement crisis." By the 1990s, it had constructed the U.S. borders as "out of control" and focused the minds of Americans on boundary and immigration enforcement. Nevins (2002, 121) states, "Rather than responding to a supposed crisis of 'illegal' immigration, the state has helped to construct the 'illegal' through the expansion of the INS' enforcement capacity as the very evidence of a policed boundary." As we will see below, the reluctance of the INS to investigate undocumented day laborers in small suburban towns such as Mount Kisco contributes to a local sense of immigration "out of control."

12.   Graciela Heymann of the Westchester Hispanic Coalition in 1997 estimated that 40% of the Mount Kisco Hispanics were undocumented.

13.   According to Harold Lasso of the Hispanic Resource Center in Mamaroneck, day laborers from different countries prefer specific towns in Westchester: Guatemalans and other Central Americans go to Mount Kisco, Mexicans predominate in Mamaroneck, Brazilians in Mount Vernon, and Ecuadorians in Ossining (Archibold 2002).

14.   In 2002, the Westchester Hispanic Coalition estimated that there were approximately 160 day laborers without a steady job, approximately 80% of whom live in Mount Kisco at any one time. What was not known, however, was the number of laborers who have a patron who gives them regular seasonal work. Such laborers may live in the village but do not come to the hiring center for work.

15.   In the 1980s and 1990s, most Central American migrants were political refugees from civil wars. While the United States has been willing to grant political refugee status to people fleeing leftist regimes such as Cuba and Vietnam, they have usually been unwilling to do so for those escaping right-wing regimes. Consequently, Central Americans have mostly been treated as economic refugees and hence candidates for deportation. Such a policy by the United States restricted the number of Guatemalans illegally entering the United States in the 1970s and early 1980s. In 1985, however, Salvadorian and Guatemalan asylum seekers filed a class-action suit against the INS asking that they be allowed to remain in the United States until their cases were heard. More important was the broad federal amnesty for all persons unlawfully in the United States in 1986. As a result of this amnesty and the suit, the INS stopped vigorously prosecuting cases against Central Americans and the numbers of immigrants grew rapidly. They began to increase even more substantially after 1990 when the suit was settled in favor of the plaintiffs and new legislation was put in place the following year. Immigrants were led to believe that even if they were denied asylum, they might eventually qualify for permanent residence. These two changes in the application of immigration law has meant that in practice undocumented immigrants from Central America are infrequently deported (Thompson 2001). The consequence is a significant growth of the Latino population in towns such as Mount Kisco, which combines the availability of low-skilled jobs requiring little knowledge of English with more affordable rentals relative to neighboring towns. Between 1990 and 1995, nearly 22,300 legal immigrants settled in Westchester County, the highest immigration level since the 1930s (Brenner 1996, 3). This is part of a trend in which job growth is greatest in low-density suburbs and the immigrant poor are settling farther from central cities in search of jobs (Gross 1997; Mahler 1995, 1996). For a survey of the impact of U.S foreign policy on migration from Latin America, see Mitchell (1992).

16.   Most illegal migrants from Central America arrive in the United States heavily in debt. Nevins (2002) and Popkin (1999, 275) estimate that the cost of a "coyote" [guide] from the mountains of central Guatemala to the United States border has risen from $1,000 in 1994 to $2,500 in 1999. Mahler (2001) cites costs for the Salvadorians she interviewed as over $4,000 in 2000. On Mexican mistreatment of non-Mexican migrants bound for the United States, see Castillo, Angel, and Palma (1996); U.S. Committee For Refugees (1991); and Thompson (2001).

17.   Besides the inevitable harassment of immigrants, such a change would cause many problems as immigrants would be unable to use police services, report crimes, or assist in the investigation of crimes.

18.   The Westchester Hispanic Coalition estimates that a day laborer in Mount Kisco can earn $13,000 per year at best, and of course he receives no benefits (Rae 1998a). This figure is in line with the $12,000 per year that Mahler (2001) estimates that Salvadorians day laborers earn in wealthy Long Island suburbs.

19. It has been estimated that in 2002 there are more than forty gathering spots for day laborers within the New York metropolitan area. Nine are found in Westchester and Putnam counties drawing more than 400 laborers daily (Archibold 2002).

20. Foner (2001, 38–41) describes Italian migration to New York between 1870 and World War I in terms that are startlingly resonant with that of the contemporary day laborer experience. Eighty percent of migrants between 1870 and 1910 were men who left their families in Italy. Many laborers arrived in the spring from Italy and returned in the winter when layoffs were most numerous. This lead to a similar type of transnationalism to the one one finds between Central America and the United States today. On these early waves of immigration more generally, see Wyman (1993).

21. Across the country many day laborers face the same problems with employers, and hiring centers are attempting to solve this problem.

22. Since 1995, they have had some assistance from the Westchester Hispanic Coalition and more recently the Neighbor's Link to help them claim unpaid wages. The problem continues, however.

23. Except where it is indicated that Luis Lujan conducted them, Jim Duncan interviewed the day laborers in Spanish.

24. We interviewed only three Latinas because their labor, although crucial to the reproduction of Bedford, is inside the home, whereas our focus is upon the reproduction of the landscape of the town. Likewise, our focus in this chapter is on the controversy in Mount Kisco over the presence of male day laborers on the street. Residents had little to say about Latinas because they are not so visible. Peggie Arriazo of the Westchester Hispanic Coalition told us that the majority of day laborers are males living without families in Westchester.

25. We use the terms "race," "racist," and "racialized" because non-Latinos largely see the Latino population in Mount Kisco in racialized terms. Latinos are a heterogeneous group ethnically, nationally, and racially. While we do not subscribe to the view that there is any biologically valid, essentialistic concept of race, we do acknowledge that as a principle of categorization race is widely subscribed to (albeit with important differences in the way it is conceptualized among the countries of Latin and North America) and thus it is performatively effective. We mean performative here in Austin's and Butler's senses (despite differences between these) that words and categories are dynamic, transformative, and transgressive; they "do things." In symbolic interactionist terms, categories "are real because they are real in their consequences"; or as those with a more psychoanalytical bent might say, they are a part of the material, unconscious dimension of language that structures world views and are inaccessible to conscious critique. We would be more inclined to say words and categories are not *easily* accessible—that words and categories that are naturalized as a part of practical consciousness must be brought into discursive consciousness before they can be subjected to critical analysis. On the concept of racialization, see Valle and Torres (2000).

26. Sibley uses the term "moral" panic to describe a situation in which a group defined as different destabilizes the social or moral order. Such panics tend to erupt when spatial and social boundaries are threatened and are often heightened by alarmist media coverage. Sibley says, "Moral panics articulate beliefs about belonging and not belonging, about the sanctity of territory and the fear of transgression. Such panics bring boundaries into focus by accentuating the differences between the anxious guardians of mainstream values and excluded others" (Sibley 1995, 43). Davis (2000, 109) describes the panic associated with the visibility of "street corner labor markets in edge cities and exurbs across the country" as "a nativist hysteria that frequently uses an occult pitch." Also see Cohen (1972) and Cresswell (1996).

27. Baxandall and Ewen (2000, 239) say of the recently immigrated Central and South Americans, "unlike their turn-of-the-century predecessors, these immigrants were not of one class. They were wealthy, educated, middle class, working class, uneducated, and poor." The immigrants who are most visible and cause concern in the village are the poor, male day laborers. Those with permanent work and middle-class families are, therefore, not the topic of our concern here.

28. Mitchell (1995, 1996b, 1997, 1998a, 1998b) in a series of articles on law and public space discusses how the poor are increasingly being marginalized in their use of public spaces.

29. Valle and Torres (2000, 13) posit "that class is far more important than the specious concept of 'race' in determining the life chances of Latinos in Los Angeles."

30. Pred (2000) illuminates the historically and geographically specific nature of racisms through his rich analysis of contemporary Sweden.

31. Young adopts Kristeva's (1982) notion of the abject as a kind of loathing and fear to explicate aversive racism. The abject is that which perpetually threatens the physical and psychological borders between the self and Others and thus undermines identity. The abject is that which upsets the proper functioning of an order, in the case of Mount Kisco a spatial or moral order. While the abject may not be intrinsically polluting or dangerous, it becomes so when deemed "out of place" and "uncontrolled" as determined by a particular historical and cultural context.

32. There is a cruel irony in the descendants of Irish and Italian immigrants to Mount Kisco protesting against these nonwhite immigrants. For as Guterl (2001, 18–19, 52, 55, 188) points out, between 1880 and 1920, tens of millions of Irish, Italian, and Jewish immigrants arrived in northeastern cities, inflaming racial sentiments among "old stock" Americans. These people were themselves deemed by "old stock" Americans to be of questionable "whiteness" and were often termed "dingy whites." In the 1920s, however, as black migrants moved north, the notion of a black/white dichotomy became seen as strategic and Italians, Irish, and East European Jews were admitted into "absolute whiteness," as evidenced by new U.S. Census definitions.

33. As Young (1990, 146) puts it,

     There exists a dissonance between group-blind egalitarian truisms of discursive consciousness and the group-focused routines of practical consciousness. This dissonance creates a sort of "border crisis" ripe for the appearance of the abject. Today the Other is not so different from me as to be an object . . . But at the level of practical consciousness they are affectively marked as different. In this situation, those in the despised groups threaten to cross over the border of the subject's identity because discursive consciousness will not name them as completely different . . . The face-to-face presence of these others, who do not act as though they have their own "place," a status to which they are confined, thus threatens aspects of my basic security system, my basic sense of identity, and I must turn away with disgust and revulsion.

34. On the concept of white privilege, also see Dyer (1997), Frankenberg (1993), and McIntosh (1988).

35. As Lipsitz (1995) points out, "As the unmarked category against which difference is constructed, whiteness never has to speak its name, never has to acknowledge its role as an organizing principle in social and cultural relations." On the reproduction of structural privileges for whites, see Lipsitz (1998). On the spaces of whiteness, see Dwyer and Jones (2000), Kobayashi and Peake (2000), and Bonnett (1997, 2000).

36. The survey consisted of sixteen questions about problems facing the village and its future growth. Some of the questions were multiple choice with "other" as a choice and a blank to fill in if desired for some of the questions. All of the answers explicitly referring to illegal immigrants and loitering were contributed by the respondents rather than suggested by the village as choices. However, the questionnaire did ask the following: Do you think there is a good **Quality of Life** in Mount Kisco? Yes_ No_ Please identify what factors contribute to or detract from the Quality of Life (emphasis in the original). This seems to be a somewhat leading question given the frequent use in the local media of the term "quality of life" as a code word alluding to the immigrant population. It was in fact in answer to this question that many people mentioned illegal immigrants, loitering, and illegal apartments.

     While many of the respondents were concerned about overcrowded housing, the way the problems were expressed (illegal apartments, illegal housing, illegal tenants, deterioration of neighborhoods, nonenforcement of housing codes) suggests that these were not people who themselves lived in overcrowded housing.

37. Included among those perceived as "rough types" are a few black teenagers as well as Latinos. Some Latinos told us they are afraid of some of the blacks who hang out across from the station. Clearly there is a class as well as a race issue here.

38. Gustavus Kirby, the father of Willamina Waller, one of Bedford's establishment grande dames who inherited his large horse farm on Guard Hill was a prominent citizen of Bedford. Kirby and his daughter were involved at the local and county levels in the politics of preservation and beautification. Waller was active at the national level (Garden Club of America and Lady Bird Johnson's Beautification of America Program). The plaza built in Kirby's memory was intended, we assume, more as visual space than as space to be heavily used as plazas traditionally have been, especially in Spanish and Latin American cultures. One interviewee felt that it was an affront to Kirby's memory that the plaza has become "overrun with Latino males."

39. This perception of very low crime rates was confirmed by our examination of the police records in 1996 and the police blotter for 2001 to 2002 in the *Patent Trader.*
40. Quality of life has long been used as a code word for "cleaning up" public space (Mitchell 2000, 231). As early as 1983 Canning (1983, 192) mentions that in Westchester "maintaining quality of life" was a code word for "keeping out undesirables," especially Hispanics.
41. For a telling parallel in Vancouver, Canada, see Ley (1995).
42. "Quality of life" is used in a similar fashion in Farmingville, Long Island, by an anti-immigrant organization called the Sachem Quality of Life Organization, which concerns itself with what residents call "visual pollution," caused by poor Latinos hanging out in the streets (Cooper 1999).
43. In Marietta, Georgia, police tried ticketing contractors who pick up day laborers: "The city is researching whether or not it can ticket the day laborers themselves. . . . The growing concern is that we want to protect our property values" (Rodriguez 1987, 19).
44. On the link between the public sphere and public space, see Howell (1993), Duncan (1996), K. Mitchell (1997), and D. Mitchell (2000, 209–13).
45. Some feminist analyses (hooks 1990; Marchand and Runyan 2000; Sen and Grown 1987; Sharp 1996; Staehli 1996; Ward 1990), however, argue that the view of politics as based primarily in public space has a gender bias because men traditionally have been more apt to equate the public sphere with public space. Women tend to spend more time in their own homes and as domestic help in the homes of other people and consequently have even less public political presence. To the extent that political gains have been made by the Latino community, it would appear that men have received more of the benefits. The community center caters primarily to the needs of male day laborers because there are many more poor Latinos than Latinas. At present Neighbor's Link is helping forty-five women and 120 men. Politically the center is a mixed blessing, for being indoors on the margins of the village it serves to make Latinos less visible in public space. Furthermore, one writer points out that many day laborers come from countries where there is a fear of organizing and public protests; either, he says, can be "a potentially deadly activity in Guatemala" (Llorente 1998).
46. On the links between spatial and social marginality, see Mair (1986) and Marcuse (1988).
47. In June 1997, perhaps with an eye to the upcoming court case, a group of day laborer who were denied access to Leonard Park collected fifty signatures on a petition to allow them access (Bonnett 1997).
48. By June 1998, more than eighty laborers had joined the Mount Kisco Workers' Project. Participants contribute a dollar per week to a fund that is available to members who need housing, food, or medical care. The project also runs workshops on work skills and civil rights (Rae 1998a, 1998b). The Westchester Hispanic Coalition says that the principal thing it is trying to convey to day laborers is that even if they are undocumented, they have rights under labor laws. Under a new state labor law in November 1997 repeated failure to pay employees has been raised from a misdemeanor to a felony and the fine increased from 25% of the amount owed to 200%. At present the U.S. Labor Department only has nine investigators to cover Westchester and six other counties, while the New York State Labor Department has six investigators handling 1,200 cases in Westchester, Putnam, Rockland, and Orange Counties (Rae 1998a).
49. By 1990 Latinos made up 12% of Addison's 32,000 people. Then in 1994 the village bulldozed eight apartment buildings occupied by Latino residents, condemned three more, and said that dozens of others were blighted. Latino residents said they were being driven out of town and launched a class-action lawsuit. The Justice Department joined them in a federal case charging the village with intentional discrimination. Village officials said the problem was one of overcrowded and dilapidated housing rather than discrimination.

   The lawyer for the plaintiffs saw it as a problem of the cultural production of space: "People hear Spanish spoken in the street and at school. They see Latinos using their front yards instead of their back yards. It reaches what some people consider an unacceptable critical mass." In a classic expression of aversive racism that sees itself as tolerant, Addison Mayor Larry Hartwig said,

   > I don't think it's a racial thing; it's a cultural thing. I see two types of Hispanics in Addison. There are those who have been here for a long time and are very acculturated. If you don't know their last name, you wouldn't know they were Hispanic. The newer ones, I don't blame them. We need to educate them. They need to adapt and adopt our ways.

In other words: they're ok as long as they "act and sound like us." The town of Addison settled out of court. They agreed to build affordable housing, to compensate families up to $1.4 million, and to put in a community center and parks in two Latino neighborhoods. The projected cost of this plan is between $20 and $25 million.

50. The practices and attitudes in Mount Kisco are probably not more racist, classist, or xenophobic than those of other towns confronted with a rapid increase in poor people of color. Some of the opponents of Latino day laborers in neighboring towns like Brewster appear even more strident. Tony Hay is the chairman of the legislature of neighboring Putnam County. He says,

> There's a cultural difference between Americans and Latinos. We don't stand on the street looking for work. The average person will wake up at 8 o'clock and go to work. They wake up and go stand on the street corner and look for work. I call it visual pollution.

But he believes that Latinos are not only culturally and aesthetically unpleasant, but potentially dangerous as well. He continues,

> The World Trade Center blew up; planes are blown out of the sky. I'm not saying it's Latinos, but they're all immigrants. The West Nile virus, they laugh at me but we don't know where it came from. If Saddam Hussein shaved his mustache and spoke Spanish, he could come here and stand on the streets of Brewster. Muammar Qaddafi, he could come here. (Purdy 1999)

Such attitudes are especially dangerous when held by an official.

51. This is one of only two hiring centers for day laborers in the metropolitan area. In 2001, Suffolk County turned down a plan to spend $80,000 on a center in Farmingville after intense lobbying by anti-immigrant groups (Worth 2001). Communities across the United States have had protracted battles over day laborer hiring sites (Archibold 2002). Toma (2001) says that communities have a choice either to follow the path that leads through "INS arrests, police harassment, court battles over anti-day-laborer ordinances, deepening divisions, even hate crimes and xenophobia" or shortcut this divisive approach and end up in the same place by setting up a hiring site in a building with toilets and a variety of social services. He says that all tactics that attempt to run Latinos out of town ultimately cost the town dearly and fail.

52. While there are over forty such hiring sites in the United States (Axtman 2001), Mount Kisco's is particularly well funded and well accepted by non-Latino locals because of its location in an "already spoilt" area away from the stores.

53. Another attempt at cultural change is the Buddies/Companeros Program, organized by the local elementary school. At first fifty immigrant parents and half as many longer-term residents (most of whom not surprisingly are children of immigrants who are bilingual) were signed up to work together. By summer of 2001 the number of students had risen to 400 (Gorman 2001a; Gross 2000b). The organizer said she hopes the American buddies will learn to see "Hispanic culture as an asset rather than an eyesore." The program appears to be a success thus far.

54. See Smith (1996) on the dark side of place-based identity by which middle-class residents attempt to drive out of their neighborhoods those who are homeless or foreign looking. He notes a tremendous increase in the United States of such reactionary, what he terms "revanchist," politics.

55. The response from the village Manager's Office raises a very important question concerning representation of racist material. This is a question we have agonized over. It became clear from interviews with Latinos and comments quoted in the newspaper that the Latinos know that many non-Latinos are hostile to them in general and toward their culture of gathering in public places in particular. They have been taught this in workshops and through the use of fliers. They are also well aware of the lawsuits. Thus, we think more is to be gained through our discussion of aversive racism and white privilege, which many people do not understand as racist. Even positively charged terms such as "exclusive" and "tolerance" need to be rethought. There is a relationship between the negative term "exclusionary" and the widely used term "exclusive," which is usually equated with prestige. Likewise, we think that the word "tolerant" should be seen as conveying the notion that there is something negative to be tolerated or "put up with."

56. See Aizenman (2001, A01) on established Latinos' negative reactions to day laborers.

57. The village of Glen Cove also issued a short flier explaining acceptable behavior to day laborers (Baxandall and Ewen 2000, 240, who cite Carvajal 1993).

58. Zavella (2000, 155) argues that the term "Latino" disrupts the black white binary familiar to Americans and calls for an analysis of Latino identity in terms of both race and ethnicity.
59. The Central Bank of Guatemala estimated that in 1995 $327 million was remitted from the United States. This constituted 66% of all private transfers and exceeded tourist income by $88 million (Velasquez de Estrada 1996, cited in Popkin 1999, 283).
60. On transnational identities, see Davis (2000), Smith (2001), and Mitchell (1997b). For an argument that Italian and Jewish migration to New York at the beginning of the twentieth century had many of the characteristics associated with transnationalism, see Foner (2001).
61. Also see Agyeman (1989).

Chapter 9

1. For other examples, see Duncan (1994, 1999) and Duncan and Duncan (1984, 1997).

Bibliography

Agyeman, J. 1989. "Black-people, white landscape." *Town and Country Planning* 58: 336–38.

Aizenman, N. 2001. "Some Hispanics live close together, worlds apart." *Washington Post*, August 14, A01.

Aldrich, N. W., Jr. 1988. *Old Money: The Mythology of America's Upper Class*. New York: Knopf.

Andersen, T. 1995a. "Village debates laborer controls." *Reporter Dispatch*, May 14.

Andersen, T. 1995b. "Mount Kisco moves to enforce day laborers law." *Reporter Dispatch*, July 11.

Andersen, T. 1995c. "Laborers worried by law." *Reporter Dispatch*, August 8.

Andersen, T. 1995d. "Hispanic day workers voice their concerns." *Reporter Dispatch*, August 30.

Andersen, T. 1996. "Day workers protest a new law that limits hiring." *Reporter Dispatch*, April 8.

Anderson, B. 1990. *Imagined Communities*. London: Verso.

Anderson, K. 2001. "The nature of 'race,'" in N. Castree and B. Braun (eds.), *Social Nature: Theory, Practice, Politics*. Oxford: Blackwell, pp. 64–83.

Anderson, T. 1997. "A mid growing region, biologist is a voice calling for more wilderness." *Reporter Dispatch*, August 7.

Archibold, R. C. 2001. "Mount Kisco agrees to extend ban on bias against Hispanics." *New York Times*, February 8.

Archibold, R. C. 2002. "Creating a bridge from the subculture of day laborers to mainstream society." *New York Times*, March 3.

Arizona Republican. 2000. "Job center considered for day laborers." July 20, B3.

Atkinson, D. and E. Laurier. 1998. "A sanitised city? Social exclusion at Bristol's 1996 International Festival of the Sea." *Geoforum* 29: 199–206.

Austin, J. L. 1975. *How to Do Things with Words*. Cambridge: Harvard University Press.

Axtman, K. 2001. "More cities switch from friend to foe of day laborers." *Christian Science Monitor*, July 5, 1.

Balibar, E. 1991. "Racism and Nationalism," in E. Balibar and I. Wallerstein (eds.), *Race, Nation, Class: Ambiguous Identities*. London: Verso, pp. 37–67.

Baltzell, E. D. 1958. *Philadelphia Gentleman: The Making of a National Upper Class*. New York: Free Press.

Baltzell, E. D. 1964. *The Protestant Establishment: Aristocracy and Caste in America*. New York: Vintage.

Barnett, G. 1995. "How can Bedford curb development?" *Patent Trader*, November 9.

Barrett, J. 1886. "Bedford," in J. T. Scharf (ed.), *History of Westchester County, New York*. Philadelphia: L. E. Preston, Vol. 2, pp. 574–608.

Barrett, R. T. 1955. *The Town of Bedford: A Commemorative History, 1680–1955*. Bedford: Town of Bedford.

Bartels, R. "Let newcomers enjoy Bedford too." *Record Review,* November 3.

Barthes, R. 1973. *Mythologies.* Trans. A. Lavers. New York: Hill and Wang.

Baudrillard, J. 1988. *America.* Trans. C. Turner. New York: Verso.

Baxandall, R. and E. Ewen. 2000. *Picture Windows: How the Suburbs Happened.* New York: Basic Books.

Beck, U., A. Giddens, and S. Lash. 1994. *Reflexive Modernization: Politics, Tradition, and Aesthetics in the Modern Social Order.* Cambridge: Polity Press.

Bedford Historic District Review Commission. 1988. "Letter to Town Board, Town of Bedford." Bedford Historical Society Library, April 5.

Bedford Historical Society. n.d. *Tour of the 1787 Bedford Court House and the Village Green.* Bedford: Bedford Historical Society.

Bedford Historical Society. 1971. *A Short Historical Tour of the Town of Bedford.* Bedford: Bedford Historical Society.

Bedford Historical Society. 1980. *Long Live the Bedford Oak.* Bedford: Bedford Historical Society.

Bedford Historical Society. 1993a. *A Campaign for the Bedford Historical Society.* Bedford: Bedford Historical Society.

Bedford Historical Society. 1993b. *In Memory of Louise.* Bedford: Bedford Historical Society.

Bedford Village Green Traffic Study, 1992. Final Report.

Belluck, P. 1997. "Landmark settlement ends Hispanic bias suit." *New York Times,* August 8.

Benanti, S. C. 1999. "Mount Kisco must be reclaimed." *Patent Trader,* October 1.

Benjamin, W. 1969. "The work of art in the age of mechanical reproduction," in H. Arendt (ed.), *Illuminations.* New York: Schocken, pp. 217–52.

Berger, J. 1993. "Bienvenidos a los suburbios: Increasingly, New York's outskirts take on a Latin accent." *New York Times,* July 29.

Berman, M. 1982. *All Thats' Solid Melts into Air: The Experience of Modernity.* London: Verso.

Bermingham, A. 1986. *Landscape and Ideology: The English Rustic Tradition, 1740–1860.* Berkeley: University of California Press.

Bianco, G. 1999. "The DEP must show mutual consideration for our community." *Record Review,* April 30. ·

Birmingham, S. 1987. *America's Secret Aristocracy.* Boston: Little Brown.

Bladen, E. "Is open space the next frontier?" *Record Review,* January 16.

Blinken, R. 1999. Correspondence, June 2. In Final Environmental Impact Statement. Rippowam-Cisqua School, Proposed High School Campus. Town of Bedford, Vol. 1, November 2000.

Bolton, R. 1848. *A History of Westchester County.* New York: A. S. Gould, Vol. 1, pp. 1–33.

Bolton, R. 1881. *The History of the Several Towns, Manors, and Patents of the County of Westchester.* Rev. ed. New York: Chas, F. Roper, Vol. 1, pp. 1–81.

Bonnett, A. 1997. "Geography, 'race,' and whiteness: invisible traditions and current challenges." *Area* 29: 193–99.

Bonnett, A. 2000. *White Identities: Historical and International Perspectives.* Harlow: Prentice Hall.

Bonnett, C. 1997. "Hispanics protest residence rule to play in park." *Reporter Dispatch,* June 24.

Bourdieu, P. 1984. *Distinction: A Social Critique of the Judgement of Taste.* Trans. R. Nice. Cambridge, Mass.: Harvard University Press.

Bourdieu, P. 1987. "What makes a social class." *Berkeley Journal of Sociology* 22: 1–18.

Boyer, M. C. 1992. "Cities for Sale: Merchandizing History at South Street Sea Port," in M. Sorkin (ed.), *Variations on a Theme Park: The New American City and the End of Public Space.* New York: Noonday Press, pp. 181–204.

Bradsell, D. and B. Bradsell 1998. Letter to the Editor. "Keep Bedford a peaceful place to live and drive, resident urges." *Record Review,* August 7.

Brandt, E. 1997. "Hispanics, Kisco settle lawsuit." *Patent Trader,* August 14.

Braun, B. and N. Castree (eds.) 1998. *Remaking Reality: Nature at the Millenium.* London: Routledge.

Breen, T. H. 1989. *Imagining the Past: East Hampton Histories.* Reading, Mass.: Addison-Wesley.

Brenner, E. 1996. "Changes in laws spur immigrants to citizenship." *New York Times,* November 24.

Brouder, P. 1999. Correspondence, June 3. In Final Environmental Impact Statement. Rippowam-Cisqua School, Proposed High School Campus. Town of Bedford, Vol. 1, November 2000.

Brown, B. 1979. "To pave or not? A thorny road." *New York Times,* April 8.

Brown, M. 1994. "The possibility of local autonomy." *Urban Geography* 13: 257–79.

Bunce, M. 1994. *The Countryside Ideal: Anglo-American Images of Landscape.* London: Routledge.

Burke, D. 2001. "Article demonstrated lack of sensitivity." *Record Review,* May 4.

Burns, A. 1993. *Maya in Exile.* Philadelphia: Temple University Press.

Butler, J. 1990. *Gender Trouble: Feminism and the Subversion of Identity.* London: Routledge.

Butler, J. 1997. *Excitable Speech: A Politics of the Performative.* London: Routledge.

Butler, J. 2000. "Restaging the Universal: Hegemony and the Limits of Formalism," in J. Butler, E. Laclau, and S. Žižek (eds.), *Contingency, Hegemony, Universality: Contemporary Dialogues on the Left.* London: Verso, pp. 11–43.

Butler, W. 1985. "Another city upon a hill: Litchfield, Connecticut and the colonial revival," in A. Axelrod (ed.), *The Colonial Revival in America.* New York: W.W. Norton, pp. 15–51.

Butlin, R. 1982. *The Transformation of Rural England, c. 1580–1880.* London: Oxford University Press.

Calvitto C. and M. Berger. 1997. "In defense of Mount Kisco." *New York Times,* July 20.

Campbell, C. 1987. *The Romantic Ethic and the Spirit of Modern Consumerism.* Oxford: Basil Blackwell.

Canning, Jeff. 1983. "Westchester Since World War II: A Changing People in a Changing Landscape," in Marilyn Weigold (ed.), *Westchester County: The Past Hundred Years, 1883–1983.* New York: Westchester County Historical Society Harbor Hill Books, pp. 188–241.

Cappa, P. 1995. "Residents look carefully toward Bedford's future." *Record Review.* November 17.

Carlebach, W. 1988. "Letter to A. J. Bauman, Regional Construction Engineer, DOT," Bedford Historical Society Library, April 11.

Carroll, F. 1994. "Sewage revisited: town considers more options." *Bedford Record,* July 21.

Carroll, F. 1995. "Bedford's large tracts: what's to become of them?" *The Bedford Record,* December 22.

Carroll, F. 1996a. "Bedford Ponds seeks water, sewage districts." *Record Review,* February 16.

Carroll, F. 1996b. "Public bashes Twin Lakes." *Record Review,* February 16.

Carroll, F. 1996c. "Regional Review League … " *Record Review,* July 5.

Carroll, F. 1998a. "Will filtration be the answer?" *Record Review,* March 27.

Carroll, F. 1998b. "A new trend? Preserving Bedford's horse trails." *Record Review,* July 10.

Carroll, F. 1999. "Finding sanity through a coalition." *Record Review,* February 5.

Carvajal, D. 1993. "New York suburbs take on a Latin accent." *New York Times,* July 29.

Castells, M. 1997. *The Power of Identity.* Oxford: Blackwell.

Castillo, G., M. Angel, and S. Palma. 1996. *La Emigracion Internacional en Centroamerica.* Guatemala: FLASCO.

Castree, N. and B. Braun (eds.) 2001. *Social Nature: Theory, Practice, Politics.* Oxford: Blackwell.

Catanzarite, L. 2000. "Brown collar jobs: Occupational segregation and earnings of recent immigrant Latinos." *Sociological Perspectives* 43: 45–75.

Chase, M. and C. Shaw (eds.) 1989. "The Dimensions of Nostalgia," in M. Chase and C. Shaw (eds.), *The Imagined Past: History and Nostalgia.* Manchester: Manchester University Press, pp. 1–17.

Chitwood, S. 1999a. "Twin Lakes: Builder wins wetland battle." *Record Review,* October 1.

Chitwood, S. 1999b. "Is it cheaper not to build? Expert calculates the cost of preserving land." *Record Review,* September 3.

Chitwood, S. 1999c. "Bedford receives 'farm aid,'" *Record Review,* October 15.

Chitwood, S. 1999d. "Go west, young riders." *Record Review,* May 14.

Chitwood, S. 1999e. "A-home neighbors fight political correctness." *Record Review,* November 12.

Citizens for the Open Space Fund. 2000. *Vote to Save Open Space.* Privately Published.

Clark, F. P. 2000. *Village/Town of Mount Kisco Comprehensive Development Plan.* New York: F. P. Clark and Associates.

Cloke, P. and Little, J. (eds.) 1997. *Contested Countryside Cultures: Otherness, Marginalisation, and Rurality.* London: Routledge.

Cohen, S. 1972. *Folk Devils and Moral Panics.* London: MacGibbon and Kee.

Cole, A. 1995. "Bedford Village traffic suit settled for $350K." *Patent Trader,* March 2.

Connerton P. 1989. *How Societies Remember.* Cambridge: Cambridge University Press.

Cooper, M. 1999. "Laborers wanted but not living next door." *New York Times,* November 28.

Cormode, L. 1999. "The economic geographer as a situated researcher of elites." *Geoforum* 30: 299–300.

Cosgrove, D. 1984. *Social Formation and Symbolic Landscape.* Totowa, N.J.: Barnes and Noble.

Cosgrove, D. 1993. *The Palladian Landscape: Geographical Change and Its Representations in Sixteenth Century Italy.* Leicester: Leicester University Press.

Cosgrove, D. and S. Daniels (eds.) 1988. *The Iconography of Landscape: Essays on the Symbolic Representation, Design, and Use of Past Environments*. Cambridge: Cambridge University Press.

Cox, K. and A. Jonas. 1993. "Urban development, collective consumption, and the politics of metropolitan fragmentation." *Political Geography* 12: 12–32.

Cox, R. 1993. "Structural issues of global governance: Implications for Europe," in S. Gill (ed.), *Gramsci, Historical Materialism, and International Relations*. Cambridge: Cambridge University Press, pp. 49–66.

Crandell, G. 1993. *Nature Pictorialized: "The View" in Landscape History*. Baltimore: Johns Hopkins University Press.

Cresswell, T. 1996. *In Place/Out of Place: Geography, Ideology, and Transgression*. Minneapolis: University of Minnesota.

Cronon, W. 1983. *Changes in the Land: Indians, Colonists, and the Ecology of New England*. New York: Hill and Wang.

Cronon, W. 1995. *Uncommon Ground: Toward Reinventing Nature*. New York: W.W. Norton.

Daniels, S. 1988. "The Political Iconography of Woodland in Later Georgian England," in D. Cosgrove and S. Daniels (eds.), *The Iconography of Landscape: Essays on the Symbolic Representation, Design, and Use of Past Environments*. Cambridge: Cambridge University Press, pp. 43–82.

Daniels, S. 1993. *Fields of Vision: Landscape Imagery and National Identity in England and the United States*. Princeton: Princeton University Press.

Danielson, M. 1972. "Differentiation, Segregation, and Political Fragmentation in the American Metropolis," in A. Kier (ed.), *The Governmental Implications of Population Change*. Washington: U.S. Government Printing Office, pp. 143–76.

Danielson, M. 1976. *The Politics of Exclusion*. New York: Columbia University Press.

Davis, M. 1990. *City of Quartz: Excavating the Future in Los Angeles*. London: Verso.

Davis, M. 1998. *Ecology of Fear: Los Angeles and the Imagination of Disaster*. New York: Henry Holt.

Davis, M. 2000. *Magical Urbanism: Latinos Reinvent the U.S. City*. New York: Verso.

DeLyser, D. 1999. "Authenticity on the ground: Engaging the past in a California ghost town." *Annals, Association of American Geographers* 89: 602–32.

Demeritt, D. 1994a. "Ecology, objectivity, and critique in writings on nature and human societies." *Journal of Historical Geography* 20: 22–37.

Demeritt, D. 1994b. "The nature of metaphors in cultural geography and environmental history." *Progress in Human Geography* 18: 163–85.

Demeritt, D. 1998. "Science, Social Constructivism, and Nature." in B. Braun and N. Castree (eds.), *Remaking Reality: Nature at the Millennium*. London: Routledge, pp. 173–73.

Demeritt, D. 2001. "Being Constructive about Nature," in N. Castree and B. Braun (eds.), *Social Nature: Theory, Practice, Politics*. Oxford: Blackwell, pp. 22–40.

Devine, P. 1989. "Stereotypes and prejudice: Their automatic and controlled components." *Personality and Social Psychology*. 56: 5–18.

Dorst, J. 1990. *The Written Suburb*. Philadelphia: University of Pennsylvania Press.

Douglas, M. 1966. *Purity and Danger*. London: Routledge and Kegan Paul.

Dowling, R. 1998. "Neotraditionalism in the suburban landscape: Cultural geographies of exclusion in Vancouver, Canada." *Urban Geography* 19: 105–22.

Downing, A. J. 1841. *A Treatise on the Theory and Practice of Landscape Gardening*. New York: Appleton.

Downing, A. J. 1842. *Cottage Residences*. New York: Appleton.

Downing, A. J. 1851. *The Architecture of Country Houses*. New York: Appleton.

Driscoll, E. 1999a. "Kisco board wants police presence downtown." *Patent Trader,* July 16.

Driscoll, E. 1999b. "Mt. Kisco settles Hispanic's lawsuit." *Patent Trader,* September 17, 1.

Driscoll, E. 1999c. "Kisco business owner gets eviction reprieve." *Patent Trader,* October 22, 1.

Driscoll, E. 1999d. "Republicans win in Kisco." *Patent Trader,* November 5.

Driscoll, E. 1999e. "Judge states race is issue in 'Ah Fun' case." *Patent Trader,* November 11, 1.

Driscoll, E. 1999f. "3 shanties found in Mount Kisco." *Patent Trader,* December 21.

Driscoll, E. 1999g. "'Neighbor's Link' site to provide for food pantry, Hispanic Coalition." *Patent Trader,* December 30.

Driscoll, E. 2000. "Laborer issue is back in spotlight." *Patent Trader,* May 11, 1.

Driscoll, E. 2001. "Neighbors link gears up for day laborers." *Patent Trader,* April 19, 1.

Driscoll, E. 2002a. "Mount Kisco, church reach settlement." *Patent Trader,* January 31.

Driscoll, E. 2002b. "Neighbors link makes strides in Kisco." *Patent Trader,* March 21.

Druse, K. 1994. "The new American garden: How to create beautiful native-plant gardens, and eco-systems in miniature in your own back yard." *USAir Magazine* June: 26–29.

Duany, A. and E. Plater-Zyberk. 1992. "The second coming of the American small town." *Wilson Quarterly* 16: 19–50.

Dugger, C. W. 1996. "Immigrants and suburbia square off: Hispanic residents of Mt. Kisco say they're being harassed." *New York Times,* December 1.

Dugger, C. W. 1997. "Settling Hispanic suit, Mt. Kisco agrees not to enforce overcrowding law." *New York Times,* August 13.

Duncan, J. S. 1973. "Landscape taste as a symbol of group identity: A Westchester County village." *Geographical Review* 63: 334–55.

Duncan, J. S. 1990. *The City as Text: The Politics of Landscape Interpretation in the Kandyan Kingdom.* Cambridge: Cambridge University Press.

Duncan, J. S. 1994. "Neighborhood Organization in an Elite Neighborhood: The Case of Shaughnessy Heights," in S. Hasson and D. Ley (eds.), *Neighborhood Organization and the Welfare State.* Toronto: University of Toronto Press, pp. 58–82.

Duncan, J. S. 1999a. "Elite Landscapes as Cultural (Re)Productions: The Case of Shaughnessy Heights," in K. Anderson and F. Gale (eds.), *Cultural Geographies.* London: Longman pp. 53–70.

Duncan, J. S. 1999b. "Placelessness," in R. J. Johnston, D. Gregory, G. Pratt, D. M. Smith, and M. Watts (eds.), *The Dictionary of Human Geography,* Fourth Ed. Oxford: Blackwell 585–86.

Duncan, J. S. and N. Duncan. 1984. "A Cultural Analysis of Urban Residential Landscapes in North America: The Case of the Anglophile Elite," in J. Agnew et al. (eds.), *The City in Cultural Context.* Boston: Unwin-Hyman, pp. 255–76.

Duncan, J. S. and N. Duncan. 1988. "(Re)reading the Landscape." *Environment and Planning D: Society and Space* 6: 117–26.

Duncan, J. S. and N. Duncan. 2001a. "Theory in the field." *Geographical Review,* 91: 1–8.

Duncan, J. S. and N. Duncan. 2001b. "The aestheticization of the politics of landscape preservation." *Annals, Association of American Geographers* 91: 387–409.

Duncan, J. S. and N. Duncan. Forthcoming. "It's in the post: The promise of culture in cultural geography." Environment and Planning A.

Duncan, J. S. and D. Lambert. 2002. "Landscape, Aesthetics, and Power," in J. Agnew and J. Smith (eds.), *American Space/American Place: Geographies of the United States on the Threshold of a New Century.* Edinburgh: Edinburgh University Press, pp. 264–91.

Duncan, N. 1986. *Suburban Landscapes and Suburbanites: A Structurationist Perspective on Residential Land Use in Northern Westchester County.* Ph.D. Thesis. New York: Syracuse University.

Duncan, N. 1996. "Renegotiating Gender and Sexuality in Public and Private Spaces," in N. G. Duncan (ed.), *BodySpace: Destabilizing Geographies of Gender and Sexuality.* London: Routledge, pp. 127–45.

Duncan, N. 2003. "Suburbs," in S. Harrison, S. Pile, and N. Thrift (eds.), *Patterned Ground.* London: Reaktion.

Duncan, N. and J. Duncan. 1997. "Deep Suburban Irony: The Perils of Democracy in Westchester County, New York," in Roger Silverstone (ed.), *Visions of Suburbia.* London: Routledge pp. 161–79.

Duncan, N. and S. Legg. 2003. "Class," in J. Duncan, N. Johnson, and R. Schein (eds.), *Companion to Cultural Geography.* Oxford: Blackwell.

Duncombe, F. 1978. *Katonah: The History of a New York Village and Its People.* Clinton, Mass.: The Colonial Press.

Dungan, N. 2000. "Letter to the editor: Decrease traffic in Bedford by letting the roads become overgrown." *Record Review,* July 28.

Dwyer, O. J. and J. P. Jones III. 2000. "White socio-spatial epistemology." *Social and Cultural Geography* 1: 209–22.

Dyer, R. 1997. *White.* London: Routledge.

Eagleton, T. 1990. *The Ideology of the Aesthetic.* Oxford: Blackwell Publishers.

Eco, U. 1983. "Travels in Hyperreality," in W. Weaver (trans.), *Travels in Hyperreality.* New York: Harcourt Brace Jovanovich 1–58.

Eddings, K. 2001. "Westchester lawmakers seek ways to clean up runoff." *The Journal News,* August 9.

Eliot, C. 1902. *Charles Eliot, Landscape Architect.* Boston: Houghton Mifflin.

Ellen, N. 1996. *Postmodern Urbanism.* Oxford: Blackwell.

Evernden, N. 1992. *The Social Creation of Nature.* Baltimore: Johns Hopkins.

Falconer Al-Hindi, K. and C. Staddon. 1997. "The hidden histories and geographies of neotraditional town planning: The case of Seaside, Florida." *Environment and Planning D: Society and Space* 15: 349–72.

Farrell, M. 1997. "Letter from the Mayor to the residents of Mount Kisco. Re: Settlement of Day Workers' Suit." *Village/Town of Mount Kisco,* September 2.

Featherstone, M. 1991. *Consumer Culture and Postmodernism.* London: Sage.

Featherstone, M. 1992. "Postmodernism and the Aestheticization of Everyday Life," in S. Lash and J. Friedman (eds.), *Modernity and Identity.* Oxford: Blackwell, pp. 265–90.

Featherstone, M. 1994. "City Culture and Politics," in A. Amin (ed.), *Postfordism: A Reader.* Oxford: Blackwell, pp. 387–408.

Fentress, J. and C. Wickham. 1992. *Social Memory.* Oxford: Blackwell.

Fernandez-Kelly, M. P. and A. M. Garcia. 1989. "Informalization at the Core: Hispanic Women, Homework, and the Advanced Capitalist State," in A. Portes, M. Castells, and L. A. Benton (eds.), *The Informal Economy: Studies in Advanced and Less Developed Countries.* Baltimore: Johns Hopkins. pp. 229–246.

Fernandez-Kelly, M. P., A. Portes, and M. Zhou. 1992. "Gaining the upper hand: Economic mobility among immigrant and domestic minorities." *Ethnic and Racial Studies* 15: 491–521.

Fillipone, T. 2001. "Singling out of house was 'mean spirited.'" *Record Review,* May 4.

Firey, W. 1945. "Sentiment and symbolism as ecological variables." *American Sociological Review* 10: 140–48.

Fishman, R. 1995. "Metropolis Unbound," in P. Kasinitz (ed.), *Metropolis: Center and Symbol of our Times.* New York: New York University Press, pp. 395–417.

Foderaro, L. 1999. "Plan for elite school in Westchester divides haves and have-mores." *New York Times* August 1.

Foner, N. 2001. "Transnationalism Then and Now: New York Immigrants Today and at the Turn of the Twenieth Century," in H. R. Cordero-Guzman, R. C. Smith, and R. Grosfoguel (eds.), *Migration, Transnationalism, and Race in a Changing New York.* Philadelphia: Temple University Press, pp 35–57.

Foster, H. 1999. "Bedford's other side." *Patent Trader,* January 29.

Frankenberg, R. 1993. *White Women, Race Matters: The Social Construction of Whiteness.* London: Routledge.

Fraser, N. 1990. "Rethinking the public sphere: A contribution to actually existing democracy." *Social Text* 25/26: 56–79.

Friedman, S. 1984. "Industrialization, Immigration, and Transportation to 1900," in M. Weigold (ed.), *Westchester County: The Past Hundred Years, 1883–1983.* Valhalla: The Westchester County Historical Society, pp. 49–89.

Fussell, P. 1983. *Class.* New York: Ballentine.

Gallagher, J. 1997. "Rippowam school's plans face wetland review." *Record Review,* February 21.

Gandy, M. 1996. "Crumbling land: The postmodernity debate and the analysis of environmental problems." *Progress in Human Geography* 20: 23–40.

Gandy, M. 2002. *Concrete and Clay: Reworking Nature in New York City.* Cambridge: Massachusetts Institute of Technology.

Garden Club Bulletin. Bedford Garden Club.

Garreau, J. 1988. *Edge Cities: Life on the New Frontier.* New York: Doubleday.

Giddens, A. 1979. *Central Problems in Social Theory Action: Structure and Contradiction in Social Analysis.* Berkeley: University of California Press.

Giddens, A. 1991. *The Consequences of Modernity.* Cambridge: Polity.

Goldring, L. 1996. "Blurring borders: Constructing transnational communities in the process of Mexico-U.S. immigration." *Research in Community Sociology* 6: 69–104.

Gonzales, C. 1997. "Day laborers glad things have changed for them in Mt. Kisco: Hispanics, Village put restrictions behind them in facing influx of Latino workers." *Reporter Dispatch,* August 17.

Goodhue, M. 1988. "Letter to A. E. Dickson, Regional Director DOT, February 11." *Bedford Historical Society Library.*

Gordon, C. 1992a. "Bedford seeks rationale for lights." *Patent Trader,* May 7.

Gordon, C. 1992b. "Judge halts Bedford Green traffic project." *Patent Trader,* July 2.

Gordon, C. 1992c. "DOT returns to work at Bedford Village Green." *Patent Trader,* July 30.

Gorman, S. 2001a. "Hispanic population doubles." *Journal News,* April 16.

Gorman, S. 2001b. "Businessman preserves land." *Journal News,* May 31.

Gorman, S. 2001c. "GOP candidates put focus on sewer systems, affordable housing." *Journal News,* June 7.

Gorman, S. 2001d. "Westchester Land Trust approves preservation of up to 64 acres." *Journal News,* June 13.

Gorman, S. 2001e. "Farmers market starts in Mount Kisco." *Journal News,* June 20.

Gorman, S. 2001f. "County legislator candidates support more affordable housing." *Journal News,* June 26.

Gorman, S. 2001g. "Mount Kisco church files lawsuit vs. village." *Journal News,* August 19.

Goss, J. 1996. "Disquiet on the waterfront: Reflections on nostalgia and utopia in the urban archetypes of festival marketplaces." *Urban Geography* 17: 221–47.

Gracia, J. and P. De Greiff. 2000. "Introduction" in Gracia, J. and P. De Greiff (eds.), *Hispanics/Latinos in the United States: Ethnicity, Race, and Rights.* London: Routledge, pp. 1–12.

Graham, B. 1994. "No place of mind: contested Protestant representations of Ulster." *Ecumene* 1: 257–82.

Graham, B., G. J. Ashworth, and J. E. Tunbridge. 2000. *A Geography of Heritage: Power, Culture, and Economy.* London: Arnold.

Gramsci, A. 1991. *Selections from the Prison Notebooks of Antonio Gramsci.* London: Lawrence and Wishart.

Greene, D. 1997. "Hispanic group leader faces down bias." *New York Times,* July 6.

Grewal, I. and C. Kaplan. 1994. "Introduction: Transnational Feminist Practices and Questions of Modernity," in I. Grewal and C. Kaplan (eds.), *Scattered Hegemonies: Postmodernity and Transnational Feminist Practices.* Minnesota: University of Minnesota Press, pp. 1–36.

Gross, J. 1997. "Poor without cars find trek to work can be a job." *New York Times,* November 18.

Gross, J. 1999. "In Westchester, trouble on the menu: As Hispanic clientele grows, a restaurant loses its lease." *New York Times,* November 8.

Gross, J. 2000a. "For Latino laborers, dual lives. Welcomed at work, but shunned at home in suburbs." *New York Times,* January 5.

Gross, J. 2000b. "Addressing the county's no.1 need: Trying to create affordable housing in a place that few can afford." *New York Times,* May 14.

Gross, J. 2000c. "Warm smiles in strange land of the S.U.V.'s: Immigrants find friendship in suburb known for hostility." *New York Times,* July 10.

Gross, J. 2001. "Change stirs hope for legal status among immigrants." *New York Times,* February 20.

Guarnizo, L. E. 1997. "Going Home: Class, Gender, Household Transformation, and Dominican Return Migrants," in P. R. Pessan (ed.), *Caribbean Circuits: New Directions in the Study of Caribbean Migration.* New York: Center for Migration Studies, pp. 13–59.

Gurney, D. F. 1979. "God's Garden," in *The Oxford Dictionary of Quotations.* Third ed. Oxford: Oxford University Press.

Guterl, M. P. 2001. *The Color of Race in America, 1900–1940.* Cambridge: Harvard University Press.

Gwynne, F. 1983. "Something Foxy: the last stroll." *Lewisboro Ledger,* March 23.

Habermas, J. 1989. *The Structural Transformation of the Public Sphere: An Inquiry into a Category.* Cambridge, Mass.: MIT Press.

Hage, G. 1998. *White Nation: Fantasies of White Supremacy in a Multi-cultural Society.* Sidney: Pluto Press.

Harding, S. 1991. *Whose Science, Whose Knowledge? Thinking from Women's Lives.* Milton Keynes: Open University Press.

Harrison, C. M. and J. Burgess. 1994. "Social constructions of nature: A case study of conflicts over the development of Rainham marshes." *Transactions of the Institute of British Geographers* 19: 291–310.

Hartsock, N. 1987. "The Feminist Standpoint," in S. Harding (ed.), *Feminism and Methodology.* Bloomington, Ind.: Indiana University Press, 157–80.

Harvey, D. 1989. *The Condition of Postmodernity: An Enquiry into the Origins of Cultural Change.* Oxford: Blackwell.

Harvey, D. 1996. *Justice, Nature, and the Geography of Difference.* Oxford: Blackwell.

Harvey, D. 2000. *Spaces of Hope.* Edinburgh: Edinburgh University Press.

Hencyey, B. 1977. "High price paid in scenery for saving Bedford Oak." *Patent Trader,* February 26.

Heppner, D. 1998. "No to pet goats." *Record Review,* August 14.

Hetherington, K. 1997. *The Badlands of Modernity: Heterotopia and Social Ordering.* London: Routledge.

Hewison, R. 1987. *The Heritage Industry: Britain in a Climate of Decline.* London: Methuen.

Higley, S. R. 1995. *Privilege, Power, and Place: The Geography of the American Upper Class.* Lanham: Rowman and Littlefield.

Hirsch, F. 1976. *Social Limits to Growth.* Cambridge: Harvard.

Hobsbawm, E. and T. Ranger (eds.) 1983. *The Invention of Tradition.* Cambridge: Cambridge University Press.

Hoelscher, S. 1998. "Tourism, ethnic memory, and the other-directed place." *Ecumene* 4, 369–98.

hooks, b., ed. 1990. "Homeplace: A Site of Resistance," in *Yearning: Race, Gender, and Cultural Politics.* Boston: South End Press, pp. 41–50.

Howard, E. 1902. *Garden Cities of To-Morrow.* London: S. Sonnennschein.

Howell, P. 1993. "Public space and the public sphere: Political theory and the historical geography of modernity." *Environment and Planning D: Society and Space* 11: 303–22.

Hughes, A. and L. Cormode. 1998a. "Theme issue: Researching elites and elite spaces." *Geoforum* 29: 2098–2179.

Hughes, A. and L. Cormode. 1998b. "Researching elites and elite spaces." *Geoforum* 29: 2098–2100.

Hugill, P. J. 1986. "English landscape tastes in the United States." *Geographical Review* 76: 408–23.

Hugill, P. J. 1989. "Home and Class among an American Landed Elite," in J. A. Agnew and J. S. Duncan (eds.), *The Power of Place: Bringing Together Geographical and Sociological Imaginations.* Boston: Unwin-Hyman, pp. 66–80.

Hugill, P. J. 1995. *Upstate Arcadia: Landscape, Aesthetics, and the Triumph of Social Differentiation in America.* Lanham, Mary.: Rowman and Littlefield.

Jackson, J. B. 1979. "The Order of a Landscape: Reason and Religion in Newtonian America," in D. W. Meinig (ed.), *The Interpretation of Ordinary Landscapes.* New York: Oxford University Press, pp. 153–63.

Jackson, K. T. 1985. *The Crabgrass Frontier.* New York: Oxford University Press.

Jacobs, J. 1998. "Staging Difference: Aestheticization and the Politics of Difference," in R. Fincher and J. Jacobs (eds.), *Cities of Difference.* New York: The Guildford Press pp. 252–78.

Jameson, F. 1984. "Postmodernism or the cultural logic of late capitalism." *New Left Review* 146: 53–92.

Jenkins, V. S. 1994. *The Lawn: A History of an American Obsession.* Washington: Smithsonian Institution Press.

Johnson, N. C. 1995. "Cast in stone: Monuments, geography, and nationalism." *Environment and Planning D: Society and Space* 13: 51–65.

Johnson, N. C. 1996. "Where geography and history meet: Heritage tourism and the big house in Ireland." *Annals, Association of American Geographers* 86: 551–66.

Jonas, A. 2002. "Local Territories of Government: From Ideals to Politics of Place and Scale," in J. Agnew and J. Smith (eds.), *American Space/American Place: Geographies of the Contemporary United States.* Edinburgh: Edinburgh University Press, pp. 108–49.

Jordanova, L. 1989. "Objects of Knowledge: A Historical Perspective on Museums," in P. Vergo (ed.), *The New Museology.* London: Reaktion Books, pp. 22–40.

Julca, A. 2001. "Peruvian Networks for Migration in New York City's Labor Market, 1970–1996," in H. R. Cordero-Guzman, R. C. Smith, and R. Grosfoguel (eds.), *Migration, Transnationalism, and Race in a Changing New York.* Philadelphia: Temple University Press, pp. 239–57.

Kant, I. 1987. *Critique of Judgement.* Trans. W. Pluhar. Indianapolis: Hackett.

Karsch, D. and S. Karsch. 1996. "Portraits of Mt. Kisco." *New York Times,* December 4.

Kasinitz, P. (ed.) 1995. *Metropolis: Center and Symbol of Our Times.* New York: New York University Press.

Katz, C. 1998. "Whose Nature, Whose Culture?: Private Productions of Space and the 'Preservation' of Nature," in B. Braun and N. Castree (eds.), *Remaking Reality: Nature at the Millennium.* London: Routledge, pp. 46–63.

Kearns, G. 1998. "The virtuous circle of facts and values in the new Western history." *Annals, Association of American Geographers* 88: 377–409.

Keiser, C. 1996. "Twin Farms development would destroy our 'little dirt road.'" *Record Review,* January 26.

Kirp, D. L., J. P. Dwyer, and L. A. Rosenthal. 1995. *Our Town: Race, Housing, and the Soul of Suburbia.* New Brunswick: Rutgers University Press.

Klein, M. 1997. "Conflict simmers behind day laborer suit." *Reporter Dispatch,* August 14.

Kobayashi, A. and L. Peake. 2000. "Racism out of place: Thoughts on whiteness and antiracist geography in the new millennium." *Annals, Association of American Geographers* 90: 392–403.

Kovacic, T. 1999. Public Hearing, Town of Bedford, May 19. In Final Environmental Impact

Statement. Rippowam-Cisqua School, Proposed High School Campus. Town of Bedford, Vol. 1, November 2000.

Kovel, J. 1984. *White Racism: A Psychohistory.* Columbia University Press.

Kristeva, J. 1982. *Powers of Horror: An Essay on Abjection.* Trans. Leon Roudiez. New York: Columbia University Press.

Kurdell, J. 1972. "Historic area established." *Patent Trader,* August 17.

Kutz, C. 2000. *Complicity.* Cambridge: Cambridge University Press.

Landzelius, M. 1999. *Dis[re]membering Spaces: Swedish Modernism in Law Courts Controversy.* Goteborg: Goteborg University Institute of Conservation.

Lapham, L. H. 1988. *Money and Class in America: Notes and Observations on our Civil Religion.* New York: Weidenfield and Nicolson.

Lash, S. and J. Urry. 1994. *Economies of Signs and Space.* Cambridge: Polity Press.

Lawrence, C. 1987. "The id, the ego, and equal protection: Reckoning with unconscious racism." *Stanford Law Review* 39: 317–88.

Ledger. 1988a. "Too precious to lose." February 10.

Ledger. 1988b. "History, traffic square off at Bedford's Village Green." February 10.

LeFebvre, H. 1991. *The Production of Space.* Oxford: Blackwell.

Levine, S. 1972. "Art values, institutions and cultures." *American Quarterly* 24: 131–65.

Ley, D. 1987. "Styles of the times: Liberal and neoconservative landscapes in inner Vancouver, 1968–1986." *Journal of Historical Geography* 13: 40–56.

Ley, D. 1993. "Past Elites, Present Gentry: Neighborhoods of Privilege in Canadian Cities," in L. Bourne and D. Ley (eds.), *The Changing Social Geography of Canadian Cities.* Montreal: McGill-Queens University Press, pp. 214–33.

Ley, D. 1995. "Between Europe and Asia: The case of the missing sequoias." *Ecumene* 2: 185–210.

Ley, D. and J. Mercer. 1980. "Locational conflict and the politics of consumption." *Economic Geography* 56: 89–109.

Lipsitz, G. 1995. "The possessive investment in whiteness: Racialized social democracy and the 'white' problem in American studies." *American Quarterly* 47: 369–87.

Lipsitz, G. 1998. *The Possessive Investment in Whiteness: How White People Profit from Identity Politics.* Philadelphia: Temple University Press.

Livingstone, D. 1995. "The polity of nature: Representation, virtue, strategy." *Ecumene* 2: 353–77.

Llorente, E. 1998. "As familiarity grows, fears ebb—day laborers find hope in Palisades Park." *The Record* (Bergen County, New Jersey), August 24.

Lloyd, M. 1999. "Performativity, Parody, Politics," in V. Bell (ed.), *Performativity and Belonging.* London: Sage, pp. 195–214.

Lombardi, K. S. 1994. "Parallel worlds collide in Mt. Kisco." *New York Times,* December 25.

Lombardi, K. S. 1997. "Private school plans new high school." *New York Times,* June 1.

Lovejoy, A. 1974. *The Great Chain of Being.* Cambridge, Mass.: Harvard University Press.

Lovejoy, S. 1999. Correspondence, May 27. In Final Environmental Impact Statement. Rippowam Cisqua School, Proposed High School Campus. Town of Bedford, Vol. 1, November 2000.

Low, S. 2000. *On the Plaza: The Politics of Public Space and Culture.* Austin: University of Texas Press.

Lowenthal, D. 1985. *The Past Is a Foreign Country.* Cambridge: Cambridge University Press.

Lowenthal, D. 1989. "Nostalgia Tells It Like It Wasn't," in M. Chase and C. Shaw (eds.), *The Imagined Past: History and Nostalgia.* Manchester: Manchester University Press, pp. 18–32.

Lowenthal, D. 1991. "British identity and the English landscape." *Rural History* 2: 205–230.

Lowenthal, D. and H. Prince. 1965. "English landscape tastes." *Geographical Review* 55: 186–222.

Lowenthal, L. 1961. *Literature, Popular Culture, and Society.* Palo Alto: Pacific Books.

Luke, T. 1995. "The Nature Conservancy or the nature cemetery: Buying and selling 'perpetual care' as environmental resistance." *Capitalism Nature Socialism* 6: 1–20.

Luman, S. 1995. "Bedford eyes future growth warily. "*Patent Trader,* October 26.

Lynch, M. 1998. "Rippowam gets planning review go-ahead." *Record Review,* February 5.

Lynch, M. 1999a. "Bedford Coalition packs community house." *Record Review,* January 29.

Lynch, M. 1999b. "Class or crass? *Vanity Fair* story riles, titillates." *Record Review,* January 15.

Lynes, R. 1980. *The Tastemakers: The Shaping of American Popular Taste.* New York: Dover.

McCabe, A. J. 1995a. "Local initiative sought for Hispanic relations." *Patent Trader,* February 16.

McCabe, A. J. 1995b. "Kisco raid reveals 52 in 1 house." *Patent Trader,* August 2.

McCabe, A. J. 1995c. "Day workers debate Kisco hiring law." *Patent Trader,* August 17.

McCabe, A. J. 1995d. "Groups wrangle over Mt. Kisco work law." *Patent Trader,* September 8.

McCabe, A. J. 1995e. "Court: N. Salem must allow affordable housing." *Patent Trader,* September 28.

McCabe, A. J. 1996. "Affordable housing to be discussed in No. Salem." *Patent Trader,* June 20.

McCabe, A. J. 1997. "Insurance could pay Kisco Hispanic suit tab." *Patent Trader,* August 21.

McCann, E. J. 1995. "Neotraditional developments: The anatomy of a new urban form." *Urban Geography* 16: 210–33.

McCarthy, E. 2001. "A rave roars its stony head." *Record Review,* August 24, 4.

McDowell, L. 1998. "Elites in the City of London: Some methodological considerations." *Geoforum* 29: 2133–46.

McIntosh, P. 1988. "White privilege and male privilege: A personal account of coming to see correspondences through work in women's studies." *Wellesley College Center for Research on Women Working Paper Series* 189. Reprinted in 1992 in M. and C. Andersen and P. Hill (eds.), *Race, Class, and Gender: An Anthology.* Belmont, Calif.: Wadsworth, pp. 70–81.

McKenzie, E. 1994. *Privatopia: Homeowner Associations and the Rise of Residential Private Government.* New Haven: Yale University Press.

Mahler, S. J. 1993. *Alternative Enumeration of Undocumented Salvadorians on Long Island.* Upper Marlboro, Md.: U.S. Bureau of Census.

Mahler, S. J. 1995. *American Dreaming: Immigrant Life on the Margins.* Princeton: Princeton University Press.

Mahler, S. J. 1996. *Salvadorians in Suburbia: Symbiosis and Conflict.* Boston: Allyn and Bacon.

Mahler, S. J. 2001. "Suburban Transnational Migrants: Long Island's Salvadorians," in H. R. Cordero-Guzman, R. C. Smith, and R. Grosfoguel (eds.), *Migration, Transnationalism, and Race in a Changing New York.* Philadelphia: Temple University Press, pp. 109–30.

Mains, S. 2000. "An anatomy of race and immigration politics in California." *Social and Cultural Geography* 1: 143–55.

Mair, A. 1986. "The homeless and the post-industrial city." *Political Geography Quarterly* 5: 351–68.

Mandelker, B. 2000. "Bedford's sheep are sheer pleasure." *Record Review,* August 11.

Marchand, M. and A. Runyan (eds.) 2000. *Gender and Global Restructurings: Sightings, Sites, and Resistences.* London: Routledge.

Marcuse, P. 1988. "Neutralizing homelessness." *Socialist Review* 18: 69–96.

Maroti, D. H. 1997. "Asking fairness for Mount Kisco." *New York Times,* August 31.

Marshall, D. W. 1980. *Bedford Tricentennial, 1680–1980: Articles on the History of Bedford in Westchester County, New York, from Its Beginnings as a Settlement of the Colony of Connecticut.* Bedford: Town of Bedford.

Martin, C. 1999. "The New Migrants: 'Flexible Workers' in a Global Economy," in T. Skelton and T. Allen (eds.), *Culture and Global Change.* London: Routledge, pp. 180–90.

Marx, L. 1964. *The Machine in the Garden: Technology and the Pastoral Ideal in America.* Oxford: Oxford University Press.

Marx, R. J. 1997. "Environmentalists hail Twin Lakes Wetland decision." *Record Review,* August 15.

Marx, R. J. 1998. "Bedford supports rural character." *Record Review,* January 23.

Marx, R. J. 1999a. "Bedford Coalition: Shaping the future of a small town." *Record Review,* January 8.

Marx, R. J. 1999b. "Bedford Coalition: Packed house weighs development costs." *Record Review,* February 12.

Marx, R. J. 1999c. "Are DEP signs just Big Brother watching?" *Record Review,* March 19.

Massey D. 1991a. "A global sense of place." *Marxism Today* June: 24–29.

Massey D. 1991b. "The political place of locality studies." *Environment and Planning A* 23: 267–81.

Massey, D. 1992. "A place called home?" *New Formations* 17: 3–15.

Massey D. 1993. "Power/Geometry and a Progressive Sense of Place," in J. Bird et al. (eds.), *Mapping the Futures.* London: Routledge, pp. 59–69.

Matless, D. 1998. *Landscape and Englishness.* London: Reaktion Books.

Mattingly, P. H. 2001. *Suburban Landscapes: Culture and Politics in a New York Metropolitan Community.* Baltimore: Johns Hopkins University Press.

Matts, E. 1999. "Quality of life issues unjustly translated into racism." *Patent Trader,* October 29.

Meinig, D. W. 1979. "Symbolic Landscapes: Models of American Community," in D. W. Meinig (ed.), *The Interpretation of Ordinary Landscapes.* New York: Oxford University Press, pp. 164–92.

Meinig, D. W. 1986. *The Shaping of America: A Geographical Perspective on 500 Years of History. Volume 1. Atlantic America, 1492–1800.* New Haven: Yale University Press.

Mianus River Gorge Preserve. n.d. *Trail Guide.*

Mianus River Gorge Preserve. 1993. *New Bulletin.*

Mianus River Gorge Preserve. 1994. *Management Survey and Recommendations.*

Milton, K. 2002. *Loving Nature: Towards an Ecology of Emotion*. London: Routledge.

Mitchell, C. (ed.) 1992. *Western Hemisphere Immigration and United States Foreign Policy*. University Park: Pennsylvania State University Press.

/ Mitchell, D. 1995. "The end of public space? People's Park, definitions of the public, and democracy." *Annals, Association of American Geographers* 85: 108–33.

Mitchell, D. 1996a. *The Lie of the Land*. Minneapolis: University of Minnesota.

Mitchell, D. 1996b. "Political violence, order, and the legal construction of public space: Power and the public forum doctrine." *Urban Geography* 17: 152–78.

Mitchell, D. 1997. "The annihilation of space by law: The roots and implications of anti-homelessness laws in the United States." *Antipode* 29: 303–35.

Mitchell, D. 1998a. "Anti-homeless laws and public space: I begging and the first amendment." *Urban Geography* 19: 6–11.

Mitchell, D. 1998b. "Anti-homeless laws and public space: II further constitutional issues." *Urban Geography* 19: 98–104.

Mitchell, D. 2000. *Cultural Geography*. Oxford: Blackwell.

Mitchell, K. 1997a. "Conflicting geographies of democracy and the public sphere in Vancouver, B.C." *Transactions, Institute of British Geographers* 22: 162–79.

Mitchell, K. 1997b. "Transnational discourse: Bringing geography back in." *Antipode* 29: 101–14.

Mitchell, W. J. T. (ed.) 1994. *Landscape and Power*. Chicago: University of Chicago Press.

Moscovici, S. 2000. *Social Representations: Explorations in Social Psychology*. Cambridge: Polity.

Mount Kisco Chamber of Commerce. 1995. *Getting to Know Mount Kisco*. Mount Kisco Mica, Inc.

Moya, P. 2000. "Cultural Particularity versus Universal Humanity: The Value of Being *Asimilao*," in J. Gracia and P. De Greiff (eds.), *Hispanics/Latinos in the United States: Ethnicity, Race, and Rights*. London: Routledge, pp. 77–98.

Muldoon, H. 1999. *Latinos in Manasquan: A Geography of Immigrant Life in Small Town New Jersey*. Unpublished M.A. Thesis. Syracuse University.

Nardozzi, F. 2000a. "Will city's water plant affect our watershed." *Record Review*, February 4.

Nardozzi, F. 2000b. "Survey says: Let's keep Bedford green." *Record Review*, March 10.

Nardozzi, F. 2000c. "Bedford Coalition: Support sought for land referendum." *Record Review*, June 30.

Nardozzi, F. 2000d. "Bedford's rural roads: Not meant for speed, just nature's charm." *Record Review*, July 14.

Nardozzi, F. 2000e. "Building stone walls: A spiritual experience." *Record Review*, July 21.

Nardozzi, F. 2000f. "Bedford runoff sites pollute the watershed." *Record Review*, August 25.

Nardozzi, F. 2000g. "Twenty percent for affordable housing?" *Record Review*, September 15.

Nardozzi, F. 2000h. "Open space meeting draws small crowd and few questions." *Record Review*, October 13.

Nardozzi, F. 2001a. "Bedford working to stem erosion." *Record Review*, February 23.

Nardozzi, F. 2001b. "Master planners ponder dirt roads." *Record Review*, March 9.

Nardozzi, F. 2001c. "Neighbors: Martha's barn objectionable." *Record Review*, March 30.

Nardozzi, F. 2001d. "Dirt roads: Distinctive and desired." *Record Review*, March 30.

Nardozzi, F. 2001e. "Is Bedford running out of drinking water?" *Record Review*, April 27.

Nardozzi, F. 2001f. "Master planners look askance at 'McManse.'" *Record Review*, April 27.

Nardozzi, F. 2001g. "Martha arrives with photo and cookies." *Record Review*, May 18.

Nardozzi, F. 2001h. "Martha's barn OK'd by Planning Board." *Record Review*, May 25.

Nardozzi, F. 2001i. "Bedford's Master Plan: Are more controls coming?" *Record Review*, June 1.

Nardozzi, F. 2001j. "Bedford proposes a moratorium on McMansions." *Record Review*, July 20.

Nardozzi, F. 2001k. "Kelly's vote aids Alaskan drilling." *Record Review*, August 10.

Nardozzi, F. 2001l. "McMansion proposal has friends and foes." *Record Review*, August 24.

Nardozzi, F. 2001m. "That 'woodsy, natural' look planned." *Record Review*, August 31.

Nardozzi, F. 2001n. "Moratoriums delayed, work session slated Monday." *Record Review*, September 21.

Nardozzi, F. 2001o. "Board accepts less strict moratorium." *Record Review*, October 5.

Nardozzi, F. 2001p. "Fields reduced in Rippowam plan." *Record Review*, October 12.

Nardozzi, F. 2001q. "Wanted: More aesthetic controls." *Record Review*, October 26.

Nardozzi, F. 2001r. "Ridges, corridors proposed for protection." *Record Review*, November 16.

Nardozzi, F. 2001s. "Affordable housing gets Bedford OK." *Record Review*, November 16.

Nardozzi, F. 2001t. "Sewer system called highest priority." *Record Review*, November 23.

Nardozzi, F. 2002a. "Albany gives support to Dinin for sewering." *Record Review*, February 8.

Nardozzi, F. 2002b. "Biding time, biting nails, Rippowam waits." *Record Review,* February 8.

Nardozzi, F. 2002c. "Rippowam FEIS approved, public hearing set." *Record Review,* March 15.

Nardozzi, F. 2002d. "Clear-cut to cost owner $58,000." *Record Review,* March 15.

Nash, R. 1982. *Wilderness and the American Mind.* New Haven: Yale University Press.

Nevins, J. 2002. *Operation Gatekeeper: The Rise of the "Illegal Alien" and the Making of the U.S. Mexico Boundary.* New York: Routledge.

Newman, G. 1993. "The lost century of American immigration law (1776–1875)." *Columbia Law Review* 93: 1833–1901.

New York Times. 1983. "If you're thinking of living in: Bedford." March 27.

New York Times. 1987. "Where freedom's not just another word." October 11, 30–31.

New York Times. 1988. "Traffic and history cross at Bedford's village Green." March 13.

New York Times. 1992. "Past and present clash over bedford traffic light." July 19.

New York Times. 1993. "'New England' 44 miles from Broadway." November 7.

Northern Westchester Times. 1950. October 19.

Oelschlaeger, M. 1991. *The Idea of Wilderness: From Pre-history to the Age of Ecology.* New Haven: Yale University Press.

Orfield, M. 1997. *Metropolitics: A Regional Agenda for Community and Stability.* Washington: Brookings Institute.

Ortiz, P. 2000. "Day laborers rattle Valley communities: Are sidewalks big enough for all?" *Arizona Republican,* December 6.

O'Shea, P. 1999. Correspondence, May 17. In Final Environmental Impact Statement. Rippowam-Cisqua School, Proposed High School Campus. Town of Bedford, Vol. 1, November 2000.

Patent Trader. 1980. Tricentennial No. "We tip our hats as we go by: Oak is most venerable citizen."

Patent Trader. 1986. "Committee to study Architecture Board." April 16.

Patent Trader. 1992. "Couple donates 30 acres to Mianus Gorge Preserve." April 2.

Patent Trader. 1993. "No one comes off well." October 14.

Patent Trader. 1995. "Things changed in Kisco." December 29.

Penrose, J. 1993. "Reification in the Name of Change: The Impact of Nationalism on the Social Constructions of Nation, People, and Place in Scotland and the United Kingdom," in P. Jackson and J. Penrose (eds.), *Constructions of Place, Race, and Nation.* London: UCL Press, pp. 27–49.

Pepper, D. 1984. *The Roots of Modern Environmentalism.* New York: Routledge.

Perin, C. 1977. *Everything in Its Place: Social Order and Land Use in America.* Princeton: Princeton University Press.

Philo, C. 1998. "A lyffe in pyttes and caves: Exclusionary geographies of the West Country tinners." *Geoforum* 29: 159–72.

Pile, S. 1994. "Masculism, the use of dualistic epistemologies, and third spaces." *Antipode* 26: 255–77.

Platt, R. H. 1995. *Land Use and Society: Geography, Law, and Public Policy.* San Francisco: Island Press.

Ploss, P. 1977. "Oak $ due Monday." *Patent Trader,* June 18.

Popkin, E. 1999. "Guatemalan Mayan migration to Los Angeles: Constructing transnational linkages in the context of the settlement process." *Ethnic and Racial Studies* 22: 267–89.

Portes, A., L. E. Guarnizo, and P. Landholt. 1999. "The study of transnationalism: Pitfalls and promise of an emergent research field." *Ethnic and Racial Studies* 22: 217–37.

Potter, J. 2001. "Day workers: Mount Kisco assesses its new Latino immigrants." *Westchester County Times,* May 7.

Pratt, G. 1981. "The House as Expression of Social Worlds," in J. Duncan (ed.), *Housing and Identity: Cross-Cultural Perspectives.* London: Croom Helm, pp. 135–80.

Pratt, G. 1998. "Grids of Difference: Place and Identity Formation," in R. Fincher and J. Jacobs (eds.), *Cities of Difference.* New York: The Guildford Press, pp. 26–48.

Pred, A. 2000. *Even in Sweden: Racisms, Racialized Spaces, and the Popular Geographical Imagination.* Berkeley: University of California Press.

Pregill, P. and N. Volkman. 1993. *Landscapes in History.* New York: Van Nostrand, Reinhold.

Price, P. 2000. "Inscribing the border: Schizophrenia and the aesthetics of Aztlan." *Social and Cultural Geography* 1: 101–16.

Price, U. 1810. *An Essay on the Picturesque, as Compared with the Sublime and the Beautiful.* London: J. Longden.

Probyn, E. 1990. "Travels in the Postmodern: Making Sense of the Local," in L. Nicholson (ed.), *Feminism/Postmodernism.* New York: Routledge, pp. 176–89.

Proctor, J. D. 1998. "Geography, paradox, and environmental ethics." *Progress in Human Geography* 22: 234–55.

Proctor J. D. and S. Pincetl. 1996. "Nature and the reproduction of endangered species: The spotted owl in the Pacific North-West and southern California." *Environment and Planning D: Society and Space* 14: 683–703.

Pulido, L. 2000. "Rethinking environmental racism: White privilege and urban development in Southern California." *Annals, Association of American Geographers* 90: 12–40.

Purdy, M. 1999. "Our town: Where laborers are handy but shunned." *New York Times,* November 21.

Purdy, M. 2001. "Laborers wanted, sometimes." *New York Times,* April 15.

Rabinowitz, C. 1996. "Whose town is it?" *New York Times,* December 4.

Rae, L. 1998a. "Unpaid and unafraid." *Reporter Dispatch,* June 7.

Rae, L. 1998b. "Solutions." *Reporter Dispatch,* June 9.

Raymond, G. M. 1999. "Municipal zoning laws are exclusionary." *Patent Trader,* January 4.

Record Review. 1996. "Editorial. An opportunity." January 26.

Record Review. 1998. "Editorial. Bigger equals better?" June 5.

Record Review. 1999. "Bedford Housing Agency accepting applications?" February 5.

Record Review. 2000. "Editorial. Survey results are call to action." March 10.

Record Review. 2001. "Editorial. Prepare for McGeorgians." August 24.

Reeves, R. 1974. "The Battle over Land," in L. Masotti and J. Hadden (eds.), *Suburbia in Transition.* New York: The New York Times Company, pp. 303–11.

Relph, E. 1976. *Place and Placelessness.* London: Pion.

Rieser, C. 1990. "North Salem zoning law declared invalid." *Patent Trader,* July 6.

Riesman, D., N. Glazer, and R. Denney. 1950. *The Lonely Crowd.* New Haven: Yale University Press.

Riso, D. 1972. "Eagle Scout Project Dealing with the Old Burial Ground." Manuscript. Bedford Village Library.

Roberts, B. R. 1995. "Socially Expected Durations and Economic Adjustments of Immigrants," in A. Portes (ed.), *The Economic Sociology of Immigration.* New York: Russell Sage, pp. 42–86.

Robertson, M. 2000. "No net loss: Wetland restoration and the incomplete capitalization on nature." *Antipode* 34: 463–93.

Rodriquez, N. 1987. "Undocumented Central Americans in Houston." *International Migration Review* 21: 4–26.

Rose, G. 1993. *Feminism and Geography. The Limits of Geographical Knowledge.* Cambridge: Polity.

Rose, G. 1995. "Place and Identity: A Sense of Place," in D. Massey and P. Jess (eds.), *A Place in the World? Place, Cultures, and Globalization.* Oxford: Open University Press, pp. 87–132.

Rosenberg, M. 2000. "Education, behind Bedford school budget fight: Economic and ethnic divisions." *New York Times.* June 18.

Samuel, R. 1995. *Theatres of Memory.* Vol. 1. London: Verso.

Sassen, S. 1989. "New York's Informal Economy," in A. Portes, M. Castells, and L. A. Benton (eds.), *The Informal Economy: Studies in Advanced and Less Developed Countries.* Baltimore: Johns Hopkins.

Sassen, S. 1995. "Immigration and Local Labor Markets," in A. Portes (ed.), *The Economic Sociology of Immigration.* New York: Russell Sage, pp. 87–127.

Satkowski, V. 1983. "Town considering tree ordinance to protect privately-owned trees." *The Ledger,* June 29.

Sayer, A. 2000. "Critical and Uncritical Cultural Turns," in I. Cook, D. Crouch, S. Naylor, and J. Ryan (eds.), *Cultural Turns/Geographical Turns.* Harlow: Prentice Hall, pp. 166–81.

Schein, R. H. 1997. "The place of landscape: A conceptual framework for interpreting an American scene." *Annals of the Association of American Geographers* 87: 660–80.

Schembari, J. 1996. "Trees fall. Whole town hears. Man's landscaping ignites leaf-loving Greenwich." *New York Times,* June 3.

Schleifer, A. 2000a. "Homeless men elude authorities." *Patent Trader,* April 13.

Schleifer, A. 2000b. "2nd time's a charm for Bedford budget." *Patent Trader,* April 13.

Schleifer, A. 2000c. "Developer seeks ok for moderate-income housing." *Patent Trader,* August 17.

Schmitt, E. 2002a. "Ruling clears the way to use state police in immigration duty." *New York Times,* April 4.

Schmitt, E. 2002b. "Administration split on local role in terror fight." *New York Times,* April 29.

Schmitt, P. J. 1990. *Back to Nature: The Arcadian Myth in Urban America.* Baltimore: Johns Hopkins University Press.

Schneider, W. 1992. "The suburban century begins." *The Atlantic,* July 3.

Schult, E. 1984. "Board debates policies for town's master plan." *The Ledger,* September 26.

Schwartz, N. 1992a. "Bedford board to present traffic plan to state DOT." *Patent Trader,* January 23.

Schwartz, N. 1992b. "Options sought for Rt.172 traffic problem." *Patent Trader,* February 13.

Schwartz, N. 1992c. "Residents rally around Bedford traffic plan." *Patent Trader,* March 19.

Schwartz, N. 1992d. "Bedford's efforts fail to stop DOT plan for Village Green." *Patent Trader,* April 2.

Scott, J. C. 1985. *Weapons of the Weak: Everyday Forms of Peasant Resistance.* New Haven: Yale University Press.

Sen, G. and C. Grown. 1987. *Development, Crises, and Alternative Visions: Third World Women's Perspectives.* New York: Monthly Review Press.

Seshhadri-Crooks, K. 2000. *Desiring Whiteness: A Lacanian Analysis of Race.* London: Routledge.

Sharp, J. 1996. "Gendering Nationhood: A Feminist Engagement with National Identity," in N. Duncan (ed.), *Body/Space Destabilizing Geographies of Gender and Sexuality.* London: Routledge, pp. 97–108.

Sharp, J. 1999. "Performance," in L. McDowell and J. Sharp (eds.), *A Feminist Glossary of Human Geography.* London: Arnold, pp. 199.

Shoumatoff, A. 1977. *Mount Kisco: Past and Present.* Mount Kisco, N.Y.: Bi-Centennial Committee.

Shoumatoff, A. 1979. *Westchester: Portrait of a County.* New York: Coward, McCann & Geoghegan.

Shoumatoff, A. 1999a. "And So to Bedford." *Vanity Fair* February: 152–68.

Shoumatoff, N. 1999b. Public Hearing, May 19. In Final Environmental Impact Statement. Rippowam-Cisqua School, Proposed High School Campus. Town of Bedford, Vol. 1, November 2000.

Sibley, D. 1995. *Geographies of Exclusion: Society and Difference in the West.* London: Routledge.

Sibley, D. 1998. "The problematic nature of exclusion." *Geoforum* 29: 119–22.

Skiba, L. and B. Vetare Civitello. 1994. "Residents abhor Kisco's decline." *Patent Trader,* October 6.

Skolnik, S. 2000. "Land development is key to Bedford Open Space Referendum." *Record Review,* October 27.

Smith, M. P. 2001. *Transnational Urbanism: Locating Globalisation.* Oxford: Blackwell.

Smith, N. 1996. *The New Urban Frontier and the Revanchist City.* London: Routledge.

Smith, N. 2000. "What happened to class?" *Environment and Planning A.* 32: 1011–32.

Soja, E. 1989. *Postmodern Geographies: The Reassertion of Space in Critical Social Theory.* London: Verso.

Sorkin, M. (ed.) 1992. *Variations on a Theme Park: The New American City and the End of Public Space.* New York: Noonday Press.

Sourby, D. 1994a. "Town submits plan: Watershed laws." *Bedford Record,* August 25.

Sourby, D. 1994b. "Dirt roads: Friend or foe." *Bedford Record,* August 25.

Staeheli, L. 1996. "Publicity, privacy, and women's political action." *Environment and Planning D: Society and Space* 14: 601–19.

Stern, R. and J. Massengale (eds.) 1981. "The Anglo-American Suburb." *Architectural Design* 50, 10/11.

Stilgoe, J. R. 1982. *Common Landscape of America, 1580 to 1845.* New Haven: Yale University Press.

Stilgoe, J. R. 1988. *Borderland: Origins of the American Suburb, 1820–1939.* New Haven: Yale University Press.

Stockbridge, J. 2000. "Quality of life in Bedford is made evident in those things natural." *Record Review* February 11.

Suarez-Orozco, M. 1998. "Crossings: Mexican Immigration in Interdisciplinary Perspective," in M. Suarez-Orozco (ed.), *Crossings: Mexican Immigration in Interdisciplinary Perspective.* Cambridge: Harvard University Press, pp. 3–52.

Teaford, J. C. 1997. *Post-Suburbia: Government and Politics in the "Edge Cities."* Baltimore: Johns Hopkins.

Thomas, K. 1983. *Man and the Natural World: A History of the Modern Sensibility.* New York: Pantheon.

Thompson, G. 2001. "Mexico's southern border: A gateway to suffering." *International Herald Tribune,* August 6, 3.

Till, K. 1993. "Neotraditional towns and urban villages: The cultural production of a geography of 'otherness.'" *Environment and Planning D: Society and Space* 11: 709–32.

Till, K. 1999. "Staging the past: Landscape designs, cultural identity, and Erinnerungspolitik at Berlin's Neue Wache." *Ecumene* 6: 251–83.

Toma, R. 2001. "Farmingville should learn a lesson." *Newsday* April 8: A25.

Town of Bedford. 1960. *Development Plan*. Bedford: Town of Bedford.

Town of Bedford, Westchester County, New York. 1966. *Historical Records, Volume 1, Minutes of Town Meetings, 1680–1737*. Bedford: Town of Bedford.

Town of Bedford. 1972. *Development Plan*. Bedford: Town of Bedford.

Town of Bedford. 1986. "Tree Preservation," in *Code of the Town of Bedford, Westchester County, New York*. Rochester, N.Y.: General Code Publishers, pp. 11201–206.

Town of Bedford. 1989a. "Subdivision of Land," in *Code of the Town of Bedford, Westchester County, New York*. Rochester, N.Y.: General Code Publishers, pp. 10701–800.

Town of Bedford. 1989b. "Historic Districts," in *Code of the Town of Bedford, Westchester County, New York*. Rochester, N.Y.: General Code Publishers, pp. 7102–106.

Town of Bedford. 1989c. "Steep Slopes," in *Code of the Town of Bedford, Westchester County, New York*. Rochester, N.Y.: General Code Publishers, pp. 10201–208.

Town of Bedford. 1991. "Wetlands," in *Code of the Town of Bedford, Westchester County, New York*. Rochester, N.Y.: General Code Publishers, pp. 12201–220.

Town of Bedford. 1992. "Zoning," in *Code of the Town of Bedford, Westchester County, New York*. Rochester, N.Y.: General Code Publishers, pp. 12501–633.

Town of Bedford. 1997. *Conservation Board Questionnaire*.

Town of Bedford. 1998. *Conservation Board Questionnaire: Summary and Findings*.

Town of Bedford. 1999. *Master Plan Questionnaire*.

Town of Bedford. 2000. *Master Plan Questionnaire Analysis of Findings*.

Town of Mount Kisco. 1995. *Report of the Mayor's Committee on Community Relations*, April 7.

Tucker, C. 1995. "Walls." *Patent Trader*, April 16.

Tucker, W. 1982. *Progress and Privilege: America in the Age of Environmentalism*. Garden City, N.Y.: Anchor Doubleday.

Tunbridge, J. E. and G. J. Ashworth. 1996. *Dissonant Heritage: The Management of the Past as a Resource in Conflict*. New York: Wiley.

Unidentified speaker. 1999. Public Hearing, May 19. In Final Environmental Impact Statement. Rippowam-Cisqua School, Proposed High School Campus. Town of Bedford, Vol. 1, November 2000.

U.S. Committee for Refugees (USCR). 1991. *Running the Gauntlet: The Central American Journey through Mexico*. Washington: American Council for Nationalities Service.

Uzzell D. and R. Ballantyne. 1998. *Contemporary Issues in Heritage and Environmental Interpretation*. London: The Stationery Office.

Valle, V. and R. Torres. 2000. *Latino Metropolis*. Minneapolis: University of Minnesota Press.

Velasquez de Estrada, D. 1996. "Impacto de las remesas familiars en el desarrollo de las comunidades Guatemaltecas analizan investigadores." *Prensa Libre* 13 Noviembre.

Vigliotti, R. M. 1993. Letter to the Editor: "Housing Editorial Unfounded." *Patent Trader*, October 21.

Vizard, M. 1993. "Trading development rights for goodwill." *New York Times*, September 19.

Walker, D. 1981. "A Theory of Suburbanisation: Capitalism and the Construction of Urban Space in the United States," in M. Dear, and A. J. Scott (eds.), *Urbanisation and Urban Planning in Capitalist Societies*. London: Methuen.

Walker, D. 1995. "Landscape and city life: Four ecologies of residence in the San Francisco Bay area." *Ecumene* 2: 33–64.

Wallace, M. 1986. "Visiting the Past: History Museums in the United States," in S. Porter Benson, S. Brier, R. Rosenzweig (eds.), *Presenting the Past: Essays on History and the Public*. Philadelphia: Temple University Press, pp. 137–61.

Walton, J. R. 1995. "How Real(ist) Can You Get?" *The Professional Geographer* 47: 61–65.

Ward, K. (ed.) 1990. *Women Workers and Global Restructuring*. Ithaca: Cornell University Press.

Warf, B. 2000. "New York: The Big Apple in the 1990s." *Geoforum* 31: 487–99.

Weiher, G. 1991. *The Fractured Metropolis: Political Fragmentation and Metropolitan Segregation*. Albany: State University Press of New York.

Weiner, M. 1981. *English Culture and the Decline of the Industrial Spirit*. New York: Cambridge University Press.

West, D. 1997. "Who needs a house in Beverly Hills? Stars now flock to wealthy but unassuming Bedford, N.Y." *New York Times*, May 11.

Westchester County Housing Opportunity Commission. 1997. "Housing Opportunities for Westchester: A Guide to Affordable Housing Development," September.

Westchester Land Trust. 2001a. www.westchesterlandtrust.org, April.

Westchester Land Trust. 2001b. "WLT preserves key pieces of County's farm country," www.westchesterlandtrust.org, August.

Westchester Land Trust. 2002. Spring Newsletter.

Whyte, W. 1956. *The Organization Man*. New York: Simon and Schuster.

Willems-Braun, B. 1997. "Buried epistemologies the politics of nature in (post)colonial British Columbia." *Annals of the Association of American Geographers* 87: 3–31.

Williams, M. 1989. *Americans and Their Forests: A Historical Geography*. Cambridge: Cambridge University Press.

Williams, R. 1960. 1988. *Border Country*. London: Hogarth.

Williams, R. 1973. *The Country and the City*. London: Chatto and Windus.

Williams, R. 1990. *The People of the Black Mountains: The Eggs of the Eagle*. London: Chatto and Windus.

Willis, P. 1977. *Learning to Labour: How Working Class Kids Get Working Class Jobs*. New York: Columbia University Press.

Wilson, A. 1992. *The Culture of Nature: North American Landscape from Disney to Exxon Valdez*. Cambridge, Mass.: Blackwell.

Withers, C. W. J. 1996. "Place, memory, monument: Memorializing the past in contemporary highland Scotland." *Ecumene* 3: 325–44.

Witherspoon, R. 2001a. "Water system may need filtration." *Journal News*, June 19.

Witherspoon, R. 2001b. "State approves agricultural district in Westchester." *Journal News*, July 18.

Wolfson, H. 1995. "Broker of 50 years to 'sell' Bedford." *Record Review*, December 8.

Wolschke-Bulmahn, J. 1997. *Nature and Ideology: Natural Garden Design in the Twentieth Century*. Washington: Dumbarton Oaks Research Library and Collection.

Wood, J. 1925. Orig. 1917. "Town of Bedford," in A. P. French (ed.), *History of Westchester County, New York*. Vol. 2. New York: J. Cass, pp. 613–61.

Wood, J. R. 1982. "Village and community in colonial New England." *Journal of Historical Geography* 8: 333–46.

Wood, J. R. 1984. "Elaboration of a settlement system: The New England Village in the Federal period." *Journal of Historical Geography* 10: 331–56.

Wood, J. R. 1986. "The New England Village as an American Vernacular Form," in C. Wells (ed.), *Perspectives on Vernacular Architecture*. Vol. 2. Columbia, Mo.: University of Missouri Press, pp. 54–63.

Wood, J. R. 1991. "'Build, therefore your own world': The New England Village as settlement ideal." *Annals, Association of American Geographers* 81: 32–50.

Wood, J. R. 1997. *The New England Village*. Baltimore: Johns Hopkins.

Wood, L. H. 1952. *Bedford Garden Club Bulletin*.

Woods, M. 1998. "Rethinking elites: Networks, spaces, and local politics." *Environment and Planning A*. 30: 2101–19.

Worster, D. 1977. *Nature's Economy: A History of Ecological Ideas*. Cambridge: Cambridge University Press.

Worth, R. 2001. "Mount Kisco center offers order to day laborers." *New York Times*, July 22.

Wright, P. 1985. *On Living in an Old Country*. London: Verso.

Wright, W. 1992. *Wild Knowledge: Science, Language, and Social Life in a Fragile Environment*. Minneapolis: University of Minnesota Press.

Wyckoff, W. 1990. "Landscapes of Private Power and Wealth," in M. P. Conzen (ed.), *The Making of the American Landscape*. London: Unwin-Hyman, pp. 335–54.

Wyman, M. 1993. *Round-Trip America: The Immigrants Return to Europe, 1880–1930*. Ithaca: Cornell University Press.

Young, I. M. 1990. *Justice and the Politics of Difference*. Princeton: Princeton University.

Zavella, P. 2000. "Latinos in the USA: Changing socio-economic patterns." *Social and Cultural Geography* 1: 155–67.

Zink, N. 1995. "Sue Kelly. The contract, the critics: Her first year in Congress." *Record Review*, November 17.

Zink, N. 1997. "New tree ordinance gets mixed reviews." *Record Review*, February 21.

Zuckerman, M. 1970. *Peaceable Kingdoms: New England Towns in the Eighteenth Century*. New York: Vintage Books.

Zukin, S. 1991. *Landscapes of Power*. Berkeley: University of California Press.

Zukin, S. 1992. "Postmodern Urban Landscapes: Mapping Culture and Power," in S. Lash and J. Friedman (eds.), *Modernity and Identity*. Oxford: Blackwells, pp. 221–47.

Index